MW01193176

Anarchist Education and the Modern School
A Francisco Ferrer Reader

Edited by Mark Bray and Robert H. Haworth

Translated by Mark Bray and Joseph McCabe

Anarchist Education and the Modern School: A Francisco Ferrer Reader
Edited by Mark Bray and Robert H. Haworth. Translated by Mark Bray and Joseph McCabe
© PM Press 2019

ISBN: 978–1–62963–509–5
Library of Congress Control Number: 2017964735

Cover by John Yates/Stealworks
Interior design by briandesign

10 9 8 7 6 5 4 3 2 1

PM Press
PO Box 23912
Oakland, CA 94623
www.pmpress.org

Printed in the USA by the Employee Owners of Thomson-Shore in Dexter, Michigan.
www.thomsonshore.com

"Neither the State, nor the Church, nor the enemies of the Modern School are capable of resisting the immense weight of Justice."

—Francisco Ferrer Guardia

Contents

Acknowledgements

Mark Bray I would like to thank my coeditor Robert H. Haworth and everyone at PM Press. Thank you also to Jelle Bruinsma, Xavi López, Dennis Bos, Jorell Meléndez-Badillo, Miguel Pérez, Kevan Antonio Aguilar, Kenyon Zimmer, Pierre Kohler, John-Erik Hansson, Sergio Higuera Barco, David R.A., Adriano Skoda, Frederick Schulze, Temma Kaplan, Ellison Moorehead, Manel Aisa and the *Ateneu Enciclopèdic Popular*, Heather Smedberg and the UCSD Special Collections, and the Fundació Francesc Ferrer i Guardia. Thank you to my amazing family—I was lucky to be raised by two fantastic teachers! Mr. Xavi, welcome to the world and to my acknowledgements! And to Senia, the love of my life, without you this book, and everything else, would be unimaginable. ("It was a moment like this, do you remember?")

Robert H. Haworth I would like to say a huge "thank you" to Mark Bray for expanding this project beyond what was originally conceived. I also would like to thank PM Press (Ramsey, Craig, Steven, Stephanie, and everyone else) for their continued efforts to publish important historical and contemporary radical literature. Additionally, I want to thank my children Dylan and Rachel for always challenging my beliefs about the purpose of education. Of course, I can't express how much I appreciate Holly for her insights, support, and love throughout life.

I would also like to dedicate this book to all the teachers who are struggling to create educational spaces that challenge the world we live in, as well as thinking and acting in ways that provide children and youth inspiration for the future.

A Note on Translation

Unless otherwise noted, all translations are entirely my own except *The Modern School*, which is an expanded and improved version of Joseph McCabe's 1913 abbreviated translation, entitled *The Origin and Ideals of the Modern School*. McCabe's 1913 translation included only about two-thirds of Ferrer's text, and he sometimes toned down Ferrer's language in an effort to appeal to middle-class English-language readers of the era. Therefore, I supplemented McCabe's work with my own translation of the remaining third of the book, modernized some of his language, and returned certain phrases to the original spirit of Ferrer's revolutionary pedagogical vision.

—Mark Bray

I

Introduction: The Three Faces of Ferrer
Mark Bray

On the morning of October 13, 1909, the famed Catalan pedagogue Francisco Ferrer found himself in front of a firing squad in the moat of Montjuich Castle overlooking Barcelona. After a military show trial plagued by judicial irregularities, the founder of the Modern School was sentenced to death as the "author and leader of the rebellion" later known as the Tragic Week that erupted over the summer against conscription for the latest Spanish war in Morocco.[1] For days, Ferrer longed for word of a pardon from the Conservative prime minister Antonio Maura, who had issued 119 pardons over the previous two years (54 of them for murder), but he would not be so fortunate.[2] Instead he spent his final day in the prison chapel where he resolutely refused religious council from the military chaplain, even making a failed plea to authorities to remove the crucifix and altar lamp from the last room he would ever inhabit. When asked if he believed in an afterlife, Ferrer replied, "No, señor. I believe that everything ends here; that everything terminates with the life of a man. Since I acquired this conviction many years ago I have adapted all of my actions to it."[3] And so, having spent his final years adapting his pedagogical actions to the certainty that nothing mattered beyond life on earth, he stared down the barrels of the rifles pointed in his direction. "Muchachos," Ferrer cried out, "aim well and fire without fear! I am innocent! *Viva la Escuela Moderna!*" Amid his final words shots rang out. Ferrer faltered briefly before collapsing to the ground.[4]

While it may have ended right there for Francisco Ferrer the man, Francisco Ferrer the martyr was actively inspiring a groundbreaking international mobilization against this "clerical judicial murder."[5] A historic

1907 postcard of Ferrer. IISG BG A61/180.

wave of protest that had had been mounting since Ferrer's arrest cascaded down upon international public opinion as marches, demonstrations, meetings, and even riots across Europe, North Africa, and the Americas defended the legacy of Ferrer and his coeducational, antiauthoritarian, student-centered Modern School. This wave of protest sparked the creation of (more or less) Ferrerian schools across the world, from Mexico to Poland, from China and Japan to Czechoslovakia and the United States, in what came to be known as the Modern School movement. Despite the surging popularity of Ferrer's "rationalist" educational ideals, however, critics argued that Ferrer was a philandering, bloodthirsty anarchist who abandoned his children and defrauded a hapless widow to gamble on the stock market, finance shadowy assassins, and construct a sacrilegious school that taught children how to construct bombs.

In order to refute these accusations and appeal to moderate allies, Ferrer's principal supporters often denied or downplayed his anarchism and constructed an image of him as a freethinking pedagogical innovator who was martyred solely for his audacious attempt to promote "rationalist" education in "clerical" Spain. As the prominent Dreyfusard and novelist Anatole France asked, "What is his crime? His crime is being a republican, socialist, freethinker. His crime is having promoted lay education in Barcelona, instructing thousands of children in independent morality. His crime is having founded a school and a library."[6] According to this depiction, the Modern School operated based on purely scientific and rational principles free from all preconceived ideology. The Spanish government's opposition to such groundbreaking pedagogy showed that Ferrer was but the latest victim of "the Inquisition." Yet his death was all the more shocking for having occurred in the twentieth century when such "barbarity" was widely thought to be a relic of the past. Many saw Ferrer as the "Spanish Dreyfus," an echo of the case of the Jewish captain Alfred Dreyfus who was wrongfully accused of treason a decade earlier in France. One pamphlet even claimed that Ferrer had taken "his place with Socrates, Christ, Savonarola, Huss, Giordano Bruno."[7]

After the chaos of the Ferrer protest movement subsided, Ferrer and his legacy were cleanly incorporated into the pantheon of anarchist martyrdom by both the Spanish and the international anarchist movements. As anarchists across the world worked to establish rationalist schools, Francisco Ferrer and the movement he catalyzed came to be associated with a sort of anarchist purity grounded in the fundamental task of combatting and uprooting the errors of authoritarian thought at their root in the minds of the youth. This was evident in the summer of 2011, when my partner Senia and I had the opportunity to meet a group of Spanish anarchist exiles who had fled to France with the collapse of the Republic in 1939. After arriving in Paris, they helped to form the French CNT labor federation and publish a periodical for the CNT in exile. By 2011, they set aside time every weekend to get together in the office of the CNT-F on rue des Vignoles. After we introduced ourselves, they happily recounted their memories of the 1930s and 1940s. While most were children when they fled, one man had been a teenager who escaped after his brother was killed. Our conversations covered a wide range of topics, but before we left they gave us postcards with the portrait of Francisco Ferrer on one side and a brief description of his life and work on the other, practically pleading with us to educate ourselves about this great figure. From the perspective of these Spanish exiles, the most important legacy of their collective struggle was Ferrer and the Modern School.

We are left with three conflicting images: Ferrer the duplicitous, diabolical mastermind of rebellion whose school poisoned young minds; Ferrer the freethinking, pacifist, pedagogical giant whose school never strayed from the scientific method; and Ferrer the epitome of anarchist martyrdom whose school was the embodiment of libertarian pedagogy in practice. Yet none of these portrayals does justice to the complexities and paradoxes of the actual human being or the institution he founded.

Despite the accolades that his admirers have lavished upon him, Ferrer made no significant pedagogical innovations. Concepts such as coeducation, student autonomy, a focus on the natural environment, and opposition to rewards and punishments had already been developed by others. Scholars concur that Ferrer was not a pedagogical genius,[8] and Ferrer agreed, writing that before founding the Modern School he was "conscious of [his] incompetence in the art of pedagogy" so he "sought the counsel of others."[9] Yet he was an autodidact who, despite ending his formal education at thirteen, became a highly motivated organizer and brought together disparate groups of radicals, educators, and freethinkers to found what became the most enduring symbol of antiauthoritarian education.

Moreover, Ferrer's political orientation could be fairly ambiguous. In the mid-1890s, Ferrer started to shift away from his revolutionary republican roots to move closer and closer to anarchism. By the first years of

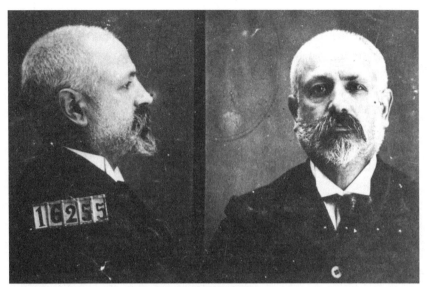

Mug shot of Ferrer in 1906. UCSD, Box 17, Folder 7.

the twentieth century his strong advocacy of revolutionary syndicalism and the general strike led him to finance the creation of the newspaper *La Huelga General* (The General Strike). Under the pseudonym "Cero," Ferrer contributed a number of articles to the paper, including "The Republicans Are Not Revolutionaries—Only the General Strike Will Make the Revolution," where he argued that "only the anarchists embark on the right path." Likewise, in his article "Property and the Anarchists: The Crazy and the Reasonable," Ferrer articulated himself in terms of what "we anarchists want." Nor was Ferrer's alter ego shy about advocating political violence. He penned an article titled "Will There Be Blood?—Yes, a Lot," which described the coming revolution undergoing the "last baptism of human blood," and another called "Preparing the Revolutionary General Strike," where he argued that "it would be better not to organize a general strike if it had to be peaceful." [See part VII.]

Yet when writing under his own name, Ferrer presented himself as peaceful and nonideological. In a 1906 article, he wrote, "I detest all party names, from Anarchist to Carlist, because all of them are obstacles to the educative work undertaken by the Escuela Moderna." Later in the same article, however, Ferrer acknowledges that if there are similarities between his perspective and anarchism then "I should be an Anarchist insofar as Anarchism adopts my ideas of education, of peace, and love, but not to the extent that I would have adopted any of its particular proceedings."[10]

Certainly Ferrer's decision to eschew political categories in public had much to do with his desire to maintain positive relations with Modern School parents and avoid prosecution, but the question of his politics goes deeper than labels.

Although Ferrer grew increasingly disgusted with republicanism, especially republican leaders, as the 1890s progressed, he never entirely left his early republicanism behind. This is reflected, for example, in the evidence that exists to suggest that Ferrer was part of a 1906 anarchist-republican conspiracy to assassinate the Spanish king in order to spark an uprising that would culminate in a republic. According to this alleged plan, it seems that the leader of the uprising and the eventual republic was Alejandro Lerroux, the radical republican demagogue and one of Ferrer's most intimate collaborators. Ferrer wrote a letter on the day of the assassination attempt that referred to Lerroux in the following terms: "If we desire a revolution, and if we want someone to personify it, this someone is Lerroux."[11] Lerroux is remembered for repressing the socialist miners' revolt in Asturias as the prime minister of a right-wing governing coalition during the second Spanish Republic in 1934.

Moreover, shortly after Ferrer's death, one of his closest friends, Charles Malato, wrote, "He would have welcomed a simply republican revolution like the one in Portugal as a first step while continuing to advance from the governmental and capitalist republic toward the ideal social and libertarian res publica."[12] This suggests that Ferrer may have considered a transitional phase of bourgeois republicanism to be a necessary stop on the way from monarchy to anarchy. Many contemporaries were keenly aware of Ferrer's liminal status in the world of Western European radicalism. Malato continues to explain that "Ferrer, who fittingly passed as an anarchist in the eyes of his republican compatriots, passed as a simple republican—a latecomer!—in the eyes of French anarchists who did not know him."[13] In Spain, as well, Ferrer's anarchist collaborators were primarily writers, publishers, and philosophers of the more literary milieu, while he was less well-known and more distrusted among anarchist workers. Although Ferrer came from a modest background, the fortune he acquired from the will of his former student Ernestine Meunié reinforced his "bourgeois" image for many. His tenuous position as a newly affluent revolutionary was clear in an article titled "The General Strike Will Enrich the Poor without Impoverishing the Rich," which he wrote under his "Cero" penname, making the unorthodox argument that after the revolution "those who call themselves rich will continue being rich because they will continue to live in their luxurious homes." As Malato phrased it, "To republican politicians, Ferrer was a bothersome anarchist; for the working masses, alas, despite his relations with militants of the revolutionary proletariat, he seemed to be a bourgeois!" Herein lies the bitter irony: the Spanish state accused Ferrer of singlehandedly instigating and leading a massive working-class rebellion that included significant numbers of republicans and anarchists, when in fact he was so marginalized and distrusted by workers and radicals that his feeble attempts to participate in the uprising were rebuffed at every turn.

Ultimately, we can conclude that although Ferrer was closer to anarchism than any other doctrine, his politics were not always entirely consistent. Although he dedicated the lion's share of his inherited fortune to his various political projects, his wealth undoubtedly rubbed some working-class radicals the wrong way. Although he founded a pioneering institution in the Modern School, he made no original contribution to pedagogical theory. Although his avowed goal was human fraternity and cooperation, he was completely certain that blood would have to be spilled to get there. Taken as a whole, we can see that Ferrer's interest in pedagogy, insurrection, the revolutionary general strike, and quite possibly carefully selected propaganda by the deed (an anarchist euphemism for attacks on oppressive figures) demonstrates that he had a multifaceted perspective on social change that involved short-, medium-, and long-term strategies.

Nor can we easily categorize the school that Ferrer founded. On the one hand, there is no question that the Modern School was one of the most emancipatory schools that Spain, and Europe as a whole, had ever witnessed when it opened its doors in 1901. To understand the magnitude of its pedagogical contribution one must situate it within the woeful state of Spanish education and compare it to earlier attempts to transcend Catholic education. Despite the Ley Moyano of 1857, which mandated primary education until the age of nine and made it free for those who could not pay, very few working-class children consistently attended school, and most of those who did enrolled in Catholic schools. In 1909, two-thirds of Spanish school districts had no government run school. As late as 1918, 325 of the 560 schools in Barcelona were religious and only 74 were public. Illiteracy rates were gradually dropping, but they only dropped from 72 percent in 1877 to between 63 and 67 percent in 1900 and 59 percent in 1910. Moreover, government run schools were chronically underfunded, overcrowded, and staffed by inexperienced, underpaid teachers in facilities that were falling apart.[14]

Educational initiatives beyond the scope of the Catholic Church emerged in Catalonia after the Napoleonic Wars in the early nineteenth century among followers of Charles Fourier and Joseph Lancaster. In the middle of the century, coalitions of republicans, democrats, and "utopian" socialists formed schools in workers' societies. Attention to working-class education soared, however, after "la Gloriosa" of 1868 (when Queen Isabella II abdicated) and the formation of the Federación Regional Española (FRE, the Spanish section of the International Workingmen's Association, or First International) in 1870. When Bakunin's comrade Giuseppe Fanelli journeyed to Spain to promote anarchism in 1868, the statutes of Bakunin's alliance that he disseminated included a provision on "integral education": a combination of intellectual and manual learning intended to break down the barriers that characterized capitalist society.[15]

The concept of "integral education" grew out of a long line of anarchist and socialist pedagogical theory. Though libertarian education certainly had precedents in Enlightenment thinkers like Locke, Rousseau, and later Godwin, Paul Avrich cites the French socialist Charles Fourier as the likely originator of the notion of "integral education." Subsequently Pierre-Joseph Proudhon argued that "labor and study, which have for so long and so foolishly been kept apart will finally emerge side by side in their natural state of union."[16] Proudhon was joined by Bakunin, Kropotkin, Marx, and many other nineteenth-century radicals in calling for education that could contribute toward the abolition of a key pillar of class rule in the classroom.

Despite their agreement on integral education in the early 1870s, the followers of Marx and Bakunin clashed over how to enact it, with the former advocating for free, mandatory state education and the latter for the autonomous creation of free schools from the bottom up.[17] While Spanish anarchists placed a great deal of emphasis on the transformative potential of education, the socialists of Pablo Iglesias's PSOE (Partido Socialista Obrero Español, or Spanish Socialist Workers' Party) did not focus on education and even eliminated the term "integral" from their program in 1888. Yet, as the party became more reformist in the 1890s, its focus on educational reform returned. In the new century, the socialists were influenced by the example of the Modern School to create a number of lay and "rationalist" schools in their clubs and centers.[18] Meanwhile, dissident intellectuals, including Francisco Giner de los Ríos, founded the Institución Libre de Enseñanza (Free Educational Institute) in 1876 to promote independent secular education. By the end of the century, free-thinking secularists were promoting their own brand of lay education across the country. For example, in the early 1880s the Confederación anticlerical organized nineteen schools.[19] Between 1882 and 1896, seventy lay schools were established in Catalonia alone.

Ferrer had been living in France since 1885, so it is safe to assume that when he decided to found the Modern School in 1900 he was more influenced by French developments than those back across the border. When he arrived in France, he was a committed republican who must have viewed the French Third Republic (established in 1870) as a model of egalitarianism. Much of Ferrer's disenchantment with republicanism grew out of the utter disgust that he developed observing the nationalist regimentation of the French secular educational program up close in Paris. Over time he came to learn that "God was replaced by the state, Christian virtue by civic duty, religion by patriotism, submission to the king, the aristocracy, and the clergy by subservience to the official, the proprietor, and the employer."[20] For Ferrer, true education had to transcend the limitations of republican secularism to target the roots of ignorance and error.

As Ferrer grew disenchanted with French republican education, he was likely intrigued by a growing focus on education in the libertarian milieu from 1897 onward in France. Although the wave of *universités populaires* (popular universities) for adults that exploded in the second half of the 1890s featured notable anarchist participation, institutionally they were "laborator[ies] for experiments in class collaboration" (unlike the Free Popular University started by Luigi Galleani and his anarchist comrades in Alexandria, Egypt, in 1901).[21] A far more revolutionary undertaking was put forth by the anarchist founders of the League of Libertarian Education, who sought to put integral education into practice. Though their efforts to create *"l'école libertaire"* foundered for a lack of money, they organized *"vacances libertaires,"* or libertarian outings, for local children. The anarchists of the League of Libertarian Education gave up their goal of raising money for a school in 1900, the same year Ferrer decided to create his own.[22]

Ferrer was strongly influenced by his comrade Jean Grave, the editor of *Temps nouveaux,* author of the 1900 *Éducation bourgeoise et éducation libertaire,* and one of the "initiators" of the "educational current" sweeping French anarchism.[23] Ferrer's most important French influence, however,

Mateo Morral. AEP.

was the anarchist educator Paul Robin, who put integral education into practice as the director of the anarchist orphanage at Cempuis from 1880 to 1894. Ferrer seems to have met Robin through his participation in Robin's neo-Malthusian Ligue de la régénération humaine, which Robin founded in 1896.[24] Neo-Malthusianism, which first developed among Owenite socialists, differed significantly from the original ideas of Thomas Malthus. Whereas Malthus disdainfully called upon the working class to show moral restraint in limiting their procreation in order to maintain the population equilibrium that he believed necessary for the well-being of society, neo-Malthusians focused on empowering working-class women to take control of their reproduction through the use of birth control. In southern Europe, neo-Malthusianism was strongly associated with anarchism and revolution, as anarchists and their allies were among its earliest advocates in Spain, Portugal, and Italy. In 1900, the first International Neo-Malthusian Congress was attended by Robin, Ferrer, and Emma Goldman, who relentlessly promoted birth control in the United States. One of the most passionate Spanish neo-Malthusians was the administrator of the Modern School publishing house, Mateo Morral, who attempted to assassinate the king in 1906.[25] According to his daughter Sol, Ferrer attempted to establish a sexual education class for the older students at the Modern School. This initiative elicited a condemnation from the archbishop and caused many parents to threaten to withdraw their children.[26]

The ideas and examples of these individuals and institutions propelled Ferrer to create a school that challenged the authority of reactionary Catholic education, that promoted science and empirical inquiry, emphasized student engagement and choice, championed mixed-gender education, and sought to forge well-rounded autonomous individuals. While these ideas were not new, Ferrer and his Modern School should be recognized as among the first, and by far the most influential, to put libertarian educational concepts into practice.

However, an examination of the Modern School textbooks, the articles of the *Boletín de la Escuela Moderna*, and Ferrer's own writings on the school makes it clear that the procedures of the Modern School went beyond the dispassionate application of the scientific method as many of Ferrer's moderate supporters claimed. Moreover, the daily activities of the Modern School were actually far more scheduled, disciplined, routinized, and traditional than many would imagine from what some have hailed as the preeminent "anarchist school." Although the practice seems to have been discontinued after the first year, students were even issued number grades that were published in the school newspaper. [See p. 167.] Similarly, at least during the first year of operation, students were not allowed to participate in Thursday and Sunday excursions if they misbehaved during the week.[27] At least initially the Modern School also implemented rewards and punishments.

When they were allowed to participate, Modern School students were taken on a variety of interactive field trips to factories and laboratories. Despite its advocacy of integral education, however, the curriculum consistently prioritized intellectual over manual activities. To some extent this may have owed to the fact that the Modern School, located in the affluent Ensanche (Eixample) neighborhood of Barcelona, attracted middle-class students who had less of a need to learn manual trades.[28] Students paid to attend the Modern School, but working-class students were given a discount.

The Modern School was well ahead of its time in advocating coeducation, but Ferrer held extremely essentialist views on gender and primarily advocated gender equality in education to stop women from imbibing Catholic dogma in their domestic isolation and train them to be "mothers in the true natural and social sense, not transmitters of traditional superstitions." Such mothers were necessary, Ferrer wrote, in order to educate the "men thus emancipated from mystery" who were to create the new society. Fundamentally, Ferrer advocated coeducation in order to shape the minds of the mothers of male revolutionaries.[29] Such views were common in Spain and beyond among the men of the left in the early twentieth century, many of whom opposed women's suffrage on the grounds that women allegedly tended to vote for right-wing parties. Moreover, some Modern School activities such as dressmaking and home economics were gender-specific.[30] Nor was the Modern School entirely horizontal. We are left with few clues as to the specific procedures that were followed to make educational decisions, but in "The Modern School" Ferrer describes having rejected a proposal from the Modern School Committee because he was "the executive power."[31]

The Modern School certainly taught its students to oppose the wars and aggression of all governments, but its faculty retained elements of the predominant European imperialist mindset of the era. For example, in 1902, the political cartoonist Miró Folguera gave a Sunday lecture about the nineteenth-century explorer David Livingstone. Though Folguera condemned the atrocities committed by the explorers and governments that followed behind Livingstone, he still claimed that in Central Africa Livingstone encountered "the poor blacks who owed him so much and paid their debt to him with so much love."[32] In another Sunday lecture, Dr. Odón de Buen argued that Africa was "the continent least suitable for human expansion, and as a consequence that with the most backward civilization."[33] Likewise Ferrer included Christopher Columbus with Copernicus, Galileo, and Darwin in his list of great figures who promoted truth against religious superstition.[34] German biologist Ernst Haeckel maintained a working relationship with Ferrer, and his work was published in the *Boletín,* despite his promotion of scientific racism. Both the achievements and the failures of the Modern School must be situated within their time and place. For too many years, English-language analysis of Ferrer and the Modern School have taken Ferrer at his word about his school without examining its actual operations or sufficiently fleshing out its context.

Certainly, the discrepancy between the more traditional, rote, and disciplinarian methods of the Modern School and Ferrer's later opposition to grades and emphasis on student initiative were in part a product of the school's evolution and a result of the interplay of a diverse array of teachers and administrators pushing and pulling in different directions in a context where rationalist education had few models to turn to. Nevertheless, it also reflects the fact that Ferrer's main critique of lay education in general, and that of the French Third Republic in particular, focused not on its educational form as much as its content: in deifying the state rather than the Church, French lay education had still not rid itself of the principle of hierarchy and its books remained "tainted with error," as Ferrer put it.[35] This suggests that if French education had simply provided students with better books and more antiauthoritarian principles, then Ferrer would have been largely satisfied. If for Ferrer "the teacher plants the seeds of ideas," then the principal goal of rationalist education was to gather the correct seeds.[36]

Ferrer's emphasis on educational content above educational form drew sharp criticism from some fellow anarchists of the era, including Ricardo Mella and Clémence (or Clemencia) Jacquinet, who argued that anarchist education should focus on form while remaining "neutral" on content *"free of all classes of isms."*[37] Yet, as the Ferrer scholar Pere Solà argued, "The nucleus of the Ferrerian approach consists in affirming that an educational vision exclusively limited to the mere innovation of form— as audacious as this may appear—ends up being recuperated by the bourgeoisie and the governments that express its interest."[38] Ferrer argued:

> If rationalist education were limited to propagating knowledge about hygiene, about natural sciences, and to training good apprentices, good employees, and good workers in all trades, we could come to live among more or less healthy and hardy atheists . . . but we would always live among slaves to capitalism.[39]

Sociologist Jaume Carbonell concurred, writing that the Ferrerian "perspective on the necessity of social revolution" made it so that Ferrer's ideas "could not be manipulated by the bourgeoisie."[40]

Anarchists on both sides of this debate stitched together their positions out of the existing intellectual cloth of the era, characterized by materialist, positivist, rationalist, and evolutionary modes of thought. Ferrer's educational project revolved fundamentally around the struggle to extirpate "error" from the human mind. Influenced by the arguments of Kropotkin and Elisée Reclus, Ferrer developed a monistic interpretation of truth that united the natural sciences, social sciences, and morality into a single conceptual apparatus. Ferrer's perspective was critically shaped by the argument put forward by the German biologist and influential figure in the development of scientific racism, Ernst Haeckel, that human reason was physiological and integrally embedded in the natural world. Influenced by Spencerian and Darwinian evolutionary theories, Ferrer joined Reclus in conceiving of "natural reason" as a kind of universal language that could redeem humanity from centuries of bondage.[41] The positivism that animated Ferrer's outlook was pervasive during his era, though his personal enthusiasm for new sociological theories was undoubtedly enhanced by sitting in on some of Émile Durkheim's lectures at the Sorbonne while he lived in Paris.[42]

(*Front*) Anselmo Lorenzo, Francisco Ferrer, and (*back*) Ignacio Clariá in 1909. IISG BG A9/31.

For Ricardo Mella, Ferrer's main anarchist critic, and his fellow advocates of "neutral" education, however, Ferrer's penchant for inculcating educational content against religion or capitalism, for example, interfered with an individual's ability to use science, understood as ontologically autonomous, to acquire "conquered truths, universally recognized, [that] will be enough to intellectually form free individuals."[43] According to Mella and likeminded anarchists, "neutral" education freed from all ideological formulations, as objectively correct as they may be, would lead students toward anarchistic outcomes. Yet Mella was also influenced by a skepticism toward science and reason that was mounting at the turn of the century. In contrast to Ferrer's rationalist élan, in 1904, Mella argued, "Modern positivism is a good example of how one can easily fall into dogmatism, even when dealing with scientific systemizations."[44] For Ferrer's close comrade and collaborator Anselmo Lorenzo, "positivism and socialism [were] twin brothers."[45] Ultimately Ferrer was secure enough in the righteousness of his political / scientific outlook to confidently dismiss his critics. In private correspondence in 1905 he wrote:

> If they want to call it dogma when we demonstrate that religions are bad because they make individuals believe that there is another life, and that politics are bad because according to the representative or parliamentary system individuals delegate to others the task of improving their situation, let them call it dogma.[46]

Anarchist Education and the Modern School is the first English-language collection of Francisco Ferrer's writings on pedagogy, the general strike, and social revolution. In addition, it features articles from the *Boletín de la Escuela Moderna* (Modern School Bulletin) and critiques from contemporary anarchist pedagogical writers, such as Ricardo Mella and Clémence Jacquinet, that provide the context necessary in order to assess Ferrer's estimation of his educational project, which has been taken at face value for many years in the English-language literature on the Modern School.

Notes

1   *Causa contra Francisco Ferrer Guardia: instruida y fallada por la Jurisdicción de Guerra en Barcelona, año 1909* (Madrid: Sucesores de J. A. García, 1911), 645.

2   Twelve of those pardons were specifically for parricide. Francisco Bergasa, *¿Quién mató a Ferrer i Guardia?* (Madrid: Aguilar, 2009), 516.

3   Ibid., 520, 524.

4   Ibid., 528.

5   Jaime de Angulo, *The "Trial" of Ferrer: A Clerical Judicial Murder* (New York: New York Labor News Company, 1911).

6   This quote is from the first Ferrer campaign, but the point applies to both. *L'Humanité*, January 6, 1907.

7   *Francisco Ferrer: His Life, Work and Martyrdom* (New York: Francisco Ferrer Association, 1910), 1.

8   Juan Avilés, *Francisco Ferrer y Guardia: pedagogo, anarquista y mártir* (Madrid: Marcial Pons, 2006), 12; Bergasa, *¿Quién mató a Ferrer i Guardia?*, 106; Maurice de Vroede, "Francisco Ferrer et la Ligue Internationale pour l'Éducation Rationnelle de l'Enfance," *Paedagogica Historica* 19 (1979): 286; Geoffrey C. Fidler, "The Escuela Moderna Movement of Francisco Ferrer: 'Por la Verdad y la Justicia,'" *History of Education Quarterly* 25, no. 1–2 (Spring–Summer, 1985): 110.

9   See p. 50 in chapter III of *The Modern School*.

10 This is from an article in *España Nueva*, November 14, 1906, translated in William Heaford, "Some Side-Lights on Ferrer's Personality," in *Francisco Ferrer: His Life, Work, and Martyrdom*, 24–25.

11 Avilés, *Francisco Ferrer y Guardia*, 172.

12 Charles Malato, *L'Assassinat de Ferrer: Eclaircissements* (Geneva: Édition du Réveil, 1911), 5.

13 Ibid., 6.

14 Carolyn P. Boyd, "The Anarchists and Education in Spain, 1868–1909," *The Journal of Modern History* 48, no. 4 (1976): 134–36; Adrian Shubert, *A Social History of Modern Spain* (London: Routledge, 1990), 182–83; Ferran Aisa, *La cultura anarquista a Catalunya* (Barcelona: Edicions de 1984, 2006), 189; Julio Ruiz Berrio, "La rénovation pédagogique en Espagne de la fin du XIXe siècle à 1939," *Histoire de l'éducation* 78 (1998): 135.

15 Alejandro Tiana Ferrer, "Movimiento obrero y educación popular en la España contemporánea," *Historia Social* 27 (1997): 128–30.

16 Paul Avrich, *The Modern School Movement: Anarchism and Education in the United States* (Princeton: Princeton University Press, 1980), 10–16.

17 Tiana Ferrer, "Movimiento obrero y educación popular en la España contemporánea," 128–29.

18 Ibid., 133–36.

19 Yvonne Turin, *La educación y la escuela en España de 1874 a 1902: liberalismo y tradición*, trans. Josefa Hernández Alfonso (Madrid: Aguilar, 1967), 264.

20 See chapter 11 of *The Modern School*.

21 Jean Maitron, *Le movement anarchiste en France: 1. Des origins à 1914* (Paris: Gallimard, 1992), 353–56; Anthony Gorman, "Anarchists in Education: The Free Popular University in Egypt (1901)," *Middle Eastern Studies* 41, no. 3 (May, 2005): 303–20; Sanford Elwitt, "Education and the Social Questions: The Universités Populaires in Late Nineteenth Century France," *History of Education Quarterly* 22, no. 1 (Spring, 1982): 55–72.

22 Maitron, *Le movement anarchiste en France*, 353–56.

23 Sylvain Wagnon, *Francisco Ferrer: une éducation libertaire en héritage* (Lyon: Atelier de création libertaire, 2013), 44–45.

24 de Vroede, "Francisco Ferrer et la Ligue Internationale, 284.

25 Eduard Masjuan, *Un héroe trágico del anarquismo español: Mateo Morral, 1879–1906* (Barcelona: Icaria editorial, 2009), 81–119; Aisa, *La cultura anarquista a Catalunya*, 119–30; C.L. James, *Anarchism and Malthus* (New York: Mother Earth, 1910).

26 Sol Ferrer, *Le véritable Francisco Ferrer: d'après des documents inédits* (Paris: L'Écran du monde, 1948), 126.

27 *Boletín de la Escuela Moderna*, May 31, 1902.

28 Pere Solà i Gussinyer, "Escuela y educación para una sociedad autogestionada: la aportación de la pedagogía racionalista de F. Ferrer," in *Ferrer Guardia y la pedagogía libertaria: elementos para un debate*, ed. Jordi Monés, Pere Solà, and Luis Miguel Lázaro (Barcelona: Icaria Editorial, 1977), 90–1.

29 See p. 124 in *The Modern School* chapter 14.

30 Aisa, *La cultura anarquista a Catalunya*, 192.

31 See p. 55 in *The Modern School* chapter 4.

32 *Boletín de la Escuela Moderna*, March 31, 1902.

33 *Boletín de la Escuela Moderna*, October 31, 1905.

34 See p. 124 in *The Modern School* chapter 14.

35 See p. 94 in *The Modern School* chapter 11.

36 See p. 57 in *The Modern School* chapter 4.

37 See p. 200 in "The Problem of Teaching."

38 Solà i Gussinyer, "Escuela y educación para una sociedad autogestionada," 67.

39 Ibid.

40 Jaume Carbonell, introduction to Monés, Solà, and Lázaro, *Ferrer Guardia y la pedagogía libertaria*, 7–8.

41 Jordi de Cambra Bassols, *Anarquismo y positivismo: el caso Ferrer* (Madrid: Centro de Investigaciones Sociológicas, 1981), 57–74.

42 Ferrer, *Le véritable Francisco Ferrer*, 49.

43 See p. 202 in "The Problem of Teaching"; de Cambra Bassols, *Anarquismo y positivismo*, 71.

44 Álvaro Girón Sierra, *En la mesa con Darwin: evolución y revolución en el movimiento libertario en España (1869–1914)* (Madrid: Consejo Superior de Investigaciones Científicas, 2005), 63.

45 Boyd, "The Anarchists and Education in Spain, 1868–1909," 128.

46 Avilés, *Francisco Ferrer y Guardia*, 107–8.

II
Francisco Ferrer: The Man
Mark Bray

On a warm June day in Paris in 1894 Francisco Ferrer stared down the barrel of a different gun. This one was not a rifle in the hands of a steely-eyed soldier. No, in front of him stood a thirty-four-year-old woman whose trembling hands pointed a revolver at his head. She was Teresa Sanmartí—his wife. How did it come to this?

It all started when Ferrer got a job as a ticket inspector for the Compañía de Tarragona, a Barcelona y Francia railroad company, at the age of nineteen, in 1878.[1] This job allowed him to consistently travel outside of the country for the first time, and it inaugurated his formal political activity. Not long after assuming the position, Ferrer became a courier for the Spanish revolutionary republican leader Manuel Ruiz Zorrilla, who had been living in exile in Paris since shortly after the collapse of the First Spanish Republic in 1874. The First Republic and the revolutionary period that preceded it formed a bedrock of inspiration for Ferrer and his generation of radicals. In a short autobiographical sketch, Ferrer claimed to have vivid memories of participating in the popular celebrations of "la Gloriosa," the abdication of Queen Isabella II, in 1868, when he was only nine years old. Writing of himself in the third person, he claimed that the events of this era "left their mark upon his spirit. From then on, he never ceased to interest himself in political struggles."[2]

While the queen's abdication may not have truly meant as much to Ferrer when he was nine as it did when he was older, it was a tremendous development for Spanish republicans who had been longing for a republic since the French Revolution. France had already experimented with two short-lived republics and would soon inaugurate its most successful yet when the Third Republic commenced its seventy years of governance in 1870. The Spanish monarchy, however, had been fighting tooth and nail to stave off the encroachment of republican ideas from across the Pyrenees since the Napoleonic invasion, while also fending off the supporters of the pretender to the throne Infante Carlos, known as Carlists, who challenged Queen Isabella's claim. That struggle collapsed in 1868 when Generals Juan Prim and Francisco Serrano and much of the military turned against the government and Isabella II stepped down. After a brief provisional government and a failed attempt to install an Italian prince, Amadeo of Savoy, onto the Spanish throne, the long-awaited Spanish Republic was proclaimed on February 11, 1873.

Months after the republic was proclaimed, at the age of fourteen, Ferrer left his home in Alella, a small village in Catalonia, to work for a fabric merchant near Barcelona. This decision likely stemmed from the economic realities of being the thirteenth of fourteen children. On January 14, 1859, Francisco Juan Ramón Ferrer Guardia was born to Jaime Ferrer and his wife María Ángela Guardia.[3] According to Francisco Ferrer's daughter Sol, his parents were conservative Catholics and fairly affluent owners of a local vineyard. She explained that the only contact Francisco and his siblings had with progressive thought came from their uncle, a freethinking soldier, whose civil burial scandalized the community. Allegedly, "Quico," as Ferrer's mother called him, was eager to attend his uncle's funeral, but this provoked a beating from the local priest. Until the age of ten, Ferrer attended the Alella municipal school. His intense disgust with how the school was run became a key inspiration for his future creation of the Modern School. Looking back, Ferrer wrote, "The school of my youth made me strive to do everything to the contrary of what it was."[4] He spent the next two years at another local school, which he described as "little better than a stable," before ending his formal education at thirteen and leaving home to work shortly thereafter.[5]

Ferrer's first job away from home would have a profound impact on the course of his life. He went to San Martí de Provençals to live and work with the republican merchant Pablo Ossorio whose wife had been a childhood friend of Ferrer's mother. Ossorio treated Ferrer with great affection, encouraging him to take night classes and initiating his political education amid the excitement of the First Republic. By the age of fifteen, Ferrer accompanied Ossorio to all of his political meetings.[6] However, the First Republic fell far short of the lofty aspirations of most republicans.

Passing through seven presidents in less than two years, the government struggled to cohere around competing centralist and federalist tendencies within the republican movement; it failed to truly mobilize popular support as the Spanish section of the First International was firing the imaginations of the dispossessed; it desperately resisted Carlist insurrection and the continual intrigue of Bourbon restoration—all the while continuing to wage the Ten Years' War to maintain colonial control of Cuba. In December 1874, General Arsenio Martínez Campos led the *pronunciamiento* that restored the Bourbon monarchy to the throne in the figure of Alfonso XII, Isabella's son.

After the restoration of the monarchy, republicans were divided between those who reluctantly accepted the monarchy and those who rejected it. The most prominent advocate of reconciliation was the final president of the First Republic, Práxedes Mateo Sagasta, who became the leader of the dynastic Partido Liberal, which alternated in power with Antonio Cánovas del Castillo's Partido Conservador. Sagasta and his followers were granted liberal concessions and guaranteed a significant parliamentary minority by the Conservatives to bring them into the fold, so they could marginalize intransigent republican elements in a power sharing system, known as the *turno pacífico*, where the two parties took turns in government.[7] Ultimately, in 1897, the Italian anarchist Michele Angiolillo assassinated Cánovas during his sixth term as prime minister, while Sagasta served seven times before dying in 1903. Over time, more and more republican leaders, including Emilio Castelar and José Canalejas, integrated their followers into the Liberal Party.[8]

Yet a significant number of republicans refused to accept the Restoration. Some, such as former prime ministers of the First Republic Nicolás Salmerón and Francisco Pi y Margall, attempted to resist with the ballot. Others resisted with the bullet. The principal revolutionary republican conspirator of the era was Manuel Ruiz Zorrilla (1833–1895). After being elected to Congress in 1858, Ruiz Zorrilla became an active conspirator against the regime of Isabella II in the 1860s. During the *sexenio democrático* (1868–1874) he occupied various high-profile government positions, culminating in two terms as prime minister in the early 1870s. After the fall of the Republic, Ruiz Zorrilla refused to capitulate. For Ruiz Zorrilla, the key to dethroning the king was to win over the military. Although he incorporated socialist elements into his various platforms, he had relatively little interest in popular politics. From exile in France, he expanded his network of sympathetic high-ranking military contacts and hatched insurrectionary plots in the late 1870s and early 1880s with the aid of French republicans like Victor Hugo and Georges Clemenceau.[9] The young Francisco Ferrer was enthralled by Ruiz Zorrilla's romantic revolutionary vision. He soon became one of Ruiz Zorrilla's most faithful operatives, entrusted with transmitting messages across the border while working as a railroad ticket inspector after parting ways with the merchant Ossorio at the age of nineteen.

One day in 1880, Ferrer was allegedly struck by the beauty of a distressed young woman on the train named Teresa Sanmartí Guiu. When Ferrer approached her, she broke down in tears and explained that she was on her way to Gerona to enter a convent. Her family had left her no other option, she explained, since her father had died and her mother and older brothers treated her like a maid. Ferrer comforted her, passionately dissuading her from becoming a nun. His efforts a success, they were married within a few months. While living in the Barcelona neighborhood of Sants, they gave birth to their daughters, Trinidad in January 1882 and Paz about twenty months later.[10] However, Ferrer's youthful desire to save an attractive young woman from the clutches of Catholicism led him to rush into a poor match, while Sanmartí's quest to avoid domestic servitude was ultimately not as fruitful as she had hoped.

Neither Francisco nor Teresa got along with their in-laws. Teresa considered Francisco's mother to be domineering and found their penchant for calling him "Quico" to be disrespectful. Moreover, Sanmartí pushed Ferrer to work his way up the ladder of the railroad company, while he was much more interested in spending his free time reading and teaching himself French. Her insistence on his career advancement seems to have stemmed from the fact that she was "possessed by ideas of grandeur and luxury," as her daughter Trinidad phrased it.[11] Most important, perhaps, was Sanmartí's hatred for republicanism. The more time Ferrer put into meetings and books, the farther apart they drifted. Increasingly, he stayed out until the early morning hours, leaving the household chores and childcare responsibilities to Sanmartí, who no longer had any time to pursue her interests in reading and playing the guitar. In an effort to break out of her domestic isolation, Sanmartí started to leave her young daughters home alone at night while she socialized with her girlfriends.[12]

To make matters worse for Sanmartí, in 1883 Ferrer joined La Verdad Masonic lodge under the Masonic name "Cero" (Zero). By the end of the nineteenth century freemasonry had come to represent a significant network for all stripes of radicals and freethinkers in Western Europe and beyond. Although freemasonry originated in London in 1717 as a network designed to promote spirituality apart from religious and political sectarianism, by the late nineteenth century it had shifted toward rationalism and liberalism, erecting a "secular cult of reason." Masonry became far more political and anticlerical when lodges in France, Belgium, and elsewhere removed the requirement that members believe in God. After 1870, Masonry became the "Church of the Republic" as many radical republican politicians and left dissidents comingled through its archaic rituals and rites. A similar shift to the anticlerical left occurred in Spanish Masonry, which became a platform for collaboration between all shades of republicans, anarchists, anticlericals, and others after it became legal again with the creation of the First Republic in 1873. The very real connections between freemasonry, anticlericalism, revolutionary intrigue, and the nightmares they provoked led Pope Pius IX to refer to Masonry as the "synagogue of Satan."[13] Notable Masons of the era included figures from around the world, including anarchists like Charles Malato, Anselmo Lorenzo, Sébastien Faure, Pedro Vallina, Belén de Sárraga, Teresa Claramunt, and Enrique Flores Magón, republicans like Ferrer's beloved Manuel Ruiz Zorrilla, Henri Rochefort, Francisco Pi y Margall, Alejandro Lerroux, and the Modern School collaborator Odón de Buen, as well as nationalists like José Rizal, José Martí, and Antonio Maceo.[14]

Around the time Ferrer became a Mason, his marriage deteriorated to the point that he moved out to live on his own in several different locations in Barcelona and then the small Catalan town of Granollers, where he had to appeal to the local Masonic lodge for financial support.[15] Although his marriage was on the decline, his political activity was on the rise. Years later, Ferrer claimed to have collaborated with Ruiz Zorrilla (who had achieved the highest rank in freemasonry) in the conspiracy behind the April 1884 republican military rising of Santa Coloma de Farnés. Three days after the start of the insurgency, government troops put down the only battalion to revolt and executed the battalion's commander and one of its lieutenants. Ferrer wrote that his role in the failed conspiracy, combined with his marital problems, prompted him to flee to Paris. Yet the fact that he remained in Spain until a year after the rising and the absence of evidence that the authorities were pursuing him for his involvement in the conspiracy, which was likely minor, suggest that Ferrer was on the run from his wife more than he was from the government.[16]

In May 1885, Ferrer quit his railroad job, brought his wife and daughters to stay with his brother José and other relatives in Alella, and set off alone for Paris. Through his connections to Ruiz Zorrilla and related transnational republican circles, in September Ferrer managed to open a wine shop on rue Pont Neuf, where he lived in the back room. Ferrer kept in touch with his wife and they managed to reconcile. In March 1886, Teresa and their daughters Trinidad, Paz, and the recently born Luz arrived in Paris. Ferrer's daughter Sol, who was born in 1892, claimed that during this period her father participated in the planning of Manuel Villacampa's failed republican rising in Madrid in September 1886, but there is no evidence to corroborate her claim. If he did, it was likely again in the role of messenger. Only three hundred soldiers out of a garrison of twenty thousand took up arms against the government.[17] Villacampa's 1886 *pronunciamiento* marked the end of the classical era of military-republican conspiracy and the last relevant gasp of Ruiz Zorrilla's insurgent politics. The abject failures of the 1884 and 1886 risings may have pushed Ferrer to take a step back over the following years and more seriously consider other modes of social transformation beyond military insurrection. This was certainly evident at the Madrid Universal Freethinkers Congress of 1892, where Ferrer made a rash attempt to hurriedly assemble a cadre of three hundred committed revolutionaries that would seek out an opportunity, such as a general strike, to overthrow the monarchy in collaboration with the Socialist Party and others. [See p. 207.]

Meanwhile, Ferrer converted his wine shop into a restaurant called Libertad (Liberty). The restaurant started to gain some popularity among local students, but business suffered in October 1886 when the anarchist Clément Duval stabbed a police agent before fleeing into Ferrer's restaurant. In 1889, Ferrer gave up the restaurant to give free Spanish lessons at the Grand Orient of France Masonic temple and paid lessons to private clients. Ferrer had continued his Masonry upon arriving in Paris in 1884, joining Les Vrais Experts lodge. Eventually Ferrer would rise to the top of Parisian freemasonry by becoming a ""Grand Inspector Inquisitor," degree 31 out of 33 possible degrees.[18] Although their family was reunited, Teresa hated Paris and loathed her husband's commitment to the Masons. On Sundays, he brought his daughters to the Grant Orient, and even had Trinidad and Paz participate in a Masonic adoption ceremony.[19]

Sanmartí was no happier with Ferrer's new line of work. Allegedly, she grew intensely jealous as he accumulated more and more upper-class

Trinidad Ferrer and her father
Francisco Ferrer. FFG.

Trinidad and Paz Ferrer in Bendigo,
Australia. UCSD, Box 17, Folder 7.

women as his students. Perhaps in an effort to get closer to him, she also started giving Spanish lessons herself.[20] Ferrer supplemented his income by copying manuscripts. His daughter Trinidad recounted how her mother was enraged when he spent the evening copying after their daughter Luz died in 1893. Trinidad defended his decision, writing that he couldn't afford to lose the work while her "mother understood no grief that did not express itself in cries and theatrical outpourings."[21] Their son Carlos also died around the same time. In total Ferrer and Sanmartí had seven children, but only three (Trinidad, Paz, and Sol) survived to adulthood.[22]

Undoubtedly the grief of losing children put an added strain on the relationship. Their eldest daughter Trinidad was all too aware of her parents' conflicts. She recounted that it got so bad that at about twelve years old she asked her father to send her to a boarding school and get divorced. That same day he took her to stay at an anticlerical school in Montreuil. Every Sunday, Sanmartí travelled to the boarding school to visit her daughter. Over the course of their conversations, Sanmartí berated Trinidad's father and pleaded with the young girl to come live with her after their inevitable divorce. "I was afraid that her tears would break down my resolution," Trinidad recounted. "It was then that I asked my father to send me to Australia."[23] Francisco Ferrer's brother José had moved to Australia years before following a curious migration pattern of

Ferrer family in Bendigo, Australia, 1898. (*from left*) Trinidad, Francisco, Paz, María (José's wife), one of José and María's children, and José (Francisco's brother). Francisco holds a copy of *El Motín*, the anticlerical paper of José Nakens. FFG.

Alella residents to the island. In 1892, Ferrer had sent his second daughter Paz, then about nine years old, around the world to live with her uncle. On June 3, 1894, he obliged his daughter Trinidad by sending her to join her older sister and uncle.[24]

That was the last straw for Teresa Sanmartí. When her attempts to have her husband arrested as an alleged anarchist bore no fruit, nine days later, on June 12, 1894, she approached him on rue Richer. For years they had lived together at 26 rue Richer, but several months earlier Ferrer had moved down the street to live on his own at number 43. That day she walked up to him and fired three shots from her revolver. Had her aim been better we would have no occasion to publish this book, but Ferrer only suffered a scratch on his head. Sanmartí was immediately arrested. When interrogated, she claimed that Ferrer had removed all of the furniture from their apartment and left her to pay the rent on her own. More importantly, she claimed that he had taken away her daughters.[25] Trinidad, however, clarified in no uncertain terms that

> My mother was never ignorant of my address. At each port of call I wrote to her (for one always loves one's mother), and she knew the address of my uncle in Australia. As to my sister Sol [then three],

who had been [sent to a wet nurse], my mother could have kept her
had she wished to, or could have gone to see her, for she knew the
address of the nurse.[26]

At first the Parisian newspaper *Le Figaro* acceded to Ferrer's request to
avoid a scandal, but before long they published Teresa's story, which gar-
nered her great public sympathy and cost Ferrer clients for his Spanish
lessons. After a few weeks in prison, Sanmartí was handed a one-year
sentence, which was subsequently suspended allowing her to walk free.[27]
After this definitive split, Sanmartí met a fabulously rich young Ukrainian
aristocrat named Mering. They moved to "a vast property near Saint
Petersburg" with Sol, got married, and had three more daughters. Sol
would grow up in Tsarist Russia, never to see her father again. The fact
that Sol Ferrer never really got to know her father seems to have motivated
her to become an archivist of his life's work and write a doctoral disserta-
tion on him at the Sorbonne in 1959.[28]

Another rupture, perhaps even more important than separating from
his wife, occurred for Ferrer in 1895 when the republican leader Manuel
Ruiz Zorrilla died. While Ferrer may have been gradually rethinking his
politics for years, the death of the man he had envisioned as the leader of
the revolution clearly forced Ferrer, then in his mid-thirties, to take account
of the broader political context. After the death of Ruiz Zorrilla, a power
struggle erupted within the Partido Progresista when the age-old question of electoral participation versus armed insurrection reemerged, split-
ting the party. None of the "impenitent careerists," as Ferrer called them,
vying for power could match the charisma of their fallen leader nor could
they find sufficient ground for a practical compromise. Although a Unión
Republicana came out of the process a year later, it amounted to little.
Regarding their lack of popular support, General Prim once quipped that
nineteenth-century Spanish republican leaders were "generals without
soldiers." In the midst of this chaos, Ferrer was increasingly uninterested
in enlisting.[29]

The bickering and ineptitude of the divided republican leadership
led Ferrer to consider socialism. Around this time, he became a member
of Jules Guesde's Parti ouvrier français (French Workers' Party, POF). In
the republican paper *El País*, Ferrer publicly advocated for revolutionary
unity between socialists and republicans back in Spain and chastised the
Socialist leader Pablo Iglesias for his "campaign against the republican

parties; something farther beyond common sense than anything that I have ever seen other than the notion of a conservative republic."[30] Over the summer of 1896, Ferrer travelled to London as a POF delegate from the 9th arrondissement of Paris to attend the fourth congress of the Second International. At the congress Ferrer proposed a resolution "in favor of the Cubans, Cretans, Macedonians, and Armenians who are fighting for their independence" that was unanimously approved.[31] Far more contentious however, was a proposal to exclude all those opposed to parliamentary action—i.e., the anarchists. Despite arguments for anarchist inclusion made by figures such as Errico Malatesta and Domela Nieuwenhuis, the congress voted to exclude the anarchists, marking a definitive break in the relations between the two camps that would only expand into the twentieth century. Although the French delegation narrowly voted in favor of anarchist participation, Ferrer was the only POF member to support their continued participation.[32] Feeling like the odd man out, Ferrer left the socialist movement behind for good after departing from London.[33]

Instead, he increasingly turned to anarchism. Ferrer got to know the influential Spanish anarchist Anselmo Lorenzo while living in Barcelona and befriended the French anarchist Charles Malato shortly after his arrival in Paris, but it wasn't until the death of Ruiz Zorrilla and his failed flirtation with socialism that he seems to have taken anarchism seriously. By 1896, French anarchism was steadily recovering from the repression brought on by a wave of anarchist "propaganda by the deed" known as *"l'ère des attentats."* After Ravachol bombed the houses of a judge and a prosecutor, Émile Henry bombed a police station and a café, Auguste Vaillant bombed the Chamber of Deputies, and Sante Caserio assassinated the president, the French government passed a series of repressive *"lois scélérates"* (villainous laws) clamping down on anarchism, the labor movement, and radicalism in general. A similar dynamic unfolded across the Pyrenees into Spain, where Paulino Pallás's attempt on the life of a general and Santiago Salvador's bombing of a theater prompted the passage of a harsh anti-anarchist law.[34] Ferrer spoke out against anarchist "propaganda by the deed" in both countries in his 1894 article "How the Spanish Republic Will End Anarchy." [See p. 209.] Yet his handwritten 1892 manifesto aimed at assembling a cadre of three hundred revolutionaries concluded with "¡Viva la dinamita!" suggesting that he may have been more inspired by the "dynamite craze" of the early 1890s than he chose to admit publicly two years later.[35]

Nevertheless, by the second half of the 1890s, French anarchism was transformed by the emergence of revolutionary syndicalism. Although the autonomous unionism and direct-action strategies of revolutionary syndicalism were part and parcel to the antiauthoritarians of the First International, in much of Europe anarchist unionism declined in the 1870s and 1880s (with the notable exception of Spain). The general inability of anarchists to influence the labor movement, paired with a fairly widespread disinterest in the "gradualism" of unionism, opened space for the growth of insurrectionary strains of anarchist communism and the spread of "propaganda by the deed." By the end of the century, however, the popularity of "propaganda by the deed" declined as revolutionary syndicalism reemerged. Influenced in part by the example of British syndicalism, French revolutionary syndicalism coalesced around the Confédération générale du travail (General Confederation of Labor, CGT), established in 1895.[36] Over the following decades revolutionary syndicalism, and its specifically anarchist variant, anarcho-syndicalism, would play a central role in the labor movements of Europe and the Americas. This was the context in which Ferrer gradually came to embrace anarchism, following in the path of many nineteenth-century Spanish republicans who made the transition, including Fermín Salvochea, Ricardo Mella, and José Prat.[37] Ferrer's decision to found the newspaper *La Huelga General* (The General Strike) upon his arrival in Spain several years later attests to the importance of revolutionary syndicalism in his adoption of anarchism.

Professionally Ferrer continued teaching Spanish and published the Spanish grammar book *L'Espagnol pratique: enseigné par la méthode Ferrer* (Practical Spanish: Taught by the Ferrer Method), which billed itself as "the simplest and fastest of all published up to today."[38] Although *L'Espagnol pratique* is a standard grammar text, Ferrer still managed to put his stamp on the work by selecting unorthodox texts, such as works by the republican, Mason, and feminist Ángeles López de Ayala, a text by Demófilo requesting the pardon of the anarchist bomber Paulino Pallás, and a series of anticlerical stories.[39] Years later Ferrer would write:

> I cannot conceive life without propaganda. Wherever I may be—in the street, in public places, in the tramway, in the train—with whomsoever I may find myself in company, I cannot but try to make a convert. I have often exposed myself to rebuffs; but I cannot help it, or rather I do not try to help it. I would rather appear indiscreet

than withhold a word or an observation whereby I may possibly make people reflect.[40]

During this time Ferrer met Ernestine Meunié, the French woman who would become his most significant "convert." In 1894, Meunié started taking Spanish lessons with Ferrer in anticipation of a trip to Spain she had planned with her mother. During the trip her mother died, leaving her the fortune that her deceased father had accumulated in construction during the mid-century urban renovation of Paris known as Haussmanization. The next year, Ferrer mailed Ernestine the autograph of the recently deceased Manuel Ruiz Zorrilla after remembering that Meunié collected autographs. This correspondence renewed the lessons. Yet, according to Ferrer, Meunié was so Catholic that her "conviction amounted to fanaticism." After waiting an entire year before challenging her beliefs, Ferrer started to gradually introduce anticlerical texts and discussions and brought up a debate about the ongoing Dreyfus Affair. Although initially offended, Meunié kept coming back for more until eventually Ferrer managed "to demolish, stone by stone, the fortress of her prejudices."[41]

Ferrer always insisted that his affairs with Ernestine Meunié were strictly platonic. The same was not true about his relationship with another one of his students, Leopoldine Bonnard. In 1897 or 1898, she started taking Spanish lessons with Ferrer and they immediately bonded over their shared interest in pedagogy. Despite, or perhaps because of, their thirteen-year age gap, they moved in together in 1899, and a year later Bonnard gave birth to their son, named Riego after the legendary leader of an early nineteenth-century liberal revolt against the crown. Though it's unclear whether Bonnard became an anarchist before or after meeting Ferrer, she heartily embraced his vision of the Modern School and became a French teacher there when it opened.[42] Ferrer would have formally divorced Sanmartí in order to marry Bonnard, but Spain prohibited divorce and he couldn't manage to become a naturalized French citizen to pursue divorce there.[43]

Over the next few years Ferrer pushed Meunié, ten years his senior, to expand her purview by organizing excursions ranging from the theater and the opera to anarchist meetings and the Parisian underworld. They even journeyed beyond France, travelling around Europe to visit England, Spain, Portugal, Italy, and Switzerland.[44] Ferrer later recounted that in "Geneva, on August 24, 1900, I told her that I did not want any longer to lead this egoistic, pleasure-seeking life, when there was so much to be done for ignorant and suffering humanity. She agreed with me, and offered to stand by me in whatever I proposed." What he proposed was the founding of a school that would teach "based *solely* upon the Natural Sciences," that would teach "the true origin of all the evils that afflict humanity: wars, pestilences, religions, etc."[45] Yet Sol Ferrer actually claimed that Leopoldine Bonnard was the first to come up with the idea of opening a school in Spain.[46]

Immediately upon his return from Switzerland, Ferrer got to work planning what he was originally going to call the Escuela Emancipadora Siglo XX (Emancipatory School of the Twentieth Century). The motto of the school appearing in promotional materials was the rather unwieldy: "To extirpate from the minds of men that which divides them, replacing it with fraternity and solidarity, which are indispensable for the liberty and well-being of all."[47] Ferrer wrote to his Barcelona comrades explaining that the idea was to create a board of directors for the school that would be ideologically diverse while all of the elements of the school itself would be "internally libertarian" but "without broadcasting it externally." To achieve this goal, Ferrer explained that "it is indispensable that the personnel of the School be favorable to our ideas and have well-developed anticlerical convictions, *at least*."[48]

In January 1901, Meunié edited her will to leave Ferrer a building at rue des Petites-Écuries 11 in Paris.[49] On April 2, 1901, less than three months later, she died.[50] Ferrer had the revenue he needed to finance the creation of a school in Barcelona (he later augmented his resources by investing in a Barcelona construction company).[51] On September 8, 1901, the first class of twelve girls and eighteen boys started their first day as students of the Modern School at calle Bailén 56 (today number 70) in Barcelona.[52] In October 1901, Ferrer founded the *Boletín de la Escuela Moderna* to promote the theories of rationalist education to the broader society, and in November he established the revolutionary syndicalist newspaper *La Huelga General*. The timing of Ferrer's return to Spain was extremely fortuitous—only a few years earlier he would have risked arrest by merely entering the country and his school might not have managed to open because of the hysteria around *el proceso de Montjuich*. While the French government reduced the scale of its anti-anarchist repression and issued an amnesty for many of those charged in the mid-1890s, the Spanish monarchy ramped up its mass arrests and torture of prisoners in Montjuich

Castle overlooking Barcelona in response to the bombing of a religious procession in 1896. It was not until 1900, after an international campaign against "inquisitorial" Spain that developed the blueprint for the Ferrer campaigns of the next decade, that the modest civil liberties that political dissidents had made use of were restored and the anarchist movement could resume publishing and organizing.[53] The period of relative calm that came over Barcelona politics was undoubtedly a factor in Ferrer's decision to open the Modern School.

Francisco Ferrer and Soledad Villafranca. FFG, IISG.

As the Modern School continued to grow, it needed to recruit more teachers to cater to its expanding student body. The decision by Soledad Villafranca and her sister Ángeles to apply to teach at the Modern School in 1902 would have a major impact on Ferrer's life. Apparently, Ferrer instantly fell in love with Soledad, twenty-one years his junior, and offered her and her sister jobs despite their lack of qualifications. Over time, their relationship grew as he distanced himself from Leopoldine Bonnard. In 1905, the relationship between Ferrer and Bonnard ended, and she took their five-year-old son Riego to live in Amsterdam with the Dutch anarchist Domela Nieuwenhuis and open a new school in the vein of the Modern School. The school did not materialize, and, after spending a brief time near Paris, Bonnard and Riego moved into Ferrer's country house outside of Barcelona called Mas Germinal, after Émile Zola's novel *Germinal*, while he moved into a new place with Soledad Villafranca in the neighborhood of Gràcia.

Although Ferrer would visit Riego on a few occasions over the following years, and apparently asked his mother for her permission to determine the content of his education, he never developed a relationship with his son. In fact, given how much time and energy he put into working for the education and well-being of children, Ferrer seems to have given his

Ferrer arriving at his trial. *Nuevo Mundo*, June 6, 1907. FFG.

own children a surprisingly small amount of his time. He did not get to know Riego or his daughter Sol, who had been taken to Russia, and Trinidad and Paz spent much of their childhood with their uncle in Australia, though Ferrer used the revenue from his grammar book to visit on several occasions in the late 1890s. It is impossible to answer the oft-repeated question of whether Ferrer was a good father, especially considering the fact that Ferrer's outlook on fatherhood was a product of his time and place. Trinidad, who adopted Ferrer's ideas, Paz, who did not, and Sol, who was sympathetic, vigorously defended their father against allegations that he was a poor father, though the dramatic conflicts surrounding his legacy may have prompted them to be more defensive than they might have been otherwise. Although some have criticized Ferrer for only leaving his daughters the minimum amount of money required by law, he explained that the fortune he was left by Ernestine Meunié was to be used for political purposes.[54] Either way, it is clear that Ferrer invested far more time in the revolutionary potential of youth education as a concept than he did in exploring the particularities of the lives of his own children.

Alongside the Modern School was the publishing house Publicaciones de la Escuela Moderna founded by Ferrer in 1901. Over the following years the publishing house issued volumes from French anarchists such as Jean Grave, Elisée Reclus, and Georges M. Paraf-Javal, as well as academics like Odón de Buen and Andrés Martínez Vargas, a professor of pediatrics at the University of Barcelona. While the school itself educated 114 students in June 1904, by 1905 Modern School books were used in fourteen Barcelona schools and thirty-four provincial schools, thereby affecting many more children.[55]

In 1906, the publishing house was administered by the young Catalan anarchist Mateo Morral. On May 31 of that year, Morral bombed the wedding procession of King Alfonso XIII in Madrid, killing twenty-six and

Masthead for the paper *Pro Ferrer* published in support of Ferrer. UCSD, FB133, Box 1, Folder 6.

injuring one hundred more, not including the king or his new English bride.[56] Days later, Ferrer was arrested as an accomplice and the Modern School was shut down, never to reopen. His arrest sparked a significant international campaign against the "clerical reaction" of the Spanish crown that spread to England, Italy, Portugal, Belgium, and most importantly France. Yet, this campaign accentuated some of the paradoxes at the heart of Ferrer's radicalism. Although his anarchist comrade Charles Malato was one of the campaign's main organizers along with Spanish republican allies, many French anarchists felt marginalized as anarchist speakers were excluded from some of the public meetings, while moderate speakers asserted that Ferrer was "not an anarchist but a reformer."[57] Moreover, some anarchists complained that Ferrer received significant support while unknown French and Spanish anarchists languished in prison, because he was rich and had powerful allies.[58] Nevertheless, the campaign persisted and ultimately succeeded in obtaining Ferrer's acquittal.

But was he really innocent? Probably not. While there is no definitive proof of his guilt, the fact that he allegedly attended a private meeting with Morral and other revolutionaries the night before Morral left for Madrid, that he sent a large check to the man who helped Morral escape, that he supposedly sat in a Barcelona café with the radical republican leader Alejandro Lerroux waiting for news from Madrid at the moment the bomb exploded, and other similar evidence suggest that Ferrer played

Postcard from the hotel in the French Pyrenees where Ferrer wrote *The Modern School*. UCSD, Box 1, Folder 40.

some role in the bombing.[59] Those who defended his reputation in public argued that such an act ran counter to his educational philosophy. But more than an educator, an anarchist, a Mason, a republican, or a freethinker, Ferrer was a revolutionary, and it is highly plausible that he saw the death of the king as a potential opening for an earthshaking political rupture.

After his release from prison on June 12, 1907, Ferrer and Villafranca moved back to Paris. Although he restarted the *Boletín de la Escuela Moderna* and founded the francophone *L'École rénovée*, Ferrer failed to reopen the Modern School because the government said the school's books didn't meet their requirements. Instead he travelled with Villafranca to Brussels to thank those who had organized a campaign on his behalf in Belgium, and then they journeyed to Prague to attend an international freethinkers' congress. Although Ferrer represented the lay teachers of Catalonia, thirty teachers renounced his representation because of his anarchist ideas.[60]

After returning to Paris, Ferrer and Villafranca relocated to the Hotel Pujade in Amélie-les-Bains in the summer of 1908 because Soledad was in poor health. According to the French police monitoring Ferrer's activities, another reason was to be closer to the Spanish border to continue his revolutionary machinations. Police agents constantly followed Ferrer after his release, but, as he told Alejandro Lerroux, he was only worried about the French because the Spanish police were so incompetent. While Ferrer doesn't seem to have been planning anything on the scale of the bombing that landed him in jail, he secretly funded the new revolutionary syndicalist labor federation Solidaridad Obrera, supported the development of his educational newspapers, cofounded a new Masonic lodge in Barcelona, and founded the International League for the Rational Education of Children. [See part IX.] Over the summer of 1908 in Amélie-les-Bains,

Ferrer also took the time to write *The Modern School*, though it would not be published during his lifetime.[61]

In March 1909, Ferrer and Villafranca visited Lisbon before travelling to London. In London, Ferrer visited his twelve-year-old son Riego, who was studying in a boarding school, and spent time with his comrades. Despite constant surveillance from French and English police agents, they met with Errico Malatesta, Lorenzo Portet, and Pedro Vallina, and they attended the May Day demonstration in Hyde Park with Fernando Tarrida del Mármol. A few days later they ate dinner with Pyotr and Sophie Kropotkin. Villafranca offered to teach Sophie Spanish. Ferrer also met with William Heaford of the International League, who helped him pick out some books for the Modern School publishing house to translate after completing translations of *L'Homme et la Terre* by Reclus and *La Grande Révolution* by Kropotkin. Their vacation was cut short on June 11, however, when Ferrer received a telegram from his brother José back in Catalonia informing him that José's wife María and his daughter Eulalia were gravely ill. On June 17, Ferrer and Villafranca were back in Barcelona. María made a full recovery, but her daughter Eulalia died several days later from tuberculosis. They buried her body in Montjuich Cemetery, not knowing that only months later Ferrer would meet his end in the nearby castle.[62]

The next month the Spanish government mobilized over twenty thousand working-class and peasant conscripts to put down an uprising in Morocco against Spanish colonial control. On July 18, 1909, a conflict broke out at the embarkation of a group of conscripts in Barcelona. When a group of affluent women started to distribute medals and cigarettes, some of the angry soldiers threw them in the water igniting the crowd to shout, "Throw down your weapons" and "Let the rich go; all or none!" The police fired into the air and hurriedly removed the gangway to the ship before the situation could escalate further.[63]

Working-class radicals responded by organizing a general strike against the war for Monday July 26, 1909. Solidaridad Obrera was the main force behind the strike, though it chose not to officially sponsor it out of fear of repression. Clashes between the Civil Guard and strikers intensified the conflict, leading to the construction of barricades and attacks on churches and convents across Barcelona and surrounding cities and towns. Despite the important role of anarchists and socialists in fomenting the general strike, the conflict that ensued took on a much more anticlerical than anti-capitalist orientation, evident in the prevalence of church arson

Barricade on Carrer de l'Hospital in Barcelona during Tragic Week. *La Actualidad*, Aug. 28, 1909. FFG.

Open coffins at the convento de las Magdalenas during the Tragic Week. *La Actualidad*, July 26, 1910. FFG.

and the paucity of workplace occupations or attacks on the upper class.[64] By Friday July 30, the violence started to wane as the authorities reclaimed control of the region. On Monday August 2, Catalan workers returned to work.[65]

In the course of what came to be known as the "Tragic Week," between 21 and 61 churches and 30 convents were burned, 104 civilians, 4 Red Cross workers, 3 clergy, and 4 to 8 police were killed, 296 civilians and 124 police were injured, 1,725 were charged and another 2,000 fled to France, primarily to evade conscription.[66] Although 1,725 people were charged with crimes pertaining to the rebellion, more than two-thirds were quickly absolved or had the charges dropped. Similarly, although the military initially handed out 17 death sentences, that number was reduced to 5. Those sentenced to death were José Miquel Baró, who was charged with leading the local revolt in San Andrés, Antonio Malet Pujol, who was charged with burning church property and shooting at the police, Eugenio del Hoyo, who was charged with shooting at an army patrol, Ramón Clemente García, who was charged with helping to build a barricade and dancing with the disinterred corpse of a nun, and the most famous and influential of the 5, Francisco Ferrer, who was accused of masterminding the entire uprising.[67]

As opposed to the 1906 bombing of the royal wedding, there is no evidence to suggest that Ferrer was the key figure behind the entire uprising, though he might have wished he were. During the early stages of strike planning, the central committee decided to avoid contact with polarizing

Courtroom for Ferrer's trial, October 1909. Ferrer has an X over his head on the left. Archer, *The Life, Trial and death*, 190. FFG.

political figures like Ferrer to give the strike broader appeal.[68] Yet when the strike began, Ferrer travelled into Barcelona from his farmhouse in Masnou outside of town to meet with the strike leadership to assuage his concerns that their plans would fail due to a lack of political direction. Motivated by loyalty to a figure who had donated a significant amount of money to labor struggles and related projects over the years, some of the strike leaders granted Ferrer short meetings where they hurriedly attempted to reassure him.[69] Others were simply aggravated by his presence. Emiliano Iglesias, the acting leader of the Radical Party, initially failed to attend a scheduled meeting with Ferrer, and then later when they finally met grew so frustrated with Ferrer that he kicked him out of the

Postcard commemorating those executed after the Tragic Week: Ramón Clemente García, José Miquel Baró, Francisco Ferrer Guardia, Eugenio del Hoyo, and Antonio Malet Pujol. © Real Academia de la Historia. España. Legajo 11/8891, Archivo Natalio Rivas.

Ferrer's grave in Montjuich Cemetery in Barcelona. According to his baptismal certificate he was actually born on January 14, 1859. Photo by Mark Bray, July 2010.

Party's social center.[70] Similarly, the socialist representative of the strike committee was so infuriated with Ferrer's attempt to influence the strike leadership that he threatened to resign from the committee if Ferrer were allowed to interfere.[71] After his attempts to influence the course of events in Barcelona failed, Ferrer attempted to rile up rebellion in some of the surrounding towns like Masnou and Premià. Although some minor incidents unfolded in those towns, it's unclear whether Ferrer had any influence on them.[72]

At the most, Ferrer was one of the hundreds or thousands of revolutionaries attempting to foment unrest and push the course of events in a more radical direction. Yet the government ascribed his influence on the Tragic Week with supreme importance despite a complete lack of evidence. Ferrer's arrest sparked protests across Europe and beyond, but they were not enough to stop his execution, merely four days after a five-hour military trial where Ferrer was not allowed to call any witnesses or even select his own lawyer.[73] The military firing squad may have eliminated Francisco Ferrer, the man, but in so doing they created Francisco Ferrer, the martyr, whose legacy would spread rationalist education around the world.

Notes

1   Juan Avilés, *Francisco Ferrer y Guardia: pedagogo, anarquista y mártir* (Madrid: Marcial Pons, 2006), 33.

2   Quote from *l'Almanach-Annuaire illustré de la Libre-Pensée international* published in 1908 and reprinted in Comité de défense des victimes de la répression espagnole, *Un martyr des prêtres: Francisco Ferrer, 10 janvier 1859–13 octobre 1909: sa vie, son ouvre* (Paris: Schleicher frères, 1909), 53. Archer clarifies that he would have been nine rather than eleven. William Archer, *The Life, Trial and Death of Francisco Ferrer* (New York: Moffat, Yard and Co., 1911), 4.

3   As Juan Avilés points out, although Ferrer's father Jaime was baptized with the Catalan name Jaume in 1813, Francisco was not given the Catalan version of his name, Francesc, in 1859. Moreover, the church Francisco was baptized in had the Castilian name San Félix de Alella at the time but has since been changed into the Catalan San Feliu. At home he spoke Catalan, learning Castilian in school. UCSD, Box 2, Folders 5 and 6; Avilés, *Francisco Ferrer y Guardia*, 31; Sol Ferrer, *Le véritable Francisco Ferrer: d'après des documents inédits* (Paris: L'Écran du monde, 1948), 14.

4   Sol Ferrer also claimed that in their youth Francisco and his brother José tried to get an abusive priest in trouble, but he was simply transferred. Sol Ferrer, *La vie et l'oeuvre de Francisco Ferrer: un martyr au XXe siècle* (Paris: Librairie Fischbacher, 1962), 47–49.

5   Archer, *The Life, Trial and Death of Francisco Ferrer*, 3–4.

6   Ferrer, *La vie et l'oeuvre de Francisco Ferrer*, 14–15; Ferrer, *Le véritable Francisco Ferrer*, 18–22.

7   José A. Piqueras Arenas, *Cánovas y la derecha española: del magnicidio a los neocon* (Barcelona: Ediciones Península, 2008), 114–15.

8   Charles J. Esdaile, *Spain in the Liberal Age: From Constitution to Civil War, 1808–1939* (Oxford: Blackwell Publishers, 2000), 166; José Álvarez Junco, *El emperador del paralelo: Lerroux y la demogogia populista* (Madrid: Alianza, 1990), 96.

9   Eduardo González Calleja, *La razón de la fuerza: orden público, subversión y violencia política en la España de la Restauración (1875–1917)* (Madrid: Consejo Superior de Investigaciones Científicas, 1998), 77–102; Raymond Carr, *Spain*

1808–1975 (Oxford: Clarendon Press, 2003), 360–2; Esdaile, *Spain in the Liberal Age*, 160, 166.

10 Ferrer, *Le véritable Francisco Ferrer*, 35–37; Avilés, *Francisco Ferrer y Guardia*, 33–34; Archer, *The Life, Trial and Death*, 11.

11 Ferrer, *Le véritable Francisco Ferrer*, 41; Archer, *The Life, Trial and Death*, 12.

12 Avilés, *Francisco Ferrer y Guardia*, 34; Ferrer, *La vie et l'oeuvre de Francisco Ferrer*, 53; Ferrer, *Le véritable Francisco Ferrer*, 38, 40.

13 UCSD, Box 2, Folder 16; Francisco Bergasa, *¿Quién mató a Ferrer i Guardia?* (Madrid: Aguilar, 2009), 88; Avilés, *Francisco Ferrer y Guardia*, 46–47. In 1864, Bakunin modeled his Alliance of International Brothers on Masonic and Carbonist models. González Calleja, *La razón de la fuerza*, 225. Romero Maura discusses how the political prominence of Masonry in Barcelona peaked in the 1880s and 1890s before declining with the new century. Joaquín Romero Maura, *La Rosa de Fuego: el obrerismo barcelonés de 1899 a 1909* (Barcelona: Ediciones Grijalbo, S.A., 1975), 66–67; Joan Casanovas, *Bread, or Bullets! Urban Labor and Spanish Colonialism in Cuba, 1850–1898* (Pittsburgh: University of Pittsburgh, 1998), 64.

14 Ángel Herrerín López, *Anarquía, dinamita, y revolución social: violencia y repression en la España de entre siglos (1868–1909)* (Madrid: Catarata, 2011), 223–24; José Luis Gutiérrez Molina, introduction to Pedro Vallina, *Fermín Salvochea: crónica de un revolucionario* (Sevilla: Editorial Renacimiento, 2012), 78; D.J. Walker, *Spanish Women and the Colonial Wars of the 1890s* (Baton Rouge: Louisiana State University Press, 2008), 47; María Amalia Pradas Baena, *Teresa Claramunt: la "virgen roja" barcelonesa, biografía y escritos* (Barcelona: Virus, 2006), 57; Claudio Lomnitz, *The Return of Comrade Ricardo Flores Magón* (Brooklyn: Zone Books, 2014), 97; Robert L. Hoffman, *More Than a Trial: The Struggle over Captain Dreyfus* (New York: Free Press, 1980), 72, 165–66; Enrique A. Sanabria, *Republicanism and Anticlerical Nationalism in Spain* (New York: Palgrave Macmillan, 2009), 141; Benedict Anderson, *Under Three Flags: Anarchism and the Anti-Colonial Imagination* (New York: Verso, 2005), 130; Lawrence Tone, *War and Genocide in Cuba 1895–1898* (Chapel Hill: University of North Carolina Press, 2006), 32, 69–70.

15 Buenaventura Delgado, *La Escuela Moderna de Ferrer i Guardia* (Barcelona: Ediciones CEAC, 1979), 21.

16 *España Nueva*, June 16, 1906; Avilés, *Francisco Ferrer y Guardia*, 35.

17 Some have claimed that Ferrer was Ruiz Zorrilla's secretary, but Álvarez Junco doubts this was literally true. Álvarez Junco, *El emperador del paralelo*, 103; Ferrer, *La vie et l'oeuvre*, 54; Ferrer, *Le véritable Francisco Ferrer*, 45–47; Avilés, *Francisco Ferrer y Guardia*, 38; González Calleja, *La razón de la fuerza*, 130–33.

18 APP, Ba 1075; Ferrer, *Le véritable Francisco Ferrer*, 49–51; Avilés, *Francisco Ferrer y Guardia*, 41; *Proceedings of the M.W. Grand Lodge of Free and Accepted Masons of the District of Columbia from November 4, A.L. 5845 to January 21, A. L. 5847* (Washington: T. Barnard Printer, 1847), 50.

19 Ferrer, *Le véritable Francisco Ferrer*, 59.

20 Avilés, *Francisco Ferrer y Guardia*, 40; Archer, *The Life, Trial and Death*, 11.

21 Archer, *The Life, Trial and Death*, 12; Ferrer, *Le véritable Francisco Ferrer*, 63–64; Avilés, *Francisco Ferrer y Guardia*, 25.

22 Sol Ferrer also claims that her father was heartbroken over the deaths of Luz and Carlos. Ferrer, *La vie et l'oeuvre*, 59; Ferrer, *Le véritable Francisco Ferrer*, 62; Bergasa, *¿Quién mató a Ferrer i Guardia?*, 87.

23 Archer, *The Life, Trial and Death*, 13.

24 Avilés, *Francisco Ferrer y Guardia*, 25–32.

25 APP, Ba 1075; Ferrer, *Le véritable Francisco Ferrer*, 66–67; Avilés, *Francisco Ferrer y Guardia*, 17–19.

26 Archer, *The Life, Trial and Death*, 13–14.

27 Avilés, *Francisco Ferrer y Guardia*, 18–19.

28 APP, Ba 1075; Ferrer, *Le véritable Francisco Ferrer*, 72–73; Ferrer, *La vie et l'oeuvre*, 12–14; Avilés, *Francisco Ferrer y Guardia*, 27–28.

29 See chapter 1 of *The Modern School* for Ferrer's disenchantment with republicans. Álvarez Junco, *El emperador del paralelo*, 108–19.

30 Francisco Ferrer, "Los enemigos del pueblo: en Francia como en España," *El País*, May 5, 1896; Francisco Ferrer, "Contrastes," *El País*, February 28, 1896.

31 Augustin Hamon, *Le socialisme et le congrès de Londres: étude historique* (Paris: P.V. Stock, 1897), 144.

32 Hamon, *Le socialisme et le congrès de Londres*, 230; Avilés, *Francisco Ferrer y Guardia*, 70.

33 Although an 1897 Parisian police report describes Ferrer as a socialist, there is no evidence of any concrete participation in the POF or related endeavors after the London congress. APP, Ba 1075.

34 Sol Ferrer claimed that her father knew Santiago Salvador "well," having met him at the home of José Nakens. There is no proof to corroborate this unlikely relationship. Ferrer, *Le véritable Francisco Ferrer*, 62.

35 John Merriman, *The Dynamite Club: How a Bombing in Fin-de-Siècle Paris Ignited the Age of Modern Terror* (Boston: Houghton Mifflin Harcourt, 2009).

36 Jean Maitron, *Le movement anarchiste en France: 1. Des origins à 1914* (Paris: Gallimard, 1992), 265–329; Constance Bantman, *The French Anarchists in London, 1880–1914: Exile and Transnationalism in the First Globalisation* (Liverpool: Liverpool University Press, 2013), 160–67.

37 Romero Maura, *La rosa de fuego*, 68.

38 Francisco Ferrer, *L'Espagnol pratique: enseigné par la méthode Ferrer* (Paris: Garnier Hermanos, 1895).

39 Avilés, *Francisco Ferrer y Guardia*, 64.

40 Translated by William Archer from *España Nueva*, June 16, 1906. William Archer, *The Life, Trial and Death*, 20.

41 Ibid., 20–22; Ferrer, *La vie et l'oeuvre*, 66; Ferrer, *Le véritable Francisco Ferrer*, 75–76.

42 Sol Ferrer thought that Meunié was in love with her father, though she asserted that nothing ever happened between them. Ferrer, *Le véritable Francisco Ferrer*, 76; Bergasa, *¿Quién mató a Ferrer i Guardia?*, 99; Avilés, *Francisco Ferrer y Guardia*, 61–62.

43 Archer, *The Life, Trial and Death*, 15.

44 Avilés, *Francisco Ferrer y Guardia*, 63–64; Ferrer, *Le véritable Francisco Ferrer*, 78–79.

45 Translated by William Archer from *España Nueva,* June 16, 1906. Archer, *The Life, Trial and Death,* 22.

46 Ferrer, *La vie et l'oeuvre,* 66.

47 Salvador Canals, *Los sucesos de España en 1909,* vol. 2 (Madrid: Imprenta Alemana, 1911), 53.

48 Canals, *Los sucesos de España en 1909,* 53–54.

49 UCSD, Box 2, Folder 10.

50 Avilés, *Francisco Ferrer y Guardia,* 67.

51 According to Malato, the building was worth one million francs and it generated an annual revenue of thirty-three to thirty-five thousand francs. APP Ba 1075; UCSD, Box 2, Folder 13; *Causa contra Francisco Ferrer Guardia: instruida y fallada por la Jurisdicción de Guerra en Barcelona, año 1909* (Madrid: Sucesores de J. A. García, 1911), 380.

52 Abel Paz et al., ed., *La Barcelona rebelde: guía de una ciudad silenciada* (Barcelona: Octaedro, 2008), 294.

53 Antoni Dalmau, *El procés de Montjuïc: Barcelona al final del segle XIX* (Barcelona: Editorial Base, 2010).

54 Avilés, *Francisco Ferrer y Guardia,* 119–21; Bergasa, *¿Quién mató a Ferrer i Guardia?,* 99–100; Archer, *The Life, Trial and Death,* 15–16; UCSD, Box 2, Folder 13.

55 Pascual Velázquez and Antonio Viñao, "Un programa de educación popular: el legado de Ferrer Guardia y la editorial publicaciones de la Escuela Moderna (1901–1936)," *Educació i Història: Revista d'Història de l'Educació* 16 (2010): 88–89.

56 Eduard Masjuan, *Un héroe trágico del anarquismo español: Mateo Morral, 1879–1906* (Barcelona: Icaria editorial, 2009), 213.

57 APP, Ba 1075; *L'Humanité,* January 6, 1907.

58 *La guerre sociale,* January 9, 1907.

59 AN F7/12725; *Regicidio furstrado, 31 Mayo 1906: causa contra Mateo Morral, Francisco Ferrer, José Nakens, Pedro Mayoral, Aquilino Martínez, Isidro Ibarra, Bernardo Mata y Concepción Pérez Cuesta,* vol. 1 (Madrid: Sucesores de J. A. García, 1911), 456, 485–89; Alejandro Lerroux, *Mis Memorias* (Madrid: A. Aguado, 1963), 460–65; Constant Leroy, *Los secretos del anarquismo* (México, DF: Librería Renacimiento, 1913), 207; Alvarez Junco, *El emperador del paralelo,* 306; Joaquín Romero Maura, "Terrorism in Barcelona and Its Impact on Spanish Politics 1904–1909," *Past and Present* 41, (December 1968): 145; *El proceso Ferrer en el Congreso: recopilación de los discursos pronunciados por various diputados durante el debate* (Barcelona: Imprenta Lauria, 1911), 140; Masjuan, *Un héroe trágico,* 195, 201; Avilés, *Francisco Ferrer y Guardia,* 167–93.

60 APP Ba 1075; Avilés, *Francisco Ferrer y Guardia,* 210; Bergasa, *¿Quién mató a Ferrer i Guardia?,* 132–34; Archer, *The Life, Trial and Death,* 82.

61 Avilés, *Francisco Ferrer y Guardia,* 197–209; Bergasa, *¿Quién mató a Ferrer i Guardia?,* 134–36; Archer, *The Life, Trial and Death,* 114.

62 Avilés, *Francisco Ferrer y Guardia,* 209–10; Bergasa, *¿Quién mató a Ferrer i Guardia?,*136–37; Archer, *The Life, Trial and Death,* 108–113.

63 Joan Connelly Ullman, *La semana trágica: estudio sobre las causas socioeconómicas del anticlericalismo en España (1898–1912)* (Barcelona: Ediciones Ariel, 1968),

295–96; Temma Kaplan, *Red City, Blue Period: Social Movements in Picasso's Barcelona* (Princeton: Princeton University Press, 1992), 94–95; González Calleja, *La razón de la fuerza*, 427.

64 In 1909 Solidaridad Obrera had a membership of ten thousand in Barcelona and two thousand in surrounding areas. Romero Maura, *La rosa de fuego*, 500, 519; Francisco Madrid, *Solidaridad Obrera y el periodismo de raíz ácrata* (Badalona: Ediciones Solidaridad Obrera, 2007), 85–112. For the particularly prominent role of women in the uprising, see Kaplan, *Red City, Blue Period*, 96.

65 González Calleja, *La razón de la fuerza*, 435; Kaplan, *Red City, Blue Period*, 101; David Martínez Fiol, *La setmana tràgica* (Barcelona: Pòrtic, 2009), 73–132; Antoni Dalmau, *Set dies de fúria: Barcelona i la setmana tràgica (juliol de 1909)* (Barcelona: Columna Edicions, 2009), 35–62.

66 Romero Maura, *La rosa de fuego*, 515; Ullman, *La semana trágica*, 508–13.

67 Ullman, *La semana trágica*, 513–14.

68 *El País*, August 13, 1909.

69 Ferrer, *Le véritable Francisco Ferrer*, 180–82; Archer, *The Life, Trial and Death*, 143–44.

70 *Causa contra Francisco Ferrer Guardia*, 35, 334–35, 370.

71 Ullman, *La semana trágica*, 379.

72 Peter Tiidu Park, "The European Reaction to the Execution of Francisco Ferrer" (PhD diss., University of Virginia, 1970), 100–8; Ullman, *La semana trágica*, 468–69.

73 Bergasa, *¿Quién mató a Ferrer i Guardia?*

III

The Modern School: Posthumous Explanation and Scope of Rationalist Education

Francisco Ferrer Guardia

Ferrer wrote The Modern School *over the summer of 1908 at the Hotel Pujade in Amélie-les-Bains in the French Pyrenees. Since the Modern School had been closed for two years, Ferrer sought to synthesize the lessons learned from the school's successes and failures in order to disseminate the principles of rationalist education as widely as possible.* The Modern School *was first published after Ferrer's execution.*

An abbreviated translation of this book was published in English in the early twentieth century as The Origin and Ideals of the Modern School. *To our knowledge, this is the first complete translation of Ferrer's text in English. It fills in the blanks left by Joseph McCabe's* Origin and Ideals *while returning Ferrer's original phrasing to some of the more incendiary passages that McCabe toned down to appeal to an early twentieth-century middle-class audience.*

1. Preliminary Explanation

My participation in the political struggles of the last part of the nineteenth century put my early convictions to a severe test. I was a revolutionary in the cause of justice; I was convinced that liberty, equality, and fraternity were the legitimate fruit to be expected of a republic. Seeing, therefore, no other way to attain this ideal but a political agitation to change the form of government, I devoted myself entirely to the republican propaganda.

My relations with Don Manuel Ruiz Zorrilla, who was one of the leading figures in the revolutionary movement,[1] brought me into contact with a number of the Spanish revolutionaries and some prominent French agitators, and my intercourse with them led to a sharp disillusion.

I detected in many of them an egoism that they sought hypocritically to conceal, while the ideals of others, who were more sincere, seemed to me inadequate. In none of them did I perceive a design to bring about a radical improvement—a reform that should go to the roots of disorder and afford some security of a perfect social regeneration.

The experience I acquired during my fifteen years residing in Paris, during which I witnessed the crises of Boulangism, Dreyfusism, and nationalism and the menace they posed to the Republic,[2] convinced me that the problem of popular education was not solved; and, if it were not solved in France, there was little hope of Spanish republicanism settling it, especially as the party had always betrayed a lamentable ignorance of the capital importance that a system of education has for a people.

Imagine what the condition of the present generation would be if the Spanish republican party had, after the banishment of Ruiz Zorrilla, devoted itself to the establishment of rationalist schools in connection with each committee, each nucleus of freethinkers, or each Masonic lodge; if, instead of the presidents, secretaries, and members of the committees thinking only of the office they were to hold in the future republic, they had entered upon a vigorous campaign of popular education. In the thirty years that have elapsed considerable progress would have been made in founding day schools for children and night schools for adults.

Would the people educated in this way be content to send members to Parliament who would accept an Associations Law presented by the monarchists?[3] Would the people limit themselves to provoking riots because of the rise in the price of bread,[4] without rebelling against the privations imposed on the worker because of the superfluous abundance enjoyed by the rich from the labor of others? Would the people incite miserable riots against *los consumos* (food taxes), instead of organizing their forces for the removal of all tyrannical privileges?[5]

My situation as a teacher of Spanish at the Philotechnic Association and in the Grand Orient of France brought me into touch with people of every class, both in regard to character and social position, and when I considered them from the point of view of their possible influence on humanity I found that they were all bent upon making the best they could of life in a purely individual sense: some studied Spanish with a view to advancing in their profession, others in order to master Spanish literature and promote their careers, and still others to enjoy themselves by travelling in countries where Spanish was spoken.

No one felt the absurdity of the contradictions between what one believes and what one knows; hardly anyone cared to give a just and rational form to human solidarity, in order that all the members of each generation might have a proportionate share in the patrimony created by earlier generations. I saw progress conceived of as a kind of fatalism, independent of the knowledge and the goodwill of men, subject to vacillations and accidents in which human conscience and energy had no part. The individual, reared in the family, with its inveterate atavism and its traditional errors perpetuated by the ignorance of mothers, and in the school with something worse than error—the sacramental untruth imposed by men who pontificate in the name of a divine revelation—entered into society deformed and degenerated; and, because of the logical relation between cause and effect, nothing could be expected of him but irrational and pernicious results.

I spoke constantly to those I met, always inspired by the idea of proselytism, seeking to ascertain the use of each of them for the purpose of my ideal. I soon realized that nothing was to be expected of the politicians who surrounded Ruiz Zorrilla; they were, in my opinion, with a few honorable exceptions, impenitent careerists. This gave rise to a certain expression that the judicial authorities sought to use to my disadvantage in circumstances of great gravity and peril. Don Manuel [Zorrilla], a man of lofty views and not sufficiently on his guard against human malice, used to call me an "anarchist" every time he saw me put forth a logical solution; he always regarded me as a deep radical, opposed to the opportunist views and the flashy radicalism of the Spanish revolutionaries who surrounded and even exploited him, as well as the French republicans, who followed a bourgeois politics and ran away from what might benefit the disinherited proletariat, on the pretext of distrusting utopias.

In a word, during the early years of the Restoration[6] there were men conspiring with Ruiz Zorrilla who have since declared themselves convinced monarchists and conservatives; and that honorable man who kept the protest against the coup d'état of January 3, 1874 alive confided in his false friends, with the result, not uncommon in the political world, that most of them abandoned the republican leader for money or an elevated position. In the end, he could count only on the support of those who were too honorable to sell themselves, though they lacked the logic to develop his ideas and the energy to carry out his work. If it had not been for Asensio Vega, Cebrián, Mangado, Villacampa, and a few others, Don Manuel would have been the toy of ambitious people and speculators disguised as patriots for many years.

Consequently, I limited myself to my pupils, selecting for my experiments those whom I thought more appropriate and better disposed. Having now a clear idea of the aim that I proposed to myself and a certain prestige from my position as teacher and my expansive character, I discussed various subjects with my pupils when the lessons were over; sometimes we spoke of Spanish customs, sometimes of politics, religion, art, or philosophy. I sought always to correct the exaggerations of their judgments and to show clearly how mischievous it is to subordinate one's own judgment to the dogma of a sect, school, or party, as is so frequently done. In this way, I succeeded in bringing about a certain agreement among men who differed in their creeds and views and induced them to master the beliefs that they had hitherto held unquestioningly by faith, obedience, or simple servile compliance. My friends and pupils found themselves happy in thus abandoning some shameful error and accepting a truth that uplifted and ennobled them.

A rigorous logic, applied with discretion, removed fanatical bitterness, established intellectual harmony, and gave, to some extent at least, a progressive disposition to their wills. Freethinkers who opposed the Church and rejected the legends of Genesis, the imperfect morality of the gospels, and the ecclesiastical ceremonies; more or less opportunist republicans or radicals who were content with the futile equality conferred by the title of citizen, without in the least affecting class distinctions; philosophers who fancied they had discovered the primordial cause of things in their metaphysical labyrinths and established truth in their empty phrases—all were enabled to see the errors of others as well as their own, and they leaned more and more to the side of common sense.

When the further course of my life separated me from these friends, some sent me their expressions of friendship to the cell where I awaited freedom confident in my innocence. From all of them I anticipate good and useful progressive action, satisfied in having been the decisive cause of their rational orientation.

2. La Señorita Meunié

Among my pupils was a certain Señorita Meunié, a wealthy woman with no family who was fond of travel and studied Spanish with the object of visiting Spain. She was a convinced Catholic and a very scrupulous observer of the rules of her Church. To her, religion and morality were the same thing, and unbelief—or "impiety," as the faithful say—was an evident sign of vice and crime.

She detested revolutionaries, and she regarded with impulsive and undiscriminating aversion every display of popular ignorance. This was due not only to her education and social position but to the circumstance that during the period of the Commune she had been insulted by children in the streets of Paris as she went to church with her mother. Ingenuous and sympathetic, without regard to antecedents, accessories, or consequences, she always expressed her dogmatic convictions without reserve, and I had many opportunities to open her eyes to the inaccuracy of her opinions.

In our many conversations I refrained from taking any definite side; so that she did not recognize me as a partisan of any particular belief but as a careful reasoner with whom it was a pleasure to confer. She formed such an excellent opinion of me that, given her isolation, she gave me her friendship and full confidence, inviting me to accompany her on her travels. I accepted the offer, and we travelled to various countries. My conduct and our constant conversation compelled her to recognize the error of thinking that every unbeliever was perverse and every atheist a hardened criminal, since, I, a convinced atheist, manifested symptoms very different from those that her religious prejudice had led her to expect.

She thought, however, that my conduct was exceptional, remembering that they say that every exception proves the rule. Yet the continuity and the logic of my reasoning forced her to bow to the evidence, and if some doubts remained for her regarding religion, she agreed that a rational education and scientific teaching would save the youth from error, would give men necessary goodness, and would reorganize society in conformity with justice. She was deeply impressed by the reflection that she might have been like those children who had insulted her if at their age she had been reared in the same conditions as they. When she had given up her belief in innate ideas, she could not satisfactorily resolve this problem that I raised: If a child were educated without any religious contact, what idea of divinity would they have upon reaching the age of reason?

After a while, it seemed to me that we were wasting time if we were not prepared to go on from words to deeds. To be in possession of an important privilege through the imperfect organization of society and by the accident of birth, to conceive regenerative ideas and to remain in inaction and indifference amid a life of pleasure, seemed to me to incur a responsibility similar to that of a man who refused to lend a hand to a person whom he could save from danger. One day, therefore, I said to Señorita Meunié: Señorita, we have reached a point at which it is necessary to search for a new orientation. The world needs us, it appeals to us for our assistance, and in good conscience we cannot refuse it. It seems to me that to enjoy comforts and luxuries that form part of the universal patrimony and that could be used to establish a useful and reparative institution is to commit a fraud; and that would be sanctioned neither by a believer nor a freethinker. Therefore, I must tell you that you cannot count on me for your further travels. I owe myself to my ideas and to humanity, and I think that you ought to have the same feeling now that you have exchanged your former faith for rational principles.

This decision surprised her, but she recognized its force and without other stimulus than her own good nature and fine feeling she gave me the resources necessary for the creation of an institute of rational education: the Modern School. Although it already existed in my mind, its realization was assured by this generous act.

All the malicious statements that have been made in regard to this matter—for instance, that I had to submit to a judicial interrogation—are sheer calumnies. It has been said that I used a power of suggestion over Señorita Meunié for my own purposes. This statement, which is as offensive to me as it is insulting to the memory of that worthy and excellent lady, is absolutely false. I do not need to justify myself; I leave my vindication to my acts, my life, and the stern judgment of the impartial. But Señorita Meunié is entitled to the respect of all people of right feeling, of those who have been emancipated from dogmatic and sectarian tyranny, who have broken all connection with error, who no longer submit the light of reason to the darkness of faith or the dignity of freedom to the vile submission of obedience.

She believed with honest faith. She had been taught that between the Creator and the creature there is a hierarchy of intermediaries whom one must obey, and that one must bow to a series of mysteries contained in the dogmas imposed by a divinely instituted Church. In that belief she remained perfectly tranquil. The remarks I made and advice I offered her were not spontaneous commentaries on her belief but natural replies to her efforts to convert me; and, from her want of logic, her feeble reasoning broke down under the strength of my arguments, instead of her persuading me to put faith before reason. She could not regard me as a tempting demon, since it was always she who attacked my convictions; and she was in the end vanquished by the struggle of her faith and her own reason, which was aroused by her indiscretion in assailing the faith of one who opposed her beliefs.

She now ingenuously sought to exonerate the boys of the Commune as poor and uneducated wretches, the fruit of perdition, the seeds of crime, and disturbers of the social order because of privilege that, in the face of such a disgrace, permits others, no less disturbers of the social order, to live unproductive lives, enjoy great wealth, exploit ignorance and misery, and trust that they will continue throughout eternity to enjoy their pleasures by paying for ritual ceremonies and works of charity. The idea of a reward for easy virtue and punishment for unavoidable sin shocked her conscience and moderated her religiosity, and, wanting to break the atavistic chain that so much hampers any attempt at reform, she wanted to contribute to the founding of a useful work that would put the youth in touch with nature in conditions that would help them to use the full the treasures of the knowledge that humanity has acquired by labor, study, observation, and the methodical arrangement of its general conclusions.

In this way, she thought, with the aid of a supreme intelligence that veils itself in mystery from the mind of man or by the knowledge that humanity has gained by suffering, contradiction, and doubt the future will be realized; and she found an inner contentment and vindication of her conscience in the idea of contributing, by the bestowal of her property, to a work of transcendent importance.

3. Responsibility Accepted

Once I was in possession of the means of attaining my object, I determined to put my hand to the task without delay. It was now time to give a precise shape to the vague aspiration that had long haunted my imagination; and to that end, conscious of my incompetence in the art of pedagogy, I sought the counsel of others. I had not a great confidence in the official pedagogues, as they seemed to me to be largely hampered by prejudices in regard to their subject or other matters, so I searched for a competent person whose views and conduct would accord with my ideals. With his assistance, I would formulate the program of the Modern School, which I had already conceived. In my opinion it was to be not the perfect type of the future school of a rational society, but rather its precursor, the best possible adaptation of our means; that is to say, an emphatic rejection of the school of the past perpetuated in the present, the true orientation toward that integral teaching in which the youth of the coming generations will be initiated in the most perfect scientific esotericism.

I was convinced that the child comes into the world without innate ideas, and that during the course of their life they gather the ideas of those nearest to them, later modifying them through reading, observation, and relations that they form with the environment that surrounds them. If this is so, it is clear that if a child is to be educated with positive and truthful ideas of all things and prepared to avoid errors, it is indispensable that they believe nothing by faith but only by experience and rational demonstration. With such a training, the child will become a careful observer and will be prepared for all kinds of studies.

When I had found the person I sought, and while the first lines were being traced of the plan we were to follow, the necessary steps were taken in Barcelona for the founding of the establishment: the building was chosen and prepared, and the furniture, staff, advertisements, prospectuses, leaflets, etc. were secured. In less than a year all was ready, though I was put to great loss through the betrayal of my confidence by a certain person who worked with me but then put me in grave danger of failure. It was clear that we should at once have to contend with many difficulties not only on the part of those who were hostile to rational education but partly on account of a certain class of theorists who urged upon me, as the outcome of their knowledge and experience, advice that I could only regard as the fruit of their prejudices. One person, for instance, who was afflicted with a zeal for regional patriotism, proposed to me that the lessons should be given in Catalan, thereby confining humanity and the world to the narrow limits of the corner formed by the Ebro and the Pyrenees. I would not, I told the enthusiast, even adopt Spanish as the language of the school if a universal language had already advanced sufficiently to be of practical use. I would a hundred times rather use Esperanto than Catalan.

This incident confirmed me more and more in my resolution not to submit the settlement of my plan to the authority of distinguished men who, with all their repute, do not take a single voluntary step in a progressive direction. I felt the burden of a responsibility freely accepted, and I wanted to fulfill it to the satisfaction of my conscience. An enemy of social inequality, I could not limit myself to lamenting its effects; rather I wanted to combat it at its roots, sure that this method has to arrive positively at justice, which is to say, at that longed for equality that inspires all revolutionary desire.

If matter is one, uncreated, and eternal—if we live on a relatively small body in space, a mere speck in comparison with the innumerable globes about us, as is taught in the universities and may be learned by the privileged few who monopolize universal science—we have no right to teach, and no excuse for teaching in the primary schools that the people go to when they have the opportunity, that God made the world out of nothing in six days and all the other absurdities of the religious legend. Truth is universal, and we owe it to everybody. To put a price on it, to reserve it as a monopoly of the powerful, to leave the lowly in systematic ignorance and—what is worse—impose on them a dogmatic and official doctrine in contradiction with science, so that they accept without protest their low and deplorable state under a democratic political regime, is an intolerable indignity. For my part, I consider that the most effective protest and the most positive revolutionary action consists in giving the oppressed, the disinherited, and all who are conscious of a demand for justice as much truth as they can receive, trusting that it will direct their energies in the great work of the regeneration of society.

Here is the first public notice for the Modern School:

Program

The mission of the Modern School is to ensure that the boys and girls who are entrusted to it shall be well-instructed, truthful, just, and free from all prejudice.

To that end, the reasoned study of the natural sciences will be substituted for the old dogmatic teaching. It will stimulate, develop, and direct the natural abilities of each pupil, so that with the totality of their own individual value they will not only be a useful member of society, but rather, as a consequence, they will proportionately elevate the value of the collectivity.

It will teach the true social duties in conformity with the just maxim: *there are no responsibilities without rights, and there are no rights without responsibilities.*[7]

In view of the good results that have been obtained abroad by mixed education and principally in order to realize the purpose of the Modern School—the formation of a truly fraternal humanity, without distinction of sex or class—children of both sexes, from the age of five upward, will be accepted.

To complete its work, the Modern School will open on Sunday mornings, when there will be classes on the sufferings of mankind throughout the general course of history and on the men who have distinguished themselves in science, in art, or in struggles for progress. The families of the children may attend these classes.

In the hope that the intellectual work of the Modern School will be fruitful, in the future, besides securing hygienic conditions at our facility and its dependencies, we have arranged a medical inspection of children upon their entrance into the school. The result will be communicated to the parents if it is deemed necessary; and others will be held periodically, in order to prevent the spread of contagious diseases during school hours.

During the week that preceded the opening of the Modern School, I invited the local press to visit the institution on its opening. It may be of historical interest to include the following report from *El Diluvio*:[8]

Modern School

Politely invited, we had the pleasure of attending the inauguration of the new school under the abovementioned title on calle Bailén.

The future must arise from the school. To build on any other foundation is to build on sand. Unhappily, the school may serve as cement for the bastions of tyranny or for the fortresses of liberty. From this point of departure begin either barbarism or civilization.

We are therefore pleased to see that patriotic and humanitarian men, understanding the transcendence of this social function, which our own governments systematically overlook, have arisen to fill such a sensible vacuum by creating the Modern School; a real school that will not seek to promote the interests of sect and to move in the old ruts, as has been done hitherto, but will create an intellectual environment in which the new generation will absorb the ideas and the impulses that the stream of progress unceasingly brings.

Moreover, this end can only be attained by private initiative. Historical institutions, contaminated with all the vices of the past and weakened by all the trivialities of the present, cannot discharge this beautiful function. To noble souls, to altruistic hearts, is it

Classroom for the *clase superior* of the Modern School. *Nuevo Mundo*, June 13, 1907. FFG.

reserved to open the new path across which the new generations will glide to happier destinations.

This has been done, or at least will be attempted, by the founders of the modest Modern School, which we have visited at the courteous invitation of its directors and those who are involved in its development. This school is not a commercial enterprise like most scholastic institutions but a pedagogical experiment of which only one other specimen could be found in Spain (the Free Institution of Education in Madrid).[9]

Señor Salas Anton brilliantly expounded the program of the school to the small audience of journalists and others who attended the small party for its exhibition and elaborated on the design of educating children in the *whole* truth and *only* the truth, or what is proved to be such. We will limit ourselves to adding, as a concluding idea among those that this señor opportunely shared, that the goal is not to add one more to the number of what are known as "lay schools," with their impassioned dogmatism, but a serene observatory, open to the four winds, with no cloud darkening the horizon and interposing between the light and human knowledge.

Needless to say, therefore, the Modern School will have proportional representation for all forms of scientific knowledge, aided by the most progressive methods known to pedagogy today and by the instruments and apparatuses that are the wings of science and the most potent conductive medium to bring about intelligence in the students. As the most succinct formula, one can say that lessons based on *things* will be substituted for lessons based on *words*, an education that has given such bitter fruits to our compatriots.

It is sufficient to take a look at the modest rooms of this incipient establishment to be sure that it offers conditions conducive to the fulfillment of such a valuable promise. The materials, so neglected in our country's education, whether official or private, are to be found in the new school represented by prints of plant and animal physiology, mineralogical, botanical, and zoological collections, a physics cabinet and a special laboratory, a projector, nutritional, industrial, and mineral substances, etc., etc. With the help and conscientious direction of teachers who are steeped in the spirit of our time, such as the known former journalist Señor Columbier, it can be hoped that we are witnessing the birth, or at least the seed, of the school of the future.

Now all that we need is imitators.

4. The Early Program

The time had come to think of the inauguration of the Modern School. Some time previously I invited a number of gentlemen of great distinction and of progressive sentiments to assist me with their advice and form a kind of Committee of Consultation.[10] They provided great help to me in Barcelona, where I had few contacts, for which I must express my gratitude. They were of the opinion that the Modern School should be opened with some display—invitation cards, a press release, a large hall, music, and speeches from orators selected from the political youth of the liberal parties. It would have been easy to do this, and we would have attracted an audience of hundreds of people who would have applauded with that momentary enthusiasm that characterizes our public functions. But I was not seduced by such ostentation. As much a positivist as an idealist, I wanted to start a work destined to reach the greatest revolutionary transcendence with simple modesty; other proceedings would have seemed like surrender, a concession to enervating conventions and to the very evil that I was setting out to correct. The proposal of the Committee was, therefore, repugnant to my conscience and my will, and I was, in that and all other things relating to the Modern School, the executive power.

In the first number of the *Boletín de la Escuela Moderna*, published on October 30, 1901, I gave a general exposition of the fundamental principles of the School.

Those imaginary products of the mind, a priori concepts and all the absurd and fantastical fictions hitherto regarded as truth and imposed as directive principles of the conduct of man have for some time past incurred the condemnation of reason and the resentment of conscience. The sun no longer merely touches the tips of the mountains; it floods the valleys, and we enjoy the light of noon. Science is fortunately no longer the patrimony of a small group of privileged individuals; its beneficent rays more or less consciously penetrate every rank of society. On all sides it dissipates traditional errors; by the confident procedure of experience and observation it enables men to attain accurate knowledge and criteria in regard to natural objects and the laws that govern them. With indisputable authority, it bids men lay aside forever their exclusivisms and privileges, and it offers itself as the controlling principle of the life of man, seeking to imbue it with a universal, human sentiment.

Relying on modest resources, but with a robust and rational faith and a spirit that will not easily be intimidated, whatever obstacles arise in our path, we have founded the Modern School. Its aim is to righteously contribute to an education based on the natural sciences without concession to traditional methods. This new method, though the only sound and positive method, has spread throughout the civilized world and has the support of innumerable workers, superior in intelligence and selfless in will.

We are aware how many enemies there are about us. We are conscious of the innumerable prejudices that oppress the social conscience of our country. This is the outcome of a medieval, subjective, dogmatic education, which makes ridiculous pretensions to the possession of an infallible criterion. We are further aware that by virtue of the law of heredity, strengthened by the influences of the environment, the tendencies that are connatural and spontaneous in the young child are still more pronounced in adolescence. The struggle is severe, the work is intense, but with a constant and perpetual desire, the sole providence of the moral world, we are certain that we will obtain the triumph that we pursue; that we will develop living brains, capable of reacting; that the minds of our pupils, when they leave the rational tutelage of our center, will continue to be mortal enemies of prejudices; that they will be solid minds, capable of forming their own rational convictions on every subject.

This does not mean that we will leave the child, at the very outset of their education, to form their own ideas. The Socratic method is wrong if it is taken too literally. The very constitution of the mind at the commencement of its development demands that education, at this early stage of life, must be receptive. The teacher plants the seeds of ideas. These will, when age and strength, invigorate the brain, bring forth corresponding flowers and fruit, in accordance with the degree of initiative and the characteristic features of the pupil's mind.

On the other hand, we may say that we regard as absurd the widespread notion that an education based on natural science stunts idealism. We are convinced that the contrary is true. What science does is to correct and direct it and give it a wholesome sense of reality. The work of man's cerebral energy is to create the *ideal*, with the aid of art and philosophy. But in order that the ideal shall not degenerate into fables or hazy daydreams, and that the structure not be built on sand, it is absolutely necessary to give it a secure and unshakable foundation in the exact and positive knowledge of the natural sciences.

Moreover, the education of a man does not consist merely in the training of his intelligence, without having regard to the heart and the will. Man, in the unity of his cerebral functionalism, is complex. He has various fundamental facets, but at the bottom he is a single energy, which sees, loves, and applies a will to the prosecution of what he has conceived or affected. It is a morbid condition, an infringement of the laws of the human organism, to establish an abyss where there ought to be a sane and harmonious continuity. The divorce between thought and will is an unhappy feature of our time. To what fatal consequences it has led! We need only refer to our political leaders and to the various orders of social life: they are deeply infected by this pernicious dualism. Many of them are undoubtedly powerful in their mental faculties and have an abundance of ideas; but they lack a sound orientation and the fine thoughts that science applies to the life of individuals and of peoples. Their restless egoism and the wish to accommodate their relatives, all of it mixed with the leaven of traditional sentiments, will form an impermeable barrier round their hearts and prevent the infiltration of progressive ideas and the formation of that sap of sentiment that is the impelling and determining power in the conduct of man. Hence the attempt to obstruct progress and put obstacles in the way of new ideas; hence, as a result of such causes, the skepticism of the multitudes, the death of peoples, and the just desperation of the oppressed.

We regard it as one of the first principles of our pedagogical mission that there is no such duality of character in any individual—one that sees and appreciates truth and goodness and one that follows evil. And, since we take natural science as our guide in education, it will be easily understood what follows: we shall endeavor to secure that the intellectual impressions that science conveys to the pupil be converted into the sap of sentiment and shall be intensely loved. When sentiment is strong it penetrates and diffuses itself through the deepest recesses of a man's being, pervading and giving a special color to his character.

And as a man's conduct must revolve within the circle of his character, it follows that a youth educated in the manner we have indicated will, when he comes to rule himself, convert science, by the conduct of his sentiment, into the unique and beneficial teacher in his life.

The school was opened on September 8, 1901, with thirty pupils—twelve girls and eighteen boys. These sufficed for a first attempt, and we had no intention of increasing the number for a time, so that we might keep a more effective watch on the pupils. The enemies of the new school would take the first opportunity to criticize our work in coeducating boys and girls.

The audience consisted of the public attracted by the notice published in the press and of families of the students and delegates of various workers' societies invited on account of their assistance to me. I was supported in the presidency by the teachers and the Committee of Consultation, two of whom expounded the system and aim of this brand-new institution. In this sober simplicity we inaugurated a work that was destined to last. We created the Modern, Scientific, and Rational School, the fame of which soon spread in Europe and America. If in time it will lose the title of modern, over the centuries it will be strengthened more and more in its titles of *rational* and *scientific*.

5. The Coeducation of the Sexes

The most important manifestation of rational education, given the intellectual backwardness of the country, and the feature that was most likely to shock current prejudices and habits was the coeducation of girls and boys.

The idea was not absolutely new in Spain. As a result of necessity and of primitive conditions, there were villages in remote valleys and on the mountains where some good-natured neighbor or the priest or sacristan used to teach the catechism, and sometimes elementary letters, to boys and girls in common. In fact, it is sometimes legally authorized, or at least tolerated, by the state among small populations that have not the means to pay both a male and female teacher. And so, a female teacher, never a male teacher, gives common lessons to boys and girls, as I had myself seen in a small village not far from Barcelona. In towns and cities, however, mixed education was not unknown. One read sometimes of the occurrence of it in foreign countries, but no one thought of adopting it in Spain, where such a proposal would have been deemed an innovation of the most utopian character.

Knowing this, I refrained from making any public propaganda on the subject and confined myself to private discussion with individuals. We asked every parent who wished to send a boy to the school if there were girls in the family, and it was necessary to explain to each the reasons for coeducation. Although the work was difficult, the result was fruitful. If we had announced our intention publicly, it would have raised a storm of prejudice. There would have been a discussion in the press, conventional feeling would have been aroused, and the fear of "what people will say"— that paralyzing obstacle to good intentions—would have been stronger than reason. Our project would have proved exceedingly difficult, if not impossible. Whereas, proceeding as I did, I was able to achieve the presentation of a sufficient number of boys and girls for the inauguration, and the number steadily increased, as the *Boletín de la Escuela Moderna* shows.

Coeducation was of capital importance for me. It was not merely an indispensable condition for the realization of the ideal that I consider to be the result of rationalist education; it was the ideal itself, initiating its life in the Modern School, developing a confidence of attaining our end. Nature, philosophy, and history teach, against all the fears and atavisms,

"Natural history class" (left) and "pre-school class" (right) of the Modern School. *Nuevo Mundo*, June 13, 1907. FFG.

that woman and man complete the human being, and ignorance of such an essential and transcendental truth has been the cause of the greatest evils.

In the second number of the *Boletín*, I extensively justified these judgments with the following article:

The Need for Mixed Education

Mixed education is spreading to all cultured peoples. Many have already recognized its excellent results. The principle of this scheme of teaching is that children of both sexes shall receive the identical education; that their minds shall be developed, their hearts purified and their wills strengthened in precisely the same manner; that feminine and masculine humanity understand each other from infancy, so that woman shall be, not in name only but in reality and truth, the companion of man.

A venerable institution that dominates the thoughts of our people declares, at one of the most solemn moments of life, when, with ceremonious pomp, man and woman are united in matrimony, that woman is the companion of man. These are hollow words, void of sense, without vital and rational significance in life, since what we witness in the Christian Church, in Catholicism particularly, is the exact opposite of this idea. Not long ago a Christian woman of fine feeling and great sincerity complained bitterly of the moral debasement that is put upon her sex in the bosom of the Church: "It would be impious audacity for a woman to aspire in the Church even to the position of the lowest sacristan."

A man must suffer from a blindness of the mind not to see that under the inspiration of the Christian consciousness the position of woman is no better than it was in Ancient History: or perhaps worse, and with heavy additional problems. It is a conspicuous fact in our modern Christian society that, as a result and culmination of our patriarchal development, the woman does not belong to herself; she is neither more nor less than an adjunct of man, subject constantly to his absolute dominion, constantly bound to him, sometimes . . . by chains of gold. Man has converted her into a perpetual minor. Once mutilated in this way, she was bound to experience one of two alternatives: man either oppresses and silences her or treats her as a child to be spoiled . . . according to the mood of the señor. If at length we note in her some sign of the new spirit, if she begins to assert her will and claim some share of independence, if she is passing, with irritating slowness, from the state of slave to the condition of a respected ward, she owes it to the redeeming spirit of science, which is dominating the customs of peoples and the designs of our social rulers.

The work of humanity for the greater happiness of the species has hitherto been defective. In the future it must be a joint action of the sexes; it must be incumbent on both man and woman, according to the point of view of each. It is important to take into account that the purpose of man in human life is neither inferior nor (as we affect to think) superior to that of woman. They have different qualities, and no comparison is possible between heterogeneous things.

As many psychologists and sociologists observe, the human race displays two fundamental aspects: man typifies the dominion of thought and of the progressive spirit; woman bears in her moral nature the characteristic note of intense sentiment and of the conservative spirit. But this view of the sexes gives no encouragement whatever to the ideas of reactionaries nor does it have anything to do with them. If the predominance of the conservative element and of the emotions is ensured in woman by natural law, this does not make her the less fit to be the companion of man. She is not prevented by the constitution of her nature from reflecting on things of importance nor is it necessary that she should use her mind in contradiction to the teaching of science and absorb all kinds of superstitions and fables. The possession of a conservative disposition does not imply that one is bound to crystallize in a certain stage of thought or that one must be obsessed with prejudice in all that relates to reality.

"To conserve" merely means "to retain," to keep what has been given us or what we have ourselves produced. The author of *The Religion of the Future*, referring to woman in this aspect, says: "The conservative spirit may be applied to truth as well as to error; it all depends what it is you conserve. If woman is instructed in philosophical and scientific matters, her conservative power will be to the advantage not to the disadvantage of progressive thought."

On the other hand, it is pointed out that woman is emotional. She does not selfishly keep to herself what she receives; she spreads abroad her beliefs, her ideas, and all the good and evil that form her moral treasures. She insists on sharing them with all those who are, by the mysterious power of emotion, identified with her. With exquisite art, with invariable unconsciousness, her whole moral physiognomy, her whole soul, so to say, impresses itself on the soul of those she loves.

If the first ideas implanted in the mind of the child by the teacher are germs of truth and of positive knowledge planted in the consciousness of the child by their first pedagogue, who is influenced by the scientific spirit of their time, the result will be good from every point of view. But if a man is fed with fables, errors, and all that is contrary to the spirit of science in the first stage of his mental development, what can be expected of his future? When the child becomes an adult, he will be an obstacle to progress. Human consciousness in children is of the same natural texture as the bodily organism; it is tender and pliant. It readily accepts what comes to it from without. In the course of the time this plasticity gives place to rigidity; it loses its pliancy and becomes relatively fixed. From that time, the ideas communicated to it by the mother will be encrusted and identified with the youth's conscience.

The acid of the more rational ideas that the youth acquires by social intercourse or private study may in cases relieve the mind of the erroneous ideas implanted in childhood. But what is likely to be the practical outcome of this transformation of the mind in the sphere of conduct? We must not forget that in most cases the emotions associated with the early ideas remain in the deeper folds of the heart. Hence it is that we find in so many men such a flagrant and lamentable antithesis between the thought and the deed, the intelligence and the will; and this often leads to an eclipse of good conduct and a paralysis of progress.

This primary sediment that we owe to our mothers is so tenacious and enduring—it passes so intimately into the very marrow of our being—that even energetic characters who have effected a sincere reform of mind and will have the mortification of discovering this Jesuitical element derived from their mothers when they turn to make an inventory of their ideas.

Woman must not be restricted to the home. The sphere of her activity must go out far beyond the walls of the house; it must extend to the very confines of society. But in order to ensure a helpful result from her activity, we must not restrict the amount of knowledge that is allowed to her; she must learn both in regard to quantity and quality, the same things as a man. When science enters the mind of woman it will direct her rich vein of emotion, the characteristic element of her nature, the glad harbinger of peace and happiness in society.

It has been said that woman represents *continuity* and man represents *change*: man is the individual and woman is the species. Change, however, would be useless, fleeting, and flimsy, with no social foundation in reality, if the work of woman did not strengthen and consolidate the achievements of man. The individual, as such, is the flower of a day, a thing of ephemeral significance in life. Woman, who represents the species, has the function of retaining within the species the elements that improve its life, and to discharge this function adequately she needs scientific knowledge.

Humanity would advance more rapidly and confidently on the path of progress and increase its resources a hundredfold if it were to combine the ideas acquired by science with the emotional strength of woman. Ribot says that an idea is no more than an idea, a simple fact of knowledge. It does not produce anything, cannot do anything, and does not function if it is not heartfelt, if it is not accompanied by an emotional state, a motive element. Hence it is conceived as a scientific truth that, to the advantage of progress, an idea does not long remain in a purely contemplative condition when it appears. This is obviated by associating the idea with emotion and love, which do not fail to convert it into a vital action.

When will all this be accomplished? When shall we see the marriage of ideas with the impassioned heart of woman? From that date, we shall have a *moral matriarchy* among civilized peoples. Then, on the one hand, humanity, considered in the home circle, will have the proper teacher to direct the new generations in the sense of ideal; and on the other hand, it will have an apostle and enthusiastic propagandist who will know how to make men feel liberty and solidarity among the peoples of the world.

6. The Coeducation of the Social Classes

There must be a coeducation of the different social classes as well as of the two sexes. I could have founded a free school, but a school for poor children could not have been a rational school, since, if they were not taught submission and credulity as in the old type of school, they would have been strongly disposed to rebel and would instinctively cherish sentiments of hatred.

There is no escape from the dilemma. There is no middle term in the school for the disinherited class alone; you have either a systematic insistence by means of false teaching on error and ignorance or hatred of those who domineer and exploit. It is a delicate point and needs stating clearly. Rebellion against oppression is merely a question of statics, of pure equilibrium. Between one man and another who are perfectly equal, as is said in the immortal first clause of the famous Declaration of the French Revolution ("Men are born and remain free and equal in rights") there can be no social inequality. If there is such inequality, some will tyrannize, the others protest and hate. Rebellion is a levelling tendency, and to that extent natural and rational, however much it may be discredited by justice and its evil companions, law and religion.

I will say it clearly: the oppressed and the exploited have to be rebels, because they have to reclaim their rights until they achieve their complete and perfect participation in the universal patrimony. The Modern School, however, has to deal with children, whom it prepares by instruction for the state of manhood, and it must not anticipate the loves and hatreds, the adhesions and rebellions, that are duties and sentiments for adults. In other words, it must not seek to gather fruit until it has been produced by cultivation nor must it attempt to implant a sense of responsibility until it has equipped the conscience with the fundamental conditions of such responsibility. Let it teach the children to be men; when they are men, they may declare themselves rebels.

It needs very little reflection to see that a school for rich children cannot be a rational school. From the very nature of things, it will tend to insist on the maintenance of privilege and the securing of their advantages. The only sound and enlightened form of school is that which coeducates the poor and the rich, which brings the one class into touch with the other in the innocent equality of childhood by means of the systematic equality of the rational school.

With this end in view I decided to secure pupils of all social classes and include them in a common class, adopting a system of payment accommodated to the circumstances of the parents or guardians of the children. I would not have a fixed and invariable fee but a kind of sliding scale, with free lessons for some and different charges for others. I later published the following article on the subject in *La Publicidad* of Barcelona on May 10, 1905 and in the *Boletín*:

Modern Pedagogy

Our friend D.R.C. gave a lecture last Sunday at the Centro Republicano Instructivo on calle de la Estrella [in the Barcelona neighborhood of] Gràcia, on the subject of this article, explaining modern education to his audience and what advantages society may derive from it. As I think that the subject is one of very great interest and most proper to receive public attention, I offer the following reflections and considerations on it. It seemed to us that the lecturer was correct in his exposition but not in the advice he gave to achieve it nor in presenting the examples of Belgium and France as models to be imitated.

Señor C., in fact, relied solely upon the state and local government for the construction, funding, and management of scholastic institutions. This seems to us to be a great error. If modern pedagogy means a new orientation toward a reasonable and just society; if modern pedagogy means that we propose to instruct the new generations in the causes that have brought about and maintain the lack of social equilibrium; if it means that we are anxious to prepare a happy humanity, by freeing it from all religious fiction and from all idea of submission to an inevitable socioeconomic inequality; we cannot entrust it to the state or to other official organisms that necessarily maintain existing privileges and support the laws that consecrate the exploitation of man by man, the pernicious source of the worst abuses.

Evidence of the truth of what we affirm is so abundant that anyone can see it by visiting the factories and workshops and wherever there are salaried workers and asking how people live on the bottom and the top of society, by attending the sessions of the so-called palaces of justice, and by asking prisoners in all types of penal institutions why they are in prison. If all this evidence does not suffice to prove that the state favors those who are in possession of wealth and persecutes those who rebel against such injustice, it will be sufficient to notice what happened in Belgium. Here, according to Señor C., the government is so attentive to education and conducts it so excellently that private schools are impossible. In the official schools, he says, the children of the rich mingle with the children of the poor, and one may at times see a rich child arm in arm with a poor and lowly companion. It is true, we will add, that children of all classes may attend the Belgian schools, but the instruction that is given in them is based on the eternal necessity of having rich and poor and on the principle that social harmony consists in the fulfillment of the laws.

Consequently, what would the masters like more than to see this kind of education spread far and wide? It is a means of bringing to reason those who might one day be tempted to rebel. Not long ago, in Brussels and other Belgian towns, the sons of the rich, armed and organized in the national militia, shot down the sons of the workers who dared to ask for universal suffrage.[11] On the other hand, the news I have heard about the quality of Belgian education differs considerably from that of the lecturer. I have before me various issues of *L'Express* from Liège, which devotes a section to the subject entitled "The Destruction of our Public Education." The facts given are, unfortunately, very similar to the facts about education in Spain, without mentioning that recently in this country there has been a great development of education by religious orders, which is, as everybody knows, the systematization of ignorance. Ultimately, it is not for nothing that a violently clerical government rules in Belgium.

As to the modern education that is given in republican France, we may say that not a single one of the books used in French schools serves the purpose of a truly lay education. On the very day that Señor C. lectured in Gràcia, the Parisian journal *L'Action* published an article with the title "How to Teach Lay Morality" in regard to the book *Recueil de maximes et pensées morales* and quoted from it certain ridiculously anachronistic ideas that offend the most elementary common sense.

We shall be asked: What are we to do if we cannot rely on the aid of the state, town councils, or municipalities? We must appeal to those in whose interest it is to change the mode of living; to the workers, in the first place, and later to the intellectuals and privileged people of good sentiments who may not be numerous but exist. I know some. Señor C. complained that the civic authorities were dilatory in granting the reforms that are needed. I feel sure that he would do better not to waste his time on them but to appeal directly to the working class.

The field has been well prepared. Let him visit the workers' societies, the republican fraternities, the centers of instruction, the workers' *Ateneos*, and all the bodies that are interested in the regeneration of humanity, and let him give ear to the language of truth, the exhortations to union and courage. Let him observe the attention given to the problem of rational and scientific instruction, a kind of instruction that shows the injustice of privilege and the possibility of making it disappear. If individuals and societies continue thus to combine their endeavors to secure the emancipation of those who suffer—for it is not only the workers who suffer—Señor C. may rest assured of a positive, sound, and speedy result, while whatever may be obtained of the government will be dilatory and will tend only to stupefy, to sow confusion, and to perpetuate the domination of one class over another.

7. School Hygiene

Regarding hygiene, Catholic dirtiness dominates in Spain. Saint Alexius and Saint Benoît-Joseph Labre are not the only nor the most characteristic swine on the list of the supposed inhabitants of the kingdom of heaven, but they are the most popular with the masters of filth [*porquería*]. With such types of perfection, in an atmosphere of ignorance, cleverly and maliciously sustained by the clergy and the royalty of the past and by the liberal (and even democratic) bourgeoisie of today, it was to be expected that the children that came to our school would be wanting in cleanliness; dirtiness was atavistic.

We carefully and systematically combatted it, demonstrating to the children the repugnance aroused by every dirty object, animal, and person, while cleanliness makes one feel esteem and sympathy. We showed how one instinctively moves toward the clean person and away from the dirty and malodorous and how we should be pleased to win the regard of those who see us and ashamed to excite their disgust.

We then explained cleanliness as an aspect of beauty and dirtiness as a part of ugliness; and we resolutely embarked upon the terrain of hygiene, presenting dirtiness as a cause of disease and a constant source of infection and epidemic and cleanliness as one of the chief conditions of health. We thus easily succeeded in disposing the children in favor of cleanliness, making them understand the scientific principles of hygiene.

The influence of these lessons spread to their families, as the new demands of the children altered the household routine. One child urgently asked for their feet to be washed, another asked to be bathed, another wanted a brush and powder for their teeth, another was embarrassed by a stain, another asked for new clothes or boots, and so on. The poor mothers, burdened with their daily tasks, sometimes crushed by the hardness of the circumstances of their lives, and furthermore influenced by religious society, tried to stop their petitions, but in the end the new life introduced into the home by the child triumphed, a welcome presage of the regeneration that rational education will one day accomplish.

I entrust the exposition of the rationale behind school hygiene to those who are perfectly competent in this matter. Therefore, I have included two articles published in the *Boletín de la Escuela Moderna*:

School Hygiene: The Details of Its Implementation

The outcry is widespread. The same exclamation emerges from everywhere: "Of the eighteen million Spaniards, ten million are illiterate; Spaniards suffer from a lack of education and instruction." The exclamation is inspired by reality and could not be more just. I would add that Spaniards have lost a routine and lack faith in labor; for both reasons, entire regions of our peninsula have a sterile, gray crust, where barely a herb of straw sprouts and bird excrement makes them look more like the plains of the desert. Neither the plow nor cultivation have broken up the earth in many years, nor shaken off the inertia of the land. There are thousands of hectares that are unproductive because of the misery of its owners and the stain of the infertility of our soil. And I don't say this about the Catalans, who here love to see olives, wine, wheat, or the carob tree on the most daring slope or on the most elevated point as a signal of a labor and a struggle that does not cease until the point where juice can be extracted from rocks.

Congratulations to those who call for obligatory education for these lazy citizens. But to impose a law, without surrounding it with a complement of certain guarantees does not seem satisfactory to me. As a doctor, I have often had the occasion to appreciate the neglect that many children suffer in school, and the grief of a father who lost a child to a preventable disease contracted in school deeply moved me. Are children sufficiently protected in our schools for a mother to calmly let their loved one go every morning, if while they are in their mother's care they grow up healthy but return from school sick?

Epidemics in the schools are proof of these risks, but there are other contagions that are quietly being discovered that target an even greater number of victims without motivating an intervention to stop them. A few months ago, as a mere coincidence undoubtedly, I attended to three children with diphtheria within a few days who all attended the same school. Whooping cough, measles, scarlet fever, and others find the most fertile ground for the explosion of an epidemic in schools. There, children are gathered and subjected to the same environment, so when they go home they infect their older and younger siblings and even newly born babies. Sometimes it even reaches their parents. Tuberculosis is transmitted this way. Apart from these terrible diseases, ringworm, eye diseases, scabies, hysteria, spinal conditions, etc., etc. always come from school.

Students live in a crowd where they all use a single toilet and a single glass, notebooks and pencils pass from hand to hand and mouth to mouth, and bread and candies are shared among them. All of this is a dangerous mixture for the collectivity. There are many parents who, against their will, have had to give up the instruction of their children in school because they would always get sick there. If school buildings and furniture were inspected, few would meet a mediocre standard of hygiene. But that's not the point. Let's be practical. Even when a large amount of capital is available to build new schools based on the dictates of a hygienist, we would not brusquely interrupt instruction while buildings were destroyed and rebuilt.

Therefore, given the need to use the resources that exist, I think conditions can be improved without great efforts simply by establishing *hygienic protection* and *instruction* in the schools. Dazzling palaces are unnecessary; spacious rooms with abundant light and clean air where the students are protected would be sufficient.

In other countries this reform has come from the government; here . . . it seems to me that the initiative for these details can make up for these deficiencies by taking advantage of their own interests. School teachers will find doctors to support them in this school hygiene campaign. The directors of schools will be able to find medical support with little effort. And even when an effort is required, they will realize that such preventative measures are beneficial. When a child gets sick and stops coming to school they will lose their monthly payment, but they lose more when a child dies and a client is erased forever.

Who knows if the credit of the establishment would suffer even more with these losses? Not long ago, a very distinguished school nearby had to send home a number of students who had been hit by an epidemic of scarlet fever to start the year. How much better would it have been to have avoided this loss of revenue and the suffering of the students with *hygienic protection*?

Therefore, the owners of schools and municipal teachers are thinking about instituting this service, completely ignoring the plans of the government. Here we are not doing well in this respect, while news like this is being published: "*The medical inspection of the schools* of New York last September resulted in the temporary exclusion of one hundred students: thirty-five of them suffered from granulations in the eyes, sixteen from conjunctivitis, fifteen had skin infections, etc." In this way parents could calmly send their children to school!

This protection of the school follows an eminently social goal, the fundamental and indispensable condition for intellectual education to be effective. The measures that doctors should put into effect in every school can be understood in the following points:

1. *The Health of the Building*—This proposal is intended to monitor the layout of educational facilities, lighting, ventilation, heat, air currents, the installation of toilets, etc. These elements of the school will be adapted as much as possible to pedagogical progress.

2. *Prophylaxis of Transmittable Diseases*—A light cough, vomiting, a minor fever, redness in the eyes, an abnormal blotch of hair will lead to a personal investigation and the separation of the child who is unwell. In this respect, it will be necessary to count on the loyal support of the families, so that measles, whooping cough, or other diseases are not hidden that could affect the siblings of the students. A prudent isolation will impede the transmission of disease at school, and, in the case of sickness, the doctor will determine after some time what precautions are necessary for the child to return to school without endangering their comrades.

3. *The Normal Function of the Organs and Growth*—Through measurements and regular weighing, it will be known positively if the child is developing well and if they are developing vicious postures that can become permanent, including myopia, scoliosis, and others. This will be very useful for families. Since the mother is focused on domestic work and the father is absorbed in his business, no one notices if their child limps, if they start to twist their spinal column, if they bring the book very close to their eyes to read; and by the time they realize, the problem is so large or so well-advanced that its remedy requires significant measures and perhaps some sacrifices. This monitoring would fill a great void in some families. The mission of the school doctor will be reduced in this case to warning the parents of the danger so that they can search for help from their doctor.

4. *Physical Education and the Adaptation of Studies to the Intellectual Capacity of Each Child*—This will be accomplished in accord with the teacher. By means of this inspection children can be spared from headaches, insomnia, childhood neurasthenia, and the effects of fatigue. Appropriate levels of physical exercise and intellectual labor will also be gauged.

5. *Hygienic Education and Instruction*—Children will be given weekly or biweekly presentations on hygiene, and they will be habituated to hygienic practices such as washing their hands, mouths, bathrooms, swimming, cleaning their nails, etc. As young as the student may be, they should receive this education and instruction. These concepts are not too advanced for

them; it's all in how they are taught. Grasping the highest importance of these matters, the most recent International Hygiene Congress held in Brussels decreed this education and many eminent foreign doctors practice it. In our country, I have tried to imitate such laudable conduct. When a child is taught to love their health, they transmit the information they have learned to their parents and friends, carrying out a proper educational dissemination. When they reach maturity, they will take care of their offspring with a better understanding. Perhaps this will be a way to remove individual and collective suicide from society. Because of the social conditions of our race [raza], this education will be more beneficial in Spain than in other countries.

6. *Keeping a Biological Logbook*—It consists of entries on the development of the student and the illnesses they have had. Apart from its ethnic and anthropological transcendence, this personal history has a very important practical application. For example, an epidemic of typhoid fever, whooping cough, or measles breaks out at a fast or slow velocity. Closing the schools as a precaution does not resolve the problem and it provokes serious criticism. When the biological logbook is in use for every student, students who have already had the epidemic infirmity, if they weren't already protected from it, can continue to attend school without any risk for them or their compañeros, and those who have not suffered from the disease can be the object of certain methods that do not interrupt the normal life of families and schools or foment idleness or the love of vacations in the students.

This is the program. At first look, it can seem like an inaccessible mountain, an unrealizable project, and here I'm not even speaking about experimental pedagogy that, founded in psychology, gauges the intellectual force of each individual and examines their special aptitudes . . . but we will apply this redemptive work to our students, and our labor and our perseverance will take us to the summit in a short time just as easily as we go up to [Mount] Tibidabo with the funicular.

—Dr. Martínez Vargas

Games

Games are indispensable for children. By looking at their constitution, health, and physical development, everyone will agree; but most only pay attention to the amount of physical development produced by games. They have been replaced with physical exercise as an excellent equivalent, and some believe that much has been gained in this substitution.

These assertions have been rejected in absolute terms by hygiene. After the inveterate belief that what we need to do is attend to our physical development, another concept in the field of scientific knowledge has come to dominate. In said field it is currently recognized, as in authority of something judged, that the pleasant state and free unfolding of the native tendencies are important, essential, and predominant factors in the strengthening and development of the being of the child.

Happiness, as Spencer affirms, "constitutes the most powerful tonic; accelerating the circulation of blood, it better facilitates the development of all functions; it contributes to the enhancement of health when one is healthy, and the reestablishment of health when one has lost it. The live interest and happiness that children feel in their pastimes are as important as the physical exercise that accompany them. Calisthenics are defective because they do not offer this mental stimulation." But we have to say along with Spencer: something is better than nothing. If we were told to choose between being without both games and calisthenics or accepting calisthenics we would opt for calisthenics.

Games deserve a different point of view and a greater consideration in pedagogy. The child should be allowed to pursue their desires. This is the principal element of the game that, as Johonnot tells us, is desire satisfied by free activity. At the same time, we do not refrain from insisting on the absolute necessity of introducing games into the classroom. That is how they understand it in more learned countries and in educational organizations that dispense with all related concerns and want nothing more than to find rational methods to achieve the congenial arrangement between health and the progress of the child. There they have done nothing more toward the achievement of this goal than to pull out by the roots from the classrooms the insufferable silence and lethargy characteristic of death and leave in its place well-being, intense happiness, delight. Delight, the intense happiness of the child in class when they share with their classmates, they consult their books, or they are in the close company of their teachers, is the infallible signal of internal health in physical and mental life.

The affirmations that we make will furrow the brows of the schoolmasters who unfortunately abound among us. How? By this path we demolish every educational organism that, by being ancient, is represented as venerable and intangible. How? By taking into account the displeasure that this causes children we rectify the conduct of our parents. We must leave an open path for the initiatives of the child as a rod that leads directly to the achievement of their culture, without damaging the typical element that individualizes their being, rather than submitting the mind of the student to the mold of the whims of parents and teachers!

There is no other solution. The truth is bitter to its enemies. A truer and more optimistic conception of the life of man has obligated pedagogues to modify their ideas. In individuals and collectivities where modern culture has penetrated, they see life from a point of view contrary to Christian education. The idea that life is a cross, an annoying and heavy weight that you have to tolerate until providence is tired of seeing you suffer, radically disappears.

Life, they tell us, is to be enjoyed, to be lived. What torments us and produces pain should be rejected as a mutilator of life. He who patiently accepts it is worthy of being considered an atavistic degenerate or an immoral wretch if they know what they do. The supreme individual right that presides over the conscience of man is the right to nourish oneself in all aspects of life. The supreme collective responsibility is to radiate life everywhere. This beautiful tendency must crystalize and develop in the generations of the future, and the only clear method to make this happen is to lend education the sentiment of Froebel: every well-organized game becomes work, as all work becomes a game.

Moreover, games serve to reveal the character of the child and their future pursuits in life. Parents and pedagogues must be *passive* up to a certain point in the educational enterprise. The observations of the parent and the advice of the teacher should not become an imperative precept in a mechanical, military, or religiously dogmatic manner. Some people impose their particular view of life on the student. The student can be governed arbitrarily; they must develop dynamically from without and from within, and nothing more should be done than to assist in the development of their native dispositions.

Because of this the educator does not have to decide a priori, without the patient and thorough prior consultation with the nature of the child, that they will study to be a sailor, a farmer, or a doctor, etc. Can one destine children, by the mere desire of the will of those who condition them, to be poets, to study to be philosophers, or to revel in music? The same premise applies.

The study of the games of children demonstrates their great similarity with the most serious occupations of adults. Children coordinate and execute their games with an interest and an energy that only abates with fatigue. They work to imitate grownups as much as they can. They build houses, they make mud pies, they go to the city, they play school, organize dances, play doctor, dress dolls, clean clothing, arrange circuses, sell fruit and drinks, plant gardens, work in carbon mines, write letters, make jokes, discuss, fight, etc.

The ardor and vehemence with which they do this shows how deeply real it is for them; and, moreover, reveals that the instincts of children do not differ absolutely from the instincts of adulthood. The spontaneous game that is the preference of the child predicts their occupation or native dispositions. The child pretends to be an adult, and when they reach adulthood what amused them as a child becomes serious.

Taylor says, "Children should be taught to play with the same care that they are later instructed to apply to their job." "Not a few women have made excellent dressmakers cutting and making dresses for their dolls; and many men learn the use of the most common tools pretending to be carpenters. A little female friend of mine became a real artist after having played with her paint and brushes. Another child recited interesting things playing comedy, and some years later he excelled in school by using the knowledge he had acquired by playing games. And so likewise many of the poetic images of some authors portray the games and adventures of childhood."

Moreover, games can develop altruism among children. The child, in general, is egotistical. Many causes factor into such an awful disposition, the most important being the law of inheritance. Yet games have the ability to counteract the natural despotism of children that makes them want to arbitrarily order around their little friends.

Children should be oriented toward the law of solidarity in games. The prudent observations, advice and reproaches of parents and teachers should guide children through games to realize that they are better off being tolerant and affable than intransigent with their friend, that the law of solidarity benefits everyone, including the one who promotes it.

—R. Columbié

8. The Teachers

The choice of teachers was another point of great difficulty. As useful as it was to create the program of rational instruction, once it was completed the need arose to choose teachers who were competent to carry it out. I found that in fact such people did not exist. How true it is that a need creates its own organ!

There were teachers, obviously! Ultimately, although it isn't very lucrative, pedagogy is a profession by which a man can support himself. There is not a universal truth in the popular proverb that says of an unfortunate man, "He is hungrier than a schoolteacher." The truth is that in many parts of Spain the teacher forms part of the local ruling clique [junta caciquil], with the priest, the doctor, the shopkeeper, and the moneylender (who is often one of the richest men in the place, though he contributes least to its welfare). The teacher receives a municipal salary equal to his neighbors and has a certain influence that may at times secure material advantages. In larger towns, the teacher, if he is not content with his salary, may give lessons in private schools, where, in accord with the provincial institute, he prepares bourgeois youth for university. Even if he does not obtain a privileged position, he lives as well as most citizens.

There were also teachers in what are called "lay schools"—a name imported from France, where they arose because the schooling was formerly exclusively clerical and conducted by religious bodies. This was not the case in Spain; however Christian the teaching may be, it is always given by civil teachers. However, the Spanish lay teachers, inspired by sentiments of free thought and political radicalism, showed themselves to be better anticlericals and anti-Catholics than true rationalists.

Professional teachers have to undergo a special preparation for the task of imparting scientific and rational instruction. This is difficult in all cases and is sometimes rendered impossible by the difficulties caused by habits of routine. Those who had no pedagogical experience and offered themselves for the work out of pure enthusiasm for the idea stood in perhaps even greater need of preparatory study. The solution of the problem was very difficult, because there was no other place but the rational school itself for making this preparation.

Yet the excellence of the system saved us! Once the Modern School had been established by individual inspiration, with its own resources and a firm determination to be guided by the ideal, the difficulties began to disappear. Every dogmatic imposition was detected and rejected, every excursion or deviation in the direction of metaphysics was at once abandoned, and experience gradually formed a new and salutary pedagogical science. This was due not merely to my zeal and vigilance but to the first teachers and to some extent to the doubts and ingenious expressions of the pupils themselves. We may certainly say that if a need creates an organ, the organ speedily meets the need.

Nevertheless, in order to complete my work, I established a rationalist normal school for the education of teachers under the direction of an experienced teacher and with the cooperation of the teachers in the Modern School. In this school a number of young people of both sexes were trained, and they worked excellently until the despotic authorities, yielding to our obscure and powerful enemies, put a stop to our work, forming the deceptive illusion that they had destroyed it forever.

As a complement to the ideas expressed in this chapter, I think it is worthwhile to include the following article on individual pedagogy by my friend Domela Nieuwenhuis, published in the *Boletín*:

> One can never do enough on behalf of children. Those who are not interested in children are not worthy of interest themselves, because children are the future. But those who take care of children should be guided by common sense; it is not enough to have good will, one also needs knowledge and experience.
>
> Who cultivates plants, flowers, and fruit without knowing something about the subject? Who takes care of animals, for example,

dogs, horses, chickens, etc., without knowing what is most beneficial to each species? Yet when it comes to the education of children, the most difficult thing in the world, almost everyone thinks they are capable by virtue of being the father of a family.

The matter is truly strange: a man and a woman agree to live together, they procreate, and all of a sudden they become educators without having bothered to instruct themselves in the most basic elements of the art of education. We are not among those who agree with Rousseau that all that comes from the creator of things is good, that everything degenerates in the hands of man.

Before everything, we cannot say that all is good, and after declare that we do not know a creator of things, and even less do we know a creator that has hands that can make a capable worker that copies a model. And moreover, we ask: Why is it said that everything degenerates? What does it mean to degenerate? What kind of self-image does a creator have whose job could be to be damaged by the men who are considered to be the product of the hands of the creator? That is to say that one of the products can destroy the others! If a worker gave a product like that to their boss, they would soon be fired for being incompetent and clumsy.

They always present two sides: the positive and the negative; and generally more is destroyed on the positive than the negative side. Doing something can be useful, but it can also be harmful. But if it hinders something, nature tends to correct what the child makes bad.

The celebrated pedagogue Froebel used to say, "We live for the children." The intention was doubtlessly good, nevertheless he did not understand the secret of education. Ellen Key, who, in her great book *The Century of the Child* gives us plenty to think about, is more correct when she says, "We let the children live for themselves."

Instruction begins when the child asks for it. All of the educational program, which is the same for all of the regions of France, for example, is ridiculous. At nine in the morning the minister of public education knows that all of the children are reading, writing, or calculating. Yet do all of the children and the teachers have the same desire at the same time? Why not allow the teacher the initiative to do what seems best to them since they know their students better than the minister or whatever bureaucrat? Shouldn't they have the liberty necessary to arrange instruction to their own liking and to the benefit of their own students? The same ration for all stomachs, the same ration for all memories, the same ration for all intelligences, the same studies, the same works.

Victor Considerant, the disciple of Charles Fourier, wrote an important book that has already been forgotten but deserves to be resurrected called *Théorie de l'éducation naturelle et attrayante*, in which he asks:

> What trainer of dogs imposes the same regimen on their show dogs, their greyhounds, their race dogs, their lapdogs, and their mastiffs? Who demands identical services of such diverse species? What gardener ignores that some plants need more shade, others more sun, others more water, others more air, without applying the same supports to all and the same cords, who prunes all in the same manner and at the same time, or who practices the same grafting on all the wild saplings? Does human nature matter less than that of vegetables or animals, so that less attention is devoted to the nurturing of children than to spinach, lettuce, or dogs?

We accustom ourselves to searching far for what is nearby if we want to see and are able to observe. Things tend to be simple, but we make them complicated and difficult. If we follow nature we will commit fewer mistakes. Official pedagogy has to cede its place to the individual. Ellen Key desired a flood that would drown all pedagogies, and if the ark were to save only Montaigne, Rousseau, and Spencer we would have progressed somewhat. And so, men would not build "schools" but rather plant vineyards in which the labor of the teachers would be to raise the bunches of grapes to the height of the lips of the children, rather than making it so that the children cannot enjoy more than the grape juice that has been weakened a hundred times over.

In the egg there is a seed. By its nature it has to open up, but it will not open unless the egg is placed in the right temperature. In the child there are many seeds of industrial abilities, of many vocations, but these vocations only show themselves in favorable circumstances. If we have organs, it is necessary that they develop. Likewise, it is necessary to give a child's nature the opportunity to unfold, and the task of parents and teachers is to avoid impeding its development. This happens the same way with plants: each has its own time; first the buds and the leaves, then the flowers and the fruit. But you will kill the plant if you subject it to artificial measures to invert the natural order of its development. Preserve, sustain, water—this is the labor of educators.

The great initiators of socialism understood that the origin of everything is education. Fourier and Robert Owen put forth ideas that were original that have not been understood or have been neglected. These names are not to be found in any pedagogical manual, yet they deserve a position of honor because all of the ideas of modern education that are currently propagated are to be found in their writings.

The greatness of these heroes of thought increases the more one delves into their works. They had great foresight that grew out of their study of nature. Once again: follow nature and you will be on the right path.

The publication of the following announcements began in the first issues of the *Boletín de la Escuela Moderna*:

To the Youth

The Modern School, in view of the great success achieved by its first institute and desiring to progressively extend its saving action, invites the youth of both sexes who want to dedicate themselves to scientific and rational teaching and have the aptitude for it to express their interest, personally or in writing, in order to prepare for the opening of branches in various districts of this capital.

To the Free Teachers

Teachers and youth of both sexes who desire to dedicate themselves to rational and scientific education and find themselves stripped of absurd traditional fears, superstitions, and beliefs can contact the director of the Modern School to fill empty positions in various schools.

9. The Reform of the School

There are two ways open to those who seek to reform the education of children: to transform the school by studying the child and proving scientifically that the current method of instruction is defective and must be improved; or to found new schools in which principles may be directly applied in the service of that ideal that is formed by all who reject the conventions, the cruelty, the trickery, and the lies that form the base of modern society.

The first method offers great advantages and is in harmony with the evolutionary conception that men of science regard as the only effective way of attaining the end. They are right in theory, as we fully admit. It is evident that the progress of psychology and physiology must lead to important changes in educational methods; that the teachers, in perfect conditions to understand the child, will be able to and will know how to conform their teaching to natural laws. I further grant that this evolution will proceed in the direction of greater liberty, as I am convinced that violence is the method of ignorance, and that the educator who is really worthy of the name will gain everything by spontaneity; they will know the child's needs and will be able to promote their development by giving them the greatest possible satisfaction.

But, in reality, I do not think that those who are struggling for the emancipation of humanity have much to hope from this method. Rulers have always taken care to control the education of the people; they know better than anyone that their power is based almost entirely on the school, and they therefore insist on retaining their monopoly of it. The time has gone by when rulers could oppose the spread of instruction and restrict the education of the masses. This tactic was open to them before because the economic life of the nations allowed popular ignorance, and this ignorance facilitated domination. But the circumstances have changed; the progress of science and our repeated discoveries have revolutionized the conditions of labor and production. It is no longer possible for the people to remain ignorant. Education is absolutely necessary for a nation to maintain itself and make headway against its economic competitors. Recognizing this, the rulers have sought to give a more and more complete organization to the school, not because they look to education to regenerate society, but because they need more competent workers to sustain industrial enterprises and enrich their cities. Even the most reactionary governments have learned this lesson; they have understood perfectly that the old tactic was dangerous for the economic life of nations, and that they had to adapt popular education to the new necessities.

It would be a serious mistake to think that the rulers have not foreseen the danger to themselves of the intellectual development of the people and have not understood that it was necessary to change their methods of domination. In fact, their methods have been adapted to the new conditions of life; they have sought to gain control of the ideas that are evolving. They have endeavored to preserve the beliefs upon which social discipline had been grounded and to give to the results of scientific research and the ideas involved in them a meaning that will not be to the disadvantage of existing institutions; and it is this that has induced them to assume control of the school. The rulers, who formerly left the education of the people to the clergy, because their instruction was usefully in the service of authority, have now themselves undertaken the direction of the schools in every country.

The danger to them consisted in the stimulation of human intelligence before the new spectacle of life, in which in the recesses of consciousness emerges a will toward emancipation. It would have been folly to struggle against the evolving forces. It was necessary to channel them, and, to do so, far from persisting in old governmental methods, they adopted others that were new and more effective. It did not require an extraordinary genius to discover the solution. The simple course of events led the men of power to understand how they had to counter the dangers before them: they founded schools, they sought generously to extend the sphere of education, and if there were at one point a few who resisted this impulse—as certain tendencies favored one or other of the political parties—all soon understood that it was better to yield, and that the best tactic was to find some new way of defending their interests and principles. There were then sharp struggles for the control of the school, which continue in every country today; sometimes the republican and bourgeois society triumphs, while other times clericalism wins out. All parties appreciate the importance of the objective, and they do not shrink from any sacrifice to win the victory. Their common cry is: "By and for the school!" The good people must be recognized in this request. Everybody seeks their elevation and happiness by education. In former times it could have been said, "Those people try to keep you in ignorance in order to better to exploit you: we want to you to be educated and free." That is no longer possible; schools of all kinds rise on every side.

In regard to this general change of ideas among the rulers regarding the school, I may state certain reasons for distrusting their good will and doubting the efficacy of the means of renewal that are advocated by certain reformers. As a rule, these reformers generally care little about the social significance of education: they are men who eagerly embrace scientific truth but eliminate all that is foreign to the object of their studies. They work patiently to understand the child and are eager to know—though their science is young—what are the best methods to promote their integral development.

But this kind of professional indifference is, in my opinion, very prejudicial to the cause that they think they serve. I do not in the least think them insensible of the realities of the social world, and I know that they believe that the general welfare will be greatly furthered by their results. "Seeking to penetrate the secrets of the life of the human being," they reflect, "and unravelling the normal process of their physical and psychic development, we shall direct education into a channel that will be favorable to the liberation of the energies. We are not immediately concerned with the reform of the school, and indeed we are unable to say exactly what lines it should follow. We will proceed slowly, knowing that, from the very nature of things, the school will transform itself by means of our discoveries, by the same force of things. If you ask us what our hopes are, we declare that we agree with you in the prediction of an evolution in the sense of an ample emancipation of the child and of humanity by science. Yet even in this case we are persuaded that our work makes for that object and will be the speediest and surest means of promoting it."

This reasoning is evidently logical. No one could deny this. Yet there is a considerable degree of fallacy in it, and we must make this clear. If the rulers had the same ideas as the benevolent reformers, if they were really impelled by a zeal for the continuous reorganization of society toward the progressive disappearance of all servitude, we could recognize that the power of science on its own is enough to improve the lot of peoples. Instead of this, however, we see clearly that the sole aim of those who strive to attain power is the defense of their own interests, their own advantage, and the satisfaction of their appetites. For some time now, we have ceased to accept the phrases with which they disguise their ambitions. It is true that there are some in whom we may find a certain amount of sincerity, and who imagine at times that they are impelled by a zeal for the good of fellows. But these become rarer and rarer, and the positivism of the age is very severe in raising doubts as to the real intentions of those who govern us.

And just as they contrived to adapt themselves when the necessity arose and prevented education from becoming a danger, they also know to reorganize the school in accord with the new scientific ideas in such a way that nothing should endanger their supremacy. These ideas are difficult to accept, but one needs to have seen what happens up close and how things are arranged in reality as to avoid falling into verbal traps. Ah! How much has been, and is, expected of education! Most men of progress expect everything of it, and, until recent years, many did not understand that instruction alone produces illusions. Much of the knowledge currently imparted in schools is useless, and the hope of reformers has been void, because the organization of the school, instead of serving an ideal purpose, has become the most powerful method of servitude in the hands of the rulers. The teachers are merely conscious or unconscious instruments of their will and have been trained on their principles. From their tenderest years, and more drastically than anybody, they have suffered the discipline of authority. Very few have escaped the tyranny of this domination; they are generally impotent against it, because the organization of the school oppresses them with such a force that they have no option but to obey. It is unnecessary here to describe that organization. One word will suffice to characterize it—Violence. The school dominates the children physically, morally, and intellectually, in order to control the development of their faculties in the way desired and deprives them of contact with nature to model them in their own manner. This is the explanation of the failure: the eagerness of governments to control the education of the people and the failure of the hopes of the men of liberty. "To educate" currently means to dominate, to train, to domesticate. I do not imagine that these systems have been put together with the deliberate aim of securing the desired results. That would be a work of genius. But things have happened just as if the actual scheme of education corresponded to some vast and deliberate conception: it could not have been done better. To achieve it, teachers have been inspired simply by the principles of discipline and authority that have guided the social organizers of all eras; such people have only one clear idea and one will—the children must learn to obey, to believe, and to think according to the prevailing social dogmas. If this were the aim, education could not be other than we find it today. There is no question of promoting the spontaneous development of the child's faculties or encouraging them to seek freely the satisfaction of their physical, intellectual, and moral needs. They try to impose ready-made ideas on them, to prevent them from ever thinking otherwise than is required for the maintenance of existing social institutions—of making them, in sum, an individual rigorously adapted to the social mechanism.

It cannot be expected that this kind of education will have any influence on human emancipation. I repeat that this instruction is merely an instrument of domination in the hands of the rulers who have never sought the elevation of the individual, but rather their servitude, and it is quite useless to expect any good from the school of today. What they have done up to the present they will continue to do in the future. There is no reason whatsoever for governments to change their system; they have resolved to use education for their purposes, and they will take advantage of every improvement of it. If only they preserve the spirit of the school and the authoritative discipline that rules it, every innovation will tend to their advantage. For this they will keep a constant watch and take care that their interests are secured.

I want to fix the attention of my readers on this point: the whole value of education consists in respect for the physical, intellectual, and moral will of the child. As in science, where all demonstrations must be based on the facts, so too the only true education is that which is stripped of all dogmatism, that leaves to the child the direction of their efforts and is content to support them in their manifestations. But nothing is easier than to alter this meaning, and nothing more difficult than to respect it. The educator is always imposing, compelling, and using violence. The true educator is the man who does not impose his own ideas and will on the child but appeals to their own energies.

From this we can understand how easily education is conducted and how easy is the task of those who seek to dominate the individual. The best conceivable methods become in their hands so many more powerful and perfect instruments of domination. Our ideal is that of science, and to it we appeal in demanding the power to educate the child by fostering their development and procuring a satisfaction of their needs as they manifest themselves.

We are convinced that the education of the future will be entirely spontaneous. It is clear that we cannot wholly realize this yet, but the evolution of methods in the direction of a broader comprehension of life and the fact that all improvement involves the suppression of violence indicate that we are on solid ground when we look to science for the liberation of the child.

Is this the ideal of those who currently control the educational system? Is this what they propose to bring about? Are they eager to eliminate violence? No, rather they employ new and more effective methods to attain the same end—that is to say, the formation of individuals who accept all the conventionalisms, all the prejudices, and all the lies upon which society is founded.

We do not fear to say that we want men who are capable of evolving continuously; men who are capable of constantly destroying and renewing themselves and that which surrounds them; men whose intellectual independence is their supreme power, which they yield to nothing; men always disposed to things that are better, eager for the triumph of new ideas; men who aspire to live multiple lives in one life. Society fears such men: you cannot, then, expect it to set up a system of education capable of producing them.

What, then, is our mission? What, then, is the method we must choose to contribute to the reform of the school?

Let us follow closely the work of the experts who study the child, and let us endeavor to find a way of applying their principles to the education we seek to establish, aiming at an increasingly complete emancipation of the individual. But how can we do this? By putting our hands energetically to the work, by promoting the establishment of new schools in which, as far as possible, there shall rule this spirit of liberty that we feel will dominate the whole education of the future.

We have already had proof that it leads to excellent results. We can destroy whatever there is in the current school that responds to the organization of violence, all the artificial methods that separate children from nature and life, the intellectual and moral discipline that has been used to impose ready-made thoughts, all beliefs that deprave and enervate the will. Without fear of tricking ourselves, we can place the child in a proper and natural environment, where they will be in contact with all that they love, and where vital impressions will be substituted for the wearisome lessons of words. If we were to do no more than this, we would have done much toward the emancipation of the child.

In such an environment we may freely and fruitfully make use of the data of science. I know that we cannot realize all our hopes in this way; that often we shall find ourselves compelled, from lack of knowledge, to employ reprehensible methods, but we shall be sustained by the confident feeling that without having achieved our entire aim, and despite the imperfection of our work, we shall have done a great deal more than is being done by the current school. I prefer the free spontaneity of a child who knows nothing to the verbal knowledge and intellectual deformation of a child that has suffered the education that currently exists.

What we have tried to do in Barcelona has been attempted in various other places. All of us have seen that the work was possible. I think, then, that it is necessary to dedicate ourselves to it immediately. We do not want to wait for the termination of the study of the child to undertake the renewal of the school; by waiting nothing will be accomplished. Let us apply what we know and go on learning. A scheme of rational education is already possible, and in such schools as we advocate children may develop freely according to their aspirations. We will work to improve and extend the work.

Those are our aims. We do not ignore the difficulties we will face, but we have begun in the conviction that we shall be assisted in our task by those who work in their various spheres to emancipate humans from the dogmas and conventionalisms that ensure the continuation of the present wicked organization of society.

10. Neither Reward nor Punishment

Rational education is, above all things, a means of defense against error and ignorance. To ignore truths and believe in absurdities is predominant in our society; to that we owe class differences and the persistence and continuity of the antagonism of interests.

Having admitted and practiced the coeducation of boys and girls, of rich and poor—having, that is to say, started from the principle of solidarity and equality—we are not prepared to create a new inequality. Hence in the Modern School there were neither rewards nor punishments, nor exams to puff up some children with the flattering grade of "outstanding," while others receive the vulgar grade of "pass," and others still suffer the shame of being scorned as incompetent.

These features of the existing official and religious schools, which are quite in accord with their stagnant environment, could not, for the reasons I have given, be admitted in to the Modern School. Since we are not educating for a specific purpose, we cannot determine the capacity or incapacity of anyone. When we teach a science, an art, a trade, or any specialty that needs special conditions, an examination could be useful, and there may be reason to give an academic diploma or refuse one; I neither affirm nor deny it. But there was no such specialty in the Modern School. The characteristic note of the school that distinguished it even from some that passed as progressive models was that in it the faculties of the children developed freely without subjection to any dogmatic model, not even to what may

72 of the 113 Modern School students with teachers. *Boletín de la Escuela Moderna*, May 31, 1904. IISG.

have been considered the body of convictions of the founder and teachers. Every pupil left there to go forth into social activity with the aptitude necessary to be their own master and guide throughout the course of life.

Hence, if we were rationally prevented from giving rewards, we could not impose punishments, and no one would have dreamed of doing so in our school if the idea had not been suggested from without. Sometimes parents came to me with the rank proverb "Letters go in with blood" on their lips and begged me to impose a regime of cruelty on their children. Others who were charmed with the precocious talent of their children wanted to see them shine in examinations and exhibit medals. But we refused to admit either prizes or punishments and sent the parents away. If any child stood out for merit, application, laziness, or bad conduct, we pointed out to them the harmony or disharmony that could result from the good or bad behavior of the student or the class, and this could serve as a topic for the teacher to address without any more consequences. The parents gradually adjusted to the system, though they often had to be corrected in their errors and prejudices by their own children.

Nevertheless, the old prejudice was constantly recurring, and I saw that I had to repeat my arguments with the parents of new pupils. I therefore wrote the following article in the *Boletín:*

Why the Modern School Does Not Hold Examinations

The conventional examinations that we are used to seeing at the end of the school year, that our parents considered to be so important, do not work at all; or, if they achieve anything it is something bad. These functions and their accompanying solemnities seem to have been instituted for the sole purpose of satisfying the vanity of parents and the selfish interests of many teachers, and in order to torture the children before the examination and make them ill afterwards. Every parent wants their child to appear in public as one of the outstanding students in school; they take pride in their child as miniature wise man. They do not notice that for a few weeks to a month or so the child suffers exquisite torture. As things are judged by external appearances, it is not thought that there is any real torture, as there is not the least scratch visible on the skin.

Parents' ignorance of the natural disposition of their children and the iniquity of putting them in unnatural conditions so that their intellectual powers, especially in the sphere of memory, are artificially stimulated prevent parents from seeing that this measure of personal gratification may, as has happened in many cases, lead to illness and to the moral and physical death of their children.

On the other hand, the majority of teachers, being mere stereotypers of ready-made phrases and mechanical inoculators, rather than *moral fathers* of their pupils, are concerned in these examinations with their own personality and their economic interests. Their object is to let the parents and the others who are present at the public display see that under their guidance the child has learned a lot, that their knowledge is greater in quantity and quality than could have been expected of their tender years and in view of the short time that they have been under the charge of such a skillful teacher.

In addition to this miserable vanity, which is satisfied at the cost of the moral and physical life of the child, the teachers are anxious to elicit compliments from the parents and the rest of the audience, who know nothing of the real state of things, as an extremely effective advertisement of the prestige of their Educational Store.

To put it bluntly, we are unrepentant adversaries of these examinations. In school everything must be done for the benefit of the pupil. Everything that does not achieve this goal should be rejected as antithetical to the nature of a positive education. Examinations do no good, and they do much harm to the child. Besides the aforementioned illnesses, above all those of the nervous system, and perhaps even an early death, the moral elements that initiate in the consciousness of the student this immoral act called an exam are: the vanity provoked in those who are placed highest; gnawing envy and humiliation, obstacles to sound growth, in those who have failed; and in all of them the germs of most of the sentiments that go to the making of egoism.

Here I have decided to include an exposition of our perspective from a professional writer published in the *Boletín*:

Examinations and Competitions

Upon finishing the school year, we have heard, as in past years, talk of competitions, examinations, and rewards. Once again, we see the parade of children with diplomas and red graduation books, adorned with green and gold ribbons; we have seen the multitude of mamas anxious with uncertainty and children terrorized by the frightful ordeals of the exam, where they have to appear before an inflexible tribunal to suffer a tremendous interrogation, circumstances that give the event a certain unfortunate analogy with those that are held daily in court.

This is the symbol of the entire current system of education. Because one is not merely interrupted during one's work to be sanctioned with grades and ratings during one part of the year, or only during one part of life, but rather during all of our years of study and for many professions during one's entire life.

This all begins when we are five or six years old, when we are taught to read: already at such a tender age, we are forced to worry not so much about the "stories" we have learned in a new exercise or the more or less interesting writing of the letters as about the prize of the lesson that we must compete for. And what's worse is that we are turned red with shame if we cannot keep up, or we are inflated with vanity if we have defeated the others, if we have attracted the envy and the enmity of our compañeros.

While we studied grammar, calculus, science, and Latin, the teachers and our parents did not rest—as if impelled by a tacit agreement, they convinced us that we were surrounded by rivals to combat, by superiors to admire or inferiors to despise. It occurred to us to ask: "What are we working for?" And we were answered that we had already obtained the benefit of our efforts or that we would have to bear the consequences of our laziness. All of the agitation and all of the functions inspired in us the conviction that if we won first place, if we managed to be more than the others, our parents, relatives, and friends, the teacher himself would give us distinguished displays of preference. As a logical consequence, our efforts were directed exclusively at the prize, at success. As a result, nothing developed in our moral being beyond vanity and egoism.

The seriousness of the problem augments considerably when one enters into life. College [*bachillerato*] is not very dangerous; it is little more than a formality, but it opens the door to a great number of careers where the right to existence is cruelly disputed. Until then the youth who works for themselves does not understand, and they are increasingly convinced that to secure their future they need to "defeat" everyone else and become the strongest or the cleverest. All of social life suffers in this way.

In society we have found men of all backgrounds and ages who would not have taken a step or made the most minimal effort if it were not for the most intimate conviction that all of their merits would be wholly counted and paid someday. The men of government know it perfectly, and so they gain much from the citizens through the rewards, promotions, distinctions, and decorations that they confer. This is an enduring remnant of Christianity. The dogma of enteral glory has inspired the Legion of Honor. At every step in life we find prizes, competitions, and examinations: Is there anything sadder, uglier, and falser?

There is something more abnormal than the preparatory work for academic programs: the excess of moral and physical labor that deforms intelligences, excessively developing certain faculties to the detriment of others that remain atrophied. The smallest reproach that can be directed against them is that they are a waste of time, and frequently they ruin lives to the point of prohibiting any other personal, familial, or social concern. Those who are serious should not be distracted by the arts or think of love or interest themselves in public concerns under the penalty of failure.

And what will we say of the competitions that isn't universally known? I will not speak of the intentional injustices, although many of them can be cited as examples; it is sufficient for the injustice to be essential to the base of the system. A grade or a rank would be different if certain conditions were to change; for example, if the jury were different, if the mood of a certain judge, in whatever circumstance, had changed. In this matter change reigns as the absolute señora and chance is blind.

Supposing one were to recognize the very debatable right of certain men, by virtue of their age or their works, to judge the value of other men, to measure them, and above all to compare their individual values, these judges would still need to establish their verdict upon solid foundations. Instead of this, they reduce the elements of evaluation to a minimum: a job of a few hours, a conversation of a few minutes, and this is sufficient to declare whether a man is more or less capable to carry out a given function, to dedicate himself to a given study or a given job.

Resting upon change and arbitrariness, competitions and the judgments that they produce enjoy a certain universal prestige and authority that are imposed not only on individuals but also on their efforts and their jobs. Even science is ruled by diplomas. There is a chosen science around which there is nothing but mediocrity; only this marked and guaranteed science can assure the man who possesses it the right to life. We denounce the vices of this system with pleasure, because in it we see an inheritance from the tyrannical past. Always the same centralization, the same official investiture.

May we be allowed, without being branded as utopians, to conceive of a society where all who want to work can, where hierarchy does not exist, and where one works for the work and for its legitimate results.

Let's start by introducing such healthy customs in school. May pedagogues inspire love for work without arbitrary sanctions, since there are already natural and inevitable sanctions that will be sufficiently evident. Above all let's avoid giving children the notion of comparison and measurement between individuals, because for men to understand and appreciate the infinite diversity that exists among characters and intelligences it is necessary to prevent students from developing the immutable conception of the *good* student that everyone ought to emulate, but which is attained *more* or *less* with greater or lesser merit.

So let's eliminate exams, prizes, and rewards from every class. This will be the practical principle.

—Emilia Boivin[12]

In number 6 of the fifth year of the *Boletín* I thought it necessary to publish the following:

No More Punishments

We have received frequent letters from workers' educational centers and republican fraternities complaining about some teachers that punish children in their schools. We ourselves have been disgusted during our brief excursions to find material proof of the fact that is at the base of this complaint; we have seen children on their knees or in other forced postures of punishment.

These irrational and atavistic practices must disappear. Modern pedagogy entirely rejects them. The teachers who offer their services to the Modern School or ask our recommendation to teach in similar schools must refrain from any moral or material punishment, under penalty of being disqualified permanently. Scolding, impatience, and anger ought to disappear with the old title of "schoolmaster." In free schools all should be peace, happiness, and fraternity. We think that this will suffice to put an end to these practices, which are most improper in people whose sole ideal is the training of a generation able to establish a truly fraternal, harmonious, and just society.

11. Laicism and the Library

In setting out to establish a rational school for the purpose of preparing children for their entry into the free solidarity of humanity, the first problem that confronted us was that of its library. The whole educational luggage of the old system was an incoherent mixture of science and faith, reason and absurdity, good and evil, human experience and divine revelation, truth and error; in a word, totally unsuited to meet the new needs that arose with the formation of a new school.

If the school had been from remote antiquity equipped not for teaching in the broad sense of communicating to the rising generation the sum of the knowledge of previous generations but for teaching in agreement with authority and the convenience of the ruling classes, and therefore destined to make obedient and submissive students, it is clear that none of the books hitherto written could be useful. But the severe logic of this position did not at once convince me. I refused to believe that the French democracy, which worked so zealously for the separation of Church and state, and that in so doing had incurred the anger of the clericals and adopted obligatory lay instruction, would resign itself to a semi-education or an education of sophistry. Yet I had to yield to the evidence against my prejudice. I first read a large number of works in the French code of secular instruction and found that God was replaced by the state, Christian virtue by civic duty, religion by patriotism, submission and obedience to the king, the aristocracy, and the clergy by respect for the functionary, the proprietor, and the boss. Then I consulted an eminent freethinker who held high office in the Ministry of Public Instruction and, when I told him of my desire to see the books they used, which I understood to be purged of traditional errors, and explained my design and ideal to him, he told me frankly that they had nothing of the sort; all their books were more or less cleverly and insidiously tainted with error, which is the indispensable cement of social inequality. When I further asked if, seeing that they had replaced the decaying divine idol with the idol of oligarchic domination, they had a book about the origin of religion, he said that there was none, but he knew one that would suit me—Malvert's *Science and Religion*. In point of fact, this was already translated into Spanish and was used as a reading book in the Modern School, with the title *Origin of Christianity.*

In Spanish pedagogical literature I found several works by a distinguished author of some eminence in science, who had written them rather in the interest of the publishers than with a view to the education of children. Some of these little books were at first used in the Modern School, but, though one could not accuse them of error, they lacked the inspiration of an ideal and were poor in method. I searched for this author to interest him in my plans and commission him to write books for the new library, but his publishers held him to a contract and he could not oblige me.

In brief, the Modern School was opened before a single work had been produced for its library, but it was not long before the first appeared—a brilliant book by Jean Grave, which has had a considerable influence on our schools. His work *The Adventures of Nono* is a kind of poem in which a certain phase of the happier future is ingeniously and dramatically contrasted with the sordid realities of the present social order; the delights of the land of Autonomy are contrasted with the horrors of the kingdom of Argirocracy. The genius of Grave has raised the work to a height at which it escapes the censures of the skeptical anti-futurists; he has depicted the social evils of the present truthfully and without exaggeration. The book enchanted the children, and the profundity of his thoughts suggested many opportune comments to the teachers. In their play, the children used to reproduce scenes from Autonomy, and the adults, in their efforts and suffering, saw their cause reflected in the constitution of that Argirocracy, where Monadio ruled.

It was announced in the *Boletín de la Escuela Moderna* and other political newspapers that competitions would be held for the best manuals of rational instruction, but no writers came forward. I confine myself to recording the fact without going into the causes of it. Subsequently, I edited two books for reading in school. They were not written for school, but they were translated for the Modern School and were very useful. One was called *The Note Book*, the other *Patriotism and Colonization*. Both were collections of passages from writers of every country on the injustices of patriotism, the horrors of war, and the iniquity of conquest. The choice of these works was vindicated by the excellent influence they had on the minds of the children, as we shall see from the little essays of the children that appeared in the *Boletín* and the fury with which they were denounced by the reactionary press and crabs of Parliament.

Many have thought that there is not much difference between lay and rationalist education, and in many articles and propagandist speeches the two have been spoken of as perfectly analogous. To correct this error, I published the following article in the *Boletín*:

Lay Education

The word *education* should not be accompanied by any qualification. It only responds to the need and to the responsibility felt by the generation that lives in the full development of its powers to prepare the rising generation and admit it to the patrimony of human knowledge. This, which is perfectly rational, will be fully practiced in some future age, when people will be free from superstitions and privileges.

Finding ourselves still on the path to this ideal, we see ourselves face to face with religious education and political education: to these we must oppose rational and scientific instruction. One type of religious education that exists, that is given in the clerical and convent schools of all countries, consists of the smallest possible quantity of useful knowledge and a good deal of Christian doctrine and sacred history. In terms of political education, there is the kind established in France after the fall of the Empire, designed to exalt patriotism and present the current public administration as the instrument of good government.

Sometimes the qualification *free* or *lay* is applied abusively and passionately to education, in order to mislead public opinion. In that way, the religious use the phrase *"free schools"* for schools that they establish in opposition to the really free tendency of modern pedagogy and many that are really political, patriotic, and anti-humanitarian are called *lay schools.*

Rational education rises above these miserable intentions. First, it has nothing to do with religious education, because science has shown that the story of creation is a legend and the gods are myths; and, therefore, religious education takes advantage of the credulity of the parents and the ignorance of the children, maintaining the belief in a supernatural being to whom people may address all kinds of prayers. This hoax, still unfortunately widespread, is the cause of great evils, whose effects will continue as long as their cause persists. The mission of education is to show the youth, by purely scientific methods, that the more knowledge we have of the products of nature, their qualities, and how to use them, the more will abound nutritional, industrial, scientific, and artistic products that are useful, convenient, and necessary for life, and with greater ease men and women will issue in larger numbers from our schools with a determination to cultivate every branch of knowledge and activity, guided by reason and inspired by science and art, which will beautify life and justify society.

We will not, then, waste time beseeching an imaginary god for things that only human labor can procure.

On the other hand, our teaching has nothing to do with politics. It is our work to form individuals in the full possession of all their faculties while politics would subject their faculties to other men. Like religions, which in extolling a divine power have created a positively abusive power and hindered human emancipation, political systems also retard emancipation by encouraging men to hope for everything from the will of others, from what are supposed to be superior men—from those who, from tradition or choice, exercise the profession of governors. It must be the aim of the rational schools to show the children that there will be tyranny and slavery as long as one man depends upon another, to study the causes that maintain popular ignorance, to learn the origin of all the traditional practices that give life to the existing social system, and to direct the attention of the pupils to these matters.

We will not, then, waste time asking others for what we can get for ourselves.

In short, our goal is to imprint on the minds of the children the idea that as they grow older they will gain more well-being in social life the more they educate themselves, the greater their efforts are to obtain it for themselves, and that the era of general happiness will be the more sure to dawn when they have discarded all religious and other superstitions, which have up to the present done so much harm. For that reason, we eliminated from our school all distribution of prizes, of gifts, of charity, of all kinds of medals, badges, and ribbons, because they are religious and patriotic imitations, fit only to encourage the children to believe in talismans instead of in the individual and collective power of beings who are conscious of their ability and knowledge.

Rational and scientific teaching must persuade the men and women of the future that they must expect nothing from any privileged being (fictitious or real), and that they may expect all that is rational from themselves and from solidarity freely organized and accepted.

In order to expand the library of the Modern School, I published the following announcements in the *Boletín* and the local press:

To the Intellectuals

The Modern School makes a vehement call to all writers who love science and are interested in the future of humanity to propose works oriented toward emancipating the spirit from all of the errors of our ancestors and guiding the youth toward knowledge of the truth and the practice of justice, liberating the world from authoritarian dogmas, shameful sophisms, and ridiculous conventionalisms, such as those that unfortunately form the mechanism of the present society.

Arithmetic Competition[13]

Considering that the way in which the study of arithmetic has been understood until the present is one of the most powerful methods of inculcating children with the false ideas of the capitalist system, the Modern School is launching a competition for the renewal of the study of arithmetic and invites those friends of rational and scientific instruction who are especially occupied with mathematics to draw up a series of easy and practical problems that make no reference to money, saving, and profit. These exercises must deal with agricultural and industrial production, the just distribution of raw materials and manufactured articles, means of communication and the transport of goods, the comparison of human labor with mechanical, the benefits of machinery, public works, etc. In a word, the Modern School wants a collection of problems showing what arithmetic really ought to be—the science of the social economy (taking the word "economy" in its etymological sense of "good distribution").

The exercises will deal with the four fundamental operations (integrals, decimals, and fractions),[14] the metric system, proportions, compounds and alloys, the squares and cubes of numbers, and the extraction of square and cube roots. As those who respond to this appeal are, it is hoped, inspired rather with the ideal of a right education of children than with the desire of profit, and as we wish to avoid the common practice in such circumstances, we shall not appoint judges or offer any prizes. The Modern School will publish the arithmetic that best serves its purpose and will come to an amicable agreement with the author as to compensation.

To Teachers

To all who dedicate themselves to the noble ideal of the rational teaching of the new generations and to their initiation in the practice of their responsibilities, to stimulate them never to abdicate the enjoyment of their rights, we plead that you fix your attention on the announcement of the *Compendium of Universal History* by Clemencia Jacquinet and *The Adventures of Nono* by Jean Grave found on the cover. The works that the Modern School edits and proposes to continue editing are intended for free institutions of rational teaching, social studies circles, and parents who resent the intellectual limitation that dogma of all kinds, religious, political, and social, imposes in order to maintain privilege at the expense of the ignorance of the disinherited. All of the enemies of Jesuitism and the conventional lies and of the errors transmitted by tradition and routine will find in our publications truth based upon evidence. As we have no desire for profit, the price of the works represents almost their intrinsic value or material cost; if there is any profit from their sale, it will be spent on subsequent publications.

In number 6 of the second year of the *Boletín*, I published the following article and the response from Reclus to a request I made of him. So it pleases me to include it here because of how it elevates a very interesting matter intimately related to my concept of rationalist education:

The Teaching of Geography

The entire history of modern science, compared to the scholastic theology of the Middle Ages, can be summed up in one phrase: "return to nature." To learn we must first try to understand. Rather than reasoning about the inconceivable, let's begin by seeing, observing, and studying what is to be found in our view, within the range of our senses and our experimentation.

Above all, in geography, which is to say, precisely, the study of terrestrial nature, it is advisable to proceed from sight, from direct observation of this land where we were born and that gives us bread to feed us. But the teaching of geography, as it is carried out in our schools, bears the mark of the scholasticism of the Middle Ages: the teacher asks the student for an act of faith, pronounced, moreover, without any meaning; like a parrot they recite the names of the "five rivers of France, three capes, two gulfs, and one strait," without referring any of these names to any specific reality. How could one do this if the teacher has never even shown them any of the things they are talking about, yet they find themselves on the same street in front of the door of the school in the streams and puddles of water formed by the rain?

Let's return to nature!

If I had the good fortune to be a geography teacher for children without being stuck in any official or particular establishment, I would make sure not to start by putting books and maps in the hands of my young compañeros. Maybe I wouldn't even utter the Greek word "geography" in front of them, but rather invite them on long walks together, happily learning in their company.

Being a teacher, but a teacher without a title, I would take great care to proceed methodically on these walks and in the conversations provoked by the sight of objects and landscapes. It is evident that the first lesson should vary in its details according to the region one inhabits: our chats wouldn't be the same in a flat area as they would be in mountainous terrain, in regions marked by granite as they would be near limestone, on a beach or a riverbank as on a barren plain; in Belgium I wouldn't speak the same as if I were in the Pyrenees or the Alps. Our language would never be absolutely identical in two different places, because all regions have particular and unique features to note, valuable observations to gather that would serve as elements of comparison with other districts.

As monotonous and poor as our area may be, we do not lack the possibility of seeing, if not mountains or hills, at least some rocks that ripped the more recently deposited layers of earth. Everywhere we would observe a certain diversity of terrains, sands, clays, swamps, and mosses—probably also sandstones and limestones. We could follow the bend of a stream or a river, see a lost current, a developing eddy, an ebb that turns back the waters, the game of the wrinkles that forms in the sand, the progress of the erosion that strips part of a bank, and the floods that develop in the lowlands. If our region were so little favored by nature that it lacked a stream nearby, at least there would be rainstorms that would create temporary streams with their banks, bluffs, rapids, supports, sluices, circuits, bends, and confluences—an infinite variety of hydrological phenomena.

And in the sky? There we can study the infinite series of movements of the earth and the stars: the morning, the midday, the dusk, and the darkness in which stars are discovered; the snow and the clouds that block out the blue sky, and later the great and strange spectacles of storms, lightning, rainbows, and maybe the aurora borealis. All of these celestial movements begin to establish themselves in our understanding by an initial mathematics, since all of the stars follow a path laid out in advance, and we see them successively pass across the meridian, thereby giving us the occasion to specify the cardinal points and recognize diverse points in space.

The circumstances of life could add long excursions to these nearby walks. True voyages could be methodically organized, because this isn't about going by chance, like those Americans who have their "return to the Old World" and usually make themselves even more ignorant by disorderly piling up places and people in their minds, confusing it all in their memories: the dances of Paris, the review of the guard in Potsdam, visits to the pope and the sultan, climbing the pyramids, and the adoration of the Church of the Holy Sepulcher. Such trips are some of the most terrible that one could imagine, because they kill the power of admiration that should grow in an individual at the same time as their knowledge, and they end up ruining it to the point where they despise all beauty. I remember the sensation of horror I experienced hearing a good-looking young man, very well-informed, very disdainful, and as stupid as he was wise, lazily remark near Mont Blanc: "Ah, yes, it's necessary that I see this falsehood!"

To avoid similar aberrations, it is important to organize excursions and trips with the same methodical care that one applies to the ordinary study of instruction, but it is also important to avoid all pedantry when directing the trips because above all else the child must have fun: the study should present itself only at the psychological moment, at the precise instant when sight and description enter directly in the mind to engrave themselves upon it forever. When this method is carried out, the child is already very advanced, although they have not followed a so-called "course." The mind finds itself open with the desire to know.

★ ★ ★

Response from Reclus

Sooner or later, always too soon, time comes for the prison of the school to trap the child within its four walls. I say *prison* because the establishment of education almost always is—the word *school* has lost much since its first Greek meaning of *recreation* or *party*.

Books appear and with them the first official lesson of geography that the teacher pronounces to their students. The moment has arrived to submit to the routine and put an atlas in the hands of the child stamped by the Board of Public Instruction. For my part, I am careful not to touch it; before all else I desire to be perfectly logical in my explanations. After having said that the earth is round, that it is a ball that moves through space like the sun and the moon, I didn't have to show an image in the form of a four-sided piece of paper with colored figures to represent Europe, Asia, Africa, Australia, the two halves of the New World!

How to escape from this flagrant contradiction? I will have to imitate the ancient magicians, asking that they believe me on faith in my word, or I will find myself obligated to try to explain to the children that the globe has changed into a planisphere; to see whether I fully understand the association between the two words "sphere" and "plain." But the explanation will remain necessarily hobbled because it is only possible by means of high mathematics still inaccessible to children. At the start of the class it is necessary that the teacher not threaten the perfect comradeship of intelligence that should exist among the students and him for the comprehension of things.

Moreover, I know from experience that these maps with unequal scales and projections would do as much damage to my students as they did to me and undoubtedly to the reader as well, because no one manages to completely erase the contradictory impressions that one receives from these diverse maps. The projections that we have already seen successively have given geographic forms a floating and indefinite appearance and the proportions between the different regions are not presented cleanly for our consideration, because we have seen them in the atlas of every class with multiple deforma-tions, inflated or narrowed, stretched, elongated, or truncated in various ways. As a consequence, our intellectual faculties are dulled: assured in advance not to reach the precision of sight, we don't even try to obtain it.

To avoid this indifference, which impedes the sincerity and the ardor of the study, it is, then, necessary, even indispensable, to proceed to fixing the forms and important points of geography for the use of school globes, in respect to which the teacher should follow

an absolute intransigence, since it is truly impossible to use traditional maps without betraying the very same cause of education
with which they were entrusted.

Which is the best globe to use as an educational object? In my
opinion, a simple ball attached to wooden apparatus beside the
teacher who moves it and trusts in their students. The lines that
one may draw on it must be simple: two points to indicate the poles,
a black line around the middle to mark the equator, later, when it
comes to speaking about the changing of the seasons a layout of the
ecliptic will be added to one point and another of the equator. Nothing
of meridians, parallels, or latitude—this comes later. It is enough to
indicate the point where one could find the school, whether it is in
Brussels or whichever other city on the face of the earth. Moreover,
one could trace an initial meridian from pole to pole across this point.
That is what the first globe has to be. It will be coated with an oily
varnish that one can draw on with chalk and erase, thereby allowing
the teacher to make their demonstrations and mark their theoretical voyages on the planetary sphere. Later students will use other
globes advantageously, above all if they have managed to draw the
continents, the seas, and everything they were taught in school with
their own hands. This is the true method: to see, to create anew and
not repeat mnemonically.

There is no doubt: the early geographical education of the child
must proceed from a direct examination of the globe, an exact and
proportional reproduction of the earth itself. Yet, this education
will soon be hindered by the limitations of the instrument. A globe
of a scale of forty-millionths with a circumference of a meter is
heavy, difficult to manage, above all for children, and the difficulty
increases in geometric proportion with the dimensions of the object.
If the globe were to a scale of twenty-millionths with a circumference of two meters, it would need to be suspended from the ceiling to
move it with a finger as is needed in education. Ultimately, a spheri-
cal instrument of larger dimensions is usually created in such an
awkward way that no one knows where to keep it, and it ends up
being forgotten in a deposit of useless junk. That's what happened
to the large globes of Olearius and Coronelli, which, moreover lacked
geographical value in our days.

But if spheres of such considerable dimensions are too unwieldy to be used in our classrooms, libraries, and auditoriums, that does not mean that they do not have educational value. To the contrary, it is worthwhile to use them as different monuments with their special and original architecture constituting a new branch of modern art (which seems to be increasingly understood already, despite the fact that the results thus far achieved in this area have not surpassed mediocrity). A large globe, especially the one with a circumference of forty meters (a millionth in scale) that was on display at the exposition in Paris in 1889,[15] did not have significance from a precisely geographic point of view. It's only merit, which was not to be disdained, consisted in showing the passersby the enormity of the seas compared with our little political territories and the relative importance of the various regions. The work of the future will impose upon every great city the construction of a globe of large dimensions to the millionth, to the 500-thousandth, to the 100-thousandth, or more even, reproducing the true form of the earth's crust in its exact relief. Detailed projects of these future constructions have already been presented to the public, and we are in an epoch in which the execution of such plans can start with full confidence. The astronomers, anticipating modern geographers, have understood the usefulness of the construction of a lunar relief in large proportions.

It is undoubtable that these scientific monuments will be indispensable for the education of the adult public, but here we are talking about lessons designed for students in our schools, where such large globes do not fit. It doesn't matter: If there is a difficulty in exhibiting the globe, who will stop us from showing pieces? If a globe is too big, one can cut segments of all dimensions. Here there is a segment to the ten-millionth! Another to the five-millionth! Even up to the hundred-millionth, the map of Switzerland by Person, part of a globe with a four hundred–meter circumference!

Since the industrial means have already been discovered, from now on disks of all scales can be made in the convenient proportion. And this does not only pertain to geography but also to astronomy, and you, researchers of what is called the "celestial sphere," you will have advantages in using concave globular disks as we have used convex disks. The errors of flat maps are the same for you as for us.

I can, then, in complete confidence count on you to take part in the peaceful revolutionary movement that we intend to launch in the schools and map rooms.

We speak of progress, but, considered from a certain point of view, we find ourselves in a period of disturbing flux if not regression, and we have to traverse much ground to reach a period comparable to the greatness of the Babylonian ages. The most distant records of antiquity present us with Chaldea, that country where a "Tower of the Stars" protruded from every town. There was always an observatory on top of all of the small homes. The beautiful aerial gardens of the legendary Semiramis poeticized with their lush vegetation and the song of the birds from the high superior tower from which the astronomers examined space. There was no complete city that did not possess one of these temples of science dedicated to the study of the earth and sky.

A well-known legend tells of a group of men in a single town working to construct one of the edifices of knowledge, the Tower of Babel. Suddenly they were afflicted by mutual ignorance of each other, and not being able to understand each other, each left to go their own way, making them foreigners and enemies. Currently we speak a new common language: science. Nothing stops us from uniting more closely than ever. We have reached the time when we can fearlessly renew the construction that had begun. Hopefully in the near future every town will build a new "Tower of Stars," where the citizens will come to comfortably observe the stars and educate themselves on the marvels of the earth, their home planet.

—Elisée Reclus

After reading the above article, I wrote to the Geographical Institute of Brussels asking them to recommend a geography textbook. My request was answered by the following letter signed by Reclus:

Señor Ferrer Guardia:
Dear friend, in my opinion there is no text for the teaching of geography in primary schools. I do not know a single one that is not infected with the venom of religion, patriotism, or, what is even worse, administrative routine.

Moreover, when children are fortunate enough, as they surely will be at the Modern School, to have teachers who are intelligent and love their profession, they benefit from not having books. Suggestive oral education given by one who knows those who learn is the best. After having planted the seed, the harvest is reaped by taking notes and making maps. Nevertheless, one can admit that, at least for teachers, geographical literature is enriched by a manual that could serve as a guide in the teaching of this science.

Do you want me to speak about it with N—————, someone who seems to me to be perfectly capable of writing this work according to the indicated criteria?

Cordial greetings from your friend,

Elisée Reclus

Brussels, February 26, 1903

In number 7 of the *Boletín* I published the following preface to our second book titled:

The Origin of Christianity

The older pedagogy, which had as its objective, though it was undeclared, to teach people the uselessness of knowledge, in order that they might be reconciled to their hard conditions and seek consolation in a supposed future life, used reading books in elementary school that swarmed with stories, anecdotes, and accounts of travels, gems of classical literature, etc. With this mix of the beautiful and the useful came the error; this pedagogy filled an iniquitous social goal. The mystical idea predominated, representing that a relation could be established between a supernatural power and men by means of priests—the chief foundation of the existence of both the privileged and the disinherited and the cause of all of the injustices that men suffer and practice, according to their position.

Among other books of this class, all tainted with the same evil, we remember one that inserted an academic discourse, a marvel of Spanish eloquence, in praise of the Bible. Its summary is expressed in the barbarous declaration of Omar when he condemned the Library of Alexandria to the flames: "The whole truth is contained in the sacred book. If all of these books are true, they are superfluous, if they are not true, they deserve the fire."

The Modern School, which seeks to form free minds with a sense of responsibility, fit to experience a complete development of the human faculties, which is the one aim of life, must necessarily adopt a very different kind of reading book in harmony with its method of teaching. For this reason, as it teaches established truth and is interested in the struggle between light and darkness, it has deemed it necessary to produce a critical work composed of positive and irrefutable facts that will enlighten the mind of the student if not during their childhood then later in manhood, when they intervene in the social mechanism and in the struggle against the errors, conventionalisms, hypocrisies, and infamies that conceal themselves under the cloak of mysticism.

This work reminds us that our books are not merely intended for children; they are destined also for the use of the adult schools that are being founded all over by many freethinking, cooperative, recreational, and workers' societies, as well as social studies circles and other progressive and enlightened groups that are eager to combat this illiteracy that sustains tradition and is naturally resistant to progress.

We believe that the section of Malvert's work (*Science and Religion*) that we have entitled *The Origin of Christianity* will be useful for this purpose. It shows the myths, dogmas, and ceremonies of the Christian religion in their primitive simplicity, sometimes as exoteric symbols concealing a truth known to the initiated, sometimes as adaptations of earlier beliefs imposed by sheer routine and preserved by utilitarian malice. As we are convinced and have ample evidence of the usefulness of our work, we offer it to the public with the hope that it will bear the fruit that we anticipate. We have only to add that certain passages that are unsuitable for children have been omitted; the omissions are indicated, and adults may consult the passages in the complete edition.

—F. Ferrer Guardia

12. Sunday Lectures

The Modern School did not limit itself to pedagogical action. Without for a moment forgetting its predominant character and its fundamental goal, it also dedicated itself to popular education. We arranged a series of public lectures on Sundays attended by the pupils, their families, and a large number of workers who were anxious to learn.

The first lectures were lacking in method and continuity, as we had to employ lecturers who were quite competent in regard to their own subjects but gave each lecture without regard to what preceded or followed. On other occasions, when we had no lecturer, we substituted useful readings. The general public attended assiduously, and our advertisements in the liberal press of the district were eagerly scanned.

In view of these results and in order to encourage the disposition of the general public, I held a consultation with Don Andrés Martínez Vargas and Don Odón de Buen, professors at the University of Barcelona. We discussed the creation of a popular university in the Modern School where the science that is given—or, rather, sold—by the state to the privileged youth in the universities should be given freely to the people, like a kind of restitution, as every human being has the right to know, and science, which is produced by observers and workers of all ages and countries, ought not to be restricted to a class.

In effect, the conferences subsequently acquired a continuity and true regularity with the help of the specialties of knowledge of the two lecturers. Dr. Martínez Vargas explained physiology and hygiene, and Dr. Odón de Buen geography and natural science, on alternate Sundays, until the persecution began. Their teaching was eagerly welcomed by the pupils of the Modern School, and the large audiences of mixed children and adults. One of the liberal journals of Barcelona, in giving an account of the work, spoke of the function as "the scientific Mass."

The eternal light haters, who maintain their privileges on the ignorance of the people, suffered greatly upon seeing this center of enlightenment shining so vigorously. They did not delay long in urging the authorities who were at their disposal to extinguish it brutally. For my part, I resolved to put the work on the firmest foundation I could conceive so it would become indestructible.

I recall with the greatest pleasure that hour we devoted once a week to the confraternity of culture. The lectures started on December 15, 1901, when Don Ernesto Vendrell spoke of Hypatia as a martyr to the ideals of Science and Beauty, the victim of the fanatical Bishop Cyril of Alexandria. Other lectures were given on subsequent Sundays, as I said, until, on October 5, 1902, the lectures were organized into regular courses of science. On that day Dr. Andrés Martínez Vargas, professor of the Faculty of Medicine (child diseases) at the University of Barcelona, gave his first lecture on school hygiene. He explained its principles in plain terms adapted to the minds of the children. Dr. Odón de Buen, professor of the Faculty of Science, dealt with the usefulness of the study of natural history.[16]

The press was generally in sympathy with the Modern School, but when the program of the third scholastic year appeared, some of the local journals, *El Noticiero Universal* and the *Diario de Barcelona*, abandoned us. Here is a passage that deserves recording as an illustration of the typical way in which the conservative press dealt with progressive subjects:

> We have seen the prospectus of an educational center established in our city that professes to have nothing to do with "dogmas and systems." It proposes to liberate the world from "authoritarian dogmas, shameful sophisms, and ridiculous conventions." It seems to us, that this means that the first thing that will be taught to the boys and girls—it is a mixed school—is to deny the existence of God, an admirable way of forming good children, especially young women destined to be wives and mothers.

The writer continues in this ironical manner for some time, and ends as follows:

> This school has the support of two doctors, one a professor of Natural Science (Don Odón de Buen) and the other from the Faculty of Medicine. We do not name the latter, as there may be some mistake in including him among the men who lend their support to such a work.

Fortunately, the damage caused by the press was remedied by the press as well, when *El Diluvio* responded to the clerical maliciousness with energy:

The Spiteful Clericals

El Brusi[17] and *El Noticiero* have both committed the most ridiculous absurdity with the publication of a short article against a lay school operating in Barcelona with the support of all liberal citizens, which are the majority of this democratic city. We are referring to the Modern School, which, motivated by the inauguration of the new year, has inserted a notice into all of the local papers except, we suppose, *el Brusi* and its appendage *El Noticiero*, which have attacked the lay institution on calle de Bailén in order to please their readers.

We will not defend the Modern School, because our readers do not need a reason to support it. These invectives have only demonstrated that *el Brusi*, with all of its religiosity, is not free from hatred or spite nor from lying as it did in this article, which oozes bad faith all over. The rancid paper says that in this school it is taught not to believe in God, to ridicule religion, and who knows what other horrors the ancient *El Diario* has been terrified to find in the words "neither dogmas nor systems," which really demonstrate that the institution in question is completely independent.

No, rancid newspaper, no; you are very confused and lacking in truth when you say that in this educational center they deny God and inculcate this belief in the children. This cannot be read in a single paragraph of the leaflet in question. What *el Brusi* has chosen in so doing, letting spill out all of its spite and bad faith (inappropriate for a true Christian), is this paragraph: "We accept neither dogmas nor systems; molds that reduce vitality to the narrowness of the exigencies of a transitory society that aspires to be definitive. Rather, our education is constituted by solutions proven by the facts, theories accepted by reason, truths confirmed by evidence. Our education is designed so that every mind may be the motor of a will and so that truths sparkle on their own in abstraction. May they establish themselves in all understanding and, applied in practice, benefit humanity without indignant exclusions or repugnant exclusiveness."

This has struck *El Diario de Barcelona* at its core, since it cannot resign itself to the fact that lay education smears clerical education; to the fact that the prayers of the convent schools are turning into hymns for Liberty and pure Science; to the fact that the ignorant parish priest and the astute monk, thieves of intelligence and tyrants of inhibited minds, may be substituted for by the independent teacher who leaves aside religion to promote absolutely lay knowledge based in Nature and Science. *El Brusi* knows with all certainty that in these lay schools, whose advance already frightens it, nothing is taught against religion nor dogma; there they don't worry about such questions, because they believe that religious sentiments should be born and inspire small children at home. In these educational centers there is the healthy conviction that their task is to form the man of science and human knowledge, and the family, and later the society, should form the man of religious beliefs if these are their inclinations.

And the rancid paper can't come with affirmations that such (atheist) schools have produced the anticlericals, because there were Voltaire, Volney, Darwin, Victor Hugo, Zola, Combes, and other groups of distinguished men and independent spirits who, all educated by Jesuits, monks, or priests, and profoundly knowledgeable of the evil disguised as good in which they were brought up, turned against them and demolished the clerical edifice with the force of their talent, the weapons of their knowledge, and the energies of their will. Nor can *el Brusi* come with concerns and baseless reasons that can leave an impression on timid families or stupid minds. Nobly recognize that clerical education loses energy as the liberal school invades the terrain of education. And at least shut up and resign yourself before the lawful propaganda that liberal citizens make in favor of lay education against monastic, retrograde, and medieval education, which struggles against today's progressive societies and knowledge. Believe us, ancient *Diario*: if you continue your stupid efforts, the void of time will surround you and leave you alone and isolated, even by those who, following you out of tradition, are not brought so far by your sanctimoniousness nor judge it prudent to show their true colors to such a degree.

13. Positive Results

At the beginning of the second school year I once more drew up a program. Let us, I said, confirm our earlier program: vindicated by success, approved in theory and practice, the principle that from the first informed our work and governs the Modern School is now firm and unshakable.

Science is the sole teacher of life: inspired with this slogan, the Modern School proposes to give the children entrusted to its care *a mental vitality of their own,* so that when they leave our rational tutelage they will continue to be the mortal enemies of all kinds of prejudices and will form their own reasoned convictions on all subjects.

Furthermore, as education does not consist merely in the training of the mind but must take into account the emotions and the will, we shall take the utmost care in the training of the student that their intellectual impressions are transformed into the juice of sentiment. When this attains a certain degree of intensity, it spreads throughout the entire being, coloring and refining the character of the person. And since practical life, that is to say the conduct of man, revolves unfailingly within the sphere of the character, the young student must similarly learn to convert science into the only beneficent teacher of life.

To complete our view, it is necessary to indicate that we are enthusiastic partisans of *mixed* education, which consists in boys and girls obtaining an identical education. In this way, feminine and masculine humanity will deeply understand each other to the point where the woman may become, in private and social life, *the companion of man* in human labor whose goal is the improvement and happiness of the species. This task, limited almost exclusively to man, has been incomplete until today, and, therefore, ineffective; in the future it must be entrusted to man and woman. To achieve this, it is necessary that the woman not be confined to the home, that she extend the radius of her action across society. Moreover, so that the compañera of man may yield intense and powerful fruit with her moral influence, the knowledge given to her must be the same as that given to man in terms of quantity and quality.

Science, penetrating the mind of the woman, will illuminate it and accurately guide the rich fountain of sentiment that is the salient and characteristic note of her life. This element, separated from the anti-progressive aims of its natural application, must in the future become good news of peace and happiness for the moral world.

Knowing how important the dissemination of knowledge of natural sciences and hygiene is in our country, particularly for children, the Modern School proposes to contribute to the achievement of this goal. Two highly qualified professors will help us: Señor de Buen, professor of Natural Sciences, and Señor Martínez Vargas, professor of Childhood Illnesses. They will give alternating lectures on their respective scientific subjects at this center of learning.

In the *Boletín* of June 30, 1903, I published the following declaration:

One Year More

We have now passed two years of life, of expounding our aims, of their justification by our practice, and of the credit and prestige enjoyed by those who have cooperated in our work. This is not yet a guarantee of triumph, but rather a positive triumph representing the fact of being able to affirm with conviction and firmness what we have proclaimed.

We have overcome the obstacles that were put in our way by interest and prejudice, animated with the idea and we intend to persevere in it, counting always on that progressive comradeship that dispels the darkness of ignorance with its strong light. We resume work next September, after the autumn vacation. We are delighted to be able to repeat what we said last year. The Modern School and its *Boletín* overflow with life, for they have filled, with some measure of satisfaction, a deeply felt need. We did not need much to persevere, since, without formulating pledges or programs, we will persevere as long as possible.

—The Editorial Team

The following list of the pupils who had attended the school during the first two years appeared in the same issue of the *Boletín*:

	Girls		Boys		Totals	
	1901–1902	1902–1903	1901–1902	1902–1903	Year 1	Year 2
Opening Day	12	–	18	–	30	–
September	16	23	23	40	39	63
October	18	28	25	40	43	68
November	21	31	29	40	50	71
December	22	31	30	40	52	71
January	22	31	32	44	54	75
February	23	31	32	48	55	79
March	25	33	34	47	59	80
April	26	32	37	48	63	80
May	30	33	38	48	68	81
June	32	34	38	48	70	82

At the beginning of the third year I published, with special pleasure, the following two articles on the progress of the Modern School in year 3, number 1 of the *Boletín*:

Inauguration of the School Year

On the eighth of the present month we celebrated the inauguration of the new school year. A large number of pupils, their families, and members of the sympathetic public who regularly attended our public lectures filled the recently enlarged rooms and before the commencement of the function inspected the collections that give the school the appearance of a scientific museum. The function began with a short address from the director, who formally declared the opening of the third school year and said that, as they now had more experience and were encouraged by success, they would pursue the goal of the Modern School with energy and conviction.

Señor de Buen congratulated us on the material improvements made to the school, confirming the ideal that education faithfully reflect nature, as knowledge can only consist in our perception of what actually exists. On the part of his children, who study at the school and live in the neighborhood, he expounded upon the fraternal comradeship among the pupils, who desire to achieve the possibility of living in the countryside, at the seashore, inland in the forest, running across the plains, climbing the cliffs of a rugged mountain, ceaselessly observing and studying natural marvels.

He said that even in official education, or rather on the part of the professors engaged in it, there were, for all its archaic features, certain tendencies similar to those embodied in the Modern School. This might be gathered from his own presence and that of Dr. Vargas and other teachers. He announced that a similar school dedicated to the same goal would soon open in Guadalajara. It was being built from funds left for the purpose by an altruist who, upon dying, wished to contribute to the redemption of children and their liberation from ignorance and superstition. He expressed the hope and strong desire that wealthy people would, at their death, finally understand that, rather than the crazy egoism of dedicating their wealth to the creation of an illusory happiness in the afterlife, they should give back to society on behalf of the disinherited.

Dr. Martinez Vargas affirmed, against all who thought otherwise, that the purely scientific and rational education of the Modern School is a positive base of good education. No better can be conceived for the relations of the children with their families and society; it is the only way to morally and intellectually form the man of the future. He was glad to hear that the school hygiene, which had been previously practiced in the Modern School by means of a periodic examination of the children to avoid infectious diseases, and theoretically expounded upon in the public lectures, had received the solemn sanction of the hygienic congress recently held in Brussels.

In order to summarize his lectures, and as a means of supporting his oral explanation with visual perception, he exhibited a series of lantern slides illustrating various hygienic exercises, certain types of disease, sick organs, etc., which the speaker explained in detail. An incident occurred with the projector apparatus (that could easily be repaired for future lectures), interrupting the presentation of images but not the oral presentation, which continued to address the mischievous effects of corsets, the danger of microbial infection by trailing dresses, by children playing with soil, unsanitary houses and workshops, etc., ending with the promise to continue his hygienic explanation during the coming year.

The audience expressed its pleasure at the close of the event, and the students, radiant with joy, offered some consolation amid the hardships of the present and the hope of a better humanity for the future.

A Class Trip to the Country of Industry

In 1903 Francisco Ferrer and Anselmo Lorenzo brought the students of the Modern School to visit a factory in nearby Sabadell. For obvious reasons, years later Ferrer did not mention that the owner of this factory was none other than the father of Mateo Morral—the administrator of the Modern School publishing house who would bomb the royal wedding only three years later, in 1906. After the class trip, Morral's progressive father was so impressed with Ferrer that he allowed his daughter Adelina to attend the Modern School. Several years earlier Mateo's father had entrusted him with the operations of the factory. Already an anarchist, Mateo took the opportunity to urge the workers to demand more pay and improved conditions. Not long after this visit, tensions with his father led Mateo to leave the business.[18]

How grand, how beautiful, how useful is labor!

Such exclamations spontaneously flowed from the lips of the girls and boys, students of the Modern School, in the happy countryside of Sabadell last July 30 after having visited various factories, where they affectionately interacted with female and male workers, who embraced their small visitors with love and respect. Ultimately, after the countryside and a fraternal banquet, where they were gathered together to reflect upon this instructional excursion, they could admire the considerations that the trip offered them.

Primitive man, formed after a very long and progressive evolution, found himself at the dawn of inexperienced humanity, without resources and with urgent needs. In the midst of nature, which is abundant and fertile though little disposed to freely concede its treasures, early man vegetated (rather than lived) on the coasts, in the forests, in the mountains, taking refuge in the caverns where he managed to free himself from the harshness of the weather and the voracity of the beasts.

When relating ideas that imperceptibly developed in his memory, he could form the first thought out of necessity, the principal (if not only) source of intellectual activity, presented by nature that was satisfied and disposed to share its gifts. And as thought progressed it produced traps and spears, which led to hunting, and with the creation of another device suitable for its use, there developed fishing, and from having devised how to plant a seed, fruit was grown. This not only prevented man from dying of hunger, but moreover he learned to fight off ferocious animals, and even conceived of the first hints of sociability.

Early man needed to dress himself, and perhaps the use of the plant fibers, after having used animal skins, which were shapeless and useless without convenient tanning, inspired them to think about using wool fibers, to weave them on that embryonic loom, where the thread stretched tightly between two sticks, and the weave was intertwined by hand, since the skein that opened the shed was unknown, as was the weaver's shuttle that deposits the thread that unites the fabric.

The spinster emerged, which entailed an immense social advance; because with her the nomadic tribe becomes sedentary. Whereas previously such tribes had to leave exhausted lands in search of abundant, virgin territory, always suffering enormous hardships on the way or having to fight wars to displace tribes that occupied desired lands—sometimes perishing in the process, the spinster entailed the family, the home, cultivated land, animal husbandry, clothing, regular food and bread, legumes, vegetables, fruit, milk, cheese, and meat. Moreover, it entailed tools, iron, forges, labor, morality, and peace.

If at this height of progress there had not emerged, like infirmities capable of deforming an organism, the priest, the bureaucrat, the warrior, progress would have continued to ascend regularly, and those ideals that today we can only glimpse as a distant aspiration would already have centuries of practice. This kind of spinster is known through artistic and even visual representation, because there are still spinsters in those remote lands where the civilizing influence has scarcely arrived. Sometimes a decrepit old woman, sometimes a beautiful matron or a timid damsel, she sits beside the upright spinning wheel that contains the washed and carded fleece, twisting and consolidating the thread that she slides rapidly and smoothly between her fingers with the spindle.

With such a representation in the mind, children can compare and appreciate the mechanical marvels that are available for their young admiration. When the guide of the expedition and the workers of the different sections explained very difficult technical details with clarity and kindness, it seemed to the children as if beneficent fairies must have been responsible for the transformation of coarse, dirty, recently sheared wool into very fine fabrics of elegant patterns and rich colors that they saw in a short period of time as they passed by different devices without having the slightest idea as to the difficulty of the operations or of the hardships of labor.

It was necessary to bring them to reality and fix their attention on the mechanism that moves the raw wool, cleans it by passing it mechanically through a series of basins, each of which cleans the wool a little more until it comes out white as snow. Later comes the carding, where the simple tuft of wool that we all know dissolves into infinite, perfectly individualized thin fibers. The thread continues with its carts that come and go full of spindles, achieving in a minute the quantity of work that it would have taken months to accomplish with the traditional spinner. Next comes the twisting that gives the thread solidity and uniformity; later the warping to prepare it for the loom. After that, the process is crowned by the ingenious mechanism of Jacquard, which, as if it were a brain with its own will, like an artist that manages paintbrushes and colors, moves needles and cards and with them produces colorful images that embellish the fabric that we use for clothing and decorations of different types.

Once this laborious process is completed, the waste, scraps, and remnants are submitted to primitive operations to renew the fiber to some extent, to be used for cheap fabrics for the poor, which is to say as a reward for the producers.

A hymn to progress, to civilization, to labor is formulated spontaneously in the exalted little imaginations of the students, expressing themselves in the exclamations of admiration that burst forth with each step, with silvery notes modulated by their fresh and youthful throats.

It was again necessary to maintain their sense of reality. An incident presented the opportunity: various girls and boys, bothered by the heat and the disagreeable smell of the materials and ingredients, did not want to enter the last department on the visit. This presented an opportunity for a final consideration. The female and male workers that labored in these factories began their apprenticeship as children, long before they had consolidated and fortified their bodies and before having completed their education and instruction. They were also bothered by the heat and the stink of the materials, but necessity imposed itself upon their discomfort. They have to be there until they die; a sad end that always occurs before the time generally fixed by the human organism.

It is clear and admirable that science and industry together have achieved marvels like those that were produced by these machines. Yet, unfortunately this observation must be accompanied by a terrible *but*: its benefits are not distributed equally. In view of this, these workers, who have to continually bear these conditions to support their children, who endure many hardships and end up dying prematurely, receive poverty wages. Regarding the legal owners of the machines, the products, and the profits, when the business does not fail they get rich and they and their families enjoy the resulting benefits, which indicates that in order for social justice to reach the height of the scientific industrial advance, we have to work with determination to elevate the human species to the height of dignity and positive happiness.

Such were the considerations summarily expressed that moved our students on this pleasant excursion, which constituted one of several instructional complements used in this school.

Eleven of the eighteen students in the pre-school class, first section, with teacher. *Boletín de la Escuela Moderna*, May 31, 1904. IISG.

14. In Legitimate Defense

Here is our program from the third school year of 1903–1904:

> To promote the progressive evolution of childhood by avoiding regressive atavisms, which are obstacles placed by the past to any real advance toward the future, is, in sum, the predominant aim of the Modern School. We accept neither dogmas nor systems; molds that reduce vitality to the narrowness of the exigencies of a transitory society that aspires to be definitive. Rather, our education is constituted by solutions proven by the facts, theories accepted by reason, truths confirmed by evidence. Our education is designed so that every mind may be the motor of a will and so that truths sparkle on their own in abstraction. May they establish themselves in all understanding and, applied in practice, benefit humanity without indignant exclusions or repugnant exclusiveness.
>
> Two years of success are a sufficient guarantee to us. They prove, in the first place, the excellence of mixed education, the brilliant result—the triumph, we could say—of an elementary common sense over prejudice and tradition. As we think it especially advisable that

the student may know what is happening around them, that physical and natural sciences and hygiene should be taught, the Modern School will continue to have the services of doctors Señor de Buen, professor of Natural Sciences, and Señor Martínez Vargas, professor in the Faculty of Medicine at the university. They will lecture from 11:00 to 12:00 on alternate Sundays on their respective subjects in the schoolroom. These lectures will complete and further explain the classes in science held during the week.

It remains only to say that, always solicitous for the success of our work of intellectual regeneration, we have enriched our scholastic material with the acquisition of new collections that will at once facilitate comprehension and give an attractiveness to scientific knowledge; and that, as our rooms are now not large enough for the growing number of pupils, we have acquired other premises in order to have more room and give a favorable reply to the petitions for admission that we have received.

The publication of this program, as I said, attracted the attention of the reactionary press, which was answered by the liberal press. In order to give them a proof of the logical strength of the position of the Modern School, I inserted the following article in the *Boletín*:

Pedagogical Antagonism

Modern pedagogy, stripped of traditions and conventionalisms, must raise itself to the height of the rational conception of man, the current state of knowledge, and the consequent human ideal. If from any cause whatever a different tendency is given to education, and the teacher does fulfill their duty, it would be just to describe them as an impostor and declare that pedagogy must not be a means of dominating men for the advantage of their rulers.

Unhappily, this is usually what happens: society is organized, not in response to the satisfaction of a general need and for the realization of an ideal, but as an institution with a strong determination to maintain its primitive forms, defending them vigorously against every reform, however rational and compelling it may be.

This element of immobility gives ancient errors the character of sacred beliefs, it surrounds them with the greatest prestige, it gives them dogmatic authority and arouses conflicts and disturbances that deprive scientific truths of most or all of their due efficacy. Instead of illuminating the minds of all and translating themselves into institutions and customs of general utility, they abusively stagnate in the sphere of privilege. The effect is that today, as in the days of the Egyptian theocracy, there is an esoteric doctrine for the superiors and an exoteric doctrine for the lower classes—the classes destined to labor, defense, and degrading misery.

On this account, we set aside the mystic and mythical doctrine, the domination and spread of which is only comprehensible and explicable in the earlier ages of human history, and embrace scientific teaching, according to its evidence. This is at present restricted to the narrow sphere of the intellectuals or is at the most accepted in secret by certain hypocrites who, so that their position may not be endangered, make a public profession of the contrary. Nothing could make this absurd antagonism clearer than the following parallel, in which we see the contrast between the imaginative dreams of the ignorant believer and the rational simplicity of the learned:

The Bible

The Bible contains the annals of the heavens, the earth, and the human race. In it, like in divinity itself, there is contained all that was, all that is, and all that will be: on its first page we read of the beginning of time and of things, and on its last page the end of things and times. It begins with Genesis, which is an idyll, and ends with Revelations, which is a funeral hymn. Genesis is as beautiful as the fresh breeze that sweeps over the world, as the first dawn of light in the heavens, as the first flower that opens in the meadows, as the first word

Anthropism

The backward philosophy of traditional dogmas draws its principal power from anthropism or anthropomorphism. I understand this word to mean "that large and powerful group of erroneous notions that tend to put the human organism, considered to be of divine essence, in opposition to the rest of nature, making of it the preordained goal of organic creation, of which it is radically different." Closer examination of this group of ideas shows it to be made up of three different dogmas, which we may distinguish as the *anthropocentric*, of love spoken by men, as the first appearance of the sun in the east. Revelations is as sad as the last palpitation of nature, as the last ray of the sun, as the last breath of a dying man. And between the funeral hymn and the idyll there pass in succession before the eyes of God all generations and all peoples. The tribes go by with their patriarchs, the republics with their magistrates, the monarchies with their kings, the empires with their emperors, Babylon with its abominations, Nineveh with its splendor, Memphis with its priesthood, Jerusalem with its prophets and temple, Athens with its arts and heroes, Rome with its crown and the loot of the world. Nothing lasts but God; all else passes and dies, like the froth that tips the wave.

★ ★ ★

A prodigious book that mankind began to read thirty-three centuries ago, and of which, if read all day and night, would not lose its richness. A prodigious book in which all was calculated before the science of arithmetic was invented, in which the origin of language is told without any knowledge of philology, in which the

the *anthropomorphic*, and the *anthropolatrous*.[19]

1. The *anthropocentric* dogma affirms that man is the center and final aim of all terrestrial life—or, in a wider sense, of the whole universe. As this error satisfies human egoism, and as it is intimately connected with the creation myths of the three great Mediterranean religions, Mosaic, Christian, and Mohammedan, it still dominates the greater part of the civilized world.

2. The *anthropomorphic* dogma compares the creation of the universe and control of the world by God to the artistic creations of an able engineer or mechanic and to the administration of a prudent head of state. God, as creator, sustainer, and ruler of the universe, is conceived in absolute conformity, in his mode of thinking and acting, with the human model. Hence it follows that man in turn is Godlike and therefore affirms the dogma: "God created man in his own image." The simple, primitive mythology is pure "homotheism," attributing human shape, flesh, and blood to their gods. The recent mystic theosophy adores a personal God as an "invisible"—properly

revolutions of the stars are described without any knowledge of astronomy, in which history is recorded without any documents of history, in which the laws of nature are unveiled without any knowledge of physics. A prodigious book, that sees everything and knows everything, that knows the thoughts hidden in the hearts of men and those in the mind of God, that sees what is happening in the abysses of the sea and in the bowels of the earth, that records or foretells all the catastrophes of peoples, and in which are accumulated all the treasures of mercy, of justice, and of vengeance. A book, in conclusion, that, when the heavens are folded like a gigantic fan and the earth sinks and the sun withdraws its light and the stars are extinguished, will remain with God, because it is his eternal word, echoing forever in the heights.

—Donoso Cortés
An academic discourse included in the volume titled La Elocuencia, *a collection of notable writings for school reading.*

speaking, gaseous—being, yet makes him think, speak, and act in human fashion; it offers us the paradoxical picture of a "gaseous vertebrate."

3. The *anthropolatrous* dogma naturally results from the comparison of human and divine activities; it ends in the apotheosis of the human organism. A further result is the belief in the personal immortality of the soul and the dualistic dogma of the twofold nature of man, whose immortal soul is conceived as the temporary inhabitant of a mortal frame. These three anthropistic dogmas, variously adapted to the respective professions of the different religions, came at length to be vested with extraordinary importance and proved to be the source of the most dangerous errors.

—Ernst Haeckel
From The Enemies of the Universe, *from which was taken an extract inserted at the end of the* Cartilla, *the first reading book of the Modern School.*

Before this antagonism, sustained by ignorance as much as interest, positive pedagogy, which proposes to teach truths for the realization of practical justice, should methodize and systematize the positive knowledge of nature, inculcate them in the youth, and thus prepare elements for the equitable society, which, as an exact expression of sociology, must work for the individual and collective benefit of all.

Moses, or whoever was the author of Genesis, and all the dogmatizers, with their six days of creation out of nothing after the creator has passed an eternity in absolute inaction, must give way to Copernicus, who showed the revolution of the planets round the sun; to Galileo, who proclaimed that the sun, not the earth, is the center of the planetary universe; to Columbus and others who, believing the earth to be a sphere, set out in search of other peoples and gave a practical basis to the doctrine of human fraternity; to Cuvier and Linnaeus, the founders of natural history; to Laplace, the inventor of the established cosmogony; to Darwin, the author of the evolutionary doctrine, which explains the formation of species by natural selection; and to all who, by means of observation and study, have discredited the supposed revelation, and with demonstrable truth show the real nature of the universe, the earth, and life.

Against the evils engendered by generations sunk in error and superstition, from which so many are now delivered, only to fall into antisocial skepticism, an effective remedy, without excluding others that are no less effective, is to educate and instruct the rising generation in purely humanist principles and in the positive and rational knowledge of this nature of which they are a part. Women educated in this way will be mothers in the true natural and social sense, not transmitters of traditional superstitions; they will teach their children the integrity of life, the dignity of life, and social solidarity, instead of a medley of outworn and sterile dogmas and submission to absolutely illegitimate hierarchies.

Men thus emancipated from mystery, miracle, and distrust of themselves and their fellows, and convinced that they were born, not to die, as the wretched teaching of the mystics says, but to live, will hasten to bring about such social conditions as will give to life its greatest possible development. In this way, preserving the memory of former generations and other frames of mind as a lesson and a warning, we will once and for all close the religious period and enter definitely into that of reason and nature.

Despite all of the difficulties, on June 30, 1904, I published the following declaration in the *Boletín*:

The Third Year

Three years of flourishing and progressive activity, with a tendency to see our method spontaneously generalized, have given the Modern School of Barcelona not only the character of a perfectly consolidated institution, but rather that of the stimulator of powerful energies and regenerative initiatives, capable of transforming the new generation, stripping them of their atavisms, and preparing them so that, upon reaching the peak of life, they overcome the dominant errors and open a path for science, reason, and justice, obtaining peace and happiness as their reward.

Upon ending this third year of our existence, and as we enter the annual period of rest, the *Boletín de la Escuela Moderna* confirms such a brilliant result with satisfaction, shows its gratitude to those who have lent their support, and repeats its goal to persevere until the fulfillment of the work set forth.

—The Editorial Staff

In the same issue I presented the following summary:

Classification by sex and number of the students present in the Modern School during the first three school years

	Girls			Boys			Totals		
	1901–1902	1902–1903	1903–1904	1901–1902	1902–1903	1903–1904	Year 1	Year 2	Year 3
Opening day	12	–	–	18	–	–	30	–	–
September	16	23	24	23	40	40	39	63	64
October	18	28	43	25	40	59	43	68	102
November	21	31	44	29	40	59	50	71	103
December	22	31	45	30	40	59	52	71	104
January	22	31	47	32	44	60	54	75	107
February	23	31	47	32	48	61	55	79	108
March	25	33	49	34	47	61	59	80	110
April	26	32	50	37	48	61	63	80	111
May	30	33	51	38	48	62	68	81	113
June	32	34	51	38	48	63	70	82	114

Locations and number of schools that use Modern School books

Location	Institutions	Number of Schools
Villanueva y Geltrú	Cooperative Society	1
Tarragona	"Education" Lay School	1
Sevilla	Lay School	1
Sestao	Lay School	1
Reus	Workers' Instructive Center	1
Portbou	"Progress" Lay School	1
Palamós	Lay School	1
Mongat	Lay School	1
Mazarrón	Lay School	2
	Various Trades Society	
Mataró	Workers' *Ateneo*	1
Malagá	Julián Vargas Lay School	1
Mahón	Workers' Federation	1
La Unión	Workers' Societies	1
Gaucín	"The Truth" Workers' Society	1
Granollers	Lay School	1
Granada	"The Work" Workers' Society	1
Esplugas	"New Humanity" Free Academy	1
Córdoba	Workers' Societies	1
Casares	Workers' Instructive Center	1
Cartagena	Workers' Federation	2
	Llano del Real Lay School	
Barcelona	Free School of Hostafranchs	9
	The "Germinal" School of the Builders' Society	
	Builders' Society of Gracia	
	Mutual Instruction	
	Free School of Poblet	
	Sansense Republican Fraternity	
	The Collective School of San Martín	
	Republican *Ateneo* of Fuerte Pío	
Aznalcóllar	Workers' Instructive Center	
Total		**32**

15. The Ingenuousness of the Child

In the *Boletín* of September 30, 1903, we published the work of the pupils in the various classes of the Modern School, which had been read on the closing day of the second school year. The students were tasked with finding a subject to which they would apply their nascent opinions. We found that their intellectual efforts—grounded in their inexpert though ingenious reasoning inspired in a sense of justice—predominated over the application of rules of form. As a result, if their judgments do not reach rational perfection that is owed only to the lack of information, to a lack of knowledge indispensable in the formation of perfect reasoning; the opposite of what occurs with dominant opinions, which have no other foundation than fear founded in traditions, interests, and dogmas.

A boy of twelve, for instance, gave the following principle for judging the value of nations: to be civilized, a nation or state must be free from the following:

Let me interrupt for a moment to point out that the young author identifies "civilized" with "just," and especially that, putting aside prejudice, he describes certain evils as curable, and regards the healing of them as an essential condition of justice. These evils are:

1. The coexistence of poor and rich and the resultant exploitation.
2. Militarism, a means of destruction employed by some nations against others due to the bad organization of society.
3. Inequality, which allows some to rule and command and obliges others to humble themselves and obey.
4. Money, which makes some rich and subjugates the poor.

It is clear that these criteria are fundamental and simple, as we should expect to find in an imperfectly informed mind, and it would not enable one to solve a complete sociological problem, but it has the advantage of keeping the mind open to whatever rational observations present themselves. It is as if one asked: What does a sick person need to recover health? And the reply is: that their pain disappear. This is a naive and natural reply and would certainly not be given by a child influenced by spiritualist metaphysics, who needs before all else to consider the arbitrary will of supposedly supernatural beings. It is clear that this simple way of putting the problem of life does not definitively exclude a reasonable solution; indeed, one logically demands the other, as the conclusion of the same child's essay shows:

I do not mean that if there were no rich people, or soldiers, or rulers, or money, people would fight amongst themselves and abuse their liberty and welfare, but that, enjoying a high degree of civilization, there would be universal cordiality and friendship, and surely science would make much greater progress, not being interrupted by wars and political stagnation.

A girl of nine made the following sensible observation, which we leave in her own incorrect language:

A criminal is condemned to death. If the murderer deserves this punishment, the man who condemns him and the man who kills him are also murderers. Logically, they ought to die as well, and so humanity would come to an end. It would be better, instead of punishing a criminal by committing another crime, to give him good advice so that he will not do it again. Besides, if we were all equal, there would be no thieves or murderers or rich people or poor people, but all would be equal and love work and liberty.

The simplicity, clarity, and importance of this thought do not allow commentary. One can understand our astonishment to hear it from the lips of a tender and very pretty little girl, who looked more like a symbolic representation of truth and justice than a living reality.

On the topic of sincerity, a boy of twelve says:

He who is not sincere does not live peacefully; he is always afraid of being discovered. When one is sincere, if one has done wrong, the sincere declaration relieves the conscience. If someone begins to tell lies in childhood, when they grow up they will tell bigger lies that may do much harm. There are cases in which one must not be sincere. For instance, if a man comes to our house, fleeing from the police, and we are asked afterwards if we have seen him, we must deny it; the contrary would be treachery and cowardice.

It is sad that the mind of a child who regards truth as an incomparable good, "without which it is impossible to live," is induced by the seriousness of authoritarian abuses to consider lying a virtue in some cases.

A girl of thirteen writes of fanaticism, and, after regarding it as a bad characteristic of a backward country, she searches for and finds its cause, saying:

Fanaticism is the outcome of the state of ignorance and backward-ness that the woman finds herself in. On that account, Catholics do not want the woman to educate herself, as she is their principal support.

A profound observation on the cause of fanaticism, and the cause of the cause, since if ignorance produces fanaticism, the ignorance of the woman perpetuates general ignorance. Against such serious damage, another girl of thirteen indicates the best remedy with this thought, which we include in its entirety:

The Mixed School

The mixed school, for both sexes, is supremely necessary. The boy who studies, works, and plays in the company of the girl learns gradually to respect and help her, and the girl reciprocally; whereas, if they are educated separately, and the boy is told that the girl is not a good companion and is worse than he, the boy will not respect women when he is a man and will regard her as a toy or a slave, which is what women are reduced to today. So we must all work for the foundation of mixed schools, wherever possible, and where it is not possible we must try to remove the difficulties.

We could add nothing to such a well-reasoned thought that was summa-rized with such temperance but to emphasize the emotion with which this thirteen-year-old thinker concludes her essay.

A boy of twelve regards the school as worthy of all respect, because that is where one learns to read, write, and think, and it is the basis of morality and science. He adds:

If it were not for the school, we would live in the forest, walk naked, eat herbs and raw meat, and take refuge in caves and trees; that is to say, we would live a brutal life. In time, as a result of the school, everybody will be more intelligent, and there will be no wars or towns burned to the ground, and people will look back on the soldier with horror, considering him the worker of death and destruction. It is a great disgrace that there are children who wander in the streets and do not go to school, and when they become men they are very disgraceful. So let us be grateful to our teachers for the patience they show in instructing us, and let us regard the school with respect.

This is just reasoning and a well-applied sentiment that indicates a psychic state in equilibrium. If this child preserves and develops the faculties that he is discovering, he will properly harmonize egoism and altruism for its own good and that of society. A girl of eleven deplores that nations destroy each other in wars and laments the difference of social classes and that the rich live on the work and privation of the poor. She ends:

> Instead of killing each other in wars and hating each other for class differences, why don't men devote themselves cheerfully to work and the discovery of things for the good of humanity? Men ought to unite to love each other and live fraternally.

Here we have a youthful reproach that should embarrass those who persist in the maintenance of the causes of damage that so sadly affect the tender heart of this girl.

A boy of ten, in an essay that is almost so correct that we could insert it whole if space permitted, and if it were not similar to the previous passages, says of the school and the pupil:

> Gathered under the same roof, eager to learn what we do not know, without distinction of classes, we are siblings guided by the same goal. . . . The ignorant man is a nullity; little or nothing can be expected of him. He is a warning to us not to waste time. On the contrary, let us benefit from him, and in due course we will be rewarded. . . . We will never forget the fruits of a good school, and honoring our teachers, our family, and society, we shall live happily.

What beautiful sense, that at ten years old they harmonize with youthful happiness.

A girl of ten philosophizes on the faults of the human species, which, in her opinion, can be avoided by instruction and goodwill. She says:

> Among the faults of the human species are lying, hypocrisy, and egoism. If men, and especially women, were better instructed, and women were entirely equal to men, these faults would disappear. Parents would not send their children to religious schools, which inculcate false ideas, but to rational schools, where there is no teaching of the supernatural, which does not exist, or to make war but to live in solidarity and work in common.

The ideal that serves as a guide for human progress comes into view in this critique of society.

We end this compilation with the following essay, written by a young lady of sixteen, which is correct enough in form and substance to quote without any changes:

The Present Society

What inequality there is in this society! Some working from morning to night without any more rest than to eat their insufficient food; others receiving the products of the workers to enjoy themselves in superfluity. Why does it have to be like this? Aren't we all equal? Undoubtedly, we are, but society does not recognize this, since some seem to be destined to work and suffer, and others to idleness and enjoyment. If a worker shows that he realizes the exploitation to which he is subject, he is blamed and cruelly punished, while others suffer the inequality with resignation. The worker must educate himself, and to do this it is necessary to found free schools, maintained by the money that the rich waste. In this way, the worker will advance more and more, until he is regarded as he deserves, since the most useful mission of society depends on him.

Whatever may be the rational value of these ideas, this collection shows the chief aim of the Modern School—namely, that the mind of the student, influenced by what it sees and informed by the positive knowledge it acquires, shall work freely, without prejudice or sectarian submission of any kind, with perfect autonomy and no other guide but reason, equal for all, and sanctioned by the cogency of evidence, before which the darkness of sophistry and dogmatic imposition is dispelled.

In Barcelona, in December 1903, the Congress of Railway Workers announced that part of its program would include a visit to the Modern School. The pupils were delighted, and to derive some utility from the visit, we invited them to write essays to be read on the occasion of the visit. The visit was prevented by unforeseen circumstances, but we published in the *Boletín* the children's essays, which exhaled a delicate perfume of sincerity and unbiased judgment, graced by the intuitive ingenuousness of the writers.

One must observe that although they started with the assignment to write a greeting to the workers of the congress who had met to try to improve their conditions of labor and existence, it turned out that the students, despite the fact that no suggestion was made to them and they did not compare notes, showed a remarkable conformity in their affirmations, differing slightly, but not much, in their argumentation. We have extracted excerpts from their writings to avoid repetition while maintaining their ingeniousness and almost always any original mistakes.

A nine-year-old girl wrote:

I salute you, dear workers, for the work you do on behalf of society. It is to you and to all workers that appreciation must be given for the production of all that is necessary for life, and not to the rich who pay you a miserable wage and do not pay you to live, but rather because if you did not work they would have to work themselves.

A nine-year-old boy, after an affectionate greeting, says:

The land should belong to the workers as well as everyone else. Nature has not created men so that a few are left with everything. The land should be cultivated without the one who works being exploited and the other eating their fruit. The worker lives in a small and dark house, eats very little food of bad quality, and does not drive in a car like the bourgeoisie. If the worker wanted, all would be theirs: if not, let them count the number of workers and bourgeoisie, of which are there more? Then since the workers are more, soon, or better said, immediately, they would obtain what they desire.

These nine-year-olds, in this simple explosion of sense, demonstrate that they could be teachers for many outdated economists whose understanding is based on respect for that which exists only by virtue of its existence, without considering if in reason or justice it has the right to be so.

An eleven-year-old girl:

The day will come when work will be more spread out, reason will dominate, science will prevail, and social classes will disappear. . . . The responsibility of man is to do all that is possible, whether by manual or intellectual means, toward this end, and he who does the contrary is inhuman. . . . Instruction is the foundation of humanity and the redemption of man, since it will reinstate him in all of his rights.

An eleven-year-old boy:

Greetings, representatives of labor! . . . You, as railroad workers, guide powerful machines as if they were harmless little animals. These machines, as products of human civilization to which they should belong, are property of some potentates who made no effort of their own to acquire them. They have been acquired through the exploitation of the workers. . . . While you suffer the sun, rain, and snow finishing your work, the satisfied bourgeoisie, complaining about the slowness of the train, stretch out in their sleeping car.

An eleven-year-old girl:

I am happy that you dedicate yourselves to working on the railroads to advance industry and so that there are trains to transport travelers, products, and many things from one town to another. Those who dedicate themselves to this work and to discoveries do a great service to humanity, and moreover there are some who consider them better than a general who has won a battle.

An eleven-year-old boy:

The worker, who should be the admiration of the world, is the most despised by our society. He provides us with clothing, a house, and furniture. He tends to the livestock that provide us with wool and meat. With trains or boats he takes us from one place to another, and provides us with many other services. To him we owe life.

An eleven-year old boy, who, agreeing with some of the previously expressed thoughts, says:

The parasites that consume and do not produce, always thinking about exploitation, despise the worker who earns a very low wage working many hours a day almost without being able to support his family. If society were organized in a different way, no one would die miserably while the rich are enjoying themselves.

In this group of eleven-year-old intellectuals one finds elements for the development of a sociological treatise. Within it one finds what is most important: an exposition of facts and the resulting critique and censure that end with a beautiful and simple affirmation of the ideal.

A twelve-year-old boy:

Who enjoy the fruits of labor? The rich. What good are the rich? These men are unproductive, which is why they can be compared to bees, except they are smart because they kill parasites.

A twelve-year-old girl:

The worker is a slave of the bourgeoisie. . . . While the rich enjoy themselves on their strolls in their gardens, there are workers whose children ask them for bread, but they have none to give. Why does this happen? Because the rich hoarded it all.

A twelve-year-old boy:

The worker, in addition to working has to go to war, which is a great evil, and while he goes to war, his parents are left without his help; he could even return unable to work. On the day that society is changed so that everyone, fulfilling their social responsibilities, is assured the satisfaction of their needs, there will be no poor or rich and everyone will be happy.

A twelve-year-old girl:

You workers who shorten distances with the railroads and one day may even perhaps be able to erase the borders that separate one nation from another, you are very welcome here because, with the railroads, industry can grow and expand and people can communicate with the most remote countries.

A twelve-year-old boy:

Poor social organization creates an unjust separation between men, since there are two classes of men—those who work and those who do not. . . . When there is a strike the Civil Guard show up at the doors of the factories ready to use their Mausers. Wouldn't it be better if they had instead chosen a useful trade?

A twelve-year-old girl:

For the worker to be respected as every man should be, and for his rights to prevail without being insulted or despised, he should educate himself.

A twelve-year-old boy:

The children of the bourgeoisie and those of the workers: Aren't they all flesh and bone? Then why do some have to be different from others in society?

Without faulting anything expressed by this group above, there is a certain note of great energy and more intensity of sentiment, highlighting a mode of thought marked by profundity, truth, and a correct and beautiful concision.

A thirteen-year-old girl:

The exploitation of man by man is ruthless, inhuman, and cruel . . . the day must come when the workers unite to demand that the bourgeoisie stop its wicked exploitation forever.

A fourteen-year-old girl:

The right of every man is to search for and discover that which can be useful for him and his fellows, helping them as much as possible and consoling them in their sorrows. He who does not do this does not deserve to be called human. Solidarity, fraternity, and equality are the utmost aspirations of the society of the future.

A seventeen-year-old girl:

I greet and congratulate the railroad workers as representatives of labor and as lovers of equality, things that correspond poorly with this egotistical, hypocritical, and vain society. I hope that the work undertaken at your congress will be a great success and that you achieve a reduction in working hours and an increase in wages, which are sorely needed for your necessities and to help with your education.

In the way that the nascent intelligences developed in the Modern School responded to the exciting prompt to express themselves freely regarding one of the most important branches of labor, one should see nothing more than a demonstration of positive knowledge and nothing less than an orientation in a determined sense of opinion—or rather the brilliant spontaneity with which the students revealed their particular manner of feeling, free from fears and conventionalisms.

Rationalist education progressed. Here I have a beautiful statement of its progress from the *Boletín*:

Educational Fraternity

The students of the Elementary Class of the Workers' *Ateneo* of Badalona wrote the following letter to the students of the Modern School:

To the Children of the Modern School—Barcelona
Dear compañeros:

Desiring to form relationships with children from other schools in order to develop friendships and mutually educate each other, we address ourselves to you to begin to achieve our goals.

A few days ago, we started to read *The Adventures of Nono*, which we like a lot, and since our teacher had told us that you also read it recently, we hope that you can share with us something that you have gotten out of reading it.

We take advantage of this occasion to offer ourselves as your good friends. Know that we are eager to meet you and that our teacher has promised to take us to Barcelona to see the zoological collection at the park; there we could see each other. We will notify you about it.

We are your friends, and we send you many hugs for all as we eagerly await your replies. We, the children of the Elementary Class of the Workers' *Ateneo* of Badalona, wish you Health and Love.
In their name,
Francisco Rodríguez
Badalona, February 16, 1904.

Reading this letter from the Badalona teacher in class greatly excited our students. All of them, from the youngest to the oldest, felt an intense affinity for those children who offered their fraternity and awaited the moment to demonstrate it practically.

Invited by the teachers to answer the happy initiative of the children from Badalona, as it corresponds to such beautifully human sentiments and thoughts, each student wrote their own reply. However, we drafted a collective response composed of the fundamental elements from the fifty-six individual letters (sixteen girls and eleven boys from the elementary class, ten girls and nineteen boys from the superior class) as must occur in all human communist acts in which, as in arithmetic, every quantity is the sum of all of the parts that form it. The happiness with which they received the greeting of love and the idea of reciprocating on a day of recreation was unanimous. The response regarding "what our students got out of reading *The Adventures of Nono*" is perhaps not very categorical, because most contented themselves with saying that they liked the book very much and referred to the scenes that they enjoyed. Nevertheless, there were various girls and boys—not only the older students—who went deeper in developing partial and even some general opinions of the work.

What is notable about this compilation of responses is that there is nothing contradictory. Each student presents their impression, and those who achieve little, although they may not know how to express it, feel the same as those who achieved more. Their thoughts could be expressed on an ascending scale with a unified direction. There are those who loved the idyll of Autonomy and those who were saddened by the tyranny and lack of solidarity in Argirocracy. Some focused on the description of Nono's familial home, others on the beauty of the practice of solidarity that the owl brilliantly expresses with these words: "Without realizing it, you have put into practice the great law of universal solidarity that wants all beings to aid each other mutually." All of this is taken into account and there is an element from every statement: freedom of labor, social equality, the problem and the consequences of vice and the lack of reciprocal sincerity, the joy that comes from general and harmonious happiness, the heroism of those who are in solidarity with each other, the pleasant sensation of natural beauty and poetry, and even comical statements: there was no shortage of students who loved the blow that Nono struck to the nose of Monadio.

With all of these elements and with textual phrases that were lightly corrected for the most part, and to avoid repetitions, the following letter was composed, which if everyone could not contribute to in their entirety, they could sign it by virtue of their shared foundation of thought and sentiment.

To the children of the Elementary Class of the Workers' Ateneo of Badalona

Dear compañeros:

The same as you, we desire to form relationships with well-educated children to practice friendship and solidarity.

We happily accept your proposal and we impatiently await the moment when we can meet you, play with you, share our knowledge, and talk about this beautiful book, *The Adventures of Nono*. We loved reading it as much as you do now that you have started it.

We must exert our minds to bring this society closer to the goals that our parents set forth but could not achieve; we are called to this.

How beautiful is the country of Autonomy! There things are very good; they work, they rest, and they play when they want; they do what they want, which is how it should be among men. There is no money, no sentries, no rural guards, no soldiers who have the face of a marten or a hyena, no rich people who live in palaces and travel in carriages alongside the poor who live in bad homes and die of hunger after working a lot. There are no thieves, because all is for everyone and the exploitation of man by man is not practiced. We would all love to live in such a delightful country. Nono dreams of this country. Today it is not possible but the day will come when it will be. We should all work for this day to come soon, because Autonomy is an example of the future society. We have deduced that this is how one must live, not how we currently live, so far from the true and complete civilization.

Argirocracy is a repetition of what happens in current society. All countries, some more than others, imitate Argirocracy, an awful country where exploitation exists, where there are those who work and those who enjoy, where some serve others and those who speak of the happiness of Autonomy are locked in jail.

In summary, *The Adventures of Nono* is an instructive book that must be read carefully. It envisions a country where all work for one and one for all, and there is no money, or thieves, or those who impose the laws that they please, or weapons, and where everyone advances science and art.

Looking forward to meeting you, we repeat our farewell:

Health and Love,

Girl and boy students [*alumnas y alumnos*] of the Modern School Barcelona

16. *Boletín de la Escuela Moderna*

The Modern School needed and had its organ in the press. The political and ordinary press, which at one time favored us and at another time denounced us as dangerous, cannot maintain an impartial attitude. It either gives exaggerated or unmerited praise or calumnious censures. The only remedy for this was the sincerity and clearness of our own statements. To allow these libels to pass without correction would have done us considerable harm, and the *Boletín de la Escuela Moderna* enabled us to respond to them.

The directors published in it the programs of the school, interesting notes about it, statistical details, original pedagogical studies by the teachers, accounts of the progress of rational education in our own and other countries, translations of important articles from foreign reviews and periodicals that were in harmony with the main character of our work, reports of the Sunday lectures, and announcements of the public competitions for the engagement of teachers and of our library.

One of the most successful sections of the *Boletín* was that devoted to the publication of the ideas of the pupils. Beyond an exposition of their advances, which never would have been published, it was a spontaneous manifestation of common sense. Girls and boys, with no appreciable difference in intellect according to sex, in contact with the realities of life as indicated by the teachers and readings, expressed themselves in simple essays that, though sometimes unsophisticated and incomplete in judgment, more often showed the clear logic with which they conceived philosophical, political, or social questions of importance.

The journal was at first distributed without charge among the pupils and was exchanged with other periodicals, but there was soon a demand for it, and a public subscription had to be opened. When this was done, the *Boletín* became a philosophical review, as well as organ of the Modern School, and it retained this character until the persecution began and the school was closed. As proof of the important mission of the *Boletín*, beyond its already demonstrated utility evident in the figures and articles previously inserted, take a look at what was published in no. 5 of year 4 of the paper to correct certain lay teachers who unconsciously initiated a deviation:

School Savings

At a school of a Workers' *Ateneo* they have introduced the novelty of establishing a savings-bank administered by the children. This news, disseminated by the press in a laudatory tone as an object of admiration and imitation, induces us to express our opinion on the subject. If some have the right to do and say, we have the same right to judge, contributing thusly to giving rational consistency to public opinion.

In the first place, we have to observe that the idea of *economy* is very different from, if not to say antithetical to, the idea of *saving*. If one is attempting to teach children the knowledge and practice of the economy, this will not be achieved by teaching them to save. *Economy* means a prudent, methodical, and foresighted use of goods; *saving* is a reduction and limitation of the use of these goods. By *economizing* one avoids waste; by *saving*, the man who has nothing superfluous deprives himself of what is necessary.

Do the children who are taught to save have anything superfluous? The very name of the organization in question assures us that they have not. The workers who send their children to this school live on their wages, the minimum sum, determined by supply and demand, which is paid for their work by the capitalists. And as this wage gives them nothing superfluous, and the social wealth is monopolized by the privileged, the workers are far from obtaining enough to enjoy regular life in harmony with the benefits given to the present generation by civilization and progress. Hence, when these children of workers, and future workers themselves, are taught to save—which is a voluntary privation under the appearance of interest—they are taught to prepare themselves to submit to privilege. While the intention is to initiate them to the practice of economy, what is really done is to convert them into victims and accomplices of the economic disorder of the capitalist society.

Working-class children are human children, and, as such, they have the right to the development of all of their aptitudes and faculties, and the satisfaction of all of their moral and physical needs. For that purpose, society was instituted. It is not its function to repress or subject the individual to its manner of being, as is selfishly attempted by the privileged, the unchanging, those who live by enjoying what others produce; it has to hold the balance justly between the rights and duties of all members of society.

Yes, because the individual is asked to sacrifice their rights, needs, and pleasures to society, because a similar disorder demands patience, suffering, and false reasoning, let us commend economy and censure saving. We do not think it right to teach children that they have to be workers in a society in which the average mortality of the poor, who live without freedom, instruction, or joy, reaches an appalling figure in comparison with that of the parasites that live in triumph on their labor. Those who, from sociolatry, would derogate in the least from the rights of man, should read the fine and vigorous words of Pi y Margall: "Who are you to impede the use of my rights of man? Perfidious and tyrannical society, I created you to defend them, not to restrict them. Go back to the abyss of your origin, the abyss of nothing."

Starting from these principles and applying them to pedagogy, we think it necessary to teach children that to squander any type of materials and objects is contrary to the general welfare; that if a child wastes paper, loses pens, or destroys books, it prevents extracting the greatest utility from them and it does an injustice to their parents and the school. Assuredly one may impress on the child the need of prudence in order to avoid acquiring useless things and remind them of lack of employment, illness, and even old age, but it is not right to insist, and it's even worse for a teacher, that with their wages, which do not achieve the satisfaction of the needs of life, they can assure their future well-being. This is false arithmetic.

The workers have no university training; they do not go to the theater or to concerts; they don't travel; they never go into ecstasies before the marvels of art, industry, or nature; they have no holiday in which to fill their lungs with life-giving oxygen; they do not have books and magazines within reach that establish the common elevation of understanding. On the contrary, they suffer all kinds of privations and may have to endure crises due to excessive production. It is not the place of teachers to hide these sad truths from the children, and to tell them that a smaller quantity can equal, and even surpass, a larger. In order that the power of science and industry be shared by all and all be invited to partake of the banquet of life, we must not teach in the school, in the interest of privilege, that the poor should servilely organize the use of crumbs and scraps. We will not prostitute education.

Following my intention to avoid deviations within popular education, I thought it my duty to publish the following censure in the *Boletín*:

Regarding Subsidies

We were sad and indignant upon reading the list of subsidies that the city council of Barcelona voted to allocate to certain popular societies that promote education. We saw sums destined for republican fraternities and similar centers; and not only have these organizations not rejected them, rather they have voted to send messages of thanks to the district council and to the city council.

That this would occur among Catholic and ultraconservative people is understandable. The predominance of the Church and the capitalist society can only maintain itself thanks to the system of charity and protection that is well understood to be a method to contain the disinherited, who are always resigned and trusting in the goodness of their masters. But we cannot watch republicans transforming themselves from revolutionaries into humble Christian beggars without raising our voices in alarm at those who are active in the republican camp in good faith.

Beware, we repeat, beware! You are educating your children badly and taking the wrong path in intending to regenerate yourselves by accepting alms. Beware! For you will neither emancipate yourselves nor your children by trusting in the strength of others and in official or private support. Let the Catholics, who vegetate in their ignorance of the reality of things, hope for everything from a god, or St. Joseph, or another similar myth, and, as they have no security that their prayers will be heard in this life, trust to receive a reward after death. Let gamblers who play the lottery fail to see that they are morally and materially victimized by their governments, who collect something from the vast sum that they lose together and trust to receive by chance what they do not earn by energy.

But it is sad to see men who are united in a revolutionary protest to change the regime hold out the hand of a beggar, to see them admitting and giving thanks for humiliating gifts, not knowing to trust in the energy that must give conviction to their reason and their power. We repeat this in sadness and outrage.

Beware, then, all men of good faith! Such measures do not lead to the true education of the youth, but rather to their domestication.

After a year of suspension, after the closing of the Modern School and during my trial and time in prison in Madrid, the *Boletín* reappeared, inserting the following declaration in the first issue of its second epoch, which began on May 1, 1908.

To Everyone

Yesterday we said. . .

There has never been a better time than the present, when we bring to light the first issue of the second epoch of our *Boletín*, to employ this historic phrase: the Modern School continues its progress without changing its procedures, methods, orientations, or goals; it continues its ascendant course toward the ideal, because it has evidence that its mission is redemptive and contributes to a better, more perfect, more just humanity than present humanity by means of rational and scientific education. This is debated among hatreds and miseries that will be the result of the work achieved over centuries for the conquest of universal peace.

We do not have to rectify a shred of our work up to today; it is our close conviction, increasingly intense, that without an absolute reform of educational methods it will be impossible to orient humanity toward the future. That is where we are going by means of schools where they can be built; by means of our books, whose library grows day after day, intensifying the dissemination of truths demonstrated by science; by means of the word, in conferences that bring the light of truth against traditional errors to the minds of listeners; by means of this *Boletín*, where our aspirations acquire life so that the serenity of study can have its influence in the vehicle of the written word.

Our friends, those who have accompanied us for the last five years in our dear Modern School and have stood in solidarity with the progressive men of the entire world to impede the injustice that the reaction intends to carry out on its founder will not have to look back. To the contrary, they will fix their gaze forward toward a dawn of justice and love and help us with even greater energy to achieve this work of true and fertile redemption.

To the press, we extend an expression of our professional solidarity and an affectionate greeting. To the good, we extend our hand in an effusive sign of peace.

Salud.

As an example of the work of the *Boletín*, I have chosen to include the following translated article that combines pedagogical competence and a clear vision of the ideal of education.

The Education of the Future

The fundamental idea behind the reform that the future of childhood education will introduce is the replacement, in all modes of activity, of the artificial imposition of a discipline of convention with the natural imposition of facts. Consider what is done at present: apart from the necessities of a child, they have created a program of knowledge that they consider to be necessary for their culture, and, by grades or by force, without fixing the means, it is necessary that they learn.

But only the teachers understand this program and are familiar with its goal and its scope, not the child. All vices of modern education stem from this fact. In effect, by severing natural reason from one's acts and volition, which is to say by attempting to replace it with artificial reason, a nonexistent, abstract duty that no one can conceive of, one must institute a system of discipline that must necessarily yield poor results: the constant rebellion of the child against the arbitrary authority of their teachers, perpetual distraction and laziness, and a clearly bad will. And what maneuvers teachers must employ to control their unyielding challenge! Through the use of all methods, some of them unseemly, they manage to capture the child's attention, activity, and will. Those who are the most ingenious at such practices are considered the best educators.

They think that they are fortunate when they achieve the appearance of success; but they never achieve more than appearances when the artificial purpose of the activity replaces the unique and superior reason of the action, the necessity that imposes necessity. Everyone has been able to feel that labor is only valid when it is determined by desire. When this reason disappears, negligence, sorrow, and ugliness ensue.

Everywhere in our societies the artificial reason of labor tends to replace the logical and healthy imposition of necessity, the natural desire to achieve a result. The conquest of money appears to the eyes of the men of our epoch as the true object of effort. But it is true that modern education does nothing to oppose this pernicious conception, rather it does the opposite. As a result, every day the unique pursuit of money grows at the expense of the beautiful instinct of observance that one finds in the few men whose wills have not been falsified, who retain the normal rationale behind their actions, and who work to achieve their goals with a noble contempt for money. How could one demand that individuals who have been habituated from childhood to work for the will of others, under the oppression of external law, for the attainment of a goal whose importance they do not understand—since the meaning of labor has already come to be defined simply as punishment and reward—be capable of taking interest in the beauty and nobility of human effort, its eternal struggle against the blind forces of Nature?

This bad conception of education has caused the organic infirmity of our societies: the need to be something, to enjoy; the contempt, the hate, of work; the yearning for life that cannot be satisfied; the horrific hostility of those who hate and attempt to mutually destroy each other. What has been forgotten is that it is essential to defend and conserve at all cost the natural game of man's activities, all of which should be directed outward and spread externally in the sense of all social forces. *The struggle for existence!* How this phrase has been abused and how deliberately it has come to excuse such iniquities! And it has been understood so poorly! It is understood in such a way that it even negates the natural principles of society: nowhere in Nature does one find an example of the aberration that they want it to express. There is no organism or animal colony where individual elements try to mutually destroy each other; to the contrary, they all struggle together against hostile influences in their environment, and the functional transformations that they carry out among them are necessary differentiations, healthy changes in the general organization, not destructions.

Above all else, it is important that life be such, that it come to be such, that man works and struggles only to be useful to his fellows. To achieve this one simply needs to guard and fortify within oneself the instinct of defense against the hostile forces of Nature, to have learned to love labor for the pleasure of fulfilling one's duties and proposals through long and hard work, to understand the immense expanse and sublime beauty of human effort. Our great men, our inventors, our wise men, our artists, are great because they have conserved the excellent quality of desiring on behalf of their fellows not against them. To the eyes of their contemporaries they are considered to be strange beings, and, being that they are those who are in greatest accord with the harmonious ensemble of laws of existence, after achieving success they are considered visionaries.

A rational education will be, then, that which conserves in man the faculty of wanting, of thinking, of idealizing, of hoping; that which is based only on the natural necessities of life; that which allows him to freely manifest these necessities; that which facilitates as much as possible the development and efficacy of the forces of the organism so that they all concentrate themselves on the same external objective: the struggle to fulfill that which thought demands.

The foundations of current education will be completely changed. Rather than basing everything on theoretical instruction, on the acquisition of knowledge that does not mean anything to the child, it will depart from practical instruction whose goal shows itself clearly, which is to say, it will begin with the teaching of manual labor.

The reason for this is logical. Instruction for its own sake has no use for the child. They don't understand why they are being taught to read and write or why their heads are being filled with physics, geography, and history. All of this seems completely useless to them, and they show it by resisting it with all of their power. They are filled with science, and they throw it away as soon as possible. Take note that this happens everywhere, as much with moral and physical education as with intellectual education: when natural reason is absent it is replaced by artificial reason.

The goal is to found everything on natural reason. To do so it is sufficient to remember that primitive man started his evolution toward civilization by means of labor determined by necessity. Suffering forced him to create means of defense and struggle, from which were gradually born the various trades. Children have within them an atavistic necessity for labor sufficient to replace their initial circumstances; it is sufficient to simply support it. Organize work around them, maintain logical and legitimate discipline for its completion, and one will easily arrive at a complete, happy, and healthy education.

We will not have to do more than wait for the child to come to us. The child will only have to have lived life a little to know that labor stimulates an irresistible desire within them. And how much is done to annihilate this good disposition within them! After that, who would dare to speak about vice and laziness? Healthy men and children need to work: the entire history of humanity proves it.

Little by little the child abandons the game, which in itself is really nothing more than a form of work, an innate manifestation of this desire for activity that has not yet even found a direction, or they base their reason for being in the atavistic enjoyment of the struggle for subsistence from the primitive periods of human life. They abandon the game under the impulse of necessity that is slowly born and the appeal of example: they work near it and aspire with all of their efforts toward labor.

Then the influence of the educator intervenes; a concealed and indirect influence. Their science of life helps them to understand what happens within the child, to distinguish their desires, to replace the uncertainty and thoughtlessness of their wills. To know how to offer them what they ask for, it is enough to study the primitive life of the savages to know what they desire to do. And in continuation everything will be easy, natural, simple. The teaching profession has its inflexible logic: guide work better than high science could achieve. It is sufficient for teachers to not allow them to deviate toward the imperfections of primitive labor, toward ignorance, but rather to impose upon them that which has arrived to the will of the child through the progress of advanced peoples, demanding from him the effort of an achievement in which all of necessary human knowledge is intertwined.

It is easily understood that today every trade, in order to be properly understood and executed, is accompanied by intellectual labor that requires the knowledge that constitutes precisely the type of instruction that at present is limited to being inculcated theoretically. As the child advances in their learning, they will be presented with the need to know, to instruct themselves, and so they will take care not to stifle this need, but rather, to the contrary, once felt and manifested they will be provided with the means to satisfy it, and subsequently they will be educated logically, according to the needs of their labor, always bearing in mind the determining reason behind this interest.

It is useless to insist on the quality of such labor and the excellent results that it must necessarily produce. With a combination of trades, they can acquire the knowledge necessary for an education that is much stronger and healthier than that entirely composed of appearances that is given currently.

Where is imposition left in all of this? The educator simply asks for help from Nature, and wherever they find difficulties they will investigate how they may have contradicted it; to nature will be entrusted the care of their discipline, which will be admirably conserved. Working in this way in the education of men, one can infallibly await a better humanity, determined in its task, conserving all of the vigor of its will, all of its moral health, always advancing toward new ideals, a humanity not meanly dedicated to a stupid struggle, not sordidly subject to the abundance of their appetites, miserably devoted to their vices and their lies, sad, spiteful, depraved, always without love, beauty, and happiness.

17. The Closing of the Modern School

I have reached the culmination of my life and my work. My enemies, who are all the reactionaries in the world, represented by the reactionaries of Barcelona and all of Spain, believed that they had triumphed by involving me in a charge of attempted assassination. But their triumph proved to be only an episode in the struggle of practical rationalism against the great atavistic and traditionalist obstacle. The stupid audacity with which they called for a death sentence against me (a claim that was refused less because of the rectitude of the court and more on account of my transparent innocence) drew to me the sympathy of all liberals, or better said, of all true progressives of the world, and fixed their attention on the meaning and ideal of the Modern School. This produced a universal and uninterrupted movement of protest and admiration for a whole year—from May 1906 to June 1907—echoed in the press of all of the languages of modern civilization of that period with their editorial articles or distinguished collaborators, and in reviews of meetings, conferences, and other popular demonstrations.

In the end, the mortal enemies of our work were its most effective supporters, as they led to the establishment of international rationalism.

I recognized my own littleness in face of such might. Illuminated always by the light of the ideal, I conceived and carried out the creation of the International League for the Rational Education of Children, in the various branches of which, scattered over the world, are found men that represent the flower of thought and the regenerative energy of society. Its organ is *L'École rénovée* of Brussels, supported by the *Boletín de la Escuela Moderna* in Barcelona, and Rome's *La Scuola Laica*. These papers explain, discuss, and disseminate all the latest efforts of pedagogy to purify science from all defilement of error, to dispel all credulity, to bring about a perfect harmony between belief and knowledge, and to destroy that privileged esoteric system that has always left a rotten exoteric doctrine.

This great concentration of knowledge, carried out by this great gathering of desire, must lead to a powerful, conscious, and combined action that will give to the future revolution the character of a practical manifestation of applied sociology, without passion or demands of revenge, with no terrible tragedies or heroic sacrifices, without sterile movements, without the weakness of fools and fanatics, without betrayals paid for by the reaction. For scientific and rational education will have dissolved the popular mass to make each woman and each man a self-conscious, active, and responsible being who will determine their will according to their own judgment, advised by their own knowledge, free forever from the passion inspired by the exploiters to respect tradition and the charlatanry of the modern framers of political programs.

If progress thus loses this dramatic character of revolution, it will gain in firmness, stability, and continuity as evolution. The vision of a rational society, which revolutionaries foresaw in all ages, and which sociologists confidently promise, will rise before the eyes of our successors not as the mirage of dreamy utopians but as the positive and merited triumph won by the revolutionary power of reason and science.

The fame acquired by the educational and instructive innovations of the Modern School attracted the attention of all who appreciated the value of sound instruction; everyone wanted to know about the new system. There were individual lay schools and others supported by societies whose directors wanted to know the difference between their practices and rationalist innovations. Individuals and commissions constantly came to visit the school and consult me. I gladly satisfied them, removed their doubts, and pressed them to enter upon the new way; and at once efforts were made to reform the existing schools and to create others on the model of the Modern School.

There was great enthusiasm and the promise of mighty enterprises, but one serious difficulty stood in the way: we were short of teachers, and what was worse, there was no way to create them. Professional teachers, which were few in number, had two disadvantages—traditional habits and dread of the contingencies of the future. There were very few, and they were honorable exceptions, who, from altruism and a love of the ideal, would devote themselves to the progressive adventure. Instructed youth of both sexes might be found to fill the gap, but how were we to train them? Where could they train to be teachers? Now and again I heard from workers or political societies that they had decided to open a school. They could acquire a good facility with the necessary materials and they could count on the Modern School library for books. But whenever I asked if they had teachers, they replied in the negative, and thought it would be easy to find them. I had to give in.

Circumstances had made me the director of rationalist education, and I had constant consultations and demands on the part of prospective teachers. This made me realize the defect, and I endeavored to meet it by private advice and by admitting young assistants into the classes of the Modern School. The result was naturally mixed. There are now worthy teachers who started their career there and continue as firm supporters of rationalist education; others failed from moral or intellectual incapacity.

Not wanting to wait for the students of the same Modern School who dedicated themselves to teaching to be ready to teach, I established a normal school, of which I have already spoken. I was convinced that if the key to the social problem is in the scientific and rational school, then to find this key, before all else, it is necessary to train teachers capable for such a magnificent destiny.

As the practical and positive result of my work, I can say that the Modern School of Barcelona was a most successful attempt that distinguished itself in two ways:

1. While open to successive improvements, it set up a standard of what education should be in a regenerated society.
2. It gave the creative impulse to this education.

Previously there had been no education in the true sense of the word. There was, for the privileged in the university, a tradition of errors and dogmatic fears of an authoritarian character, mixed with truths discovered by exceptional geniuses on account of their dazzling brilliance. For the people there was primary instruction, which unfortunately was, and is, a type of domestication. The school was a sort of riding school, where natural energies were subdued in order that the poor might suffer their hard lot in silence. Real education, separated from faith—education that illuminates the mind with the light of evidence, because it finds itself constantly checked and proven by experience, that possesses the infallibility falsely attributed to the mythical creator, though it cannot fool itself or us—is that initiated by the Modern School.

In its ephemeral existence it produced notable benefits: children admitted to the school and kept in contact with their companions rapidly changed their habits, as I have already observed. They cultivated cleanliness, avoided quarrels, ceased to be cruel to animals, in their games they did not imitate the barbarous spectacle that we call the *fiesta nacional* [bullfight], and, as their minds were uplifted and their sentiments purified, they deplored the social injustices that abound everywhere. They also detested war and would not admit that national glory, instead of consisting in the highest possible moral development and happiness of a people, should be placed in conquest and violence.

The influence of the Modern School extended to other schools that had been founded on its model and were maintained by various workers' societies and centers and penetrated families by means of the children. Once they were touched by the influence of reason and science they were unconsciously converted into teachers of their own parents, and these in turn diffused the better standards among their friends and relatives.

The spread of our influence attracted the hatred of Jesuitism of short and long habits, like vipers in their dens, who took shelter in the palaces, temples, and convents of Barcelona, and this hatred inspired the plan that closed the Modern School. It is closed still, but it is currently concentrating its forces, defining and improving its plan, and gathering the strength for a fresh attempt to promote the true, indispensable work of progress.

That is the story of what the Modern School was, is, and must be.

Notes

1   Manuel Ruiz Zorrilla (1833–1895) was a former prime minister who was exiled to France for his vigorous opposition to the Bourbon Restoration after the fall of the Republic. As opposed to other republican figures who made peace with the

monarchy, Ruiz Zorrilla continued to organize insurrectionary plots from Paris through his Partido Republicano Progresista.

2   Boulangism was a populist, authoritarian, antisemitic political movement in fin de siècle France oriented around the minister of war General Georges Boulanger. Richard D. Sonn, *Anarchism and Cultural Politics in Fin de Siècle France* (Lincoln: University of Nebraska Press, 1989), 31. Dreyfusism refers to the movement that developed in defense of Alfred Dreyfus, the Jewish captain wrongfully accused of treason. For the anarchist involvement in this movement, see Jean-Marc Izrine, *Les libertaires dans l'affaire Dreyfus* (Paris: Éditions d'Alternative libertaire, 2012); Jean Maitron, *Le movement anarchiste en France: 1. Des origins à 1914* (Paris: Gallimard, 1992), 331.

3   In 1887, the Liberal Sagasta government passed the first Ley de Asociaciones governing freedom of association for unions, religious groups, and other public bodies. An ongoing struggle developed between the Church and anticlerical factions over the degree to which this and subsequent laws governed religious orders. Joan Connelly Ullman, *La semana trágica: estudio sobre las causas socio-económicas del anticlericalismo en España (1898–1912)* (Barcelona: Ediciones Ariel, 1968), 30, 53, 60, 124, 602.

4   McCabe's translation read: "Would the people confine itself to holding meetings to demand a reduction of the price of bread." This mistranslation was an effort to present Ferrer as a nonviolent figure. Bread riots were a mainstay of nineteenth-century Spanish rural unrest. They erupted in Old Castile in 1856, Granada in 1868, across Andalusia in 1882 (leading to the *Mano Negra* episode), and across Spain (as well as Italy) in 1898, among other instances. For many political commentators and future historians, the bread riot represented a "premodern," "proto-political" expression of popular discontent preceding the more "advanced" formation of unions and political parties. Here Ferrer's frustration at the futility of the bread riot reflects a bit of that perspective. Guy Thomson, *The Birth of Modern Politics in Spain: Democracy, Association and Revolution, 1854–75* (New York: Palgrave Macmillan, 2010), 244; Enrique A. Sanabria, *Republicanism and Anticlerical Nationalism in Spain* (New York: Palgrave Macmillan, 2009), 27; Eduardo González Calleja, *La razón de la fuerza: orden público, subversión y violencia política en la España de la Restauración (1875–1917)* (Madrid: Consejo Superior de Investigaciones Científicas, 1998), 229–33, 257; Mary Vincent, *Spain, 1833–2002: People and State* (Oxford: Oxford University Press, 2007), 99.

5   McCabe's translation read: "Would they waste their time in futile indignation meetings." Again the goal was to avoid a reference to violence. Riots against *consumos* (food taxes) were similar and often overlapping with those against high bread prices. The abolition of the consumos was perhaps the most significant demand of the nineteenth-century Spanish peasantry. A significant anti-consumos riot occurred in Asturias in 1897, when eight thousand people stormed city hall and two people were killed by the Civil Guard. Adrian Shubert, *A Social History of Modern Spain* (London: Routledge, 1990), 194–95. Anti-consumos riots also spread across Spain in the wake of the Spanish-American War. Sebastian Balfour, "Riot, Regeneration and Reaction: Spain in the Aftermath of the 1898 Disaster," *The Historical Journal* 38, no. 2 (1995): 409.

6   On December 29, 1874, General Arsenio Martínez Campos led the *pronunciamiento* that toppled the First Spanish Republic and restored Alfonso XII and the Bourbon monarchy. The period of the Restoration ended in 1931 with the proclamation of the Second Republic.

7   This slogan came out of the Mazzinian republican movement for Italian unification and was subsequently adopted by the First International and many anarchist and other socialist groups thereafter to emphasize that in capitalist society workers had duties without rights, while the ruling class had the inverse. Robert Graham, *We Do Not Fear Anarchy, We Invoke It: The First International and the Origins of the Anarchist Movement* (Oakland: AK Press, 2015), 65, 248; M. Teresa Martínez de Sas, ed., *Cartas, comunicaciones y circulares de la Comisión Federal de la Región Española*, vol. 7 (Barcelona: Edicions de la Universitat de Barcelona, 1987), 304.

8   *El Diluvio* was a republican newspaper somewhat sympathetic to anarchism.

9   The Institución Libre de Enseñanza (ILE) (1876–1936) was founded by Francisco Giner de los Ríos and his fellow "*Krausistas*" who followed the ideas of the German philosopher Karl Christian Friedrich Krause. In 1881, a Catalan equivalent opened that lasted until 1895. Enrique M. Ureña, "Sociedad, economía y educación en K. C. F. Krause, Albert Schäffle y Francisco Giner de los Ríos," in *Francisco Giner de los Ríos: actualidad de un pensador krausista*, ed. José Manuel Vázquez-Romero (Madrid: Marcial Pons, 2009), 129–33; Eduard Masjuan, *Un héroe trágico del anarquismo español: Mateo Morral, 1879–1906* (Barcelona: Icaria editorial, 2009), 39–40.

10   They included Jaime Peiró, Edualdo Canibell, Juan Salas Antón, J. Peiró, and Jaime Brossa. Juan Avilés, *Francisco Ferrer y Guardia: pedagogo, anarquista y mártir* (Madrid: Marcial Pons, 2006), 101–2.

11   In 1893, there was a general strike in Belgium for universal manhood suffrage.

12   Emilia Boivin was a teacher at the Modern School. Antonio Nadal Masegosa, "Análisis y valoración de la vigencia de los principios pedagógicos de la Escuela Moderna de Francisco Ferrer Guardia en el estado español en el siglo XXI. Estudio de casos" (PhD diss., Univerdidad de Málaga, 2015), 91.

13   This appeal was published in *Les Temps nouveaux* 39, January 26–February 1, 1902, with the heading "To the partisans of libertarian education."

14   The reference to four fundamental operations followed by a list of only three is an error in the original.

15   Here Reclus is referencing the Exposition Universelle of 1889, a world's fair held in Paris, highlighted by the recently constructed Eiffel Tower.

16   Despite his early collaboration with the Modern School, by 1906 Odón de Buen had started to distance himself from Ferrer to embrace more "neutral" education. Pere Solà i Gussinyer, "Escuela y educación para una sociedad autogestionada: la aportación de la pedagogía racionalista de F. Ferrer," in *Ferrer Guardia y la pedagogía libertaria: elementos para un debate*, ed. Pere Solà, Jordi Monés, and Luis Miguel Lázaro (Barcelona: Icaria Editorial, 1977), 100.

17   *El Diario de Barcelona* was commonly referred to as *El Brusi*, referring to the name of the family that owned the paper. Thomas S. Harrington, *Public Intellectuals*

and Nation Building in the Iberian Peninsula: The Alchemy of Identity (Lewisburg, PA: Bucknell University Press, 2015), 71.

18 Masjuan, *Un héroe trágico*, 54–78.

19 *Anthropos* (man), a radical word combined with the terms c*entro*, *morpho* (form) and *latria* (adoration).

IV

The Modern School Bulletin

Shortly after the grand opening of the Modern School in Barcelona on September 8, 1901, the Boletín de la Escuela Moderna *(Modern School Bulletin) published its first issue on October 30, 1901. Although readers might imagine that a school newspaper would focus on publishing information on the students, their teachers, and class activities, the purpose of the* Boletín *was to create a platform for the promotion of the theory of rationalist education. The* Boletín *published educational and more broadly theoretical articles from international intellectuals (especially French thinkers) such as Émile Zola, Herbert Spencer, Georges Clemenceau, Ernst Haeckel, Maxim Gorky, Alfred Naquet, Rousseau, and Charles Albert, foreign anarchists such as Elisée Reclus, Ferdinand Domela Nieuwenhuis, Sébastien Faure, Paul Robin, Charles Malato, Jean Grave, and Octave Mirbeau, as well as pieces from Modern School collaborators such as Ferrer, Anselmo Lorenzo, Clémence Jacquinet, and Leopoldine Bonnard. While most articles addressed questions of education and pedagogy, the* Boletín *also ranged out to cover anthropology, feminism, criminology, neo-Malthusianism, religion, patriotism, history and classics, and hygiene and medicine, among others.*

On the surface, the paper maintained a "nonideological" commitment to scientific truth, but the Boletín's *anticlerical, anti-capitalist, and anti-state politics featured prominently in its articles. For example, the* Boletín *published an excerpt of a speech attacking the religious education of children from the republican politician Nicolás Salmerón but clarified that "in copying this in the* Boletín, *we disregard its political character and invocation of the state, which completely disinterest us."[1] The first era of the* Boletín de la Escuela Moderna *ended after its May 31, 1906 issue, when it was shut down along with the school itself when Ferrer was charged as an accomplice in the royal bombing in Madrid that same day. After his acquittal, the paper published a new issue in July 1907, before returning to regular publication from May 1908 until its final issue in 1909.*

1. Modern School Daily Schedule

(Boletín de la Escuela Moderna, October 30 and November 30, 1901)
This early schedule for one of the youngest classes at the Modern School gives us special insight into the school's day-to-day operations and the content and focus of its activities. Published months after the Modern School's opening, we can see how it attempted to infuse libertarian values into a largely traditional framework. Teachers were instructed to build up the confidence of the weaker students, rather than shower praise on the "brilliant students"; they were advised to avoid telling stories that promote the "passion for any type of idols"; and they were told to safeguard against the children developing the "horrible instinct of property" by hoarding toys. Although the published schedule for the final year of the Modern School in 1905–1906 lacks a thorough description of course contents, we can see that the school's structure and contents changed little during its short life, despite the resignation of Clémence Jacquinet, the original director. The reader may be surprised to find such a strong emphasis on hygiene. This focus reflected the growing importance of hygiene in European perspectives on societal progress and modernization since the early nineteenth century and the fact that the Modern School's student body came from a range of class, and therefore hygienic, backgrounds. Moreover, physical exercise had come to be considered to be a key component of educational hygiene after the emerging popularity of calisthenics in the 1820s and 1830s and the "Rational Recreation" movement of the late nineteenth century.[2]

First Preparatory Class
Morning
9:00–9:15—hygiene examination—order in the class
The hygiene examination is very necessary for the preparatory classes; the teacher will not tolerate any negligence on this point and will make sure that all students present themselves irreproachably in their appearance and in their clothing. But since this examination, like everything else in education, requires much tact, it must be meticulous without degenerating

into humiliation. I have seen teachers who, from an excess of zeal, have shown a grave lack of respect in this matter.

To achieve the desired goal, a special effort will be made on the first day of class to explain to the children the benefits of hygiene and the drawbacks of dirtiness, as much in their straightforward meaning as in their moral sense, using language that they understand. The children will be warned that every day in the morning and afternoon their heads, faces, and hands will be examined. This inspection will not be carried out with a severe tone, and the child will not be sent to their family under the pretext of improving their hygiene, because this would have the opposite effect of what is desired, since the punished child will probably not return to class all day. This would be the worst outcome, since the attendance and precision of the students is of the utmost importance. It's a good idea to support the ignorant child who doesn't know how to be clean and who should be sent to the teacher's assistant to be taught how one cleans oneself, bearing in mind that it is very beneficial for the child to learn to do it themselves.

The greatest circumspection is necessary with clothing, because a lack of quality garments could be the result of circumstances. It is preferable to take note of the situation and express any observations to the school's administrators. Teachers should refrain from reprimanding or questioning the student, while the administrators, who are more in touch with the family, will inform them and work with them.

In their class lectures the teacher will frequently insist on the importance of bodily hygiene and cleanliness, expounding upon the benefits of baths, washing in general, etc., and even, if it were possible, recommending the system that I have seen practiced in various European cities, where the school is in charge of giving the children a bath at least once a week.

The hygiene examination should be done outside of the classroom, for example, on the recess patio, only allowing children who have been judged worthy to enter.

This brings me to speak about a sentiment that I recommend to the teacher to effectively inspire the student: respect for the class. It is necessary, indispensable, that the children understand the importance of what the school signifies, and, given their tender age, this sentiment should manifest itself in a way that is somewhat material. For example, one can speak in class but never shout; it is always necessary to maintain a regular attitude and reject without tolerance any careless or lazy posture, and, considering that the best lesson is always an example, the teacher will take great care to avoid committing any of the errors that they should criticize in the children: always in a correct attitude, the teacher should never show weakness or fatigue or show themselves to be affected by the cold or the heat. But despite everything, such accidents are liable to occur, so when they do it is preferable that the teacher momentarily step out of the class (this being an excessive concession that a good teacher will never abuse). I repeat, the teacher should constantly show that they are in control of themselves and disregard these annoyances as insignificant things, with an even greater motive since in many occasions, instead of a constructive suffering, it is nothing more than a bad habit that is necessary to get rid of at all cost, which is easy if one constantly sustains a little bit of goodwill.

It is equally recommended that the student be inspired to have love for their class: that they make sure not to have papers on the floor or books scattered in a disorderly fashion on the desks or ink stains on the floor or the walls. Every object that has been used must be carefully put back where it belongs before taking another, and if there is a need to point to something on a map or a painting then the student will use a special pointer designated for that purpose, rather than touching anything with their finger.

Moving to another set of ideas of capital importance, it is advisable that the students not use as their personal property any of the class materials: pens, pencils, chalkboards, etc. will be distributed among the children for the time of the lesson, and afterwards they will return them to special boxes, since it is prohibited to bring in and use outside objects. Also, the toys will be used in common, and there will be no tolerance for a child who tears a toy out of the hands of another who had it first or for a child who holds onto a toy after having taken others. This will make the students accustomed to considering the necessities of life as the domain of all, and it will work toward the disappearance of this horrible instinct of property against which one has to struggle mightily. For the same reason the teacher will not designate assigned seats to the students; each will take their place based on when they arrive.

9:15–9:45—questions about the work of the previous day
This is very important work, because it is essential to continually connect the work of the day before with that of the following day, and, generally speaking, everything that the students have learned should be solidly linked to the next lesson they are to be taught. This questioning is not only about exercising the memory of the children but also and principally

about inculcating the custom of not doing anything without taking perfect account of what one is doing. In effect, if during the lesson a child gets distracted or does not understand, then the child needs to take a step back, reflect, and make use of the active faculties of their intelligence, and the teacher can complete their education with explanations of the more confusing points of their lesson at the same time that the teacher learns to know the extent of the ingenuity of their students. Sometimes something difficult will be understood immediately, while something else that was considered so easy that it did not even require an explanation is confusing or has inadvertently given the students a false idea.

I do not vacillate, then, in considering this review work as the most important of the day, as much for the students as for the teacher, because it constitutes an ample and fertile field of personal experiences; at the same time a good teacher has to give it their utmost attention.

This is not easy work: the teacher attempts to create something vivid and concrete to imprint on the moral being of the students, conserving its character of summary memory. The practice will clarify the simple advice that I am giving without being able to elaborate further, limiting myself to adding that the teacher should greatly vary their lines of questioning to maintain the interest of the whole class; as such sometimes students will be questioned individually, while the rest are allowed to speak about whatever they want, although, at the same time, if done properly this will not produce confusion and will stimulate the classroom. It's all a question of tact and professional ability.

My last recommendation is that the teacher refrain from always asking the same students to answer questions. Rather than revealing the *brilliant students*, it is important, on the contrary, to give preferential treatment to the lazy children, to force them to come out in the open and participate. This must be done with tact so that the child does not suspect that the teacher is pursuing them: there are students who are inclined to believe that the insistence on their participation is a violent injustice, and as a result they obstinately enclose themselves in a rebellious silence. Prior knowledge of the exact point up to which it makes sense to push the student constitutes for the teacher an art that they must master at all cost.

9:45–10:00—recreation—10:00–10:30—hands-on exercises
Understand that after such a beneficial lesson the students feel a need for some free time; and so the teacher will let the little birds loose, so to speak,

for fifteen minutes, allowing them to make a lot of noise (even allowing them to imitate animal noises) and move as they want. After, when the flock is calm, it silently returns to class in an orderly fashion. Next are the hands-on exercises, which appeal to the children's double ability of invention and creation. These exercises are quite varied, including drawing on the chalkboard to building with blocks, to knitting, to the folding and cutting of paper with their fingers.

We don't set a day for each activity, we let the children freely choose which they prefer. With a little bit of skill, the teacher makes suggestions to the students with the goal of introducing some variety into their work. In effect, having prepared two or three exercises in advance, the teacher will propose the adoption of one of them; all the better if it works out that the students prefer the one that the teacher considered the best. Next, leading by example, the first student begins to work on the project as the other students watch, increasingly excited to see who will complete the task with flying colors. What happiness when the students overtake the teacher! This happens frequently because of the flexibility of their fingers and their fresh and inexhaustible imagination. The teacher applauds the students generously, taking great care that the less fortunate don't get down on themselves, warmly showing them what they should have done and giving them hope for greater success the next day. The teacher will not allow the rest to enjoy an excessively noisy triumph, reminding them of other lessons when their compañeros were or are superior, pushing them to understand that they possess different aptitudes and that, given that each has their special ability, levels of talent and usefulness even out for everyone.

10:30–11:00—lesson of things [lección de cosas]
The lesson of things is only advisable for the students of the preparatory class. Under its modest title, it includes a multitude of knowledge regarding what is necessary to know in life, while at the same time it is the best gymnasium for intelligence. Its plasticity allows it to be completely adapted to the children and to be varied enough that it never becomes boring and tedious.

I do not vacillate in affirming that the lesson of things is the most difficult form of education, because it constitutes the ideal form of the lesson. One can be sure that the teacher who knows how to organize a lesson of things has mastered pedagogy.

In effect, it's not about talking as clearly as possible for a certain period of time about whatever topic taken from the program, but rather about having the children reflect on the things they are learning about and having them talk about what they can discover through their own experience; and since every object that we look at can be considered from a thousand different perspectives, it is necessary to know how to deduce the unique aspects that can interest the young students, the only ones they are already familiar with. It's not as important that the children get to know new things as it is to establish in their intelligence what they already know and teach them to take note of all that surrounds them, to not let anything pass them by with indifference, because the most common facts deserve to be closely examined. How many interesting discoveries can one suggest that they make about the different parts of the body, the house, the city, the animals that live near us, and the plants that are harvested in the fields! I remember when a five-year-old little man, astonished and happy, came to tell me one morning that the enormous bunch of poppies that he had collected during his last field trip had cured his mother's cough. What an excellent topic for a lesson!

Because without forgetting the order of the lesson, we shouldn't squander incidents that can provide useful lesson topics, the teacher won't vacillate in postponing the prepared lesson when an unforeseen circumstance presents another that shouldn't be wasted.

Although the schedule indicates a half hour for the lesson of things, the teacher will change the exercise if they see the class languishing. If it is certainly true that it is up to the teacher to infuse their lesson with sufficient liveliness to retain the attention of the children, there are moments of general weariness, and when they occur the teacher and students uselessly exhaust themselves persisting in a boring exercise. Children only retain what they hear with pleasure: this is a truth that all teachers should understand.

11:00–11:15—recreation—11:15–11:35—hands-on exercises
This section is about exercises that we have already discussed so it's useless to go on about them. It is sufficient to observe that the second session of hands-on exercises should be of a different type than the first. For example, if earlier they did knitting or building, now they will work on the chalkboard. It is known that children enjoy handling a pencil or pen; for these first attempts, which are designed to further the education of the hand and the eye, the teacher will propose that the students draw a simple object, familiar to all, which the teacher will demonstrate, detailing

the general forms at the same time that they draw an easy-to-imitate sketch. Then the teacher will go from table to table pointing out the defects that students have to correct. The teacher's advice revitalizes excessively shapeless work, always trying to encourage and arouse personal effort.

With their sketch completed, each student is left free to follow their imagination and draw on their slate whatever their imagination dictates. The teacher will applaud the discoveries of happy ideas and the morning class will come to an end.

Afternoon
2:00–2:15—hygiene examination—2:15–2:45—story time [narración]
This hygiene examination intends for all of the students to go to the bathroom to clean up after recreation.

The first lesson of the afternoon is allotted to story time. It is known that one of the greatest pleasures for children is listening to stories. They can spend hours quietly listening in astonishment, but the teacher should not spend this time simply keeping their students immobile. Moreover, they shouldn't run over the half hour time slot, and they should use it to maximize the educational benefit for their young audience.

What kind of stories should be chosen? I think it is easier to answer the question by addressing its inverse—by describing the kind of stories that should be avoided: the teacher will refrain from speaking about so-called illustrious men whose fame stems from the spilling of human blood to the detriment of his fellow citizens, nor will the teacher address those who have exercised a stupefying despotism on intelligence. Those who for the goodness of their work would deserve to be addressed will not enter into our program for now, because we want to protect our students from developing passion for any type of idols and habituate them to avoid considering any of their peers to be extraordinary people. Later there will be time to teach them about what can be accomplished by an active and perseverant will oriented toward its own abilities. The teacher will also abstain from telling more or less edifying stories about good little docile children or about terrible punishments that await the recalcitrant, because all of these stories are contrary to our objective, which consists in educating a generation that is very free in all manifestations of its activity, endowed with a strong and extremely original will.

After these caveats, the field is open for the teacher to take their students to the four ends of the real and imaginary world, on the condition that they do not moralize, which in no way is suitable for the age of their audience. What enthusiasm among the children; we don't ask for anything more or anything less.

3:15–4:00—review questions—recitation from memory
In a quick review, the teacher will assure that the students have understood and retained the principal points of the day's lessons; that they remember the most important observations that have been made about their work and conduct. Later the children will recite some short, beautiful piece of prose or poetry within the scope of their intelligence.

The session will begin with the recitation of the piece that the students are to learn in an intelligible and pleasant manner. The teacher will carefully explain the meaning and make sure that all have understood it well. Next, they will turn to the mechanical work of recitation, attentively assuring proper pronunciation and expression.

Pronunciation should be clear and correct: the children have to accustom themselves to sufficiently opening their mouth and cleanly articulating the syllables, not using more of their voice than is necessary to be heard without effort, not allowing them to shout. The voice of the teacher who recites with them to guide them should always dominate theirs; if, with the hope of giving them greater inspiration, the teacher raises their voice even more, the students will not delay in crossing the line and the lesson won't produce anything more than an irritation of the larynx that can cause inflammation and, for the teacher, constitute a danger.

The teacher will not allow the children to recite mechanically or allow them to sing; it is important to always preserve the tone of a regular conversation. If the text is poetry, the rhythm should not degenerate into singsong. A simple, sober, clear diction accompanied by a sweet voice; that is the goal that all of our efforts should be directed toward.

Regarding the selection of texts, I recommend short pieces of prose that are generally easier to understand for the children and above all easier to recite intelligently. This should always be done in relation to what a child in the first preparatory class can understand.

4:15–4:45—gymnasium
Needless to say, our students do not have access to anything more than the simplest gymnasium without any equipment. Our program is composed of walking, running, and various diverse movements.

I expressly recommend that the session never reach the point of exhaustion and that any exercise that demands significant effort be eliminated; to ensure this, every student should be monitored attentively, because not all of them are equally capable of handling physical exercises.

1905–1906—Schedule

(*Boletín de la Escuela Moderna*, September 30, 1905)

Subjects taught and the distribution of time: Fifth School Year: 1905–1906[3]

PRESCHOOLERS

	9–9:10	9:10–10	10–10:15	10:15–11	11–11:15	11:15–12
Mon	Hygiene & Gym	Arithmetic	Rest	Reading	Rest	Grammar
Tues	Hygiene & Gym	Writing	Rest	Reading	Rest	Zoology
Wed	Hygiene & Gym	Writing	Rest	Reading & Drawing	Rest	Geometry
Thurs	Hygiene & Gym	Arithmetic	Rest	Reading	Rest	Grammar
Fri	Hygiene & Gym	Writing	Rest	Reading	Rest	Minerology
Sat	Hygiene & Gym	Arithmetic	Rest	Reading	Rest	Grammar

	2:30–3:30	3:30–3:45	3:45–4:30	4:30–4:45	4:45–5:30
Mon	Writing and Sewing	Rest	Hands-On Activities	Rest	Geography
Tues	Music Study	Rest	French	Rest	Moral stories from the teacher
Wed	Music Study		Field Trip		
Thurs	Writing and Sewing	Rest	Physiology	Rest	Geography
Fri	Music Study	Rest	French	Rest	Lesson of Things or stories from students
Sat	Writing and Sewing	Rest	Physics or Chemistry	Rest	Hands-On Activities or Botany

ELEMENTARY

	9–9:10	9:10–10	10–10:15	10:15–11	11–11:15	11:15–12
Mon	Hygiene & Gym	Arithmetic	Rest	Reading with explanation of words (*Adventures of Nono*)	Rest	Grammar

Tues	Hygiene & Gym	Writing from Dictation	Rest	Reading with explanation of words (León Martín)	Rest	Zoology
Wed	Hygiene & Gym	Writing from Dictation	Rest	Drawing	Rest	Geometry
Thurs	Hygiene & Gym	Arithmetic	Rest	History of Spain	Rest	Grammar
Fri	Hygiene & Gym	Writing from Dictation	Rest	Calligraphy	Rest	Minerology
Sat	Hygiene & Gym	Arithmetic	Rest	Reading with explanation of words (First Manuscript)	Rest	Grammar

	2:30–3:30	3:30–3:45	3:45–4:30	4:30–4:45	4:45–5:30
Mon	Writing and Sewing	Rest	Physics	Rest	Geography
Tues	Music Study	Rest	French	Rest	Lesson of Things
Wed	Music Study		Field Trip		
Thurs	Writing and Sewing	Rest	Physiology	Rest	Geography
Fri	Music Study	Rest	French	Rest	Arithmetic or stories from students
Sat	Writing and Sewing	Rest	Chemistry	Rest	Botany

ADVANCED

	9–9:10	9:10–10	10–10:15	10:15–11	11–11:15	11:15–12
Mon	Hygiene & Gym	Arithmetic	Rest	Drawing	Rest	Grammar
Tues	Hygiene & Gym	Narrative Writing	Rest	Reading & Discussion (Patriotism & Colonization)	Rest	Zoology
Wed	Hygiene & Gym	Writing (Commentary from Reading)	Rest	Reading & Discussion (Origin of Christianity)	Rest	Geometry
Thurs	Hygiene & Gym	Arithmetic	Rest	World History	Rest	Grammar
Fri	Hygiene & Gym	Writing (Free Theme)	Rest	Calligraphy	Rest	Minerology
Sat	Hygiene & Gym	Arithmetic	Rest	Reading & Discussion (Second Manuscript)	Rest	*Substancia Universal*

	2:30–3:30	3:30–3:45	3:45–4:30	4:30–4:45	4:45–5:30
Mon	Writing and Sewing	Rest	Physics	Rest	Geography*
Tues	Music Study	Rest	French	Rest	Lesson of Things
Wed	Music Study			Field Trip	
Thurs	Writing and Sewing	Rest	Physiology	Rest	Geography*
Fri	Music Study	Rest	French	Rest	Lesson of Things or stories from students
Sat	Letter-Writing and Sewing	Rest	Chemistry	Rest	Botany

*There will be shorthand classes on Mondays and Thursdays from 5:45–6:30.

Soon we will begin night classes to train teachers for free schools. Registration is open from 5:00 p.m. to 7:00 p.m. on weekdays and 11:00 a.m. to 1:00 p.m. on Sundays.

Students from the "First Year Normal Preparatory" class who "have studied with interest," alongside their teacher. *Boletín de la Escuela Moderna*, June 30, 1903. FFG.

Students of the Modern School "Middle Course." *Boletín de la Escuela Moderna*, June 30, 1903. FFG.

2. Students' Personal Grades

(*Boletín de la Escuela Moderna*, April 30, 1902)

This is the first and the last time that the Boletín de la Escuela Moderna *published student grades. Subsequently the practice was halted as the school moved closer to Ferrer's ideal of "no reward or punishment." Nevertheless, it is startling to see children described publicly as "lazy" or "a talker." It is unclear if or how the students were evaluated over the next four years of the school's existence. It's also worth noting that every issue of the* Boletín *published during the 1902–1903 academic year included a list of tardy students with the number of times they had been late, but this stopped the next year.*

First Year Normal Preparatory

Vicente Bonacasa—His conduct is somewhat irregular; but his work continues to be good—Grade: 8.

Carlos Turrez—Doesn't keep to himself—Grade: 5.

Arturo Boada—He wastes time, and the result is that he generally responds poorly to questions—Grade: 4.

Luis Auber—He would work well if he were alone in the class, but he is distracted easily and this hampers his progress—Grade: 4.

Middle Course
María Ruizcapilla—Good student, studious—Grade: 7.
Juan Carmany—Identical evaluation—Grade: 7.
Mario García—Good work, average conduct—Grade: 7.
Enriqueta Ortega—Good student—Grade: 8.
Enrique Reales—Good work, his conduct has improved—Grade: 7.
Pedro Ortega—Good student—Grade: 7.
Manri Montoro—He remains in the middle of his class; he could do more—Grade: 6.
Genoveva Padrós—Identical observation; has made progress in French—Grade: 6.
Pedro de José—Talks a lot; works less than the previous month; undoubtedly he remains in the middle of the class—Grade: 6.
Marina Canibell—She is also in the middle of her class; she is frequently absent and this hurts her progress—Grade: 6.
José Boyer—He could advance a lot but does not apply himself—Grade: 5.
Isidro Viñals—He is lazy—Grade: 5.
Dolores Valls—A new student to whom we will grant some time before grading her—Grade: 5.

Second Preparatory Class
First Division
The following *good students* have earned the grade of 8:
Encarnación Batlle, Sadi de Buen, Alejandro Solana, Sara Casas, Ida Montoro, Iarosslawa Turka, Juan Cebamanos, José Goytia, Teresa Arenys, José Camps.
To these names we would add José Berche, if he were less distracted, and Enrique Lasauza, who works well but whose conduct leaves much to be desired.
The following students deserve a grade of 6:
Ramón Guiu, Constancia Reales, Enriqueta Tormo, whose progress is slow.
Students of moderate effort and a grade of 5:
Feliciana Alfageme, Domingo Soulé, Asunción Abad, Francisco Badía.
Students whose work is insufficient and have a grade of 4:
Josefa Tormo, Andrés García.
And finally, with a grade of 3, José Garriga, who doesn't apply himself with anything nor does he make even the most minimal observation.

Students of the Modern School "Second Preparatory Class" with their teacher. They are classified into those with good and bad conduct. *Boletín de la Escuela Moderna*, June 30, 1903. FFG.

Second Division
Grade of 5:
Aurora Fontecha—Very intelligent but a talker.
María Molinas—A satisfactory new student; next month she will surely obtain a higher grade.
Amadeo Amorós—He has made something resembling progress, but his conduct continues to be irregular.
Francisca Abad—Her work is not very beneficial and her conduct is inappropriate—Grade: 3.
The following students have not obtained a grade this month:
Manuel Molés—Diligent student of good conduct; we are confident that he will advance.
Antonio Capdevila—Very distracted; not very conscientious with his work.
José Valls—Very diligent; we hope he will improve.
Gustavo Sainz, Juan Sainz—Too early to tell.

Preschool Class
Good students with a grade of 6:
Ramón Gironés, Dolores Molas, Fernando de Buen, Virgilio García.

Talkers with a note of 5:
Mariano García, Mercedes Molas.
Grade: 3—Lazy students:
Carmen Arenys, Daniel García, Aurea Canibell, Joaquín Berche.
Grade: 2—The laziest:
Vicente García, Juan Armengol.

3. Discord in the Family by Alicia Maur
(*Boletín de la Escuela Moderna*, May 31, 1903)
Articles like "Discord in the Family" demonstrate how Ferrer and his fellow Modern School educators aspired to influence education and childhood development beyond the classroom. In this article, Maur entreats parents to realize that they too are educators, and that their domestic conduct plays a significant role not only in how their children learn but in their entire psychological and moral development. Maur concludes with a gender analysis of how standards of domesticity often trap young women in oppressive social settings.

The gravest mistake that can be committed in a discordant home is for the children to take care of the parents more than the parents take care of the children.

At the age when a child's character is formed and all should take part in seriously forming it, the quarrels of the mother and father are detrimental to the happy result of this interior labor, which the child will resent for the rest of their life.

In effect, education is impossible if educators are not in agreement. A reprimand from one is followed by praise from another, and the child, according to their temperament, takes advantage of the family's disunion to do whatever they want.

If the child is affectionate, they will be inclined to be partial toward their mother, who is the most affectionate, crying with her, growing distant from their father who makes her cry. As a result, the father, rather than finding another bond to connect him to the home, will only find hostility.

If the child is violent, they will also be partial and not see anything more than the bad sides of their father or mother, of whichever of the two isn't to their preference. All of the backbiting that the child hears from their disliked parent will increase their rancor, and in this way they will arrive at these cruel relations between father and child where love is converted into hate.

If the child is intelligent, they will understand that both their father and mother are behaving poorly, because the child will judge the insults that they hurl at each other. The child will be able to appreciate in great detail the exaggerations produced by rage as much as the emotional scars produced by hate and ultimately develop the most contemptible idea of those who brought them into this world.

If the child is astute, they will flatter one or the other, according to their momentary convenience, enjoying having tricked them for their own benefit, thereby resulting in the most perverse moral deviation.

In every case the character of the child distorts and deviates from itself in a bad sense. A similar deterioration unfolds for their emotions; it destroys their good judgment. Sensibility, not reason, will guide their conduct and they will learn that the best way to have their whims fulfilled is to impose their will by crying, using hurtful words, and using all of the more or less shameful methods at their disposal.

It is little less than impossible that the child raised in discord will be sensible. Their nascent judgment has not been offered any moral certainty or any moderating norm for their impulses, and if they aren't a truly exceptional creature, their guide will be their caprice and circumstances.

With the family bond broken, they will be isolated before the difficulties of existence and poorly prepared to get through them.

Another problem for the child is that in conflictive families different personalities get irritated and the child bears the burden; they suffer the rebukes, they are scolded without reason, and since they have barely any philosophy and even less psychology to discern the causes of the injustice, they rebel against it. All of their moral force, rather than developing under the influence of conscientious learning, is exhausted in vain anger against that which harms them. They won't want to accept undeserved censure or punishment, but they will fight uselessly against an order of things that they find unacceptable, finding their parents as they are to be found, far too unhinged from their discord to be able to guide the conduct of their child.

. . .

One can say that the man who has lived well is he who has found the opportunity to usefully exercise all of his faculties. Perhaps one could say that the key to happiness is finding affection during every stage of one's life. Yet, as there is no affection that is more necessary for us than that of our parents, when this is lacking an emotional disillusionment lingers for one's entire life. The result is a kind of inability to enjoy happiness, and if, against all probability, happiness presents itself, it will be received with doubt, with distrust. The deception of the young heart is so profound when it is directed toward one's parents, and they respond with indifference if not repulsion, so that it is never cured completely for the rest of the child's life.

And how many incompetent, negligent parents unworthy of having children can't see the delicate sensibility of some children that is withering away in their tender and passionate little hearts!

As the years pass, the distance between child and parents increases and harmony becomes more difficult. The generation gap produces a difference in tastes. Parents have come to the point in their existence when material well-being becomes their priority. Their dreams have faded, whether for having fulfilled them or because they dissipated into vain illusions, and they value wealth, comfort, food on the table, and serious relations, while the child, who is twenty years old, needs enthusiasm more than bread and is seduced by the glory of thought and the delights of love more than the comfort of their parents' home.

The heart and the mind energetically aspire to live in the youth: they want to be heroes, and the parents advise them to be practical. Each thinks they are right, and in effect they are from their point of view. When harmony reigns in the family, each at least accepts the other, even if they don't understand each other.

What dramas unfold inside so many affluent families that present a respectable image to the outside world!

The antipathy and lack of benevolence of spouses continue in their children and, above all, they continue from mother to daughter with an excessive cruelty. That is because ultimately the father and his sons can leave the house, while the daughter always stays home. Even when she can leave, she has to go with her mother who can dominate her at a whim.

It is well-known and frequently (perhaps excessively) repeated that there are wonderful mothers. But there are others who are worse than the legendary stepmother and use every excuse to tell themselves that they don't know what they do. With their character poisoned, they take out their rage against their husband on the children who look like him and sometimes aggravate their wickedness by showing preference to the child they see themselves in.

. . .

Ah, if only the youth spoke! Perhaps they would not find the words to express all of the bitterness that they feel. And the unfortunates who silence themselves, who docilely follow their mothers to the salons, where their mothers answer questions directed toward them on their behalf, while they wear a mask of placidness and kind indifference. And when their friends spy them or visibly murmur about them or make a deliberate remark whose dark undertones allude to one of their most intimate secrets, although their heart feels injured, the fools continue to smile, eager for the instant when their loneliness can give way to the comforting relief of tears.

4. Student Presentations
(*Boletín de la Escuela Moderna*, September 30, 1904)
At the end of the 1903–1904 school year, the Modern School organized a formal presentation attended by parents and community members who regularly attended the school's Sunday presentations. One by one, twenty-eight students (ten girls and eighteen boys) took turns reading a short original writing "formulated freely and spontaneously." Although these are some of the more overtly ideological presentations, every presentation reflected the values and politics of the Modern School.

(Boy)—*The Microscope*—Ancient science was held back because as a method of examination it only had natural vision. Today there is the microscope, and with it we see the germs behind sicknesses the same as we see organs and parts in animals and plants. The microscope is an invention of free men. Fanatics are incapable of inventing anything because they attribute everything to their god.

(Girl)—*The Police*—The police arrest poor wretches who steal bread for their family; they throw them in jail, increasing misery.

(Girl)—*War*—Men should not fight. Weapons were invented by men to dominate and torment their fellows, rather than inventing scientific instruments so that humanity could progress. Many search for glory in war, but this glory is won by the bosses, while the soldiers, who are the ones who do the work, if they don't die on the battlefield, only win the ability to go home with one eye, a missing arm or leg. The inventor of an instrument of war shows pride in their work, which has won them awards that they accept, and so men stupefy themselves with war rather than civilizing themselves.

(Boy)—*Religion*—Religions have always led humanity down the wrong path. Rather than teaching children to reflect and to love their fellow

Students of the Modern School "Second Division" and "*clase infantil*." They are divided into "those who have advanced in their studies," those "who apply themselves" and those who "do not apply themselves so much." *Boletín de la Escuela Moderna*, June 30, 1903. FFG.

human beings, they teach them to pray and to admire those who kill. They make children believe in miracles when it is proven that everything takes place because of natural causes. Religion has always been the disgrace of humanity. It is the cause of exploitation and war. If we ask one of the believers of any of the infinite religions which is true, they will all respond that it is theirs, which proves the falsity of them all.

(Boy)—*Parasites*—Certain animal or plant organisms called parasites live at the expense of others and expend no effort to live. There are also parasites in human society. There is the worker who is fed upon by the rich people and the priests until they are completely exhausted.

(Boy)—*The Running of the Bulls*—I don't understand how there are people who get excited and enjoy themselves watching animals suffer. This diversion continues because of ignorance; if everyone were given proper education, as we are given, it would not exist.

(Boy)—*Politicians*—In all countries, in our epoch, there are many politicians who promise to help the people if they are elected, and the people, in their ignorance, vote, as one can see in Barcelona, and once the deputy wins

THE MODERN SCHOOL BULLETIN

things continue as always, sometimes worse. But the people are very igno-rant since they always appoint deputies, and so society does not change. If the people had more knowledge they would say: we do not want to be governed by anyone, we can govern ourselves.

5. Money

(*Boletín de la Escuela Moderna*, April 30, 1904)
This article is indicative of some of the questionable aspects of the Modern School. Rather than quoting directly from student writings, this article prioritizes the presentation of a unified exposition on the evils of money by summarizing their thoughts. In part, the unanimity of the class can be ascribed to the fact that these students would have been influenced by their leftist and freethinking families. Yet such complete uniformity of thought suggests that the spectrum of acceptable opinions on the matter may have been restricted. The author of this article (likely Ferrer) lauds the fact that the summary of the student responses "seems like a response from a single mind." Ultimately, they prioritize the dissemination of the "rational and the just" perspective through "our educational system, which consists of always giving verifiable and demonstrable positive knowledge so that natural logic simply carries them to the only conclusion." Clémence Jacquinet critiques this lesson in her Sociology in the School.

The students have been asked to share their opinions on money by answer-ing the following questions: *Is money beneficial or detrimental for society? Is it indispensable? If it were abolished, how could we satisfy our needs?*

We collected responses from thirty-two girls and boys ages nine to thirteen, who unanimously agreed that money is detrimental. All found it to be essentially unnecessary—although some recognized that in our current society it is indispensable—and therefore ought to be eliminated and replaced with something more rational and just.

Ignoring what we find repeated in the statements and arguments of many of the students, without doubt because they have not yet been affected by a certain type of concerns and are dominated by pure common sense, which consequently results in the natural flourishing of intelligence, the spontaneous bursts of good sense from these children are beautiful and as ingenious as just. They contain lessons that halt the man whose reason has been polluted by the dominant conventionalisms and preju-dices, making him submit his deeply rooted beliefs to examination by a new act of judgment. He is put in a position to discard his old opinions or feel the debilitation and deterioration of his old faith.

Corresponding to the three questions, there are three orders of response that we have summarized below:

1. Money is detrimental to society; because of it tyrannical capitalism and exploitation exist; because of it there are people who tell you that you have to be my servant and my worker. Money has facilitated the exchange of products, but it has also made the accumulation of capital possible. Without it the needs of all could not be satisfied, but capitalist accumulation makes possible the monopoly that produces hunger and misery. Money is a stimulant for evil, since money is used to pay for bad deeds; it excites envy and greed; it impedes progress; it is the foundation of the current society. Among other evils it has produced the notion that another more just society is impossible. Finally, money causes the waste of the opulent and the humiliation imposed on the poor who receive charity.

2. Money is not indispensable, because you can't eat money, you can't drink it, you can't clothe yourself with it, nor does it provide shelter, nor is it a work implement. With or without money, the things that are useful for our subsistence will always have the same properties. He who lives in a desert with a bag full of money will die lacking everything.

3. Without money and working in common we could meet our needs, collectively enjoying the fruits of labor. Without money equality would exist, everyone would help each other mutually, no one would lack any necessities, and everyone would consume everything without limit or abuse. Without money, there would exist solidarity that would make everyone rich.

In this extract, which seems like a response from a single mind, there is the principal thought of each student and part, and in some cases the totality, of the rest. All of the students have the same order of ideas because of their naturally carefree attitude and because of our educational system, which consists of always giving verifiable and demonstrable positive knowledge so that natural logic simply carries them to the only conclusion. As a result, the students think and assert with energy. As if they did not exist, the students pass by the conventional distinctions and circumlocutions used for these matters, which are nothing more than concessions to injustice and error, and head directly for what they consider just and true.

This was the outcome of this project that has important elements of criticism and social economy.

6. Direct Action by Dr. Meslier[4]

(*Boletín de la Escuela Moderna*, November 30, 1905)

This article from the French socialist deputy Adrien Meslier seeks to mobilize the intellectual prestige of evolutionary science and historical conceptions of "progress" to argue for direct action as an essential element of human development. He attempts to appeal to a moderate republican audience by situating direct action within the revolutionary canon of French republicanism. Meslier even goes so far as to justify propaganda by the deed when carried out under dire circumstances. The decision to publish this article in the Boletín *reflects the desire of Ferrer and his comrades to link pedagogical work to revolutionary struggle.*

Here we have a new name that expresses an idea whose reality is to be found in the history of all peoples; one of the forms of human activity, frequently the most glorious and productive.

We cannot and should not ban it, because throughout the centuries it has been the most active factor of progress. When reason, trampled underfoot by force, was at the point of succumbing, the desperate power of direct action assured its triumph.

No one can say of a tried and tested method: "You shall not pass beyond this point."

Evolution, in its thousand forms of life, drags men and things along an indefinite path of progress. Our action is limited to investigating the conditions of these transformations to adapt ourselves to them in an action of intelligent will.

We continually struggle against atavistic fears, the poor influences of education: fears from the familial or collective environment.

In this constant struggle, we choose the weapons that we consider the most suitable for our triumph.

Flint, broken by the action of fire or coarsely carved and strongly held in the hand or tied to a stick, was the preferred weapon of our remote ancestry at the end of the Cenozoic Era. The conference, the book, the newspaper, associations, strikes are the weapons that are adapted to our time and to our societies: they are more numerous than before because of the complex forms of individual and social life in the twentieth century, marking time passed and progress realized.

But pain, and sometimes even death, was always the price of such progress. The poet has been able to say that the great geniuses have cleansed themselves in the crucible of disgrace: the same happens with our humanity, which progresses through history by the force of revolutions.

We would be weak and ungrateful if we didn't recognize this.

But revolutions, small and large, involving the city or the nation, were always manifestations of direct action.

The poets of ancient Greece sang of the eternal honor of Harmodius and Aristogeiton, who killed the tyrant. The knife that pierced Caesar gave Brutus immortality.

The Bible glorifies the action of Judith. Spartacus, the leader of the rebellious slaves against their legal masters, cast the seed of liberty into Rome.

★ ★ ★

Without direct action the monarchy would not have fallen: Louis XVI would have completed his negotiations with foreign powers and realized his attempts to corrupt the army and the parliament. The Austrian Marie Antoinette, abandoning her ordinary [sexual] favorite, the Swede Fersen, would have further seduced Barnave. But the people of Paris wouldn't give them time; they made demands and they won them.

Also the republicans, on December 2, 1851, turned to direct action, although without success, calling on the workers of the lower neighborhoods to rise en masse against the destroyer of the constitution.[5] And when Victor Hugo, in *Les Châtiments*, wrote the famous verse "you can kill this man with tranquility," no one protested against this rebellious but just cry of conscience.

Recently, in miserable Russia, which moans under the throne of the tsars and finds itself at the mercy of these birds of prey known as grand dukes, acts of vengeance have written the preface of the liberatory revolution.

Grand Duke Sergei and the representative Plehve fell.[6] Who would have dared to protest against these executions?

Yes, we admit that a constitutional country with its parliament assures freedom of speech and of protest, and in this case the means of violent brutality are not right or excusable. But are these freedoms assured for tomorrow? The forces of reactionary perversity may slumber but an unexpected circumstance can awaken them.

A dictator, today occupying a seat in parliament, may rise tonight. . . . And so how can we combat him and overthrow him without the insurrectionary direct action of the people?

The Declaration of the Rights of Man and Citizen calls us to resist oppression: we will plaster it on the walls to realize it in our actions. It is good to read and even better to enact.

We do not forget it; woe to those who do!

An innocent man named Malato[7] has been imprisoned for many days. The judges know it. The government knows it as well as the people. The right to free thought is frightfully violated in his person.

When a citizen is a victim in this way, their immanent and personal right, preceding and superseding all law, is torn apart by the power of dominant iniquity.

When this just man suffers, all citizens should suffer and defend him . . . or they are despicable and cowardly!

And if one day the criminal force of the bankers of the cosmopolitan reaction causes its victims to rise up with a surge of direct action, I will count myself among them.

7. The Renewed School of Tomorrow, the Rebellious School of Today
by Grandjouan
(*Boletín de la Escuela Moderna*, January 1, 1909—originally published in *L'École rénovée*, November 15, 1908)
This article from the French anarchist illustrator Jules Grandjouan[8]
addresses how revolutionary educators can sow the seeds of rebellion within the confines of "bourgeois" education. Grandjouan makes a notable contribution to discussions of prefiguration in education by arguing that, given existing conditions in France, the first step toward libertarian education should be a combination of educational reforms to shrink the growing class divide, "for the same reasons that [workers] pursue the eight-hour day," and agitational pedagogical methods to spread class resentment. His argument is reminiscent of the newly popular revolutionary syndicalist perspective that the militant working-class conquest of reforms could grow popular power and open spaces for radicalization that would pave the way toward the revolution of the future. For Grandjouan, the "rebellious school of today"

was a necessary prerequisite for the establishment of the "renewed school of tomorrow."

We who read the articles about rational pedagogy in this periodical with great joy and are determined to help the beautiful endeavor of Ferrer and his friends with all of our strength ask for an expansion of the framework of the "renewed school of tomorrow," based on the projects, votes, and resolutions of the "rebellious school of today."

For us the question of youth education is divided into two parts that distinctly correspond to the two stages of the freedom of the individual with respect to society: the first period when the individual, tangled up in the nets of a poorly designed society, tries to break their bonds; and the second period when, free from all hindrances, they establish according to a rational and harmonious plan the foundations of a healthy education, the cornerstone of a well-organized society.

Currently we are in the first phase: that of the struggle against oppression, of daily combat and rebellion in formation. Necessarily we find ourselves obligated to recognize our weakness.

The bourgeois government provides the education that it wants in *its* schools. The efforts of the reformers of good will who want to improve administrative standards are halted before an impassible barrier: every book that can lead to reflection or rebellion is rigorously rejected, because at school, as everywhere else, the coalition of the rich against the poor ensures that all of the children of the community are exploited without defense.

Such is the situation at the present moment without any hope of change.

The different attempts to create rationalist schools over the past years only have relative value and have not allowed us to say that we have entered into the second phase, that of the general and total organization of rational education.

They are effectively artificial milieux created by the will of some individuals, helped by all of the sacrifices and possible enthusiasms and supported by favorable circumstances. But restricted in its development, its power of social modification appears very weak and without immediate efficacy.

These free schools are, nevertheless, indispensable and hopefully a great number of this kind of initiative will develop, because they are the preliminary proof that is necessary for the production of the renewed school of tomorrow.

When we begin to study this second question, we anticipate that it will be necessary, in order to have practical information and to support the birth of other similar initiatives, that each of the men who have attempted to create a school of this kind, known or not, come to this forum.

Here we will thoroughly expound upon all of the circumstances that have surrounded their attempt at a renewed school; figures and the most material details will be presented in addition to articles of their educational program. I am sure that this will give rise to a great number of initiatives inspired by the same intention, it will fortify those with good will, and it will influence workers' organizations to support these indispensable attempts at free education.

For the moment, we will occupy ourselves with the first question although we can only sketch it in broad strokes and deal with a minimal part of the whole. For me the question poses itself in this way: *What can the rebels of today do against bourgeois education?*

Who are these rebels of today? First, they are those who are exploited by capital, who see their children subjugated and systematically stupefied from their first years, and who think with horror that the bourgeois school has as its only objective to cut every bud of emancipation at the root and destroy all sources of rebellion.

Second, they are the conscious teachers, as exploited as their brothers the manual laborers and courageous enough to rise up against the iniquity that has been committed.

What can be done?

Workers can take action in different ways. The most complete solution would be for them to pull their children out of school and entrust their education to teachers of their choice, since education is still free thanks to the Falloux Law. Yet what is possible for the privileged is impossible for the workers, because syndicalist schools still do not exist in workers' centers. Regarding the schools formerly run by the Christian Brothers and other congregations that hide behind the title of free schools, it's a disgrace; if possible it's even worse than the lay school. Everyone agrees on this. But since the worker doesn't have the time or the capacity to instruct their children, they feel obligated to bring them to the local school.

There, books of bad faith and depressing tendencies obscure the burgeoning intelligence of the young student.

There, state employees, whose lives are as painful as those of workers, have to entertain . . . to teach fifty, sixty, and up to eighty students, forcing them to stay quiet.

There, the education given to the child of the worker is abruptly interrupted in the middle of puberty, at the moment when the body, definitively formed, gives all of its available strength to the mind; when the child is starting to reflect, their physical and moral development is halted as they are hurled into the factory. Because lay education, as bad as it may be, has already started to become dangerous.

Here I have three demands: 1) examine the books; 2) limit the number of children in a class; and 3) prolong the education of a child until the age of eighteen or twenty. These are three principal demands that I merely gesture toward, because the development of each of them would require an entire article. Yet, by this point they demand the most rapid and direct action on the part of workers for the same reasons that they pursue the eight-hour day.

It is absolutely necessary to do this work right away. Who knows if it's already too late.

The observer who passes through workers' milieux is appalled at their level of degeneration in comparison to the bourgeoisie of the same age.

The moat between the two classes is getting deeper and wider, and the school, the local school that ends when the students are thirteen years old, digs the first and the deepest trench.

Measure the height, weight, and the arc of the chest of the little girls of a local school in Charonne or Grenelle and compare them with a corresponding class at a bourgeois lycée. Above all, this disparity has been aggravated by the adoption of sports that have been in vogue among the bourgeoisie for about twenty years now.[9]

Check out a class at the law school, and then head over to a night class for apprentices: in one you will see agile, vigorous, well-nourished men, and in the other beings exhausted before their time, sick and emaciated. When the physical differences between the young bourgeois and the young worker intensify, the abyss of separation between the two classes expands.

School is where it has to begin to be filled.

The power and the consciousness of rebellion will provide the means.

Moreover, without waiting for the development of such an urgent campaign, and even to help prepare it, what can teachers do? State employees are tied to the bourgeois school by a stingy and fragile salary. They are prisoners of odious and complicated rules. They are constantly under the vigilance of two cops, one permanent, which is His Uselessness the Director, and the other intermittent, which is His Falsity the Inspector. In addition, there is the class exercise book that attests to the course of the lessons.

But despite everything, despite the precautions taken by bourgeois society, there is an immense field open to the rebellious teacher.

This field is the explanation of the words, the commentary that accompanies the text.

"I do the lesson," a teacher told me, "in the most passive, most official, and also most honorable manner. I slide through the program and through the texts that they impose on me; it's sufficient for me to fill the memory of my students with the rudimentary knowledge that they will have to regurgitate to the letter before the inspector. Sometimes I make them learn them word for word, which earns me a good official evaluation.

"But I dedicate all of my energy and all of my ardor to the explanation of the smallest details of social life. The word spoken in the course of a lesson is a pretext: it's enough to know how to choose it. So, regarding any topic, such as an image from the stupid history of France, a word from a civic instruction manual, or a piece of coal, I explain class struggle as precisely as I can. I bring before their eyes the most stimulating illustration of this terrible truth: the rich are armed against the poor.

"Of course, I do not deduce the consequences. I am careful not to for two reasons: first because doing so would delve too deeply into the mind of the child and, extended beyond the lesson, I would be transferred or censured; second because it is the child who should deduce the consequences when they enter into conflict with the wicked society. In the meantime, I give as many examples as the children can understand. I take them from their daily lives, especially their lives outside of school, but I introduce in the mind of the child a feeling of distress, of discomfort, the sense of something false or incongruous, the sensation of unbreathable air."

How right is this rebellious teacher! We offer this adolescent a little fresh air, a gust of rebellious wind toward a better society, and then, in a magnanimous impulse, he will march with us.

Precisely with examples that are lived, constructive, not invented for the necessities of the cause, but rather taken from the practices of teachers, with the desire that they be propagated and multiplied and that each school, each teacher, presents a sensational example every day, because that is how one forms class consciousness.

I—a teacher in a school in a very poor neighborhood was once dictating a summary of natural history when he came to this phrase: "*The pheasant and the guinea fowl provided the man with delicious meat.*" At this point he interrupted the dictation and asked his students: "What do you prefer, pheasant or guinea fowl?"

The children, surprised, looked at themselves, murmured, laughed but did not respond. And so, the teacher said: "Let's stop here for now. Today is Saturday so we'll continue next Monday. Since we can see that none of you have tried pheasant or guinea fowl, tomorrow ask your father, your mother, your uncle, ask your neighbors which they like better: pheasant or guinea fowl."

The following Monday each child came up to the teacher to tell him with perfect unanimity: "Mr. teacher, I asked about the pheasant and the guinea fowl, and everyone responded by asking me, 'What is that eaten with?'" Then the teacher, continuing dictation from the previous Saturday, said: "Now we can see clearly that there are men, such as myself, who never eat pheasant or guinea fowl, and so in that case it's necessary to correct the book in this way; copy: "*The pheasant and the guinea fowl provided* certain men *with delicious meat.*"

II—A teacher in a large city in the south taught a short class on electricity and machines that use motors. When he came to the fan, he explained that the propeller, in motion from electricity transformed into movement, creates a suction of hot air that consequently produces a current of fresh air. "In certain very laborious industries," he said, "the fan would be a relief from the harshness of work. The glassmakers, for example, work in a temperature that, at the mouth of the oven, reaches 75°C to 80°C. If we add the thirty or so degrees that come with the summer, the result is an unbearable heat. A few fans spinning over the heads of these workers would give them a little fresh air, and as such they have requested them, but they were denied based on the excuse that they would be too expensive. . . . [H]ere you can see the parts of a fan. When you pass by the large cafes on the main streets of the city, look at the ceilings and you will see fans spinning over the heads of elegant gentlemen who pass their time pleasantly enjoying refreshing beverages."

III—In a logic class a teacher in a suburb of Paris came to the phrase *to live in comfort.* Here she stopped and made the following remark: "I would like to explain to you, my dears, what it means to live in comfort, because you have no idea."

A girl, daughter of a foreman, stood up and vigorously interrupted her: "Miss, let me tell you that in my house we live in comfort."

And the teacher responded: "Ah my dear! I am so happy to hear that! So then when your mother comes back from her morning shopping she just has to get in the elevator rather than walking up six flights of stairs. And for light she just has to press a light switch. And you use a vacuum cleaner to get the dust out of your carpets. The rooms in your home are bright with high ceilings, and you can't smell the odors of the kitchen from the bedrooms. In your bathroom, you have hot and cold water and a large bathtub that is heated instantly. In. . ." The laughter of the children interrupted the teacher. All of the little girls looked at the daughter of the foreman asking her, "Is it true that you have all of this in your house?"

And the examples go on! By now it's clear where such methods can lead.

Always, with the monotony of a clock that separates the seconds and hammers time, this chorus must fall on the minds of poor children to mold their rebellious mentality: rich and poor! rich and poor! rich and poor!

Oh! It is necessary that a piercing and obstinate drop of water fall incessantly on the same spot and methodically dig a furrow and open a breach in the toughest granite.

Yes, may it be the smallest drop that makes the glass of cholera overflow!

You are one of us, child worker; we have struggled so much for you! You come with new vigor and a heart full of hate; you see us exhausted and worn out; you take over for us with renewed energy! Multiply your blows against this wall of inquisitors until it tumbles down!

Let's boldly acknowledge it: today we should create a generation of hate in the rebellious school! May this instinctive hate, created in the heart of the child, take form the day they enter into contact with the poorly constructed society! May it not cease until the fall of this society! May a better society sparkle on its ruins! In the meantime, it is evident that Hate and Violence are the only two weapons that can destroy all-powerful Money.

Notes

1   *Boletín de la Escuela Moderna*, January 31, 1903.
2   Virginia Smith, *Clean: A History of Personal Hygiene and Purity* (Oxford: Oxford University Press, 2007), 250–78.

3   The grammar class likely used *Epítome de Gramática Española* by Fabián Palasí, which was described as a "work freed from religious and social sophisms." The French class likely used the textbook *Nociones de Idioma Francés*, written by Ferrer's compañera and Modern School teacher Leopoldine Bonnard, *Nociones de Idioma Francés* (Barcelona: Escuela Moderna, 1903). *The Adventures of Nono* was a children's book written by the French anarchist Jean Grave in 1901. Anselmo Lorenzo's Spanish translation was first published in 1905. Pascual Velázquez and Antonio Viñao, "Un programa de educación popular: el legado de Ferrer Guardia y la editorial publicaciones de la Escuela Moderna (1901–1936)," *Educació i Història: Revista d'Història de l'Educació* 16 (2010): 88; Jean Grave, *Las aventuras de Nono* (Barcelona: Escuela Moderna, 1907). *León Martín, ó, La miseria: sus causas, sus remedios* (*León Martín, or, Misery: its causes, its remedies*) was written by one of Ferrer's closest friends, the French anarchist Charles Malato. Charles Malato, *León Martín, ó, La miseria: sus causas, sus remedios* (Barcelona: Escuela Moderna, 1905). The Spanish history class likely used *Resumen de la Historia de España* by the revolutionary republican and frequent anarchist collaborator Nicolás Estévanez. Estévanez also penned the lyrics to the Modern School song "Los juguetes" (Toys). Nicolás Estévanez, *Resumen de la Historia de España* (Barcelona: Escuela Moderna, 1904). *Patriotism and Colonization* was a collection of writings from figures including Voltaire, Dumas, Séverine, Octave Mirbeau, Herbert Spencer, and Victor Hugo, prefaced by the famed anarchist geographer Elisée Reclus. Its promotional blurb described the book as providing "more than sufficient details to reject the horrors that are committed in defense of miserable interests, sheltered under high-flown conventionalisms." *Patriotismo y colonización: con un prefacio de E. Reclus* (Barcelona: Escuela Moderna, 1904). *Science et Religion* by Malvert was translated into Spanish as *El orígen del cristianismo* by the anticlerical editor José Nakens. Malvert, *El origen del cristianismo* (Barcelona: Escuela Moderna, 1903); Velázquez and Viñao, "Un programa de educación popular," 99. *La substancia universal* (Barcelona: Escuela Moderna, 1904) was a book of ontology and philosophy of science written by Albert Bloch and Georges M. Paraf-Javal and translated by Anselmo Lorenzo.

4   Adrien Meslier was a medical doctor and parliamentary deputy from the Socialist Party in the early twentieth century. René Samuel and Georges Bonet-Maury, *Les parlementaires français: II, 1900–1914: dictionnaire biographique et bibliographique des sénateurs, députés, ministres* (Paris: Georges Roustan, 1914), 288.

5   On December 2, 1851, Louis Napoleon, president of the French Second Republic, launched a coup, to become Emperor Napoleon III.

6   In Moscow, on March 4, 1905, Ivan Kalyaev, a poet involved in the "Combat Squad" of the Party of Socialist-Revolutionaries, assassinated Grand Duke Sergei Alexandrovich by throwing a bomb into his carriage. Many were sympathetic to the deed because of the unpopularity of Alexandrovich's repression. John Keep, "Terror in 1905," in *Reinterpreting Revolutionary Russia: Essays in Honour of James D. White*, ed. Ian D. Thatcher (New York: Palgrave Macmillan, 2006), 20. Like Alexandrovich, the repressive Russian interior minister Viacheslav Konstantinovich Plehve was assassinated on July 28, 1904, when Egor Sazonov of the Party of Socialist-Revolutionaries threw a bomb into his carriage. Fredric

S. Zuckerman, *The Tsarist Secret Police in Russian Society, 1880–1917* (New York: New York University Press, 1996), 120.

7   The prominent French anarchist Charles Malato was one of Ferrer's closest collaborators and friends. Most of Ferrer's final correspondence from prison was directed to Malato. This reference is to Malato's inclusion in the "Trial of the Four," along with Pedro Vallina, Eugène Caussanel, and Bernard Harvey, for their alleged participation in the failed bombing of a carriage transporting the Spanish king Alfonso XIII and the French president Loubet. They were acquitted. Though the true identity of the bomber was never proven, some suspect it was actually the man who bombed the king's wedding a year later, Mateo Morral.

8   Jules Grandjouan was a prolific illustrator for the anarchist, revolutionary syndicalist, and satirical press of France at the turn of the century. He contributed to papers such as *Le Libertaire, L'Assiette au Beurre, Les Temps nouveaux*, and many others. He was prosecuted six times between 1907 and 1911 for his anti-militarist images. Grandjouan was also an adherent of Ferrer's Ligue Internationale pour l'éducation rationnelle de l'Enfance and collaborated with *L'École rénovée*. After the Russian Revolution, he became a communist. Robert Justin Goldstein, *Political Censorship of the Arts and the Press in Nineteenth-Century Europe* (New York: Palgrave Macmillan, 1989), 108; Comité de défense des victimes de la répression espagnole, *Un martyr des prêtres: Francisco Ferrer, 10 janvier 1859–13 octobre 1909: sa vie, son ouvre* (Paris: Schleicher frères, 1909), 28; Jordi de Cambra Bassols, *Anarquismo y positivismo: el caso Ferrer* (Madrid: Centro de Investigaciones Sociologicas, 1981), 54–55.

9   Grandjouan is referencing the growth and expansion of modern sports, which first developed in Great Britain during the Industrial Revolution. As the historian Robert F. Wheeler phrased it, modern sports "began as elitist preserves, spread to the masses as a consequence of industrialization, and came to serve as something of an integrating factor for the nation-state." Yet, as Grandjouan notes, in early twentieth-century France, sports had not yet descended from the realm of bourgeoisie masculinity to attain the popularity that they would achieve by the end of the century. Robert F. Wheeler, "Teaching Sport as History, History through Sport," *History Teacher* 11, no. 3 (1978): 314.

V

Anarchist Critiques of Ferrer and the Modern School

The commemoration of Ferrer's martyrdom over the decades follow-ing his execution has obscured the lively debates that emerged within the Spanish anarchist movement over his model of "rationalist" educa-tion. This section features anarchist critiques of the Ferrerian model from Clémence (Clemencia) Jacquinet, the first director of the Modern School, and the prominent anarchist theorist Ricardo Mella. While their points of emphasis vary slightly, both attack Ferrer and his school, though without explicitly naming either, for being dogmatic, ideological, and attempting to indoctrinate the youth. Mella argues, "Not even absolute liberty should be imposed, but rather freely pursued and accepted." Rather than teaching the children anarchism or any other doctrine, Jacquinet and Mella advocate what Mella refers to as educational "neutralism," designed to allow the "free and complete development of individuals" by starting from the first principles of science and discarding preconceived opinions. They evince a strong belief that the inherent righteousness of their beliefs will "inevitably" shine through for anyone who has had a truly neutral, scientific educa-tion, thereby rendering educational indoctrination unnecessary as well as authoritarian. Jacquinet and Mella also make a strong historicist argument that it is impossible to know what ideals future generations will value, so one must not risk getting mired in the prejudices that inevitably accom-pany the limitations of one's historical position. The "neutral" perspective represented a tiny current in Spanish anarchism until the Second Republic, when more critiques of Ferrer's rationalism emerged. Even so, they were a minority within the movement as Ferrer's ideas still animated libertarian educational practices in the 1930s.[1]

1. Excerpt of Letter from Jacquinet to Ferrer, November 11, 1900

Ferrer spent the fall of 1900 corresponding with potential Modern School collaborators. Among his most important early collaborators was Clémence Jacquinet, who would become the first director of the Modern School. Jacquinet had taken Spanish lessons from Ferrer in Paris in 1897, before travelling to Egypt with her mother in 1898 to become the governess for the children of Pasha Hassan Tewfik and teach in his school. Jacquinet claimed that the British authorities shut down the school because it taught in French more than English and included girls and poor children, while the authorities claimed it simply ran out of money. Jacquinet spiraled into a suicidal depression in 1900 when her mother died. In her early correspondence with Ferrer, he attempts to comfort her and talk her out of suicide. Most importantly, perhaps, he offered her the director position of his new school. Jacquinet claims she attempted to create a school for girls years earlier but lacked the resources.[2]

Tensions emerged between Jacquinet and Ferrer as soon as they started to discuss the details of the school. The Sorbonne-educated Jacquinet argued that the school should have the students read the classics, such as Kant, Montaigne, Rousseau, Spencer, Froebel, and, "the greatest of all," Rabelais. Ferrer, whose formal education did not continue beyond age thirteen, was skeptical and more inclined to make a clean break with the past. More fundamentally, however, Jacquinet was concerned from the very start that the Modern School ran the risk of becoming ideological. In this letter, written about two months before she arrived in Barcelona to start working on the Modern School, Jacquinet counsels Ferrer to prioritize the creation of "free minds" and avoid the dangers of "dogmatism." As we will see, her fears would not be alleviated.[3]

Everyone agrees in recognizing the poor distribution of property around the world, the abuse of authority, the injustice of all social edifices, but when we talk about putting something else in its place a diversity of opinions immediately emerges from all angles. It is, then, essential to apply oneself to forming, for now, *absolutely free* spirits, but, precisely for this reason, *prudently and discretely*. To see clearly is our first necessity; to spread science, pure science, without concern for opinion, for theories. This is what the youth needs, and when they leave school, then they will begin their apprenticeship in social life, the study of the problems that pose themselves to the formed man.

Regarding religions, it seems to me that one should treat them like goblins and other creatures no one believes in that used to scare children. With the help of true science, if one is a little skilled, it is very easy to put intelligence on guard against superstition. And as such the school will be popular and do its work of healthy education without rejecting anyone. How would it serve progress to only recruit among followers? This is not about hiding the flag in the pocket, but rather about not flaunting it unnecessarily.

The more I study the idea of your school, the more I firmly maintain this idea: you should train teachers but not with these or those works conceived of in a determined sense. It is essential to have confidence in the superiority of our ideal, to not fear putting it into contrast with works developed under a different spirit. That is how free minds that know how to think for themselves are formed without the need of any catechism to distinguish between truth and error.

Because, after all, whether with the atheist, anarchist, or theocratic idea, when you reduce a philosophy to a manual, you turn it into a dogmatic work. . . . Only the experimental sciences founded on proven facts and that can be reproduced and verified can be taught as such, and, nevertheless, it's not done. How is one to do that with knowledge whose only base is opinion?

2. Sociology in the School

(Speech read at the Centro Fraternal de Cultura in August 1903)[4]
Clemencia Jacquinet
Following the 1901–1902 academic year Clémence (Clemencia) Jacquinet resigned from her position as director of the Modern School, though she continued on as a teacher during the following year. By the summer of 1903, however, her frustration with what she considered to be the "dogmatic" and "ideological" nature of the school's education drove her to break ties with Ferrer and the institution. Months after, she delivered the following address, published a year later as the pamphlet Sociology in the School, *where she critiques anarchists and other radicals who believe that "social science is entirely contained in their newspapers" and refuse to look beyond the limitations of their ideologies. In a revealing passage, Jacquinet recounts intervening in the Modern School's lesson on the evils of money described above in the* Boletín *article "Money" and using the shortcomings of the Modern School method to articulate her perspective that education should built up from first premises to empower independent thinking.*

Also included is the original prologue to Sociology in the School *from the prominent anarchist writer José Prat (1867–1932). During this period, Prat was the editor of the anarchist journal* Natura *and "the great priest of the new school" of anarcho-syndicalism that was slowly gaining popularity in Spain. Prat was among the first Barcelona contacts that Ferrer reached out to when he was planning his school (they may have met for the first time in 1896 at the London Congress of the Second International). When the school opened, Prat served on the Modern School board and acted as an administrator. Some have suggested, however, that the relationship between Ferrer and Prat may have soured over time.[5] Regardless, Prat endorsed Jacquinet's perspective in* Sociology in the School *and published a series of articles Jacquinet wrote on education in his journal a few years later.[6] Prat argued that the dissemination of information must be different for adults and children. Yet he also made the fascinating argument that even if some adults blindly adopt egalitarian outlooks out of faith, this belief is important to defend against reaction, even if it may not be fully liberating personally.*

Prologue

José Prat

They asked me for some pages to serve as a prologue to this speech on *Sociology in the School*, and I accepted.

It occurred to me that you have to be brave to venture into such deep waters without knowing anything about pedagogy, but ignorance is adventurous, and I will take the blame for my own ignorance in daring to accept such a large enterprise, before rudely apologizing, blaming it on their request that I do them the special favor of approaching the ravines of unknown material, ravines I will hopelessly plummet into if the benevolence of the reader does not lend me a hand.

I naively confess that the first reading of *Sociology in the School* left me with a less than pleasant impression. A party man,[7] a mediocre propagandist of an ideal that others inculcated in me and in which I have faith, my love of being a propagandist suffered a rude blow upon reading certain affirmations that seemed to go categorically against my opinion and against my method of propagating it.

"For many people," the speaker says, or is about to say, "social science is entirely contained in their newspapers, in the problems of emancipation that concern us today. . . . All of their knowledge amounts to inculcating preferred opinions in order to create an inerasable impression on the minds of others. They found nothing better to create libertarians than to work in the way of the priests of all religions."

"No," exclaims the author in the following line, "the emancipation of humanity does not consist in professing such and such opinions, but rather in searching for their free and complete development."

Is it possible, I thought, that we have all been mistaken, that to inculcate ideas in the minds of those who know nothing constitutes a danger for the emancipation of humanity, that it could be an obstacle for the future, as the author fears, as much as we may have faith in the potential of our ideas, as developed as our conviction in justice and the truth that incarnates it may be?

Is it possible, I continued thinking, that emancipation rests precisely in the *non-profession* of such and such opinions that we today believe to be redemptive?

For whom, then, do ideals serve if it is dangerous to transmit them from mind to mind in such a manner that they leave an inerasable impression? Why the proselytism, why the preaching, why the newspapers if, as the author advises, we have to limit ourselves to waiting for "the child to think according to their own initiative" so that what is taught does not end up being converted into a new dogma?

Is there not, perhaps, a similarity between the man who knows nothing, or very little, and the schoolchild?

How is it possible to make it so that those individuals who currently need "others to explain things to them" can be in favor of an opinion, of an ideal, that "should not be inculcated in them," because this means snatching away the "faculty of thinking according to their own initiative"?

This leaves us with two possible conclusions: either we have to *wait* for the men of today to think according to their own initiative, and in this case there is no need for all of the proselytism and ideals, and the social revolution will come when hell freezes over, when capitalist exploitation and governmental tyranny will have already destroyed everyone; or the method employed up until the present to teach sociology to men can and should be applied to the teaching of sociology in the schools.

This would have been a real dead end for me if I hadn't run into some clarifying distinctions.

Thinking it over, I began to see things more clearly.

1. The street and the school are not the same.

2. The mind of a man for whom "it is necessary to remove errors so that truths can enter later" is not the same as the mind of a child who doesn't even have any notions of anything, a truly blank slate upon which anyone can write what they want as they please . . . and although they may not want to write anything, they involuntarily run the risk of *philosophizing* about the things of life in the presence of the child.

3. Opinions held by older people, even if they are simply professed as an article of faith and as such do not always serve to truly advance the mind of the "individual" that professes them, constitute, nevertheless, a force of opposition to the currently enthroned error. They are a factor of social progress when they oppose the antisocial factor of prevailing opinions that attempt to retard or halt progress, the evolution of the "collectivity." Meanwhile the child is a combatant in formation for the battles of tomorrow. As such, they have their current radius of action limited to the "acquisition of knowledge that will put them on the path to truth that they will fight for when they are older." It is a nascent social factor in preparation not an active and immediate factor like the followers who, with greater or lesser consciousness, fight to destroy the obstacles to their ideal that are posed by evil or the ignorance of their adversaries.

And the method of education put forth by the author of the conference has the merit of realizing the *difficulty* of the struggle faced by the propagandists of new ideas whose generous efforts almost smash the routine of the multitudes. They confront the intellectual weakness of past and present generations, whose individuals, in their immense majority, are incapable of the slightest initiative and have a spirit distorted by the prejudices imposed by a defective education that has spent or atrophied cerebral energies. Today they are almost incapable of absorbing the principles of sociology, and propagandists have to turn to the use of energetic stimulants taken from the passions if they want to obtain sufficient cerebral reactions.

Therefore, there is no contradiction between the two methods that my initial doubts had put in conflict. There is a perfect parallelism of efforts between the school, as the author claims, and the propagandists, efforts that come together toward the same goal: to save the minds of the men of today and tomorrow from any longer being the secure, manageable, and malleable prisoners of the whims of all reactionary spirits.

In fact, to recommend that the child not be taught sociology in the same way as the multitudes are taught does not mean that the multitudes should be taught the way that the author wants to teach students.

And so, just as the man needs meat and certain stimulants to his vital functions and the child needs milk and sedatives, in the same way the man of our generation, weighed down by prejudices that make him stuck in his ways, is not the same as the child whose mind is virgin to all prejudice, and consequently, the stimulants that are good for the first are not so for the second.

And . . . but why continue to follow me through the ravine as I get lost in the darkness and hesitation brought on by my incompetence in this matter, when the reader can leave for the plain, well-lit, and precise, by reading and reflecting upon the pages of *Sociology in the School*?

I recommend it to teachers and non-teachers alike. To the first so that they can see for themselves, without the need for any strange digressions, the usefulness of the text. To the second in case they want to help the first.

When all is said and done, the emancipation of humanity will not come about without this harmonization, without this coordination of multiple efforts that although they seem to lead down different paths bring us, whether we think so or not, whether we want them to or not, to the same end: liberty.

Sociology in the School
My dear compañeros:

It is impossible for me to put up a fight when what I am asked to do pleases me to such an extreme. I truly find it to be an immense pleasure to come here and speak a little with you all. Anyway, I'm not going to speak to you about my limited worth or of the honor that you provide me; all phrases of false modesty that often hide a great depth of vanity.

I'll say to you, simply, fraternally: Do you want to listen to me? Very well, I will take the floor on your behalf and at your risk.

Permit me to start with some general reflections on the matter of instruction.

It has been thoroughly recognized for a long time that the worse ignorance does not consist in not knowing, but rather in knowing things poorly.

The most disastrous errors are those that are born from a poorly understood truth.

Every moment we come upon difficulties that are born from an error of evaluation, from a false point of departure in the interpretation of an idea or principle. How many people are there who call themselves adversaries of opinions that they have misinterpreted and from which they draw such absurd and unexpected consequences?

The evil caused by false science is so great that ignorance is preferable.

In effect, it is not strange to encounter completely uneducated people whose good sense marvels us. Meanwhile, we are surrounded by highly educated people who are incapable of the slightest initiative and whose university baggage has only served to divert their intelligence from the straight, easy, and agreeable path upon which it was advancing.

Where does this apparent contradiction come from?

It will seem like I am expressing a paradox when I affirm to you that our uneducated man is one hundred times better educated than this sad, dried fruit that comes out of our schools; nevertheless it is true. Here is why.

It can be said that the man dedicated to his own impulses has not encountered the world around him with indifference. He has observed its particularities, established certain comparisons between events and their causes; in a word, he has received lessons of inestimable value from the things around him. Habituated in this way to confront the real and the tangible with all of their consequences, it would be strange if he were to pass by truth without recognizing it, at least within the limits of the utilitarian side of things, upon the fatally narrow terrain of the events of his coarse existence.

Let me hasten to add that I do not generalize with this example; unfortunately, it is all too true that ignorance is always a cause of error and of evils of all kinds. I simply wanted to demonstrate the power of observation as an educational method.

. . .

It has been said that men, from the intellectual point of view, can be divided into three categories: those who understand things through their own natural faculties, others who need things to be explained to them, and finally those who understand nothing at all.

The great majority of those who have attended school have to be placed in the second category as a consequence of the disastrous management of their education rather than their natural capabilities. This is because their

minds are disciplined since the start of their studies, because they are habituated to receive the word of the teacher as an unshakeable truth, because
they are habituated to bow to authority, in this way suffocating the intellectual activity that an intelligent gymnasium would have developed in them.

We all agree on this matter; it's just that unfortunately there are very
few who are brave enough to overcome their daily routine, that comfort-
able, delicious routine, to apply that universally recognized theory.

. . .

On the contrary, beyond the loss of our initiative, there is another danger
that comes from dogmatic education. Every idea that is inculcated in us
by force and by surprise, when our mind is not even disposed to receive
it freely by choice; when, above all, this very same ideal has also been
received docilely and superficially by the same individual that transmits it
to us, without having been sufficiently prepared and elucidated; this idea,
which is submitted to us without defense from the able sophisms of those
who seek to bring confusion to an inexperienced intelligence can launch
us onto a path totally contrary to that which we sought to follow.

These reflections bring me to the question that I have proposed to
study with you.

Should we teach sociology in the schools or not?

The answer is clear. If it is true that the goal of education consists in
helping men to form themselves; it will also be true that they should be
taught social science. We just have to agree on this point.

For many people, and unfortunately for many teachers, social science
is entirely contained in their newspapers, in the problems of emancipation
that so deeply concern our epoch.

All of their knowledge consists in inculcating their disciples in their
preferred opinions in order to create an inerasable impression in their
minds that implants and expands itself just like a weed. The best method
they found to create libertarians is to work like the priests of all religions.

They don't realize that forging minds according to their favorite model
is anti-libertarian, since it snatches away from the child in their most
tender youth the ability to think according to their own initiative. Since no
one and nothing can assure us that the ideal that currently corresponds to
our aspirations will necessarily be the ideal desired by generations to come,
when the natural environment may have transformed the conditions of
life of the men of the future, then isn't it perhaps possible that what we
call emancipation today may be an obstacle for the future?

No a thousand times [to such errors]. The emancipation of humanity does not consist in professing such and such opinions, but rather in searching for the free and complete development of individuals.

What is important is to immerse children in an atmosphere where they can spontaneously collect a large number of impressions that they will continue to organize to the degree that they are capable of reflecting upon them.

Why, then, do teachers, even those who profess libertarian opinions, have such little confidence in freedom? If they have done enough to evade error in the school, then why do they fear simply leaving free space for the truth?

Tell them to take a careful look at the past. Perhaps the minds of the first to articulate social demands were formed deliberately for that purpose?

All, or almost all who have fomented the most fruitful and magnanimous revolutions were educated, on the contrary, in the most authoritarian traditions, under the dispiriting discipline of both the Church and the state designed to turn them into docile instruments of their ambitions by means of the most effective methods to kill intelligence. How could they consequently free themselves from bonds that seemed so strong? Simply: by rejecting their education through an admirable act of will; by passing through the sieve of intelligent and disinterested observation all that they had learned.

Moreover, if our aspirations are just, if our social critiques are founded in the truth, then it stands to reason that they will be spread on their own, inevitably, from a sincere study of nature observed in all of its aspects according to a rigorously scientific method in order to deduce the consequences from the social point of view.

This eminently productive study has been given the name of sociology, and this study is what our children, and we as well, must learn.

Permit me an example to explain what I mean by school sociology.

I have heard students reflect on why money is harmful for society. Surprised by the superficiality of the propositions of these young thirteen- and fourteen-year-old sociologists, I wanted to develop a real impression of this baseless affirmation, purely dogmatic, in children of this age, and here is what I found:

"What," I asked, "does an exchange of products mean to you?"

"It is the exchange," they responded, "of a surplus material for
another that one lacks."

"And how is this exchange carried out?"

"Very simply. For example: he who needs bread trades some of his
wine, which he has in excess."

As you can see, the children had not transcended the conception of
individual exchange.

Then I had them observe that in primitive times exchanges were
carried out that way, and even today there exist various societies that
conduct trade in this way because they have no other form of exchange.
Nevertheless, in these societies there are rich people and poor people.
Their society is as poorly constituted as ours. I explained that money was
invented to facilitate exchange over great distances.

The children listened to me with great attention and soon interrupted
me to draw the conclusion that money is necessary.

But since I was determined not to give them a false idea, I made them
understand as clearly as I could that individual exchange is bad and that
this trade had to be substituted for the equitable distribution of the products of the earth and of labor.

And then I thought that if, instead of prematurely speaking to the
children about things that require a prior illustration, they were taught
to know the natural regions of the earth, its climate, its products, and the
ways of life of its different peoples, if, instead of mechanically teaching
them the names of the states and their capitals, they were taught how
parallel to the apparent luxury of the great cities exists misery that is
hidden in its heart, and that alongside the sumptuous buildings of London
or Paris there are hovels where hundreds of thousands of working-class
families vegetate, this would bring serious and real sociology within reach
of the children.

There would have been no need to draw out the future consequences
of these facts that, grouped with other facts from each branch of science,
are by themselves eloquent and speak directly to the enthusiastic heart of
the children, causing them an impression that is as unforgettable as it is
true, an impression that can be brought face to face with any discussion,
and this very same discussion strengthens it.

And if to this knowledge we add not zoology, botany, physics, etc., with
each taken in detail, as is the custom in the program of a school where

children generally don't attend more than two or three years, but rather the knowledge of matter itself, of its functioning, of its conditions of equilibrium, following step by step the transformations of living beings, their kinship patterns, we would come away with the following principles that the children would discover and use later:

1. That the equilibrium between the energies that exist between living beings and their external environment produces life.
2. That in a living colony, all of the colonists, which is to say, all of the cells that compose it, have to be able to integrally carry out their exchanges with the external environment.
3. That no organ can, under pain of death, acquire preponderance in a living being. The equilibrium of functions has to be perfect.
4. That every cell, every colony, should transfer a certain volume; the contrary leads to the rupture of the vital equilibrium, which is to say, death.

If, regarding history, children were taught how man has acquired, at the price of long centuries of effort, all that today distinguishes him from the other animals, including speech; if children were educated about the first human societies, the communist classes in which man gradually acquired all of the altruistic sentiments that most honor him when he practices them; if, on the other hand, the child were made to see that all of the benefits that the regular evolution of the clan could have provided for humanity have been lost because of wars, daughters of our states founded on authority; if they were made to see and sound out, century after century, the long and terrible combat between dominating, military, and religious power and civilization, the daughter of popular labor, produced and sustained by the proletariat despite all of the miseries, despite all of the killings, breaking all of the obstacles, destroying all of the artificial barriers erected by ambition, pride, and vice—then tell me what power would all of the absurd affirmations of all of the subtle reasons have against this shield so well forged by this teaching?

. . .

There are teachers, certainly, who do not recoil at education and dedicate their spare time to personal investigations in the field of pedagogy. But they are the exception, unfortunately. The majority of teachers constantly have the word "science" on their lips, they revere it like a deity that is very high or very distant, as an inaccessible idol, and so as the wise man said: nothing as well-known as the name; nothing as strange as the thing.

Let's stop here. I could have been able to pass through a review of all of the orders of knowledge and teach that, prohibiting all questions of opinion in the school, which is a topic of study for fully developed men and not for children, one can and one should teach sociology in the school; to teach, in sum, by means of the fluctuations of natural evolution, the means of life that are at our disposal in nature, the causes of death that come from the rupture of the equilibrium, as much physical as social, leaving for later the task of learning what has to be and the means to realize the humanitarian ideal.

My conclusion, dear compañeros, will be easy to deduce: we should all wage a ruthless war against routine, work to teach ourselves first with our own personal experience, and later pursue this same reform in the school.

If, wanting to construct a shelter for ourselves against the elements, we were to content ourselves with a magnificent roof that was only sustained by four posts, we wouldn't have anything more than a bad covering under which we would be exposed to the wind, and the slightest gale would quickly carry away a similar building.

Let's agree that to construct a durable building, it is necessary to first do a thorough inspection of the land, then construct the foundations, use good materials, and raise the walls solidly so that they can support the roof that completes the building.

That is how we should proceed in the matter of sociological education.

3. The Problem of Teaching
Ricardo Mella
(*Acción libertaria*, Gijón 5 and 11, December 16, 1910 and January 27, 1911)
Ricardo Mella (1861–1925) was a leading theoretician of anarchist collectivism in the nineteenth century and a giant of Spanish anarchist history. In this two-part essay published after Ferrer's death, Mella builds upon Jacquinet's work to continue her argument that anarchists ought to develop "neutral" forms of "teaching free of all classes of isms." It is unsurprising that Mella took an interest in Jacquinet's Sociology in the School, *since his close friend and collaborator José Prat penned its introduction. When Ferrer started his correspondence with Prat about the Modern School in 1900, he asked Prat to invite Mella to participate, but Mella seems to have*

declined. Mella's argument for nonideological education would reemerge in debates with Ferrerians over anarchist education over the following decades in Spain.[8]

I

Those who oppose religious teaching, increasingly unyielding people of very diverse political and social ideas, advocate and practice lay, neutral, and rationalist teaching.

At first laicism sufficiently satisfied popular aspirations. But when it was understood that in the lay schools they merely substituted civics in place of religion, the state in place of God, the idea emerged of a form of teaching as much unconnected to religious as political doctrines. And so some called this the neutral school, while others called it rationalist.

There is no shortage of objections to these new methods, and so as to delay no further I will challenge these corresponding names.

Because, strictly speaking, as long as they don't distinguish perfectly between teaching (*enseñanza*) and education (*educación*), any method will be defective. If we were to reduce the question to teaching, properly stated, there wouldn't be a problem. There is a problem because the goal in every case is to *educate*, inculcate in children a special mode of behaving, of being, and of thinking. And against this tendency of imposition will always be raised the objections of those who prioritize the intellectual and corporal independence of the youth over whatever other objective.

The question isn't whether the school is called lay, neutral, or rationalist, etc. This would be a simple game of words transferred from our political concerns to our pedagogical opinions.

Rationalism will vary, and varies at present, based on the ideas of those who propagate or practice it. Neutralism, on the other hand, even in the relative sense that it should be understood, remains free from and above the ideas and sentiments of those who teach it. As long as teaching and education are confused, the tendency, if not the intention, will be to model the youth in conformity with particular and determined ends.

But fundamentally the question is simpler if we focus on the real purpose rather than outward appearances. It is laudable to oppose religious teaching and promote the emancipation of children and youth from all imposition and all dogma. But later the political and social prejudices come to confuse and mix with the instructive function, the educational mission. Moreover, everyone knows clearly that real instruction is given only where there is no attempt to disseminate biased politics, sociology, ethics, and philosophy, whatever name it may be called.

And precisely because each method proclaims itself capable not only of teaching but also of educating according to preestablished principles, and consequently waves an ideological banner, it is necessary that we make it clear that if we limited ourselves to instructing the youth in acquired truths, inculcating these ideas through experience and understanding, the problem would be resolved.

As righteous as we consider ourselves, as much as we esteem our own goodness and our own justice, we have neither a lesser nor a greater right than our opponents to mold the youth in our image and likeness. If no one has the right to suggest, to impose any religious dogma on children, neither does anyone have the right to teach them a political opinion, a social, economic, and philosophic ideal.

Moreover, it is evident that to teach early writing, geometry, grammar, mathematics, etc., as much in their practical sense as in the purely artistic or scientific, there is no need to rely on lay or rational doctrines that suppose determined tendencies and, as a result, are contrary to the instructive function in itself. In clear and precise terms: school should be neither republican nor Masonic nor socialist nor anarchist, just as it cannot and should not be religious.

The school cannot and should not be anything more than the appropriate gymnasium for the total development of the individual. There is no need to present the youth with prefabricated ideas, whatever they may be, because this implies the castration and atrophy of the very same faculties that they attempt to stimulate.

Apart from all bias, it is necessary to introduce teaching, ripping the youth from the power of all ideologues, although they may call themselves revolutionaries. Conquered truths, universally recognized, will be enough to intellectually form free individuals.

We are told that the youth needs more comprehensive forms of teaching, that it is necessary for them to know all about mental and historical development, that they learn about events and ideals without which their learning and knowledge would be incomplete.

Without any doubt. But this knowledge does not correspond to a school. Here is where neutrality claims its jurisdiction. Presenting young people, previously instructed in proven truths, with the development of all metaphysics, of all theologies, of all philosophical systems, of all forms of organization, present, past, and future, of all the established facts and all ideals is precisely the necessary objective of the school, the indispensable method to arouse an understanding not to impose a real conception of life. May everyone form themselves before this immense arsenal of rights and ideas. The teacher will be easily neutral if they are obligated to teach not to instill dogmas.

There is a big difference between explaining religious ideas and teaching a religious dogma; to expound upon political ideas and teach democracy, socialism, or anarchy. It is necessary to explain it all but not impose anything, as true and just as it is thought to be. Only at this price will intellectual independence be effective.

And we who put liberty and the freedom of thought and action above all else, who proclaim the real independence of the individual, cannot advocate methods of imposition, or even doctrinaire methods of teaching for the youth.

The school that we want, without denomination, is that which best arouses in children the desire to learn for themselves, to form their own ideas. Wherever that takes them, that's where we will be with our modest support.

All the rest, to a greater or lesser extent, is to go back over the same worn-out roads, to voluntarily confine yourself to a single path, to change from one set of crutches to another but not to get rid of them.

And what's important is precisely to get rid of them for once.

II

We know that there is no lack of freethinkers, radicals, and anarchists who understand liberty in the same way as the religious sectarians. We know that when it comes to teaching, they act the same as they do with everything else in life, like the inquisitors acted years ago and how the lay or religious Jesuits, their worthy heirs, act today. And because we know this, we tackled the problem of teaching in our previous article.

Since we oppose any fanaticism, even anarchist fanaticism, since we don't compromise with any imposition, even if it is scientific, we will insist on our points of view.

Sectarianism takes matters so far afield that one is presented with a dilemma: with me or against me. Those who speak like that call themselves libertarians. They are bothered by the euphony of one word: rationalism. And we ask: What is rationalism? Is it the philosophy of Kant, is it pure and simple science, is it atheism and anarchism? How many voices would clamor against such assertions!

Rationalism can be whatever they want it to be, but for some of us it is the imposition of a doctrine on the youth. Their own language denounces it. They say and they repeat that rationalist teaching will be anarchist or it will not be rationalist. They emphatically affirm that the mission of the rationalist teacher *is to make beings ready to live in a society of happiness and liberty.* Science, rationalism, and anarchism are identified with each other, and they take their first step converting teaching into propaganda, into proselytism. More logical are those who later argue that one should resolutely say anarchist teaching and leave aside the rest of the sonorous adjectives that please the simpletons who don't have a spark in their brain.

Don't pay attention to those libertarians, because no one has the mission of *forming* everyone else in this or that way, but rather the duty to not disturb the opportunity everyone has to make themselves as they desire. They don't realize that it's one thing to instruct in the sciences and another to teach a doctrine. They don't stop to consider that what is for adults simply propaganda becomes imposition for children. And in the ultimate extreme, although rationalism and anarchism can be as identical as they want, we anarchists should guard ourselves well against deliberately engraving any belief onto the tender brains of children, thereby impeding or trying to impede their future development.

"For many people," said Clemencia Jacquinet, in a Barcelona conference on sociology in the school, "and unfortunately for many teachers, social science is entirely contained in their newspapers, in the problems of emancipation that so deeply concern our epoch."

"All of their knowledge consists in inculcating their disciples in their preferred opinions in order to create an indelible impression in their minds that implants and expands itself just like a weed. The best method they have found to form libertarians is to work like the priests of all religions."

"They don't realize that forging minds according to their favored model *is anti-libertarian,* since it snatches away from the child in their most tender youth the ability to think according to their own initiative."

It will be insisted, despite what has been said and written, that anarchy and rationalism are the same thing, and it will even be said that they are the indisputable truth, complete science, absolute evidence. Set on the track of the dogmatic, they will decree the infallibility of their beliefs.

But even if that were the case, what will become of free choice, of the intellectual independence of the child? Not even absolute liberty should be imposed, but rather freely pursued and accepted, if absolute truth were not absurd and impossible in the fatally limited terms of our understanding.

No, we do not have the right to stamp our particular ideas onto the virgin minds of children. If they are true, it is the child who should deduce them from the general knowledge that we have put at their disposal. Not opinions, but rather well-proven principles for everyone. What properly calls itself science should constitute the program of the true teaching, yesterday called integral, today lay, neutral, or rationalist, the name matters little. The substance of things is what interests us. And if in this substance there is, as we believe, the fundamental truth of anarchism, then the youth instructed in scientific truths will be anarchists as adults, but they will be from their free choice, by their own conviction, not because we have shaped them, following the routine of all believers, according to our faithful knowledge and understanding.

The evidence is clear. What kind of anarchism would we teach in the schools under the supposition that science and anarchism are the same thing? A communist teacher would emphasize the very simple and idyllic anarchism of Kropotkin. An individualist teacher would teach the ferocious egoism of figures like Nietzche and Stirner or the complicated mutualism of Proudhon. A third teacher would teach syndicalist anarchism influenced by the ideas of Malatesta and others. Which is the truth, the science, to firmly establish this uncontrollable absurdity of the rationalist absolute?

It is easily forgotten that anarchism is nothing more than a body of doctrine, and as solid and reasonable and scientific as its base may be, it does not escape the terrain of the speculative, of the debatable, and, as such, it can and should be understood, like all of the other doctrines, but not taught, which is not the same. It is forgotten that the truth of one day is the error of the next, and that it is impossible to solidly establish that the future won't keep other aspirations and other truths for itself. And finally, it is forgotten that we are ourselves prisoners to a thousand prejudices, a thousand anachronisms, a thousand sophisms that we will necessarily transmit to the coming generations if the sectarian and narrow criteria of the doctrines of anarchism have to prevail.

Like us, there are thousands of men who think that they are in possession of the truth. They are probably, surely, honorable and think and feel honestly. They have the right to neutrality. Neither they nor we have to impose our ideas on the youth. We teach acquired truths and may *everyone make of themselves as they can and want*. This will be more libertarian than the dismal labor of giving children premade ideas that can be, that will often be, enormous errors.

The figureheads of anarchism should be careful not to consider themselves the sole owners of the truth. Attacking others should be kept for a better occasion, for it is already too late to revive ludicrous dictatorships and to deny licenses that no one orders and no one accepts.

As anarchists, precisely as anarchists, we want teaching free of all classes of *isms*, so that the men of the future can make themselves free and happy for themselves and not through supposed modelers, which is to say, saviors.

Notes

1   Jordi Monés i Pujol-Busquets, "Ferrer en la tradición del pensamiento educativo libertario," in *Ferrer Guardia y la pedagogía libertaria: elementos para un debate*, ed. Jordi Monés, Pere Solà, and Luis Miguel Lázaro (Barcelona: Icaria Editorial, 1977), 44.

2   Salvador Canals, *Los sucesos de España en 1909*, vol. 2 (Madrid: Imprenta Alemana, 1911), 64–70; Francisco Bergasa, *¿Quién mató a Ferrer i Guardia?* (Madrid: Aguilar, 2009), 103–4.

3   Canals, *Los sucesos de España en 1909*, 67–71. For information on what Ferrer read, see Sol Ferrer, *Le véritable Francisco Ferrer: d'après des documents inédits* (Paris: L'Écran du monde, 1948), 39.

4   Clemencia Jacquinet, *La sociología en la escuela* (Barcelona: José Miguel Junqueras, 1904). Available at IISG.

5   Joaquín Romero Maura, *La rosa de fuego: el obrerismo barcelonés de 1899 a 1909* (Barcelona: Ediciones Grijalbo, S.A., 1975), 464; Jordi de Cambra Bassols, *Anarquismo y positivismo: el caso Ferrer* (Madrid: Centro de Investigaciones Sociologicas, 1981), 51; Miguel Íñiguez, *Enciclopedia histórica del anarquismo español* (Vitoria: Asociación Isaac Puente, 2008), 1377–78; Canals, *Los sucesos de España en 1909*, 54.

6   "Los factores de una educación social" was a six-part article published in *Natura* from April 1 to August 15, 1905.

7   *Hombre de partido*—meaning not that he was literally part of a political party, but that he staunchly stood by his political position.

8   Íñiguez, *Enciclopedia histórica del anarquismo español*, 1103–4; Canals, *Los sucesos de España en 1909*, 50–52.

VI

Ferrer and the Republic

Francisco Ferrer began his political life as a republican loyal to Manuel Ruiz Zorrilla's Progressive Republican Party (Partido Republicano Progresista). However, while living in Paris, his firsthand experience of the French Third Republic would gradually diminish his republicanism in favor of a brief sojourn with a more socialist orientation, before he finally turned to anarchism (though without necessarily leaving republicanism behind entirely). This section includes two of Ferrer's republican texts from the early 1890s.

1. Manifesto of the Three Hundred

In October 1892, Ferrer attended the Universal Freethinkers' Congress in Madrid as a delegate representing Les Vrais Experts Masonic lodge of Paris. He arrived with the hope of "taking advantage of the meeting of so many good patriots to unite the revolutionary forces" that were assembled. Yet Ferrer grew impatient with the lack of focus on revolutionary politics, writing that "one, two, three, and four days passed without having managed to begin what I considered the most practical of all." He recounts that he spent a troubled night tossing and turning over what to do, before deciding to write a revolutionary tract to distribute to the entire congress. Unfortunately for Ferrer, the printer would not print the text "because it was illegal," so he decided to "make propaganda among those that seemed to me to be the most revolutionary."

The call to arms reproduced below was Ferrer's attempt to cater his revolutionary message to the most "advanced" sectors of the congress and spearhead the creation of a secret revolutionary network. The police found this text and others related to the congress when they searched his belongings in 1909. When they were used against him at his trial, Ferrer acknowledged their authorship but argued that they were written so long ago that they did not represent his views. Subsequently, this appeal was referred to as the "Manifesto of the Three Hundred" in the press. It shows how Ferrer's politics were in flux between the elitist military conspiracies of Ruiz Zorrilla and his later interest in socialism and the general strike. Although his effort to enlist a cadre of three hundred committed revolutionaries failed, this endeavor put him in contact with his lifelong collaborator, the radical republican leader Alejandro Lerroux. Lerroux signed his follow-up manifesto as "the first of the three hundred," while Ferrer was "Cero" (Zero), his Masonic and pen name, implying that he saw himself as the primary initiator of the three hundred.[1]

To the congregated,
Some of you have read the speech that I wanted to distribute to all of the delegates but could not because I couldn't get it printed. You all agree with us in believing that to make the revolution we, the revolutionaries, should work together.

We do not intend to unite everyone nor do we need to. We are searching for only three hundred, who, like ourselves, are willing to stick their necks out to start the movement in Madrid.

We will search for the propitious moment, like, for example, during a general strike or on the eve of May 1.

We have relations with the workers' party [PSOE] and with other revolutionary forces to prepare the terrain.

We are completely convinced that on the day when the heads of the royal family and their ministers roll or the buildings that shelter them collapse, the panic will be so great that our friends will only have to struggle a little to seize public buildings and organize the revolutionary juntas.

To you, the first adherents, will go the glory of being the initiators and of being the first to die for the cause; a death a thousand times more honorable that living under the shameful oppression of a gang of thieves led by a foreigner and sustained by priests and exploiters.

Let's go, noble and valiant hearts, sons of El Cid. Don't forget that Spanish blood runs through your veins. ¡Viva la revolución! ¡Viva la dinamita!

★ ★ ★

All who want to be part of the first three hundred should send their names and addresses to Monsieur Ferrer, general delivery, rue Lafayette, Paris.

2. How the Spanish Republic Will End Anarchy
(*El País*, April 8, 1894)
Ferrer wrote this article well before transitioning away from his early republicanism. At this time, France was experiencing "l'ère des attentats" of the early 1890s, when anarchist bombers and assassins such as Ravachol, Émile Henry, and Auguste Vaillant stalked elite society. Here Ferrer publicly denounces the use of dynamite, despite his conspiratorial glorification of the revolutionary potential of the explosive two years earlier. His republicanism notwithstanding, one can still discern Ferrer's keen sensitivity to how economic despair and state repression could drive desperate people to lash out violently. Rather than pure repression, Ferrer calls for alleviating the social ills at the root of the violence. This article may provide a small clue regarding Ferrer's political metamorphosis—after all, he argues that the solution is a republic in Spain at the same time as he rails against the repression and brutality of the republic in France.

The new explosion last night at the Foyot restaurant[2] in front of the senate moves me to write what I think about anarchism.

Is the government of the French Republic following the right path to combat the anarchists?

Not at all.

The first thing that it should do is to organize a special tribunal to judge the authors of these *atentados* [attacks] and condemn them within twenty-four hours so that the press won't have time to fill their columns with the words, actions, and gestures of those who, with or without reason, call themselves *apostles* of anarchy.

Second, the police should be very careful not to arrest the innocent, as they have been doing since they began carrying out mass arrests. There is nothing to justify arresting honorable workers, dignified heads of households, merely because they were seen buying an anarchist newspaper; and even, as occurred within the past few days, arresting someone because they went to visit the home of a foreigner who lived next to the editorial office of an anarchist newspaper.

When I read the daily list of arrests carried out in Paris, composed almost entirely of workers and employees[3] who have been working for months or years at the same company, I could not help but think of the abuses that this produced. I thought of the thousands of families who, thanks to vile denunciations perhaps or the government's desire to seem strong, found themselves without their only means of support or unable to find work because their father, brother, son, or relative was arrested as an anarchist.

Third and finally, what should most concern governments is to avoid infuriating any class of society to prevent the reprisals that never fail to produce themselves.

It is an enormous error to think that anarchist ideas can be combated through any other method than education, persuasion, and, above all, with justice.

The workers of Andalusia consider themselves obligated to take bread when, tired of asking and being ignored, hunger propels them to commit acts that they surely would refrain from if the current society practiced that solidarity that is indispensable for life.

We wouldn't have deplored the catastrophe of the Liceo if public opinion had compelled the government to spare the life of Pallás,[4] who, in short, wanted to demonstrate how a *pueblo* should carry out justice when it finds itself oppressed, ridiculed, and dishonored, as Martínez Campos is doing.

And, returning to France, it is known that if Ravachol placed those two bombs in the houses of the two judges,[5] it was to avenge the severe, which is to say, unjust, sentences handed down to prisoners who were unknown to him.

I have been told that it is barbaric to risk the innocent, as the anarchists do when they pursue vengeance.

I don't support them or approve of their deeds, nor is this even about that. The question is to search for the causes that induce them to carry out such barbarities and eliminate them. When there aren't causes there won't be an effect.

A bomb was detonated at the Le Véry restaurant to avenge the denunciation that they made against Ravachol,[6] whose bomb could have been directed against all of society that approved of it.

The bomb of the rue des Bons Enfants targeted the director of the Carmaux mines,[7] who was at the time in a conflict with thousands of his miners, whose families were relegated to misery because of his intransigence.

Vaillant's bomb was thrown at the deputies, according to what he said, because they refused to amnesty workers who were imprisoned for going on strike.[8] The press in northern France was full of horrific details of entire families who died of hunger thanks to the protection that the government, presided over by Casimir-Perier, gave to the company. Not coincidentally, Casimir-Perier was one of the company's main stockholders.

What surprise is it that every day bombs explode like yesterday if the government commits new injustices, rather than preventing the causes of the explosions?

Was the bomb thrown by an anarchist or by a relative or friend of someone who committed suicide in prison because they had been incarcerated unjustly?

Was it thrown by a son to avenge his father or by a father to avenge his son?

This will not happen under the Spanish Republic. Don Manuel Ruiz Zorrilla, in a few words, puts the question on its true terrain. Speaking about it in his letter-manifesto, he says, "We, trusting in the potential of ideas, can and will allow peaceful propaganda in favor of the greatest utopias, but we will have to oppose the propaganda of deeds with the most severe repression."

Agreed.

We would give them freedom of the press and public assembly. We would listen to them when they denounce injustices to us. We would protect them just as we would protect landowners, and tranquility would be a fact.

During the celebration of the freethinking congress, I had the opportunity to get to know the Barcelona anarchists who attended, and through meeting I was convinced of the truth of what I am saying, had I not been sure before.

Anarchism will not be a danger for the Spanish Republic because the Progressive Republican Party will as a rule promote the general welfare of the country. This will end all of the irritating privileges and make it so that the Spanish *pueblo* will only consist of one caste [*casta*], united to achieve, in union with the rest of the Iberian race, the end of the frightening state of violence that all nations find themselves in because of the exploitation of the majority carried out by the minority.

F. Ferrer

April 5, 1894

Notes

1   *Causa contra Francisco Ferrer Guardia: instruida y fallada por la Jurisdicción de Guerra en Barcelona, año 1909* (Madrid: Sucesores de J. A. García, 1911), 382–89; José Álvarez Junco, *El emperador del paralelo: Lerroux y la demogogia populista* (Madrid: Alianza, 1990), 104–6; Francisco Bergasa, *¿Quién mató a Ferrer i Guardia?* (Madrid: Aguilar, 2009), 91; Juan Avilés, *Francisco Ferrer y Guardia: pedagogo, anarquista y mártir* (Madrid: Marcial Pons, 2006), 61–62.

2   On April 4, 1894, the anarchist literary critic Félix Fénéon detonated a bomb just outside the Hôtel Foyot in Paris. Ironically, the anarchist poet Laurent Tailhade was dining in the restaurant and lost an eye in the explosion. Earlier in response to Vaillant's bombing of the chamber of deputies, Tailhade had notoriously asked, "What do the waves of humanity matter so long as the gesture is beautiful!" John Merriman, *The Dynamite Club: How a Bombing in Fin-de-Siècle Paris Ignited the Age of Modern Terror* (Boston: Houghton Mifflin Harcourt, 2009), 172–73.

3   By "employees" (*empleados*) he is referring to the common distinction of the era between manual laborers and office workers or other non-manual workers.

4   On September 24, 1893, Paulino Pallás bombed the Virgin of Mercy procession in Barcelona in an attempt to target General Martínez Campos. The bomb caused one death and sixteen injuries (including the general, who survived). Shortly thereafter Pallás was executed. To avenge him, his comrade Santiago Salvador bombed the Liceo [Liceu in Catalan] Theater in Barcelona on November 7, 1893, killing twenty and injuring twenty-seven to thirty-five more. Antoni Dalmau, *Set dies de fúria: Barcelona i la setmana tràgica (juliol de 1909)* (Barcelona: Columna Edicions, 2009), 63–64, 116.

5   The French anarchist Ravachol was the first of many anarchist "propagandist by the deed" martyrs of the nineteenth and twentieth centuries. In March 1892, he and his comrades blew up the residences of the judge and prosecutor (not two judges as Ferrer writes) involved in the trial of the anarchists who had been arrested and abused after a shootout with police in Paris on May 1, 1891. Two of these anarchists received what were considered to be extremely harsh sentences of three and five years in prison. Merriman, *The Dynamite Club*, 71–78.

6   After bombing the homes of the judge and the prosecutor, Ravachol was arrested at Le Véry restaurant following an anarchist rant to his waiter. To avenge Ravachol's arrest, two anarchist cabinetmakers from a group called the Flat Feet brought a bomb into the restaurant concealed in a suitcase. The bomb killed two, including the owner. Merriman, *The Dynamite Club*, 80–81.

7   On November 8, 1892, the French anarchist Émile Henry left a bomb at the offices of the Carmaux Mining Company in Paris as retribution for a coal mining strike that began over the summer. The package aroused suspicion, so it was brought to the police station on *rue des Bons-Enfants*, where it exploded killing four police officers and an office worker. Merriman, *The Dynamite Club*, 99–105.

8   On December 9, 1893, Auguste Vaillant threw a bomb into the French Chamber of Deputies, injuring a few people but killing no one.

VII
Ferrer and the General Strike

Ferrer's political interests and strategic orientations ranged from rationalist pedagogy through popular insurrection, to the general strike (and quite possibly targeted propaganda by the deed as well). After about sixteen years living in Paris, Ferrer returned to Spain, where he used the fortune that his former student Ernestine Meunié had left him when she died in April 1901 to fund the creation of the Modern School, which opened on September 9, 1901, the Boletín de la Escuela Moderna, *which appeared on October 30, 1901, and the anarchist labor periodical* La Huelga General: Periódico Libertario *(The General Strike: Libertarian Periodical), whose first issue was released on November 15, 1901.*[1]

Ferrer's interest in the general strike was undoubtedly influenced by the growth of revolutionary syndicalism in France and the rise of the CGT (Confédération générale du travail) as the era of French propaganda by the deed faded. Conditions were also ripe for the promotion of the general strike in Spain, where restrictions on political activity were lifted in 1900 after four years of repression in response to the bombing of a religious procession in Barcelona in 1896. In October of that year, the predominantly anarchist Federación Regional de Sociedades de Resistencia de la Región Española was formed with an initial membership of fifty-two thousand—the largest anarchist-oriented labor federation in Spain since the collapse of the FTRE (Federación de Trabajadores de la Región Española) in 1888 and the collapse of its successor, Pacto de Unión y Solidaridad de los Trabajadores de la Región Española, in 1896. Before long the new Federación adopted La Huelga General *as its official organ.*[2]

La Huelga General *was an eight-page biweekly paper (later weekly) financed by Ferrer and directed by Ignacio Clariá, with illustrations from Fermín Sagristá.[3] The paper boasted an all-star team of turn of the century libertarian collaborators, ranging from Spaniards such as Teresa Claramunt, Federico Urales (Joan Montseny), Anselmo Lorenzo, Soledad Gustavo (Teresa Mañé), Fermín Salvochea, Fernando Tarrida del Mármol, and Luis Bonafulla to foreigners like Pyotr Kropotkin, Errico Malatesta, Elisée Reclus, Domela Nieuwenhuis, Jean Grave, Charles Malato, and Paraf-Javal.[4] Yet Ferrer's wealth led some anarchist labor organizers to question his participation in this venture, while, on the other side, some individualists were critical of his interest in unionism.[5] Certainly some eyes might have rolled in response to his article "The General Strike Will Enrich the Poor without Impoverishing the Rich," which argued that the wealthy would be allowed to continue living in their extravagant homes after the revolution. Ferrer's fortune generated tension in the movement and perhaps internally as well.*

In February 1902, the long awaited general strike arrived, when groups affiliated with the new Federación in Barcelona declared the largest general strike Europe had witnessed since 1893, with between eighty and a hundred thousand workers walking off the job. The authorities brought in the army, which fired machine guns at workers' barricades. By the end of the month the strike was broken with little to show for it.[6] During the strike La Huelga General *editor Ignacio Clariá was seriously injured and arrested for distributing anti-militarist and general strike pamphlets and sentenced to twelve years in prison.[7] With Clariá and many other collaborators in prison and Ferrer laying low, the paper suspended publication, reappearing on January 25, 1903.*

The first edition printed after the strike included Ferrer's article "Preparing the General Strike," attributed to his usual pseudonym "Cero" (Zero), which he used in order to advocate violent insurrection without alienating any of the Modern School parents or risking prosecution.[8] In this article, Ferrer argues that any gain in wages won through a strike would be cancelled out by rises in the cost of living. Therefore, reflecting upon the failure of the previous year, he insists that strikes are really only worthwhile if they are revolutionary, and they are only revolutionary if they meet the violence of the state with the violence of the working class. Throughout the pages of La Huelga General *Ferrer used his pseudonym to abandon the public "respectability" that undergirded his educational ventures and urge readers onward toward the "last baptism of human blood" necessary for the creation of a new world. This supports the arguments of historians Juan Avilés and Joaquin Romero Maura that Ferrer and most of his Spanish anarchist comrades were not yet interested in the philosophy of revolutionary syndicalism per se as much as they saw the general strike as an opportunity to jump toward popular insurrection. Such revolutionary syndicalist ideology would not really solidify itself in Spain until the formation of Solidaridad Obrera (Worker's Solidarity) in 1907.[9] Ultimately* La Huelga General *would print its last edition, twenty-first overall, on June 20, 1903.*

1. God or the State: NO—The General Strike: YES

(*La Huelga General*, November 25, 1901)

You won't find anyone of good faith, as unintelligent as they may be, who would confess that religion, whether Catholic, Protestant, Muslim, or Buddhist, has achieved peace and goodwill among men.

No politician, of whichever party or however independent, will be able to assure that their system of government guarantees the absolute freedom to speak or write or assures the right to life.[10]

Those who want to give supremacy to the clergy believe just as strongly as those who put all of their faith in a more or less lay state that there have to be poor and rich, masters and servants.

Neither pursues the economic and political emancipation of the individual.

We can excuse the first liberals, who, upon realizing the religious hoax, dedicated themselves to founding a state free from contact with Rome, because they could believe that all evil came from the Church.

But those who practice the parliamentary system today, monarchists, republicans, or socialists, trick their voters just as the priests abuse the credulity of their parishioners. These politicians make the people hope that they will bring liberty and peace to the heart of the nation with the government of their party or through the program of their invention.

No voter exists who can name a good government.

Neither from the centuries when religions were born nor from the kings who used their parliaments and assemblies for their own purposes, not even from the past century, which was almost completely marked by parliamentary governments, can we find an example of the usefulness of delegating the care of our interests to others. We need not look farther than the year of electoral struggle waged by the governmental socialist party.[11] What good has voting done workers?

On the other hand, if whatever time the socialists had spent on electoral struggles had been dedicated to the organization of the productive classes and anti-military propaganda, we would already have had a general strike that would have destroyed bourgeois society.

It is up to the libertarians to explain these truths to those thoughtless people who believe in the panacea of the vote, as if it were the host that would take them to paradise.[12]

The complete emancipation of the workers will come neither from the Church nor the state, but rather from the general strike that will destroy both.

Cero [Ferrer]

2. The General Strike Will Enrich the Poor without Impoverishing the Rich

(*La Huelga General*, December 5, 1901)

The belief that the rich allow the poor to survive, and that without them there would be even more misery, is so deeply rooted that it takes a lot of work to convince people of its falsity.

Neither the poor need the rich nor vice versa.

A rational organization of work and an equitable distribution of its products will suffice to eliminate the two classes that today's society of producers and consumers is divided into; that is to say, of the poor and the rich.

Only a well-planned and organized general strike can achieve the golden age dreamed of by past and present altruists.

It will benefit everyone who is today deprived of something: beggars, workers, employees, small shopkeepers, and the majority of those who hold university degrees.

In contrast, those who call themselves rich will continue being rich, because they will continue to live in their luxurious homes, moreover being provided with life's necessities.

The incorporation of their superfluous wealth (land, subsoil, and machines) into the universal patrimony will allow production to satisfy the needs of all.

Ok now.

Is a general strike possible?
Yes.

How will it happen?

When a sufficient number of workers and employees make themselves capable of logically organizing society.

What measures should be adopted from the first moment to assure its triumph?

The trade federations will *only* start the production and exchange of products once they have dissolved, demolished, and exterminated the cogs that compose the capitalist regime: the state, sustained morally by the Church and materially by the army; the courts, sustained by the police.

What will happen to the cops, to the judges and lawyers, soldiers, priests, and public employees?

Being the weakest after the general strike, they will have to adapt themselves to the new state of things and they will be the first to accept the new mode of being, which will assure them a dignified life without any other obligation than to contribute to the development of the regime of human solidarity.

The rich will be happier than today, because they will continue to enjoy without seeing others suffer.

The poor won't envy the rich, because they won't lack anything.

Cero [Ferrer]

3. Will There Be Blood?—Yes, a Lot

(*La Huelga General*, January 5, 1902)

It's not that we desire a bloody revolution. We have provided too much proof of our love for humanity for anyone to think that we are bloodthirsty.

This publication that honors us by printing our simple writings joins the ranks of the press precisely to study the capital matter of the general strike, not in a warlike fashion but with a fervent desire to find an effective solution for the tremendous social conflict that makes the life of the majority into an existence filled with suffering and deprivation.

We will bring to light as many theoretical and tactical articles and pamphlets as are necessary for the workers and the most disinherited to realize their force and their power. We are not impatient, and there is no reason to be. We know well that our journey will be long, but we do not doubt that working methodically we will find abundant fruit at the end.

Like the advice from Cruz in another article in this issue,[13] the same as given by other compañeros, it cannot be ignored, there is no doubt that the day will come when the proletariat considers itself sufficiently organized to confront the bourgeoisie triggering the greatest phenomenon that history will have recorded.

The hoarders of wealth—landowners, manufacturers, bankers, etc., etc.—and their supporters—soldiers, priests, judges, police, etc., etc.—rather than being reasonable and intelligent by trying to support the change of regime from one of exploitation to another of fraternity and solidarity, want to put up resistance by hiding behind the chests of the Civil Guard and the soldiers who have not been contaminated by our propaganda. And so, naturally, the reprisals will be terrible.

What unchained furies, as if suddenly the thousands of victims who died from hunger or were murdered by all of the governmental injustices burst out of their tombs, eager for ferocious revenge. What a devastating torrent will be unleashed by the popular masses upon all obstacles that oppose their supreme vindication. And so, yes, the blood will run and spill everywhere.

What laments! What curses, now that it's too late!

Serene, firm, and unperturbed, the Revolution follows its triumphant path. Perhaps without deploring spilled blood, it fixes the mind on the new era of peace and justice that, with the last baptism of human blood, will be established for the first time, giving rise to a society that is really worth living in.

Cero [Ferrer]

4. The Republicans Are Not Revolutionaries—Only the General Strike Will Make the Revolution

(*La Huelga General*, February 15, 1902)

In this article Ferrer gives the reader a brief glimpse into his personal political evolution from revolutionary republican to libertarian. He rails against his former comrades for either cozying up to the monarchy or spending all of their time conspiring in small hierarchical committees entirely removed from popular struggles and putting all of their faith in winning over the army in the nineteenth-century tradition of the pronunciamiento.[14] *After witnessing the personal failures of republican politicians and the shortcomings of existing republics, most notably France, Ferrer concludes that "the Republic isn't enough anymore" for society or for himself.*

During the first years of the Restoration, Don Manuel [Ruiz Zorilla] conspired in Paris with figures like Martos, Montero Ríos, and Canalejas.[15]

When many generals offered him their sword, and even Sagasta[16] and Serrano[17] were about to enter into the conspiracy, the republican revolution was the constant concern of Cánovas[18] and his master [King Alfonso XII].

Far too honorable to doubt the good faith of his then friends, Señor Ruiz Zorilla confided in them, and the result was what always happens when dealing with politicians: the majority abandoned the republican leader to accept an elevated position or post that the monarchy always offers as a sign of peace to opportunists.

And the impenitent [Ruiz Zorilla] stayed with figures like Muro, Llano y Perso, Santos de la Hoz, Ezquerdo, etc., all furious revolutionaries according to themselves despite having done nothing yet.

If it weren't for Asensio Vega, Cebrián, Mangado, Villacampa,[19] and some others, for twenty years Don Manuel would have been a toy for men who weren't more than candidates for cushy jobs, when they weren't stock market speculators who could have served as a model for the current councilman of this city.

After the military uprisings of Badajoz and Madrid,[20] Martínez Campos and Cánovas devoted all of their energy to preventing their repetition. Toward that end they dissolved the sergeant corps and purged from the army every leader or official who had affectionately served the Republic or was simply branded a liberal.

The monarchy could then sleep tranquilly.

And it has been able to sleep tranquilly ever since, because the revolutionary fervor of the republicans has consisted of forming committees, waiting for orders from the junta, which waits for orders from the *jefe*, who, for his part, continues promising everything to the army.

And the people?

In general, lambs like before: they vote, form coalitions, retreat, return to vote, and look for leaders, who always make themselves directors and masters.

Only the anarchists embark on the right path: to arouse individual valor, educate themselves about social questions, win over converts, self-organize, and federate with the purpose of making the social revolution that will bear the fruit of years of propaganda in favor of the general strike.

If the republicans had united with the people to go forward with the real revolution, the loyalty of the soldiers to the monarchy would have meant nothing. But they didn't do it, and now it's too late to try.

Libertarian propaganda has penetrated the masses too much for them to support career politicians who have no way to make the revolution nor do they dare to promise anything but *what the other republics have conceded.*

For this reason, conscious workers don't pay attention, knowing too much about what is going on in republics that are nearby and distant. They are also convinced that with half the time that the republican leaders have spent enjoying banquets and foretelling the exact day of our next victory, they would be prepared for the great battle.

But it will be a revolution in fact rather than name; not to elect constituent deputies to vote for new laws, sophists all of them, but rather to seize all of the social wealth and organize labor in such a way that the products are the property of all and not of some to the detriment of others, as necessarily happens under every government.

When the bourgeoisie finds itself faced with the social revolution it will try to stop it by offering the republic, the eight-hour day, minimum wage, and however much drivel may be put up for discussion by the politicians. Just as the Revolution of 1830 in France sent Charles X and his delayed reforms packing, we anarchists will send away the exploiters with their deceitful concessions.

The Republic isn't enough anymore.

We prepare the general strike.

Cero [Ferrer]

5. Preparing the Revolutionary General Strike

(*La Huelga General*, January 25, 1903)

Experience, our greatest teacher, has amply demonstrated to us that if in some cases workers can somewhat improve their condition using the only weapon that their current level of power provides—the strike—they will not be able to turn to it peacefully to emancipate themselves from wage labor, their most oppressive yoke.

In effect, even with as many strikes as workers organize and as many demands as they present, they will always find themselves faced with the following problem: either the bosses see the possibility to take with one hand what they give with the other, in which case they give in more or less quickly, or they fear that acceding would give up too much, and so they don't give in, thereby subjecting the workers to hunger and governmental outrages.

In the first scenario, the worker will have gained nothing, although at the moment they think they have, since the fatal increase in the price of basic necessities makes it so that the workers face the same misery after the victory that they faced before. The idea of the general strike was born in the second scenario, when the workers became conscious of their weakness before hunger, the brutal police, the murdering Civil Guard, the biased judges, and the inhuman prisons.

Yet many strikers participate in the general strike like republicans at the February 11 banquets,[21] thinking that the mere fact of the strike will be enough to bewilder their enemies. We have to be on guard against this error.

We could spend thirty years organizing general strikes like the ones that have been carried out until now, and we would find ourselves as far from social emancipation as the republicans are from achieving the republic by force of their incessant banquets.

A general strike means the common, instant action of all workers not to ask for this or that improvement from their masters, but rather to eliminate the masters. It is about replacing the regime of wage labor, which is always necessarily unjust and exploitative, with a regime of solidarity and general well-being. That is the meaning of the general strike.

That is how a group of manufacturers from a city near Barcelona understood it when the February general strike erupted. Terrified, they met to offer their workers all of the improvements that they had rejected up until that day and make even better promises for the future, because they expected to see their factories engulfed in flames and their reign of exploitation ended.

It would be better not to organize a general strike if it had to be peaceful, and preferable not to make the revolution if we had to content ourselves with burning buildings and carrying out reprisals against our tormentors. No, dear compañeros. We need to aim higher.

May every conscious worker study for themselves what a society without masters, authorities, or money could look like; may they exchange ideas with their compañeros in the resistance societies;[22] may they promote the discussion of the general strike in the labor federations. May we arrive at an agreement about the mode of production, exchange, and distribution of products for the day after the general strike, and the rest, which is to say, the methods to make the revolutionary strike victorious. Cero [Ferrer]

6. Property and the Anarchists: The Crazy and the Reasonable
(*La Huelga General*, November 15, 1901)

It is well-known that most popular knowledge is based in what people need to know on a daily basis. Very few reflect on what they read, and few have been able to understand the anarchist ideal.

Anarchists are commonly thought to be ferocious murderers funded by the Jesuits or deceitful parasites; that if one day the impossible should occur and they come to *govern*, nothing would be safe and no one would possess the smallest object for themselves since they pursue the destruction of property.

It is necessary to comprehend, and it will have to be repeated frequently, that in a reasonable society, which is to say anarchist, everyone will have their own house, their own furniture, their own clothing, their own works of art, their own instruments of labor. In short, they will have whatever makes life worth living.

Naturally we won't transition from a regime of lunatics like the one based on authority and property that we live in today to one based on solidarity and true fraternity as easily as one changes sets in a theater. Rather, it's necessary that all of the propaganda, education, and living examples that the logical among us have to offer be given to the illogical, to the unthinking, to the irrational, to the crazy people who today compose the immense majority.

We anarchists want to destroy property as it currently exists, because it is the product of the exploitation of man by man, of the privilege granted by governments, and of the right of the strongest.

We anarchists do not want there to be landowners with large tracts of land next to families that don't have anywhere to rest their bodies. We oppose a world where there are inheritors of fortunes and inheritors of miseries.

We libertarians do not want a title or a will to allow anyone to spend their life without working.

In the ideal anarchist society, education and instruction of the youth will be designed so that all understand the necessity of labor without any exceptions apart from unavoidable physical ailments. And since we won't have the current bad example of some working while others go for a stroll, of some eating while others yawn with hunger, everyone will contribute to the production of the common wealth according to their abilities and all will eat according to their appetites. It will be easy for educators to incul-cate children with the pleasure and general obligation of labor.

Since men are reasonable, as opposed to what occurs today, in the future they will easily find the way to be the proprietors of that which surrounds them without this right to property harming anyone or creating any kind of supremacy.

Precisely, the craziness of those who don't understand anarchy is based in their inability to conceive of a truly reasonable society.

Cero [Ferrer]

Notes

1   Juan Avilés, *Francisco Ferrer y Guardia: pedagogo, anarquista y mártir* (Madrid: Marcial Pons, 2006), 65. Not to be confused with a paper of the same name published clandestinely out of Paris during the same era. José Álvarez Junco, *El emperador del paralelo: Lerroux y la demogogia populista* (Madrid: Alianza, 1990), 295–96.

2   The Federación was essentially defunct by 1905. Ángel Herrerín López, *Anarquía, dinamita, y revolución social: violencia y repression en la España de entre siglos (1868–1909)* (Madrid: Catarata, 2011), 203–4, 208; George Esenwein, *Anarchist Ideology and the Spanish Working-Class Movement in Spain, 1868–1898* (Berkeley: University of California Press, 1989), 118, 199.

3   Diego Abad de Santillan, foreword in *La Huelga general: periódico libertario* (Vaduz-Georgetown: Cabildo, 1975). Available at the IISG.

4   *La Huelga General*, November 15, 1901.

5   Herrerín López, *Anarquía, dinamita, y revolución social*, 204.

6   Eduardo González Calleja, *La razón de la fuerza: orden público, subversión y violencia política en la España de la Restauración (1875–1917)* (Madrid: Consejo Superior de Investigaciones Científicas, 1998), 316; Joan Connelly Ullman, *La semana trágica: estudio sobre las causas socioeconómicas del anticlericalismo en España (1898–1912)* (Barcelona: Ediciones Ariel, 1968), 131–33.

7   According to Urales, Clariá received the antimilitarist tract from Mateo Morral. Eduard Masjuan, *Un héroe trágico del anarquismo español: Mateo Morral, 1879–1906* (Barcelona: Icaria editorial, 2009), 153–54.

8   It was not widely known that "Cero" was Ferrer until Anselmo Lorenzo published the writings of "Cero" in a pamphlet with Ferrer's name after his death. Avilés, *Francisco Ferrer y Guardia*, 129–30.

9   Ibid., 128; Joaquín Romero Maura, *La rosa de fuego: el obrerismo barcelonés de 1899 a 1909* (Barcelona: Ediciones Grijalbo, S.A., 1975), 205–6.

10   This is not a reference to the present-day abortion debate. Rather, he means the right to be able to live one's life with all of the rights and resources that entails.

11   Referring to the Partido Socialista Obrero Español (Spanish Socialist Workers' Party, PSOE), founded in 1879.

12   The host of the Catholic mass.

13 A. Cruz, "La Federación de Oficios y la Huelga General," *La Huelga General*, January 5, 1902.

14 In an 1896 article in the republican *El País*, Ferrer expresses early concern that the people were getting fed up with the ineptitude of republican leaders. Ferrer writes: "We have not lacked [political] unions and coalitions; but I believe that we have not seen practical results. We must keep an eye on the present Unión. This is not about distrust or discouragement; but we must keep an eye, I repeat. The *pueblo* is tired. It has been tricked so many times that it is always afraid. May the central junta of the Unión Republicana work with energy and continue to do so. But it better work. The *pueblo* demands it." F. Ferrer, "Los enemigos del pueblo: en Francia como en España," *El País*, May 5, 1896.

15 Cristino Martos, Eugenio Montero Ríos, and José Canalejas were prominent republican politicians who eventually joined the dynastic Liberal Party. This was viewed as a betrayal by Ferrer, Ruiz Zorrilla, and other intransigent republicans.

16 Práxedes Mateo Sagasta was the main republican to make peace with the monarchy after the fall of the Republic, by leading the Liberal Party and serving as Spanish prime minister five times.

17 Francisco Serrano was a prominent military politician and the prime minister during the reign of Amadeo of Savoy and again under the First Republic.

18 Antonio Cánovas del Castillo was the main architect of the Restoration regime and a six-time prime minister before his assassination at the hands of the Italian anarchist Michelle Angiolillo in 1897.

19 Military figures who helped plan republican coups during the Restoration.

20 Military uprisings for a republic in Badajoz on August 5, 1883 and Madrid on September 19, 1886.

21 Anniversary of the proclamation of the First Republic in Spain, often celebrated by republicans with banquets.

22 Essentially a synonym for a union during this period.

VIII

Ferrer's Prison Poems

Ferrer spent about a year imprisoned in Madrid's Cárcel Modelo while awaiting trial for his alleged participation in Mateo Morral's bombing of the royal wedding procession on May 31, 1906. Although he was trapped behind the prison walls, Ferrer maintained an active correspondence with his comrades, especially with his close friend Charles Malato, who often sent him newspapers so he could keep abreast of the international campaign in his defense. In September 1906, Ferrer grew extremely agitated when Millán Astray, the prison director whose son of the same name would become Francisco Franco's "military mentor,"[1] decided that the light in Ferrer's cell should be left on all night and that guards should monitor him nearly constantly. Ferrer wrote to Malato that he was suffering "two martyrdoms: the moral martyrdom of be surveilled at my door by the guard and the material martyrdom of suffering an electric light over my head all night." He was so agitated that he asked Malato, "Was this how it started in Montjuich?"[2] referring to the torture of anarchist prisons in Montjuich Castle in the 1890s.

In November 1906, however, Astray was removed from his post in favor of the relatively progressive sociologist and criminologist Rafael Salillas.[3] The next day, Salillas turned off Ferrer's light at night and removed the guards who were watching him. Over the following months Salillas, who was a great admirer of the criminological works of Cesare Lombroso, observed Ferrer's activities with a special focus on how he decorated his prison walls by plastering images from magazines and writing poems. After Ferrer's acquittal, Salillas published an article analyzing Ferrer's conduct that included his poems and photographs of the magazine pages on his walls.[4] Below is a selection of Ferrer's prison poems.

As long as there exists a *cuerpo de penales*[5] and prisons
where they provide their services,
no nation can call itself civilized that harbors them.

★ ★ ★

Don't expect anything from others
for although the wise and the powerful
may offer you beautiful things,
if they give they also enslave.

★ ★ ★

To seek accord among men
based in love and fraternity
without distinction of sex or class
is the great task of humanity.

We dedicate everything to it
in the rationalist schools
teaching our students
only scientific truths.

★ ★ ★

The same truths proven
by experience and history
give the disinherited classes
the good path toward their victory,
and without finding themselves cheated
we give them another notorious truth:
the workers will emancipate themselves
when, convinced of their strength,
they take control by themselves
without relying any more on the elected.

★ ★ ★

A Thought:
If men were reasonable
They would not allow injustices
Against themselves, nor against their fellow men
Neither would they want to produce them.

★ ★ ★

Let no more gods or exploiters be worshipped or served!
Let us all learn instead to love each other![6]

Notes

1   Astray the son founded the Spanish Foreign Legion in Morocco, giving it the slogan "Long Live Death!" Peter Anderson, *The Francoist Military Trials: Terror and Complicity, 1939–1945* (New York: Routledge, 2010), 13, 19.
2   Ferrer to Malato, September 23, 1906 in UCSD, Box 1, Folder 4.
3   Ferrer attributed this change to the intervention of the liberal politician Count Romanones, who occasionally lent a sympathetic ear to radicals. During this period Federico Urales (Joan Montseny) acted as an intermediary between Ferrer and Romanones. As the Ministro de Gracia y Justicia, Romanones had Ferrer's potential punishment reduced from death to sixteen years. Ferrer to Malato, November 18, 1906 in UCSD, Box 1, Folder 4; RAH, Archivo Romanones, Leg. 52, exp. 59 and Leg. 53 exp. 12; Juan Avilés, *Francisco Ferrer y Guardia: pedagogo, anarquista y mártir* (Madrid: Marcial Pons, 2006), 176.
4   Rafael Salillas, "La celda de Ferrer," *Revista penitenciaria*, Año IV, Tomo IV, Entrega 1a (Madrid: Eduardo Arias, 1907), 321–47.
5   *Cuerpo de penales* referred to the entire prison staff not only the guards. "El cuerpo de penales," *Revista de la Prisiones*, August 15 and September 1, 1895.
6   Translation from: *Francisco Ferrer: His Life, Work and Martyrdom* (New York: Francisco Ferrer Association, 1910), 89.

IX

The International League for the Rational Education of Children
Boletín de la Escuela Moderna, **November 1, 1908**

While sitting in jail awaiting trial for his alleged participation in the bombing of the royal wedding, Ferrer wrote to his friend and ardent defender William Heaford, secretary general of the English Freethinkers' League, about his idea to create "a league for the defense of the liberty of rationalist education throughout the world."[1] His experience being subjected to the monarchical judicial system of Spain seems to have enhanced his focus on expanding the cause of rationalist education to a more prominent international level. To that end, after his acquittal he set about establishing an international league and (re)founding papers to disseminate its principles. Ferrer rees-tablished the Boletín de la Escuela Moderna *under the leadership of Juan Colominas.[2] After printing a single issue in July 1907, it ran regularly from May 1908 through April 1909. In April 1908, he also founded its francophone counterpart* L'École rénovée *(The Renewed School) in Brussels. Edited by J.F. Elslander, it soon became the official organ of the* Ligue internationale pour l'éducation rationnelle de l'enfance *(International League for the Rational Education of Children) founded around the same time.[3] Soon thereafter, Ferrer funded affiliated periodicals such as* La Scuola Laica *(The Lay School), edited by Luigi Fabbri in Rome starting in May 1908.[4] The new edition of the* Boletín *and* L'École rénovée *published many of the same articles.* L'École rénovée *was originally published out of Brussels before being moved to Paris. Despite Ferrer's aspirations, the paper did not surpass 360 subscribers.[5] After Ferrer's death,* L'École rénovée *ceased publication and was replaced by* L'École émancipée, *which became the organ of the French teachers' union.[6]*

Unfortunately for Ferrer, the Ligue did not fare much better. Although it boasted prestigious international adherents, such as Paul Robin, Pyotr

Kropotkin, Charles Malato, Sébastien Faure, Georges Yvetot, Marcel Sembat, Alfred Naquet, and Lucien Descaves, in addition to the board members listed below, by the end of 1908 there were only 442 Ligue members, half of them in the four French groups (Paris, Toulon, Charente, Loir-et-Cher).[7] The conclusion of the following announcement includes news about the creation of a Barcelona branch. Eventually one was constituted under the presidency of José Casasola, a former Modern School teacher and Solidaridad Obrera organizer who ran a rationalist school in Catalonia. Ferrer's partner, Soledad Villafranca, was the treasurer, and her brother-in-law José Robles, the director of a rationalist school in the El Poblenou district of Barcelona, was the vice president. Cristóbal Litrán, who would take over the Modern School publishing house after Ferrer's death, was branch secretary. As this list of Barcelona officers indicates, the Barcelona branch of the Ligue did not extend beyond Ferrer's social circles and had little impact on the city.[8] The Cuban branch of the Ligue seems to have had a wider reach, with the participation of a variety of anarchist, socialist, republican, and labor leaders. It opened three rationalist schools in 1909.[9] National sections were also formed in Uruguay (Montevideo), Italy (Rome and Milan), Belgium (Anvers), and Germany (Frankfurt). After Ferrer's death, Soledad Villafranca took over the presidency of the Ligue Internationale as the organization fizzled out over the next few years.[10]

This announcement of the formation of the Ligue lays out the basic tenets and purposes of the new organization. The Ligue committee issues a cross-class appeal to all who hold "rational thoughts and humanitarian sentiments." The authors of the text emphasize distinguishing between enseñanza *and* educación—*two nearly identical Spanish words that are both routinely translated as "education." For the Ligue committee,* enseñanza *entailed the routinized ingestion of outdated information, while* educación *embodied modern, rationalist education freely chosen by the student. Because the specific meanings loaded into these two terms in this text are difficult to fully capture through translation,* enseñanza *and* educación *(as well as their infinitives,* enseñar *and* educar, *and related conjugations) have been left untranslated.*

Headquarters: Boulevard Saint-Martin, 21, Paris
Board of Directors:

| F. Ferrer Guardia | (Spain) | *President* |
| C.A. Laisant | (France) | *Vice President* |

Ernst Haeckel	(Germany)	*Board member*
J.F. Elslander	(Belgium)	*Board member*
Giuseppe Sergi	(Italy)	*Board member*
William Heaford	(England)	*Board member*
H. Roorda Van Eysinga	(Switzerland)	*Board member*
Henriette Meyer		*Secretary*

This League aims to substitute general *enseñanza*, whether traditionally dogmatic or modernized or lay, with rational *educación*. It has the object of putting an end to error, the child of ignorance, perpetuated by routine and by the interest of the privileged. It seeks to clear the path for the truth, demonstrated or induced, so that, accepting only the positive and the rational, human relations may be the faithful expression of equity and possess the character of the most beautiful fraternity as they emerge from the freedom of physiologically and morally balanced individuals.

It has been said with truth that all political and social problems are essentially pedagogical; which is to say that it has been recognized that to extirpate the effects of error it is necessary to delve below the man, the governor and the governed, the rich or the poor, to focus on the ingenuity of the boy and the girl, and from this truly natural and human perspective separate them from the conventionalisms and lies of the current mentality, free them from arrogance and servility, from vanity and hypocrisy, put them face to face with things and facts, methodically develop their faculties of observation and comprehension with the goal of having them see, judge, know, and create in a perfectly experimental and rational mode, never by the authority of a teacher, of prestigious authors, or even less by public opinion.

Until now, *enseñar* and *educar* have been considered to be equivalent ideas, without taking into account that enseñanza is the transmission of acquired knowledge and also of dominant ideas, while educación is the development of physical, intellectual, and moral faculties. In *enseñanza* there can be, and surely always is, violence, because the teacher, in the service of an authority and a doctrine, imposes a belief and a submissiveness; *enseña* to believe and obey. In *educación* there can and should be respect for the human personality. This is because the educator, attentive to whatever may facilitate knowledge acquired through one's own observation and ready to supply the requested information, allows the attention of the student to sustain itself through its own sensations and naturally run free. Although at first the student's attention is incoherent, later it fastens to manifestations of desire and necessity until finally, with a sufficient degree of development and supplied with multiple and various forms of knowledge, it relates to, connects with, and discovers laws and finds itself in a state of making applications relative to the specialty to which it is dedicated.

Our reason for being is essentially located in this difference: the International League for the Rational Education of Children seeks to establish itself on firm terrain and head directly toward the truth, avoiding confusions and false analogies or equivalences, precursors of the fatally anti-progressive and irrational deviations of the future. Moreover, to further clarify the dividing line, we insist:

> *Enseñanza* regulates knowledge; it submits the infinite variety of individual aptitudes to a systematic unity; it disregards the mental initiative of the student; it makes the student learn outdated orthodoxies and whatever is inadequate and useless must be forgotten; it provides a negligible amount of useful knowledge and covers its deficiencies with the farce of the exam and the degree that in many cases serves to exploit a privilege—because it provides an official capacity it often opposes a positive capacity.
>
> *Educación*, by means of the educator and the broad environment created by modern pedagogy, puts the child in the position to develop their inclination and their capacity to freely take part in the knowledge that is needed by the universal treasure of science, today monopolized and unnecessarily complicated by the systems of *enseñanza*, rather than being provided for everyone for the benefit of the individual and society.

With this foundation and these goals, we address ourselves to all of the lovers of truth and justice,[11] asking them to join the International League for the Rational Education of Children.

Given the fact that simply by educating children rationally there can emerge generations capable of religious, political, and economic emancipation, we want to dedicate our efforts to the propagation, development, and defense of this educación as far as our radius of action will reach.

We call for membership, desiring to make this League strong and numerous, and we do it not hiding the fact that we face a tremendous struggle not only against our popular atavism and the classical enemies of all progress, but moreover against those who have made a business out of enseñanza. We also face the supporters of some schools that are copying French laicism, which despite their attractive titles and certain practices that have a scientific and liberal appearance are barely any different than the official and traditional schools, all of them aimed at forming mentalities that are more or less submissive to social prejudices. They will incapacitate the children of today, the men of tomorrow, by preventing them from being able to freely and rationally judge and solve the conflicts of private and social life.

Our mission is clear and precise:

To disseminate books in pure harmony with rationalist education;
To support the teachers that use them in their schools;
To inform teachers unfamiliar with these books about their value, encouraging them to adopt them;
To aid existing rationalist schools;
To work so that those schools that are not rationalist come to be;
To found them wherever possible;
And, finally, to gain members for the League and found groups so that little by little rationalist education will not be ignored anywhere.

We direct ourselves particularly to those employees, small business-people, and all of those who suffer without compensation under the regime of religious, political, and above all economic tyranny. We also appeal to the privileged who, despite their position, have rational thoughts and humanitarian sentiments, and in general to the workers who we call upon to, in addition to working to emancipate themselves from capitalism, think about how greatly it interests them that their children receive an educación that suits their aspirations for the liberty and well-being of all.

The League has set annual membership dues at 1.20 pesetas for administrative expenses.

The International League for the Rational Education of Children, which has as its organ in French-language countries the periodical *L'École rénovée*, of Brussels, and in Italy the *Scuola Laica*, of Rome, will have as its organ in Spanish-speaking countries the *Boletín de la Escuela Moderna*, of Barcelona; but League members will be up to date on matters of interest without needing to subscribe to the *Boletín* by virtue of notices or other publicity.

Men and women of goodwill, think of how progress is not indolent "laisser-faire," neither is it the realization of a providential miracle, of an effect without a cause, but rather a result, a product in a time of many incidents and events initiated more or less consciously. May each of our activities be in harmony with our ideal. Heed our call as one of many methods of progressive action and, just as you contribute to a useful and necessary work, feel the satisfaction that is experienced when one has fulfilled a duty.

★ ★ ★

The formation of a Barcelona group of the International League for the Rational Education of Children is in progress.

Those who sympathize with the goals of this institution and want to cooperate with it can contact this administration.

Notes

1   Francisco Bergasa,*¿Quién mató a Ferrer i Guardia?* (Madrid: Aguilar, 2009), 129; William Archer, *The Life, Trial and Death of Francisco Ferrer* (New York: Moffat, Yard and Co., 1911), 82.

2   Bergasa, *¿Quién mató a Ferrer i Guardia?*, 134.

3   See the letter from Ferrer to Laisant on November 20, 1907 about his prioritizing getting the review going before the Ligue. UCSD, Box 1, Folder 16. Originally Ferrer was going to call the paper *l'École nouvelle*. He was also planning on opening a "normal school" to train teachers who would teach in the "*école nouvelle*." He also proposed creating a museum. "Correspondances et Communications," *Les Temps nouveaux*, December 14, 1907.

4   There may also have been affiliated papers called *La Razón* and *Rayo* out of Peru. Peter Tiidu Park, "The European Reaction to the Execution of Francisco Ferrer" (PhD diss., University of Virginia, 1970), 57; Comité de défense des victimes de la répression espagnole, *Un martyr des prêtres: Francisco Ferrer, 10 janvier 1859–13 octobre 1909: sa vie, son ouvre* (Paris: Schleicher frères, 1909), 28; Sol Ferrer, *Le véritable Francisco Ferrer: d'après des documents inédits* (Paris: L'Écran du monde, 1948), 158; Maurice de Vroede, "Francisco Ferrer et la Ligue Internationale pour l'Éducation Rationnelle de l'Enfance," *Paedagogica Historica* 19 (1979): 290.

5   Juan Avilés, *Francisco Ferrer y Guardia: pedagogo, anarquista y mártir* (Madrid: Marcial Pons, 2006), 200–3.

6   IISG, Augustin Frédéric Adolphe Hamon Papers, 105, Ligue Internationale pour Éducation; André Henry, *Serviteurs d'idéal: histoire de la longue marche, des associations, des coopératives, des mutuelles et des syndicats* (Paris: Centre fédéral FEN, 1987), 251; Bergasa, *¿Quién mató a Ferrer i Guardia?*, 134.

7   On June 21, 1908, *Boletín* editor Juan Colominas wrote to Ferrer saying of his work with the Ligue, "Your activity does not have many imitators." *Causa contra Francisco Ferrer Guardia: instruida y fallada por la Jurisdicción de Guerra en Barcelona, año 1909* (Madrid: Sucesores de J.A. García, 1911), 402–3; Comité de

défense des victimes de la repression espagnole, *Un martyr des prêtres: Francisco Ferrer, 10 janvier 1859–13 octobre 1909: sa vie, son ouvre* (Paris: Schleicher frères, 1909), 28; Park, "The European Reaction," 56–57; de Vroede, "Francisco Ferrer et la Ligue Internationale," 290. To make matters worse, Ferrer had a conflict with Ligue secretary Henriette Meyer. Avilés, *Francisco Ferrer y Guardia*, 205. For the statutes of the Ligue, see IISG, Augustin Frédéric Adolphe Hamon Papers, 105, Ligue Internationale pour Education.

8   Other board members of the Barcelona branch included Alfredo Meseguer, Pascual Camps, and Agustín García. *Boletín de la Escuela Moderna*, April 1, 1909; Avilés, *Francisco Ferrer y Guardia*, 205. Casasola's rationalist school was called Colegio de la Place. Joan Connelly Ullman, *La semana trágica: estudio sobre las causas socioeconómicas del anticlericalismo en España (1898–1912)* (Barcelona: Ediciones Ariel, 1968), 175. *La Enseñanza Moderna: revista quincenal pedagógico-racionalista* was founded in Irún in 1908 and was loosely affiliated with the Ligue. UCSD, FB 133, 134.

9   One school existed in Regla, while two others were about to open in Matanzas and Marianao. Organizers also opened a subscription for a school in Havana. *Les Temps nouveaux*, February 20, 1909; *¡Tierra!*, November 13, 1909; Amparo Sanchez Cobos, *Sembrando ideales: anarquistas españoles en Cuba, 1902–1925* (Sevilla: Consejo Superior de Investigaciones Científicas, 2008), 233–35. For the membership and mission statement of the Cuban committee, see *¡Tierra!*, March 13, 1909.

10 The Italian section had fifty-two members, while there were fifty-eight in Belgium. De Vroede, "Francisco Ferrer et la Ligue Internationale," 290. For the membership of the Ligue committee in 1910, see *Les Temps nouveaux*, May 28, 1910. There are scattered references to Ligue activity in 1910 and 1911. *Les Temps nouveaux*, August 20, 1910, December 10, 1910, April 1, 1911.

11 The slogan "Truth and Justice" became so powerfully associated with the pro-Dreyfus faction of the French Dreyfus Affair at the turn of the century that they came to be known as *"les Véritards-justiciards."* This phrasing was likely intended to appeal to veterans of the Dreyfus Affair. Richard Griffiths, *The Use of Abuse: The Polemics of the Dreyfus Affair and its Aftermath* (New York: Berg, 1991), 19.

X

Francisco Ferrer: The Martyr
Mark Bray

Francisco Ferrer's arrest and subsequent execution by firing squad on October 13, 1909 sparked protests across Europe and beyond, transforming him into a widely vaunted martyr for lay education, anticlericalism, and "progress." The Ferrer movement of 1909 built upon years of transnational activism among unionists, lawyers, journalists, freethinkers, Freemasons, and radicals in defense of the victims of the Spanish crown, primarily in Europe and the Americas, including the 1906 Ferrer campaign and the groundbreaking movement of 1896–1900 in support of anarchists and other radicals who were imprisoned, tortured, and executed in Montjuich Castle. The rhetorical strength of these protest movements against the Spanish government was built upon the motif of the revival of the "medieval barbarity of the Inquisition" in Spain, an updated version of the Black Legend of the sixteenth century that had been steadily promoted abroad for years.

As a result, the Ferrer campaign found eager adherents in historically Catholic countries, including France, Belgium, and Italy, among anticlerical militants and in historically Protestant countries, among them England and the United States, by tapping into longstanding anti-Catholic sentiments. In both campaigns, Ferrer was often referred to as the "Spanish Dreyfus," since the outrage his arrest provoked echoed the infamous Dreyfus Affair of turn of the century France. The movement also benefitted from the fact that many moderate and liberal sympathizers thought that Ferrer was a republican freethinker, rather than a revolutionary anarchist. This misconception stemmed from Ferrer's decision to publish his incendiary perspectives under a pen name, and it was strategically deployed by anarchist and radical supporters to garner mainstream support. This angered

Kiosk toppled during Paris protest on the day of Ferrer's execution. FFG.

some anarchists, including Rudolf Großmann (aka Pierre Ramus), who complained that Ferrer was being described as "merely a bourgeois free-thinker and reformed pedagogue" and his image being used "exclusively for anticlerical and anti-Catholic purposes."[1] Nevertheless, the 1909 Ferrer movement established a powerful precedent for the transnational activism of the following decades, as represented in the Sacco and Vanzetti campaign among others.

The Ferrer Protest Movement of 1909

As in 1906, the Ferrer campaign was strongest in France where Ferrer had lived for fifteen years. Not long after his arrest, Ferrer's Parisian comrades formed the Comité de défense des victimes de la répression espagnole to coordinate pro-Ferrer activities. The Comité united various factions including prominent international anarchists like Pyotr Kropotkin, Jean Grave, Fernando Tarrida del Mármol, and Charles Malato, socialists like Séverine, Victor Merio, and Guy Bowman of the Social Democratic Federation, unionists like Émile Pouget, academics like Ernst Haeckel and the Italian anthropologist Giuseppe Sergi, and poets and artists like Charles Morice and Pierre Quillard. Another notable signatory was the Mexican revolutionary Manuel Sarabia of Ricardo Flores Magón's Partido Liberal Mexicano.[2] The

Innovative automobile pro-Ferrer protest in Paris. *Nuevo Mundo*, Oct. 1, 1909. AEP

Ligue des droits de l'homme (League of the Rights of Man) and the CGT labor federation soon officially endorsed the campaign, and pro-Ferrer intellectuals organized a petition of university professors that managed to obtain 152 signatures, including that of Émile Durkheim. Even Captain Alfred Dreyfus of the infamous Dreyfus Affair publicly supported the Ferrer committee. Labor demonstrations and innovative motorcade protests involving thousands were organized across France over the following weeks, in addition to sporadic attempts at coordinating a boycott of Spanish goods.[3] The political breadth of pro-Ferrer organizers in France was largely equivalent in other national movements showing how his execution offended a very widely held sense of justice. Yet many more moderate and liberal elements only really threw their support behind the campaign in the weeks after Ferrer's execution.[4] The night of the execution, a riot broke out at the Spanish embassy in Paris, where protesters tore up benches and trees, extinguished streetlamps, broke bank windows, mounted barricades, with one protester fatally shot a police officer.[5] Four days later, the largest pro-Ferrer event of the campaign occurred when Parisian socialists organized a calm, peaceful procession of fifty to sixty thousand, which drew the ire of some anarchists for its disavowal of conflict.[6]

Pro-Ferrer protest in Rome. *Nuevo Mundo*, Oct. 21, 1909. AEP.

After France, the most vibrant protest movement developed in Italy where general strikes, demonstrations, protest resolutions, boycotts, and sporadic anticlerical violence gripped seemingly every city in the country for a week. The day after Ferrer's execution, work ground to a halt in cities such as Milan, Florence, and Turin, where strikers attacked non-striking street cars in an effort to shut down their cities. The strike was equally successful in Rome, where 760 protesters were arrested amid a sea of tumult that included attempts to burn down six churches (the first church burnings in modern Italian anticlerical history), the mob assault of two French priests on October 14, and a separate stoning of twenty German priests five days later. The evening of Ferrer's execution, thousands marched through Genoa shouting, "Viva Ferrer" and "Death to King Alfonso." When the police were unable to slow the march, they opened fire, injuring several demonstrators. The marchers responded by throwing rocks. In Naples, clashes with police and attacks on non-striking streetcars were punctuated by the explosion of a bomb during mass that produced no injuries. One of the most prominent defenders of Francisco Ferrer in the Italian town of Forli was a young socialist named Benito Mussolini. The prestige he generated in supporting Ferrer played a key role in allowing him to attain the position of editor of the local socialist paper, thereby propelling the career of the future founder of Fascism.[7]

Pro-Ferrer demonstration in Brussels, 1909. FFG.

On the same day in Brussels, large demonstrations were organized by predominantly socialist and liberal coalitions. During one evening demonstration, marchers smashed the windows of a Spanish jewelry shop that displayed a portrait of King Alfonso XIII and beat up a plain-clothesman they thought was the royalist jeweler. A violent clash with the police ensued when some marchers attempted to move on to the Spanish embassy. Two days later, marchers in a demonstration organized by the Belgian Jeunes Gardes Socialistes broke windows at a Catholic school, burned Alfonso XIII in effigy, and assaulted two priests. Demonstrations were also organized in the Belgian cities of Namur, Verviers, La Louvière, and Liège, where some protesters broke the windows of a convent and ransacked a church sacristy.[8] Similarly, large demonstrations were organized in Dutch cities such as Rotterdam, The Hague, and Amsterdam, where three to four thousand marchers smashed the windows of the Catholic newspaper *De Tijd* after police prevented them from reaching the Spanish consulate following a large anarchist protest. Protests were organized by coalitions of republicans and socialists across Portugal, where troops were stationed to protect Spanish consulates. A bomb exploded outside a French church in Lisbon causing minor damage to the building, and another bomb was found before it could explode in an Irish Dominican church in the same city about a week later.[9]

Postcard commemorating Ferrer's execution. Caption: "The last vision of Ferrer." © Real Academia de la Historia. España. Legajo 11/8891, Archivo Natalio Rivas.

Many protests were organized in London and elsewhere in England. On October 19, Errico Malatesta and a group of fifty Italian comrades attended one such demonstration of ten thousand people at Trafalgar Square organized by the Social Democratic Party. Eleven thousand people marched through the streets of Berlin, and thousands more organized demonstrations and protest meetings in Frankfurt, Munich, Düsseldorf, and many other cities across Germany for over a week. Although significant protests developed in Germany, they never reached the fevered pitch of their French, Belgian, and Italian counterparts. What is more striking and horrifying, however, is to read how the German right-wing press often attacked Ferrer and the newspapers that defended him for being "Jewish." Even a centrist parliamentary deputy argued that Ferrer was a "murderer, Jew, anarchist, and Freemason who was sentenced and executed in an orderly manner." Nevertheless, thousands more protested in several events in Copenhagen, Denmark, and a protest meeting was organized in Bucharest, Romania. In Russia, the Socialist Revolutionary Party called for a one-day general strike and students protested in Saint Petersburg. Several attacks were launched against Spanish consulates in the Swiss cities of Geneva and Zurich, allegedly organized by Italian and Russian anarchist exiles. Protests also developed in the Bulgarian capital of Sofia, in Athens, Greece, and in Thessaloniki (then still part of the Ottoman Empire). Attempts by the Young Turks to organize a protest in Istanbul were thwarted by authorities, however. Allegedly Ferrer sympathizers burned a Catholic church in Spek (present-day Albania). Demonstrations, general strikes, attacks on Spanish consulates, and protest resolutions also spread across the Austro-Hungarian empire in present-day Austria, Hungary, Czech Republic, Slovakia, Ukraine, Slovenia, and Croatia, as well as German-controlled Poland. The protest movement even extended as far as Teheran, where several thousand marched for Ferrer, and Beirut, where the playwright Daud Muja'is cowrote a play about the Ferrer case that caused him to flee into exile to avoid a seven-month prison sentence.[10]

Across the Atlantic, mobilizations, attempted general strikes, and boycotts developed in Uruguay, Argentina, Paraguay, Chile, Peru, Cuba, and Brazil. Likewise, protest events were held in New York City, Los Angeles, San Francisco, and Wilkes-Barre, in the United States.[11] Demonstrations and commemorations for Ferrer continued over the following years before being overwhelmed by the outbreak of the First World War.[12]

The campaign did not reach mass proportions in Spain itself, however. In part, this is because Ferrer was actually more well-known and highly regarded abroad than at home but also because of the censorship and repression that immobilized any potential campaign. With thousands in and out of jail or in exile in the wake of the most serious insurrection Spain had witnessed since the start of the Restoration, it was not easy to organize a massive campaign in a matter of weeks before Ferrer's rushed execution. Moreover, a number of republican leaders were anxious to distance themselves from the Tragic Week. Eventually some momentum developed among republican and liberal politicians for a revision of Ferrer's case and especially for the ouster of the conservative Maura administration. After some heated debates in Parliament, Prime Minister Maura offered his resignation to the king, thinking he would be turned down. To his utter surprise, the king accepted his resignation as a way to diffuse tensions. Years later the king told Maura's son that he had been forced to "sacrifice" Maura, because it was impossible to "prevail against half of Spain and more than half of Europe."[13] While the fall of the Maura government pleased liberal and republican politicians, the king's amnesty for all Tragic Week prisoners in February 1910 appeased popular indignation, effectively ending the turmoil.[14]

Postcard of Ferrer monument in Brussels. IISG BG A4/856.

Immortalizing Ferrer

Although Ferrer certainly approved of the protest movement that developed in his defense, as he had approved of the earlier movement of 1906, he was very clear in his last will and testament that he thought that "the time dedicated to the dead would be better devoted to improving the condition of the living." He then added, "I also want my friends to speak very little about me or not at all, because idols are created when men are worshipped, which is a great evil for the future of humanity."[15] Given these words, Ferrer might have been horrified to learn that after his death several monuments and hundreds of plaques were created for him, in addition to the renaming of countless streets and plazas.

Certainly, some of his comrades shared his perspective. For example, "A Group of Spanish Anarchists" called for a protest against a commemoration of Ferrer's death in 1910 in the pages of the French anarchist newspaper *l'Anarchie* arguing:

> We believe that the best way to honor the memory of Ferrer would have been to take his wishes into account. The focus should be on his work not on his person. . . . And that is why today we will attend the nauseating spectacle of a Général Peigné [and others] "honoring" the memory of one who would have excoriated them through all his indignation, and whom they would have hunted and shot themselves had it been necessary! Because there is nothing in common between those who live from political and social lies and he who gave even his life for truth and liberty.

When the meeting in question began, anarchists interrupted the Masonic Général Peigné with shouts of "Murderer! Draveil!" (referring to the bloody suppression of a CGT strike in 1908) before they started to sing the *Internationale* over his words. As the disruptions mounted, a

Group of actors in Stará Bělá, Czechoslovakia honor Ferrer on the 25th anniversary of his execution, Oct. 13, 1934 as part of a national day of commemoration across the country.

"general melee developed that degenerated into a brawl." The chaos gave the police an excuse to shut down the meeting before anyone, including Soledad Villafranca, could speak. Ultimately this conflict had much more to do with the sectarian politics that Ferrer's commemoration exacerbated than a specific interpretation of his final wishes.[16]

Similarly, Ferrer's close comrade Charles Malato pointed out that plans to construct a statue to Ferrer in Brussels conflicted with Ferrer's wishes. Ultimately, however, Malato supported its construction as a testament to the Modern School, rather than Ferrer as a man. In 1911, the Brussels statue was erected, but its inscription was removed before the First World War because the Spanish government protested, and during the war German soldiers destroyed it. Other Ferrer statues were erected in São Paulo, Brazil, and in Ostrava, Czechoslovakia, in 1936. Streets were named after Ferrer and the Modern School across France, Belgium, Uruguay, and Italy, where three hundred different cities and towns named a street or square after Ferrer and about two hundred bronze or marble plaques were created in his honor, according to his daughter Sol Ferrer. However, almost all were removed by Mussolini, a one-time Ferrer supporter, following the Lateran Treaty with the Vatican in 1929.[17] In 1934, commemorations of the twenty-fifth anniversary of Ferrer's execution were organized by socialists across Czechoslovakia.[18] During the Spanish

Revolution, many Barcelona streets were renamed for prominent revolutionaries and artists, including Plaça Urquinaona, which was renamed Plaça de F. Ferrer i Guardia.[19] In 1990, a Ferrer monument was constructed on Montjuich.[20] Today Ferrer lies in a grave in Montjuich Cemetery alongside the anarchist legends Buenaventura Durruti and Francisco Ascaso.

The Birth of the International Modern School Movement

Ferrer would have been much happier about the tribute to his legacy that was represented by the vast proliferation of (more or less) rationalist educational initiatives around the world over the decades following his execution. Since those who sought to emulate his efforts around the world did not always have access to his writings, it's unsurprising that the schools they created manifested varying degrees of fealty to the original Barcelona institution. They also struggled to raise money, to find capable teachers, establish quality facilities, and avoid state repression. Nevertheless, they were united in their goal of promoting coeducational, student-centered, participatory education for children (and often adults as well). In this section, I will survey the rise and fall of Ferrerian education around the world until the middle of the century.

The high degree of exchange between Spanish anarchists and radicals and the former Spanish colony of Cuba influenced the development of a significant Ferrerian surge on the island. Although Cuban anarchists had created schools, educational centers, and libraries in Havana and elsewhere since the late nineteenth century, starting around 1905–1906 the "rationalist" ideas of Ferrer and his followers started to influence what had been a relatively traditional view of education despite its anarchist content. In 1905, anarchists created a coed primary and secondary school in Havana called Verdad, which joined an earlier anarchist school named La Enseñanza. By 1908, anarchists created an avowedly Ferrerian school in Regla. In response to this development, Ferrer sent Miguel Martínez Saavedra to Regla to help organize the school, whose directors formed the Cuban section of the Ligue Internationale pour l'Éducation Rationnelle de l'Enfance. In May 1909, Martínez stepped down from the Regla school to help organize a night school in Havana with the anarchist group Redención Social. During this period, more "rationalist" schools were created in Pinar del Río, El Cobre, Sagua la Grande, Cruces, Manzanillo, Matanzas, and Havana. By 1910, however, internal conflicts brought the Regla school to an end. Over the following years, several more groups formed to promote

Ferrer's work such as 13 de Octubre (the date of his execution), the "Soledad Villafranca" group in Matanzas (named after his compañera), and the Agrupación Racionalista Ferrer. The latter group created a new school with forty students that folded in the summer of 1912, when Juan Francisco Moncaleano, a Colombian anarchist professor who directed the school, left to create a rationalist school in Mexico amid the Mexican Revolution. At this point, the Cuban anarchist educational movement stalled before resurfacing in the early 1920s, when anarchists used their influence in the labor movement, through unions such as the Sindicato Fabril, the Unión de Obreros Industriales (a Cuban IWW group), and most importantly the Federación Obrera de la Habana (FOH), to create rationalist schools across the country. By 1923, the FOH school had more than seventy students in both its day school for children and its night school for adults. Yet, by 1925, the anarchist schools had been shuttered by President Gerardo Machado.[21]

When Moncaleano arrived in Mexico in 1912 he formed an anarchist group called Luz, later renamed Lucha, that sought to create a joint workers' center and rationalist school. After some setbacks from police repression, the first Casa del obrero and Escuela Racionalista was opened in September 1912. Soon the new venture grew to become a significant anarcho-syndicalist union representing 150 thousand workers that was renamed the Casa del Obrero Mundial (COM). During the Mexican Revolution, the predominantly urban COM fought against the rural forces of Emiliano Zapata in a tragic clash that antiauthoritarians have lamented. Nevertheless, the expansion of the COM entailed the proliferation of proletarian educational projects influenced by Ferrer. In 1918, one of the Casas del obrero mundial was named "Francisco Ferrer Guardia of Nuevo Laredo," and in the 1920s a Grupo Francisco Ferrer Guardia formed in San Luis Potosí.[22]

Anarchist schools such as Nueva Humanidad de Corrales had been operating in Buenos Aires, Argentina, since the turn of the century, but from the middle of the decade onward specifically Ferrerian institutions started to appear with the support of the anarcho-syndicalist union Federación Obrera Regional Argentina (FORA). Modern Schools were organized in Rosario, Bahía Blanca, Luján, Villa Crespo, Mendoza, Plata, and Buenos Aires. Most of these schools were shut down by authorities in 1909. After Ferrer's death, the mantle of rationalist education was carried forward by Julio Barcos, his most ardent Argentine supporter and the former director of the anarchist Escuela Laica de Lanús and the Escuela Moderna de Buenos Aires. In 1912, Barcos helped create the Liga de

Educación Racionalista (Rationalist Education League), whose organ was called *Francisco Ferrer* before being renamed *La Escuela Popular*. Yet the Liga members developed hostile relations with the anarchist movement, and little of substance came from their efforts.[23]

A very strong Ferrerian current swept across Chile in the 1920s, when at least twenty rationalist schools were created by a variety of labor organizations with anarcho-syndicalist and communist influences. Examples included the Escuela Federal Racionalista de Peñaflor, whose five- to seven-year-old students often attended classes in the evening after working during the day, and the Escuela Federal de Puente Alto, which eschewed rewards and punishments. It also offered a "social action" class oriented around "lessons about proletarian social activities" to inculcate in its seventy students "an appropriate aversion to things unjust." During the early 1920s, the Chilean IWW even organized a Unión Infantil IWW (Union for Children). By the end of the decade, however, some schools were shut down by the liberal Alessandri government and more by the dictatorship of Carlos Ibáñez del Campo soon thereafter.[24]

Several Modern Schools were founded in Brazil during this era. For example, on May 13, 1912, Brazilian anarcho-syndicalists and anarchist communists founded the Escola Moderna de São Paulo, which offered coeducational day and night classes out of its two branches. More Modern Schools were organized in the greater São Paulo area including São Caetano, Campinas, Bauru, and Cândido Rodrigues. The Escola Moderna dos Navegantes was founded in 1914 in Porto Alegre, but unlike other Modern Schools it segregated its students by gender. An Associaçao da Escola Moderna was also founded in Río de Janeiro. Many of the schools were shut down by the government after José Alves, director of the Escola Moderna de São Caetano, and his anarchist comrades accidentally blew themselves up on October 19, 1919.[25] There was a Francisco Ferrer Guardia school in Bolivia as well in the 1920s.[26]

An early Ferrerian school was founded in Liverpool, England, in 1908, by the anarchist and syndicalist James Dick. A year earlier, Lorenzo Portet had introduced Dick to Ferrer following his acquittal for the 1906 calle Mayor bombing in Madrid. At first, the school was a communist Sunday school run by the anarchist-oriented Liverpool Communist Group, before becoming the International Modern School in November 1909, after Ferrer's death. In 1912, the school moved to London where another Ferrerian school had opened in the East End over the summer. A Ferrer

Adult School had also been founded in London in 1910. The International Modern School collapsed shortly thereafter, though it was revived for a time in Whitechapel in the early 1920s. Moreover, in 1905, Italian and Spanish anarchists, including Malatesta and Tarrida del Mármol, had organized a Università Popolare (Popular University) in London.[27]

Years later, James Dick and his wife Nellie became important figures in the Ferrer school with the greatest longevity: the Modern School of Stelton, New Jersey. Originally the school was part of the New York Ferrer Center, which was created in 1911 by the Francisco Ferrer Association (later renamed the Modern School Association of North America). The Ferrer Association formed shortly after Ferrer's execution. Its first president was Leonard Abbott, and Harry Kelly and Emma Goldman were among its charter members. The evolution of the New York Ferrer Center underwent an unexpected jolt, however, when an explosion rocked a Lexington Avenue tenement near the center on July 4, 1914. A bomb that was designed to punish John D. Rockefeller Jr. for his company's massacre of the families of striking miners in Ludlow, Colorado, had exploded prematurely, killing anarchists Arthur Caron, Carl Hanson, and Charles Berg. Since the plot had been hatched at the Ferrer Center with the collaboration of Ferrer Association founder Alexander Berkman, police swarmed the center, making its operations untenable. Therefore, on May 1915, the school was moved to a rural area in Stelton, New Jersey, where it lasted for nearly four decades. Yet, as with most Ferrer schools, the degree of direct influence from Ferrer's writings and works was mixed. Some have even claimed that in Stelton, "Ferrer was seldom mentioned." Memories of the Stelton school vary widely, with some revering it as the epitome of free education, while others, such as the anarcho-syndicalist and Wobbly Sam Dolgoff and his partner Esther, published a mimeo sheet called *Looking Forward* in the early 1930s to protest what they considered to be oppressive elements of the school. Either way, the Stelton school certainly had far less structure than Ferrer's Barcelona school. After supervising the boarding house in Stelton, James and Nellie Dick founded a Modern School on Lake Mohegan, New York, in 1924, and another in Lakewood, New Jersey, in the early 1930s that lasted twenty-five years. In 1910, Josef Jülich, a writer for the anarchist newspaper *Freiheit*, founded the first German Modern School in New York, which lasted about ten years. German anarchists had also organized free schools in Brooklyn and Jersey City in the early 1890s. Most American Modern Schools created shortly after Ferrer's execution lasted little more than a few years, however.

Twenty Modern Schools were founded in American cities, including New York, Philadelphia, Detroit, Seattle, Portland, Chicago, Salt Lake City, Boston, Paterson, San Francisco, and Los Angeles.[28]

In 1910, the anarchist professor Dr. Jean Wintsch founded the École Ferrer in Chailly, outside of Lausanne in Switzerland, with the support of the Fédération des Unions ouvrières de la Suisse romande and the Genevan Anarchist-Communist Circle. Wintsch also created a Société de l'École Ferrer to promote rationalist education in Switzerland. Ultimately the school closed in 1919.[29] In the Netherlands, a series of Ferrerian Ontspanningsschool (literally "Schools of Relaxation") were founded in the first decade of the century. At least three schools were created in Amsterdam, including the Ontspanningsschool in Oosterpark and Ontpanningsschool Haarlemmerpoort en omstreken, which had its own publishing house called De Kinderbibliotheek, in addition to schools in Sneek, Emmer-Compascuum, and Koog aan de Zaan.[30] Moreover, the German anarchist Gustav Landauer designed a Ferrerian educational program during the Bavarian Revolution of 1919, and during the Russian Revolution the anarchist Makhnovschchina of Ukraine were planning a Modern School before they were attacked by the Bolsheviks. Other schools were opened in Italy (La Scuola Moderna Razionalista di Clivio and La Scuola Moderna Francisco Ferrer in Turin), France, Belgium, Germany, Poland, Portugal, Czechoslovakia, Yugoslavia, China, and Japan.[31]

Although most English-language histories of Ferrer and the Modern School emphasize the global spread of rationalist pedagogy, it's strongest and most faithfully Ferrerian impact was felt in Spain itself. Even before his execution, in 1906, the Modern School had forty-seven affiliates in Spain.[32] One of the more prominent schools of this era was the Escuela Moderna of Valencia, which persevered from 1906 to 1914 under the direction of anarchist teachers Samuel Torner, who had taught previously at the Modern School of Vilanova i la Geltrú, and José Casasola, who had taught at Ferrer's Barcelona school and served as the president of the Barcelona branch of the Ligue Internationale. The Valencian Modern School managed to promote the creation of another dozen similar institutions in the Valencia area during this time.[33] Although the period between the Tragic Week of 1909 and the advent of the Second Republic in 1931 was difficult for the development of rationalist education, especially during the dictatorship of General Miguel Primo de Rivera from 1923 to 1930, a number of schools carried on Ferrer's legacy in the years after his execution. In 1914, the famous birth control campaigner Margaret Sanger travelled to Spain to meet with Lorenzo Portet, one of Ferrer's closest collaborators and the inheritor of the Modern School publishing house. Sanger was an anarchist at the time and had come to place a high value on libertarian education. She enrolled her children in the New York Ferrer school, where she also lectured on birth control.[34] In Spain, Portet, whom she described as "a born teacher," took her on a tour of Modern Schools in Sabadell, Granada, and Sevilla, where the students "were being taught the processes of life from the cell up, and their instructors were really trying to give them a scientific instead of a theological attitude." According to Sanger, who clearly received her information from Portet, there were forty-six Ferrer schools in Spain in 1914 and others that used Modern School books.[35] Between 1901 and 1939 at least 160 anarchist educational institutions were established. The actual total was undoubtedly much higher.[36]

More importantly, however, was the fact that Ferrer's ideas were largely adopted by the burgeoning anarcho-syndicalist movement. This was reflected in the original mission statement of the revolutionary syndicalist Solidaridad Obrera, which advocated "rational and scientific education for our children." In 1932, the CNT, its successor organization, added "modern" to this description.[37] One of the most important anarchist schools of the era was the Natura del Arte Fabril y Textil school created in the Clot neighborhood of Barcelona in 1918. This school was directed by the *cenetista* (CNT member) pedagogue Joan Puig Elías, who later ran the Escuela Natura, known as La Farigola, from 1922 to 1936. During the Civil War, he became president of the somewhat Ferrerian Consell de l'Escola Nova Unificada (Council of the New Unified School, CENU), which organized education in Catalonia.[38] Yet, regarding Ferrer's "rationalist" pedagogy, he wrote:

> For me the word "rationalist" has the flavor of another century, an aftertaste of a disciple of Robespierre and of the admirers of the Goddess of Reason. I respect . . . all that comrades have suffered to sustain their school, and when they give it that name it's because they want to signify that they base their teaching in reasoning and not in dogma and imposition. . . . [But] we need a school that above all else cultivates sentiment in the child, that turns every boy into a man with a character capable of knowing how to translate their thoughts into actions.[39]

In response to a similar critique expressed at a congress held in the midst of collectivized Barcelona in October 1936, Floreal Ocaña Sánchez, who ran a Modern School with his sisters Igualdad, Natura, and Fraterna in Hospitalet from 1934 to 1939,[40] defended a more charitable interpretation of Ferrer's rationalism:

> Whoever affirms that the Modern School is only dedicated to the cultivation of reason in the absence of sentiments is completely ignorant of the work of Francisco Ferrer. The custom of speaking constantly about the rationalist school rather than the Modern School has served as a pretext for those who see the strengthening of the human will as a danger for their miserable personal interests . . . and as such they have deceived the *pueblo* and mocked Francisco Ferrer. He always paired the word "rationalist" with the word "humanitarian." . . . The meaning of the school's name is a synthesis of the universal ethic, human and scientific.[41]

Interestingly, many of the most important anarchist educators of the era were *faístas*—members of the Federación Anarquista Ibérica (Iberian Anarchist Federation, FAI)—including Floreal Ocaña Sánchez, José Alberola, Higinio Noja Ruiz, and the anarchist individualist pacifist José Torres Tribó (aka Sol de la vida), who ran a rationalist school in the Guinardó area of Barcelona from 1932 to 1936, when he left the school to help with the process of collectivization of industry. He helped create schools at a number of collectivized workplaces. Although Ocaña Sánchez and Torres Tribó were both faístas, they could not have disagreed more about Ferrer. Torres Tribó spurned Ferrerian rationalism in favor of a Nietzschean individualism. In a quote that would have turned Ferrer's stomach, Torres Tribó argued, "The truth, empirical and ancestral nature, faithful at first, tyrannical, is rectilinear and mechanical. The lie is art, beauty, life created and overcome." Nevertheless, his school bore some resemblance to the Modern School in its emphasis on its students, ages seven to fourteen, learning through exposure to nature. Torres Tribó was known as a tireless worker who taught adults in the evenings after teaching children during the day and devoted his free time to gardening. Tragically, he was murdered in the Mauthausen Nazi concentration camp several years later after being taken prisoner while fighting in the French resistance.[42]

Despite occasional debates on anarchist education, the majority of the Spanish anarcho-syndicalist movement of the 1930s adopted Ferrer's

Barcelona CNT-FAI vendors selling busts of revolutionary figures, including Ferrer (far left), in 1936. IISG BG A37/26.

pedagogy almost entirely and implemented it in a variety of schools for children and adults in *ateneos*, union halls, collectivized workplaces, and other facilities. One notable difference was a marked departure from Ferrer's advocacy of cross-class education in favor of a solidly and self-avowedly proletarian educational agenda. Another was the fact that the anarcho-syndicalist schools took the concept of integral education more seriously than Ferrer by incorporating a far greater focus on learning skills applicable to working-class trades, in addition to more intellectual pursuits.

When the revolutionary combatants of the anarchist militias marched to the front to face Franco's forces during the Spanish Civil War, they carried hopes in their hearts that someday their children could build a new world based on the rationalist, egalitarian, and libertarian principles embodied in Ferrer and the schools he inspired.

On the Death of Ferrer

(*L'École rénovée*, October 20, 1909)

Francisco Ferrer died. He died gloriously in the moats of Montjuich, victim of the terror of governments, victim of the hate that his work aroused.

He had dreamed of a Spain finally liberated from the Inquisition; he had dreamed that one day, in this classic land of intolerance, free thought and triumphant reason would flourish. He had placed all of his confidence in the coming generations; he did his utmost so that they would form free of the prejudices and superstitions that caused his downfall. He gave all of his strength to the education of the youth; he wanted them to be happy and free.

With an absolute selflessness, he lived for them. For them, he fell crying, "*Vive l'École moderne!*" Others will avenge him. If we loved him, we must continue his work.

L'École rénovée was dear to him. For him it was the extension of his Barcelona school. Barely three months ago, he drew up a plan for the next three years with us. Alas! Little did we expect his demise, so awful and so soon!

Now he is dead. He lived courageously: he died a hero. To the howls of the jackals of Spain relentlessly bringing about his downfall, the hyenas of France have responded with their growls. The vermin of all countries always form a holy alliance. He, so sweet and so good, would have scorned it: we will remember.

Ferrer died; he will live in our hearts. *Vive Ferrer! Vive l'École moderne!*

M.D.

Rudolf Rocker on Ferrer[43]

Rudolf Rocker (1873–1958) was a prominent German anarchist known for his organizing work among the Jewish working class of the East End of London as the editor of Arbeter Fraint *and his role in the formation of the anarcho-syndicalist International Workers Association (IWA) in the 1920s. In this excerpt from his memoir, Rocker remembers his first impressions of Ferrer and the lively conversations the two men shared with a diverse group of European anarchist exiles.[44]*

I met Ferrer personally at the May Day demonstration in Hyde Park during his stay in London a year and a half before his execution. Like every year, we had a special platform in the park where orators used to speak in English and other languages. On this occasion, my friend Tarrida del Mármol[45] told me that Ferrer and his compañera had just arrived in London and that they were in the crowd. The name Ferrer had already been familiar to me for a few years. I was a regular reader of the *Boletín de la Escuela Moderna* and *L'École rénovée*, and I also had the occasion to familiarize myself with some of Ferrer's textbooks. Naturally I was quite familiar with the story of his first trial in Madrid, and I had written about him in the *Arbeter Fraint*. I had also published an article about him in September 1908 in *Germinal*, along with a letter from Kropotkin to Ferrer about new methods of education. It was therefore a great surprise for me to get to personally know a man whose work had incurred so much persecution in Spain.

When along with Tarrida I stepped down from the platform after the event, he introduced me to Ferrer and Soledad Villafranca. I saw before me a man of medium stature, dressed in a light gray suit, with a straw hat in his hand. The front of his head was already entirely bald. His hair was trimmed slightly and graying at the temples, as was his short, pointy beard. His somewhat wide face conveyed the impression of calm resolve, and his fiery eyes, which radiated vividly, immediately gave away that he was from southern Europe. Soledad Villafranca was an attractive woman of perfect beauty. Tarrida, upon introducing us, explained that I had participated actively in the protest movement [on behalf of Ferrer] two years earlier, for which Ferrer extended his hand with vigor thanking me cordially.[46] Later we went to a tearoom near the Marble Arch with Malatesta, Tcherkesov,[47] Schapiro,[48] and some other comrades. There we spent several hours in animated conversation that revolved mainly around our magnificent demonstration. When we parted ways Tarrida invited me to visit him a few days later and told me that he would be with Ferrer and his companion as well.

When I entered the cozy home of the kind Tarrida the night of the invitation, I encountered a small group of familiar comrades who were speaking intensely with Ferrer, among them Malatesta, Tcherkesov, Recchioni,[49] and Lorenzo Portet, whom Ferrer named his successor in his educational endeavors in his will the night before his death. The conversation of that night was entirely spontaneous, which is to say that we spoke about diverse topics raised by one or another of those present. The main topics of the conversation, however, were the political situation in Spain, the experiences of Ferrer before and during his Madrid trial, and the perspectives of the Modern School. Ferrer was of the opinion that the monarchy in Spain had lost all moral credibility a while back and that it advanced uncontrollably toward its ruin, which could not be avoided since the old regime was incapable of any internal renewal. Nevertheless, he said that the current state could hold on for perhaps another ten, or even fifteen, years unless unexpected events occur in the meantime that might accelerate the process of internal dissolution. He saw the reason behind the delay in the desperate atomization of the republican parties, which since the death of Pi y Margall had not produced a single man of comprehensive political vision and an equivalent depth of thought.

Ferrer was of the opinion that the first stage of political transformation in Spain had to lead to a federative republic with broad municipal and regional rights and freedoms, since that was the most appropriate for the conditions and traditions of the country. But such a decomposition of the political conditions of power by the decentralization of the social administration would entail in itself a profound alteration of the existing economic conditions, especially since the great majority of the Spanish workers' movement distrusts all of the political parties, including the republicans, and considers its unions to be the best point of departure for all new economic aspirations. For this reason, it was inevitable that the unions would have great influence in a system of federated towns and regions, which would lead to completely new economic experiments. A purely political revolution, Ferrer said, would be too late for Spain, because it was probable that the abolition of the monarchy would lead to years and years of tension and serve as a crucial point for a new social development.

When asked about his personal experiences in prison during his Madrid trial, Ferrer said that he had been treated well. They had allowed him to receive all of the books that his friends had sent him except two French editions. The first was *A Confession* by Tolstoy, and the other was *In Praise of Folly*, an essay by Erasmus, the world-famous humanist from Rotterdam. When he asked the judge about the motive behind such a strange prohibition, he responded with an evasive gesture, without fixing on an explanation.

. . .

What struck me most strongly about Ferrer was the simplicity of his words and the charming way that he expressed his thoughts. Each of his words breathed a spirit of inner sincerity, which made his every pose singular. One could see this most clearly when he spoke about his work and the people who were closest to him. He spoke with great enthusiasm about his new plan to found a free university in Barcelona. He knew he could not escape the fact that he would have to overcome some serious challenges, particularly the selection of the professoriate, but he believed that little by little he would manage to defeat these challenges as well. When asked about the current situation of the schools in existence, Ferrer explained that more than eight thousand children attended them. It is not difficult to fill the schools with children; it is much more difficult to suppress the counterproductive influences that children often face at home, especially in families where diverse interpretations of life exist between parents. To avoid this, they have organized regular meetings with parents and teachers that have proven excellent. "Principally it is important to develop entire beings and not only fragments," he said smiling. "A complete Catholic is generally better than a semi-freethinker."

It was a very pleasant soiree, and we spent many hours before finally deciding to end it and say goodbye. Who could have thought then that this sincere man, animated by such philanthropic ideas, would end his laborious life five months later in the moats of Montjuich Castle?

Ferrer as His Friends Saw Him by Renato Rugieres[50]

It is almost impossible to write or to speak of a loved friend when the wound of his death is still fresh in our heart, and our eyes full of tears. But, in spite of all, I feel it my duty to consecrate some lines to the martyr's memory.

The last long chat I had with him was in "Mas Germinal," near Mongat, on July 3, 1909, viz., some days before the general strike protesting against the war, which strike ended in an unexpected manner.

I had received a letter inviting me to spend a day with him. I well remember him. It seems as though I see him now at the Mongat station waiting for me. It was ten o'clock. He was wearing a simple linen suit and a straw hat, like an ordinary farmer. He received me with his accustomed amiability, and embraced me very affectionately. On the road to "Mas Germinal" he spoke to me about his stay at his brother's.

"You know," he said, "that my dear niece died, and on account of her illness I am here. I intended to stay in London some months more in order to improve my knowledge of the English language, and search for something good and useful for our schools. In England there are many thinkers, and although their writings are intended for their own people, we can use them by making a few explanations in the translations of them. When we reach home, I will show you a book I have already read, and I should like to publish it. Have the kindness to translate into Spanish, if you consider it in accordance with our aims. The passages marked with blue pencil, and others with ink, you may take out; they touch upon religious matters, and our books are for laical teaching."

The good man who politely begged for my opinion and my help, was helping me by giving me that work of translation! The "dangerous" book, which I had no time to finish before I left Barcelona, was *The Children's Book of Moral Lessons* by Gould; printed by a publishing firm in Fleet Street, London. English people should know the book so that they may be able to judge the "terrible evil" educationist Ferrer was doing in the land of Maria Santisima.

On arriving at the farm "Mas Germinal," I met Soledad Villafranca, also wearing the plain country dress, and managing the house; in the garden I encountered Ferrer's brother bending over his beloved soil, gathering his strawberries to carry to Barcelona market early next morning; his wife was also busily employed. Everybody was producing something, and I wondered if the martyr was really rich. The house was a modest one, built in the old-fashioned Spanish style; the furniture was certainly neither choice nor expensive. The happiness of those people, who, instead of living in the stupid manner of the *riches cochons*, preferred to be useful to their fellows by enlightening their minds—I marvel now that it could be destroyed, and in the name of justice!

Before dinner we chatted incessantly about "our" schools—as he called them—encouraging me to take charge of a small one, to make my initiation or debut, because I had never made special pedagogic studies. "Don't worry about those trifles," he said to me kindly; "the aims of the modern teacher ought to be to teach the child how to use his brains; to form from every child a being with his own will, able to know by his own conscience what is wrong and what is right. We do not intend to make lawyers or physicians; we desire only to give the first instructions, free, absolutely free, of religious and some social prejudices. It is a fact," he continued, "a thousand times proved, that the greatest educationists were not professional teachers. You are still young, and maybe someday you will become one of my best collaborators," he finished, smilingly, putting his hand affectionately on my shoulder.

Our unfortunate friend, indeed, is a proof of the truth of his opinions, because he was in his country one of the pioneers of the mode of instruction in the future.

At dinnertime on the table was a big dish containing rice and chicken—chickens are cheap in the Spanish country—and Ferrer said to me laughingly, "Let me help you well, because there are no more dishes besides this one."

The conversation during dinner was chiefly carried on by his brother José, about the farm, potatoes, onions, etc. Then I understood quite well the origin of the saying of their friends. Francisco's friends said, "He is a fanatic about his schools," and José's friends said, "He is a fanatic about his ground and his potatoes." Certainly, they were two fanatics, but their fanaticism could never be like that of the capitalists and priests, who only desire money and power. Nevertheless, one brother has been dispossessed of his farm, and the other martyred by the blind vengeance of priest and capitalist.

In the afternoon we went to the cultivated piece of land, and again the conversation turned on "our" schools. Ah! this noble fanatic, always thinking of the welfare of others. "I have an idea," he said suddenly, taking me by the arm, "merely a dream, even Soledad does not know it. You know," he added, "that I intend to extend my publishing business, and to establish in Barcelona another "Modern School," better than that which was closed years ago, furnished with the most modern material and with the staff who have improved their knowledge in Paris. Afterwards, and *this* is my dream, I should like to build here a country house, where the teachers of our schools could enjoy their last years. Do you think the place is nice? Look at these beautiful views, the trees, the sea, and overall plenty of sun. It is only a dream," he said sadly; "I do not know if it will be possible or not. One finds so many difficulties in carrying out educational work in a country where the priests are in power!"

At five o'clock we entered the cottage to take tea, English tea, which reminded me of my first day in this country last year. The brother José and his wife were in Australia for many years, and therefore they speak English like natives. Soledad was trying to compete with me in my broken pronunciation of English, and they were all very much amused at our efforts.

When about six o'clock my regretted friend and I reached Mongat station, he pointed out to me a man of repulsive appearance on the platform, and in a low voice, and smiling, said to me, "That is 'my man'"—this was the name he gave to the secret policeman ordered by the Government to follow him everywhere when in Spain. "Do you not think it is a funny affair? Happily, this one is very lazy, and he does not like to disturb himself to follow me up to 'Mas Germinal.' Only when I go to Barcelona, he accompanies me."[51]

The train arrived; we shook hands, and I entered a second-class car of the Spanish "tortoise railway." The train departed. Once more my feelings of admiration and love for that noble man increased. In his private life and in his public affairs he was the same. He *practiced* his ideals. No wonder he lost his life for them! This is the "terrible criminal" who, according to Maura's Cabinet, was at that time arranging the burning of the convents and the profanation of the graves!

One of the most frequent, and at the same time unjust, charges made against him by the Jesuits and the rotten Catalonian capitalists of the so-called "Liga Regionalista," is that in the laical schools dangerous doctrines were taught against the "pure" society, home life, order, holy jingoism, and so on. I was in one of the best Rationalist schools in Barcelona for some months, serving what one may call my "apprenticeship" at the modern teaching; therefore I am able to testify that not a word was said there which the most strict and severe judge, if honorable, could call lawbreaking. No incitement to violent methods, no insults against the priests. Nothing, absolutely nothing, which was not perfectly within the limits of justice and truth.

The Jesuits, the Catalonian capitalists of the "Liga," Maura and his friends, I am almost sure know as well as I what kind of instruction was given in the schools, which caused the murder of the noble founder and supporter; but they were anxious to crush Ferrer at any cost, because his schools might destroy the power of that black confederation of tyrants. Therefore, they were, and are, trying to confound the educationist Ferrer with the "Apaches" who have been given the very much calumniated name of Anarchist.

Truth will shine someday, and those who now approve the murder of Ferrer, because they did not know him personally or his work, will be the first to render homage to this martyr of modern civilization. The man whose death can cause tears, even to those who only knew him by his work and good deeds, and can arouse an almost international protest against the murderers, certainly was not an "Apache."

Rest in peace, beloved friend; thy memory will always live in my heart and in the hearts of all those who in any way fight for freedom.

—From London *Freedom.*

The Significance of Ferrer's Death by Emma Goldman[52]

Never before in the history of the world has one man's death so thoroughly united struggling mankind.

Never before has one man's death called forth such a universal cry of indignation.

Never before has one man's death so completely torn the veil from the sinister face of the hydra-headed monster, the Catholic Church.

Never before in the history of the world has one man's death so shaken the thrones of the golden calf, and spread ghastly fear among its worshipers.

One solitary death, yet more powerful than a million cringing lives. More powerful even than that black specter which, for almost two thousand years, has tortured man's soul and poisoned his mind.

Francisco Ferrer stretched in the ditch at Montjuich, his tender, all-too-loving heart silenced by twelve bullets—yet speaking, speaking in a voice so loud, so clear, so deep. . . . Wherein lies the secret of this wonderful phenomenon?

Francisco Ferrer the Anarchist and teacher? Yes, but there were other Anarchists and teachers, Louise Michel and Elisée Reclus, for instance, beloved by many. Yet why has their death not proved such a tremendous force?

Francisco Ferrer, the founder of the Modern School? But, then, the Modern School did not originate with Francisco Ferrer, though it was he who carried it to Spain. The father of the Modern School is Paul Robin, the latter-day Dr. Pascal—old in years, with the spirit of Spring, tender and loving, he taught modern methods of education long before Ferrer. He originated the first Modern School at Cempuis, near Paris, wherein children found a home, a warm, beautiful atmosphere.

Again, there is Sébastien Faure and his Beehive (La Ruche). He, too, has founded a Modern School, a free, happy, and harmonious place for children. There are scores of modern schools in France, yet no other man's death will act as a fertilizing force as that of Francisco Ferrer.

Was Ferrer's influence so great because of a lifetime of devoted effort? During eight years his heroic spirit strove to spread the light in the dark land of his birth. For eight years he toiled, ceaselessly, to rescue the child from the destructive influence of superstition. One hundred and nine schools with seventy thousand pupils crowned the gigantic efforts of our murdered comrade, while three hundred and eight liberal schools spring into being, thanks to his beneficial influence. Yet all this and more fails to account for the tremendous volcano that swept the civilized world at Francisco Ferrer's death.

His trial was a farce. The evidence against him perjured. But was there ever a time when the State hesitated to resort to perjury when dealing with opponents? Was there ever a time when it exercised justice toward those who endangered its stronghold? The State is the very embodiment of injustice and perjury. Some make a pretense at fairness: Spain was brazen, that is all.

What, then, is the secret of the phenomenon?

★ ★ ★

Driven from its omnipotent position of open crime by the world's progress, the Catholic Church has not ceased to be a virulent poison within the social body. Its Borgia methods merely became more hidden, more secret, yet nonetheless malignant and perfidious. Cowed into apparent submission, it had not dared since the days of Huss and Bruno to openly demand a noble victim's blood. But at last, blinded by arrogance and conceit and the insatiable thirst for martyrs' blood, the Catholic Church forgot the progress of the world, forgot the spirit of our age, forgot the growth of free ideas. As of old, it was the Jesuit hand that stretched forth its bloody fingers to snatch its victim. It was the Archbishop of Barcelona who, in a statement signed by the prelates of the Church, first denounced Ferrer and demanded his life. As of old, Inquisition methods were used in the incarceration and mock trial of Ferrer. No time was to be given the progressive world to check the premeditated murder. Hastily and secretly was the martyr assassinated. Full well the Church knew that the dead cannot be saved.

In vain the frantic efforts of Church and State to connect Francisco Ferrer with the uprising at Barcelona. In vain their delirious cries defaming the character of the dead. In vain the scurrilous attacks of their harlots upon the ideas and comrades of Ferrer—attacks which have now reached even the American press.

Before the awakened consciousness of mankind the world over the Catholic Church stands condemned as the instigator and perpetrator of the foul crime committed at Montjuich. It is this awakened human consciousness which has resurrected Francisco Ferrer.

Therein lies the secret of the force of one man's death, of one solitary man in the ditch of Montjuich.

Francisco Ferrer by Voltairine de Cleyre[53]

In all unsuccessful social upheavals there are two terrors: the Red—that is, the people, the mob; the White—that is, the reprisal.

When a year ago today the lightning of the White Terror shot out of that netherest blackness of Social Depth, the Spanish Torture House, and laid in the ditch of Montjuich a human being who but a moment before had been the personification of manhood, in the flower of life, in the strength and pride of a balanced intellect, full of the purpose of a great and growing undertaking—that of the Modern Schools—humanity at large received a blow in the face which it could not understand.

Stunned, bewildered, shocked, it recoiled and stood gaping with astonishment. How to explain it? The average individual—certainly the average individual in America—could not believe it possible that any group of persons calling themselves a government, let it be of the worst and most despotic, could slay a man for being a teacher, a teacher of modern sciences, a builder of hygienic schools, a publisher of textbooks. No: they could not believe it. Their minds staggered back and shook refusal. It was not so; it could not be so. The man was shot—that was sure. He was dead, and there was no raising him out of the ditch to question him. The Spanish government had certainly proceeded in an unjustifiable manner in court-martialing him and sentencing him without giving him a chance at defense. But surely he had been guilty of something; surely he must have rioted, or instigated riot, or done some desperate act of rebellion; for never could it be that in the twentieth century a country of Europe could kill a peaceful man whose aim in life was to educate children in geography, arithmetic, geology, physics, chemistry, singing, and languages.

No: it was not possible!—And, for all that, it was possible; it was done, on the 13th of October, one year ago today, in the face of Europe, standing with tied hands to look on at the murder.

And from that day on, controversy between the awakened who understood, the reactionists who likewise understood, and their follow-ers on both sides who have half understood, has surged up and down and left confusion pretty badly confounded in the mind of him who did not understand, but sought to.

The men who did him to death, and the institutions they represent have done all in their power to create the impression that Ferrer was a believer in violence, a teacher of the principles of violence, a doer of acts of violence, and an instigator of widespread violence perpetrated by a mass of people. In support of the first they have published reports purporting to be his own writings, have pretended to reproduce seditious pictures from the walls of his classrooms, have declared that he was seen mingling with the rebels during the Catalonian uprising of last year, and that upon trial he was found guilty of having conceived and launched the Spanish rebellion against the Moroccan war. And that his death was a just act of reprisal.

On the other hand, we have had a storm of indignant voices clamoring in his defense, alternately admitting and denying him to be a revolution-ist, alternately contending that his schools taught social rebellion and that they taught nothing but pure science; we have had workmen demonstrat-ing and professors and litterateurs protesting on very opposite grounds; and almost none were able to give definite information for the faith that was in them.

And indeed it has been very difficult to obtain exact information, and still is so. After a year's lapse, it is yet not easy to get the facts disentangled from the fancies—the truths from the lies, and above all from the half-lies.

And even when we have the truths as to the facts, it is still difficult to evaluate them, because of American ignorance of Spanish ignorance. Please understand the phrase. America has not too much to boast of in the way of its learning; but yet it has that much of common knowledge and common education that it does not enter into our minds to conceive of a population 68% of which are unable to read and write, and a good share of the remaining 32% can only read, not write; neither does it at all enter our heads to think that of this 32% of the better informed, the most powerful contingent is composed of those whose distinct, avowed, and deliberate purpose it is to keep the ignorant ignorant.

Whatever may be the sins of Government in this country, or of the Churches—and there are plenty of such sins—at least they have not (save in the case of negro slaves) constituted themselves a conspiratical force to keep out enlightenment—to prevent the people from learning to read and write, or to acquire whatever scientific knowledge their economic circumstances permitted them to. What the unconscious conspiracy of economic circumstance has done, and what conscious manipulations the Government school is guilty of, to render higher education a privilege of the rich and a maintainer of injustice is another matter. But it cannot be charged that the rulers of America seek to render the people illiter-ate. People, therefore, who have grown up in a general atmosphere of thought which regards the government as a provider of education, even as a compeller of education, do not, unless their attention is drawn to the facts, conceive of a state of society in which government is a hostile force, opposed to the enlightenment of the people—its politicians exercising all their ingenuity to sidetrack the demand of the people for schools. How much less do they conceive the hostile force and power of a Church, having behind it an unbroken descent from feudal ages, whose direct interest it is to maintain a closed monopoly of learning, and to keep out of general circulation all scientific information which would tend to destroy the superstitions whereby it thrives.

I say that the American people in general are not informed as to these conditions, and therefore the phenomenon of a teacher killed for instituting and maintaining schools staggers their belief. And when they read the assertions of those who defend the murder, that it was because his schools were instigating the overthrow of social order in Spain, they naturally exclaim: "Ah, that explains it! The man taught sedition, rebellion, riot, in his schools! That is the reason."

Now the truth is, that what Ferrer was teaching in his schools was really instigating the overthrow of the social order of Spain; furthermore it was not only instigating it, but it was making it as certain as the still coming of the daylight out of the night of the east. But not by the teaching of riot; of the use of dagger, bomb, or knife; but by the teaching of the same sciences which are taught in our public schools, through a generally diffused knowledge of which the power of Spain's despotic Church must crumble away. Likewise it was laying the primary foundation for the overthrow of such portions of the State organization as exist by reason of the general ignorance of the people.

The Social Order of Spain ought to be overthrown; must be overthrown, will be overthrown; and Ferrer was doing a mighty work in that direction. The men who killed him knew and understood it well. And they consciously killed him for what he really did; but they have let the outside world suppose they did it, for what he did not do. Knowing there are no words so hated by all governments as "sedition and rebellion," knowing that such words will make the most radical of governments align itself with the most despotic at once, knowing there is nothing which so offends the majority of conservative and peace-loving people everywhere as the idea of violence unordered by authority, they have willfully created the impression that Ferrer's schools were places where children and youths were taught to handle weapons, and to make ready for armed attacks on the government.

They have, as I said before, created this impression in various ways; they have pointed to the fact that the man who in 1906 made the attack on Alfonso's life, had acted as a translator of books used by Ferrer in his schools; they have scattered over Europe and America pictures purporting to be reproductions of drawings in prominent wall spaces in his schools, recommending the violent overthrow of the government.

As to the first of these accusations, I shall consider it later in the lecture; but as to the last, it should be enough to remind any person with an ordinary amount of reflection, that the schools were public places open to anyone, as our schools are; and that if any such pictures had existed, they would have been sufficient cause for shutting up the schools and incarcerating the founder within a day after their appearance on the walls. The Spanish Government has that much sense of how to preserve its own existence, that it would not allow such pictures to hang in a public place for one day. Nor would books preaching sedition have been permitted to be published or circulated—all this is foolish dust sought to be thrown in foolish eyes.

No; the real offense was the real thing that he did. And in order to appreciate its enormity, from the Spanish ruling force's standpoint, let us now consider what that ruling force is, what are the economic and educational conditions of the Spanish people, why and how Ferrer founded the Modern Schools, and what were the subjects taught therein.

Up to the year 1857 there existed no legal provision for general elementary education in Spain. In that year, owing to the liberals having gotten into power in Madrid, after a bitter contest aroused partially by the general political events of Europe, a law making elementary education compulsory was passed. This was two years before Ferrer's birth.

Now it is one thing for a political party, temporarily in possession of power, to pass a law. It is quite another thing to make that law effective, even when wealth and general sentiment are behind it. But when joined to the fact that there is a strong opposition is added the fact that this opposition is in possession of the greatest wealth of the country, that the people to be benefited are often quite as bitterly opposed to their own enlightenment as those who profit by their ignorance, and that those who do ardently desire their own uplift are extremely poor, the difficulty of practicalizing this educational law is partially appreciated.

Ferrer's own boyhood life is an illustration of how much benefit the children of the peasantry reaped from the educational law. His parents were vine dressers; they were eminently orthodox and believed what their priest (who was probably the only man in the little village of Alella able to read) told them: that the Liberals were the emissaries of Satan and that whatever they did was utterly evil. They wanted no such evil thing as popular education about, and would not that their children should have it. Accordingly, even at 13 years of age, the boy was without education—a circumstance which in after years made him more anxious that others should not suffer as he had.

It is self-understood that if it was difficult to found schools in the cities where there existed a degree of popular clamor for them, it was next to impossible in the rural districts where people like Ferrer's parents were the typical inhabitants. The best result obtained by this law in the 20 years from 1857 to 1877 was that, out of 16,000,000 people, 4,000,000 were then able to read and write—75% remaining illiterate. At the end of 1907 the proportion was altered to 6,000,000 literate out of 18,500,000 population, which may be considered as a fairly correct approximate of the present condition.

One of the very great accounting causes for this situation is the extreme poverty of the mass of the populace. In many districts of Spain a laborer's wages are less than $1.00 a week, and nowhere do they equal the poorest workman's wages in America. Of course, it is understood that the cost of living is likewise low; but imagine it as low as you please, it is still evident that the income of the workers is too small to permit them to save anything, even from the most frugal living. The dire struggle to secure food, clothing, and shelter is such that little energy is left where-with to aspire to anything, to demand anything, either for themselves or their children. Unless, therefore, the government provided the buildings, the books, and appliances, and paid the teachers' salaries, it is easy to see that the people most in need of education are least able, and least likely, to provide it for themselves. Furthermore the government itself, unless it can tax the wealthier classes for it, cannot out of such an impoverished source wring sufficient means to provide adequate schools and school equipment.

Now, the wealthiest classes are just the religious orders. According to the statement of Monsignor José Valeda de Gunjado, these orders own two-thirds of the money of the country and one-third of the wealth in property. These orders are utterly opposed to all education except such as they themselves furnish—a lamentable travesty on learning.

As a writer who has investigated these conditions personally, observes, in reply to the question, "Does not the Church provide numbers of schools, day and night, at its own expense?" "It does—unhappily for Spain." It provides schools whose principal aim is to strengthen superstition, follow a mediaeval curriculum, *keep out* scientific light—and prevent other and better schools from being established.

A Spanish educational journal (*La Escuela Española*), not Ferrer's journal, declared in 1907 that these schools were largely "without light or ventilation, dens of death, ignorance, and bad training." It was estimated that 50,000 children died every year in consequence of the mischievous character of the school rooms. And even to schools like these, there were half a million children in Spain who could gain no admittance.

As to the teachers, they are allowed a salary ranging from $50.00 to $100.00 a year; but this is provided, not by the State, but through voluntary donations from the parents. So that a teacher, in addition to his legitimate functions, must perform those of collector of his own salary.

Now conceive that he is endeavoring to collect it from parents whose wages amount to two or three dollars a week; and you will not be surprised at the case reported by a Madrid paper in 1903 of a master's having canvassed a district to find how many parents would contribute if he opened a school. Out of one hundred families, three promised their support!

Is it any wonder that the law of compulsory education is a mockery? How could it be anything else?

Now let us look at the products of this popular ignorance, and we shall presently understand why the Church fosters it, why it fights education; and also why the Catalonian insurrection of 1909, which began as a strike of workers in protest against the Moroccan war, ended in mob attacks upon convents, monasteries, and churches.

I have already quoted the statement of a high Spanish prelate that the religious orders of Spain own two-thirds of the money of Spain, and one-third of the wealth in property. Whether this estimate is precisely correct or not, it is sufficiently near correctness to make us aware that at least a great portion of the wealth of the country has passed into their hands—a state not widely differing from that existing in France prior to the great Revolution. Before the insurrection of last year, the city of Barcelona alone had 165 convents, many of which were exceedingly rich. The province of Catalonia maintained 2,300 of these institutions. Aside from these religious orders with their accumulations of wealth, the Church itself, the united body of priests not in orders, is immensely wealthy. Conceive that in the Cathedral at Toledo there is an image of the Virgin whose wardrobe alone would be sufficient to build hundreds of schools. Imagine that this doll, which is supposed to symbolize the forlorn young woman who in her pain and sorrow and need was driven to seek shelter in a stable, whose life was ever lowly, and who is called the Mother of Sorrows—imagine that this image of her has become a vulgar coquette sporting a robe where into are sown 85,000 pearls, besides as many more sapphires, amethysts, and diamonds!

Oh, what a decoration for the mother of the Carpenter of Nazareth! What a vision for the dying eyes on the Cross to look forward to! What an outcome of the gospel of salvation free to the poor and lowly, taught by the poorest and the lowliest—that the humble keeper of the humble household of the despised little village of Judea should be imaged forth as a Queen of Gauds, bedizened with a crown worth $25,000 and bracelets valued at $10,000 more. The Virgin Mary, the Daughter of the Stable, transformed into a diamond merchant's showcase!

And this in the midst of men and women working for just enough to keep the skin upon the bone; in the midst of children who are denied the primary necessities of childhood.

Now I ask you, when the fury of these people burst, as under the provocation they received it was inevitable that it should burst, was it any wonder that it manifested itself in mob violence against the institutions which mock their suffering by this useless, senseless, criminal waste of wealth in the face of utter need?

Will someone now whisper in our ears that there are women in America who decorate themselves with more jewels than the Virgin of Toledo, and throw away the price of a school on a useless decoration in a single night; while within a radius of five miles from them there are also uneducated children, for whom our School Boards can provide no place?

Yes, it is so; let them remember the mobs of Barcelona!

And let me remember I am talking about Spain!

The question naturally intrudes: How does the Church, how do the religious orders manage to accumulate such wealth? Remember first that they are old, and of unbroken continuance for hundreds of years. That various forms of acquisition, in operation for centuries, would produce immense accumulations, even supposing nothing but legitimate purchases and gifts. But when we consider the actual means whereby money is daily absorbed from the people by these institutions we receive a shock which sets all our notions of the triumph of Modern Science topsy-turvy.

It is almost impossible to realize, and yet it is true, that the Spanish Church still deals in that infamous "graft" against which Martin Luther hurled the splendid force of his wrath four hundred years ago. The Church of Spain still sells indulgences. Every Catholic bookstore, and every priest, has them for sale. They are called *"bulas."* Their prices range from about 15 to 25 cents, and they constitute an elastic excuse for doing pretty much what the possessor pleases to do, providing it is not a capital crime, for a definitely named period.

Probably there is no one in America so little able to believe this condition to exist, as the ordinary well-informed Roman Catholic. I have myself listened to priests of the Roman faith giving the conditions on which pardon for venal offenses might be obtained; and they had nothing to do with money. They consisted in saying a certain number of prayers at stated periods, with specified intent. While that may be a very illogical way of putting things together that have no connection, there is nothing in it to offend one's ideas of honesty. The enlightened conscience of an entire mass of people has demanded that a spiritual offense be dealt with by spiritual means. It would revolt at the idea that such grace could be written out on paper and sold either to the highest bidder or for a fixed price.

But now conceive what happens where a people are illiterate, regarding written documents with that superstitious awe which those who cannot read always have for the mysterious language of learning; regarding them besides with the combination of fear and reverence which the ignorant believer entertains for the visible sign of Supernatural Power, the Power which holds over him the threat of eternal punishment—and you will have what goes on in Spain. Add to this that such a condition of fear and gullibility on the side of the people, is the great opportunity of the religious "grafter." Whatever number of honest, self-sacrificing, devoted people may be attracted to the service of the Church, there will certainly be found also, the cheat, the impostor, the searcher for ease and power.

These indulgences, which for 15 or 25 cents pardon the buyer for his past sins, but are good only till he sins again, constitute a species of permission to do what otherwise is forbidden; the most expensive one, the 25-cent one, is practically a license to hold stolen property up to a certain amount.

Both rich and poor buy these things, the rich of course paying a good deal more than the stipulated sum. But it hardly requires the statement that an immense number of the very poor buy them also. And from this horrible traffic the Church of Spain annually draws millions.

There are other sources of income such as the sale of scapulars, Agnus Deis, charms, and other pieces of trumpery, which goes on all over the Catholic world also, but naturally to no such extent as in Spain, Portugal, and Italy, where popular ignorance may be again measured by the materialism of its religion.

Now, is it reasonable to suppose that the individuals who are thriving upon these sales, want a condition of popular enlightenment? Do they not know how all this traffic would crumble like the ash of a burntout fire, once the blaze of science were to flame through Spain? *They educate!* Yes; they educate the people to believe in these barbaric relics of a dead time—*for their own material interest.* Spain and Portugal are the last resort of the mediaeval church; the monasticism and the Jesuitry which have been expelled from other European countries, and compelled to withdraw from Cuba and the Philippines, have concentrated there; and there they are making their last fight. There they will go down into their eternal grave; but not till Science has invaded the dark corners of the popular intellect.

The political condition is parallel with the religious condition of the people, with the exception that the State is poor while the Church is rich.

There are some elements in the government which are opposed to the Church religiously, which nevertheless do not wish to see its power as an institution upset, because they foresee that the same people who would overthrow the Church, would later overthrow them. These, too, wish to see the people kept ignorant.

Nevertheless, there have been numerous political rebellions in Spain, having for their object the establishment of a republic.

In 1868 there occurred such a rebellion, under the leadership of Ruiz Zorilla. At that time, Ferrer was not quite 20 years old [he was actually nine]. He had acquired an education by his own efforts. He was a declared Republican, as it seems that every young, ardent, bright-minded youth, seeing what the condition of his country was, and wishing for its betterment, would be. Zorilla was for a short time Minister of Public Instruction, under the new government, and very zealous for popular education.

Naturally he became an object of admiration and imitation to Ferrer.

In the early eighties, after various fluctuations of political power, Zorilla, who had been absent from Spain, returned to it, and began the labor of converting the soldiers to republicanism. Ferrer was then a director of railways, and of much service to Zorilla in the practical work of organization. In 1885 this movement culminated in an abortive revolution, wherein both Ferrer and Zorilla took active part, and were accordingly compelled to take refuge in France upon the failure of the insurrection.

It is therefore certain that from his entrance into public agitation till the year 1885, Ferrer was an active revolutionary republican, believing in the overthrow of Spanish tyranny by violence.

There is no question that at that time he said and wrote things which, whether we shall consider them justifiable or not, were openly in favor of forcible rebellion. Such utterances charged against him at the alleged trial in 1909, which were really his, were quotations from this period. Remember he was then 26 years old. When the trial occurred, he was 50 years old. What had been his mental evolution during those 24 years?

In Paris, where, with the exception of a short intermission in 1889 when he visited Spain, he remained for about fifteen years, he naturally drifted into a method of making a living quite common to educated exiles in a foreign land; viz., giving private lessons in his native language. But while this is with most a mere temporary makeshift, which they change for something else as soon as they are able, to Ferrer it revealed what his real business in life should be; he found teaching to be his genuine vocation; so much so that he took part in several movements for popular education in Paris, giving much free service.

This participation in the labor of training the mind, which is always a slow and patient matter, began to have its effect on his conceptions of political change. Slowly the idea of a Spain regenerated through the storm blasts of revolution, mightily and suddenly, faded out of his belief, being replaced, probably almost insensibly, by the idea that a thorough educational enlightenment must precede political transformation, if that transformation were to be permanent. This conviction he voiced with strange power and beauty of expression, when he said to his old revolutionary Republican friend, Alfred Naquet: "Time respects those works alone which Time itself has helped to build."

Naquet himself, old and sinking man as he is, is at this day and hour heart and soul for forcible revolution; admitting all the evils which it engenders and all the dangers of miscarriage which accompany it, he still believes, to quote his own words, that "Revolutions are not only the marvelous accoucheurs of societies; they are also fecundating forces. They fructify men's intelligences; and if they determine the final realization of matured evolutions, they also become, through their action on human minds, points of departure for newer evolutions." Yet he, who thus sings the paean of the uprisen people, with a fire of youth and an ardor of love that sound like the singing of some strong young blacksmith marching at the head of an insurgent column, rather than the quavering voice of an old spent man; he, who was the warm personal friend of Ferrer for many years, and who would surely have wished that his ideal love should also have been his friend's love, he expressly declares that Ferrer was of those who feel themselves drawn to the field of preparative labor, making sure the ground over which the Revolution may march to enduring results.

This then was the ripened condition of his mind, especially after the death of Zorilla, and all his subsequent life and labor is explicable only with this understanding of his mental attitude.

In the confusion of deafening voices, it has been declared that not only did he not take part in last year's manifestations, nor instigate them; but that he in fact had become a Tolstoyan, a non-resistant.

This is not true: he undoubtedly understood that the introduction of popular education into Spain means revolt, sooner or later. And he would certainly have been glad to see a successful revolt overthrow the monarchy at Madrid. He did not wish the people to be submissive; it is one of the fundamental teachings of the schools he founded that the assertive spirit of the child is to be encouraged; that its will is not to be broken; that the sin of other schools is the forcing of obedience. He hoped to help to form a young Spain which would not submit; which would resist, resist consciously, intelligently, steadily. He did not wish to enlighten people merely to render them more sensitive to their pains and deprivations, but that they might so use their enlightenment as to rid themselves of the system of exploitation by Church and State which is responsible for their miseries. By what means they would choose to free themselves, he did not make his affair.

How and when were these schools founded? It was during his long sojourn in Paris, that he had as a private pupil in Spanish, a middle-aged, wealthy, unmarried, Catholic lady. After much conflict over religion between teacher and pupil, the latter modified her orthodoxy greatly; and especially after her journeys to Spain, where she herself saw the condition of public instruction.

Eventually she became interested in Ferrer's conceptions of education, and his desire to establish schools in his own country. And when she died in 1900 (she was then somewhat over 50 years old) she devised a certain part of her property to Ferrer, to be used as he saw fit, feeling assured no doubt that he would see fit to use it not for his personal advantage, but for the purpose so dear to his heart. Which he did.

The bequest amounted to about $150,000; and the first expenditure was for the establishment of the Modern School of Barcelona, in the year 1901.

It should be said that this was not the first of the Modern School movement in Spain; for previous to that, and for several years, there had sprung up, in various parts of the country, a spontaneous movement towards self-education; a very heroic effort, in a way, considering that the teachers were generally workingmen who had spent their day in the shops, and were using the remainder of their exhausted strength to enlighten their fellow workers and the children. These were largely night schools. As there were no means behind these efforts, the buildings in which they were held were of course unsuitable; there was no proper plan of work; no sufficient equipment, and little coordination of labor. A considerable percentage of these schools were already on the decline, when Ferrer, equipped with his splendid organizing ability, his teacher's experience, and Señorita Meunié's endowment, opened the Barcelona School, having as pupils eighteen boys and twelve girls.

So proper to the demand was this effort, that at the end of four years' earnest activity, fifty schools had been established, ten in Barcelona, and forty in the provinces.

In 1906, that is, after five years' work, a banquet was held on Good Friday, at which 1,700 pupils were present.

From 30 to 1,700—that is something. And a banquet in Catholic Spain on Good Friday! A banquet of children who have bade goodbye to the salvation of the soul by the punishment of the stomach! We here may laugh; but in Spain it was a triumph and a menace, which both sides understood.

I have said that Ferrer brought to his work splendid organizing ability. This he speedily put to purpose by enlisting the cooperation of a number of the greatest scientists of Europe in the preparation of textbooks embodying the discoveries of science, couched in language comprehensible to young minds.

So far, I am sorry to say, I have not succeeded in getting copies of these manuals; the Spanish government confiscated most of them, and has probably destroyed them. Still there are some uncaptured sets (one is already in the British Museum) and I make no doubt that within a year or so we shall have translations of most of them.

There were thirty of these manuals all told, comprising the work of the three sections, primary, intermediate, and superior, into which the pupils were divided.

From what I have been able to find out about these books, I believe the most interesting of them all would be the *First Reading Book*. It was prepared by Dr. Odón de Buen, and is said to be at the same time "a speller, a grammar, and an illustrated manual of evolution," "the majestic story of the evolution of the cosmos from the atom to the thinking being, related in a language simple, comprehensible to the child."

Twenty thousand copies of this book were rapidly sold.

Imagine what that meant to Catholic schools! That the babies of Spain should learn nothing about eternal punishment for their deadly sins, and *should* learn that they are one in a long line of unfolding life that started in the lowly sea slime!

The books on geography, physics, and minerology were written in like manner and with like intent by the same author; on anthropology, Dr. Enguerrand wrote, and on evolution, Dr. Letourneau of Paris.

Among the very suggestive works was one on *The Universal Substance*, a collaborate production of Albert Bloch and Paraf Javal, in which the mysteries of existence are resolved into their chemical equivalents, so that the foundations for magic and miracle are unceremoniously cleared out of the intellectual field.

This book was prepared at Ferrer's special request, as an antidote to ancestral leanings, inherited superstitions, the various outside influences counteracting the influences of the school.

The methods of instruction were modeled after earlier attempts in France, and were based on the general idea that physical and intellectual education must continually supplement each other. That no one is really educated, so long as his knowledge is merely the recollection of what he has read or seen in a book. Accordingly, a lesson often consisted of a visit to a factory, a workshop, a studio, or a laboratory, where things were explained and illustrated; or in a class journey to the hills, or the sea, or the open country, where the geological or topographical conditions were studied, or botanical specimens collected and individual observation encouraged.

Very often even book classes were held out of doors, and the children insensibly put in touch with the great pervading influences of nature, a touch too often lost, or never felt at all, in our city environments.

How different was all this from the incomprehensible theology of the Catholic schools to be learned and believed but not understood, the impractical rehearsing of strings of words characteristic of mediaeval survivals! No wonder the Modern Schools grew and grew, and the hatred of the priests waxed hotter and hotter.

Their opportunity came; indeed, they did not wait long.

In the year 1906, on the 31st day of May, not so very long after that Good Friday banquet, occurred the event which they seized upon to crush the Modern School and its founder.

I am not here to speak either for or against Mateo Morral. He was a wealthy young man, of much energy and considerable learning. He had helped to enrich the library of the Modern School and being an excellent linguist, he had offered to make translations of textbooks. Ferrer had accepted the offer. That is all Morral had to do with the Modern School.

But on the day of royal festivities, Morral had it in his head to throw a bomb where it would do some royal hurt. He missed his calculations, and the hurt intended did not take place; but after a short interval, finding himself about to be captured, he killed himself.

Think of him as you please: think that he was a madman who did a madman's act; think that he was a generous enthusiast who in an outburst of long chafing indignation at his country's condition wanted to strike a blow at a tyrannical monarchy, and was willing to give his own life in exchange for the tyrant's; or better than this, reserve your judgment, and say that you know not the man nor his personal condition, nor the special external conditions that prompted him; and that without such knowledge he cannot be judged. But whatever you think of Morral, pray why was Ferrer arrested and the Modern School of Barcelona closed? Why was he thrown in prison and kept there for more than a year? Why was it sought to railroad him before a court-martial, and that attempt failing, the civil trial postponed for all that time?

Why? Why?

Because Ferrer taught science to the children of Spain—and for no other thing. His enemies would have killed him then; but having been compelled to yield an open trial, by the outcry of Europe, they were also compelled to release him. But I imagine I hear, yea hear, the resolute mutter behind the closed walls of the monasteries, the day Ferrer went free. "Go, then; we shall get you again." And then—

And then they would do what three years later they did—*damn him to the ditch of Montjuich.*

Yea, they shut their lips together like the thin lips of Fate and—waited. The hatred of an order has something superb in it—it hates so relentlessly, so constantly, so transcendently; its personnel changes, its hate never alters; it wears one priest's face or another's; itself is identical, inexorable; it pursues to the end.

Did Ferrer know this? Undoubtedly in a general way he did. And yet he was so far from conceiving its appalling remorselessness, that even when he found himself in prison again, and utterly in their power, he could not believe that he would not be freed.

What was this opportunity for which the Jesuitry of Spain waited with such terrible security? The Catalonian uprising. How did they know it would come? As any sane man, not overoptimistic, knows that uprising must come in Spain. Ferrer hoped to sap away the foundations of tyranny through peaceful enlightenment. He was right. But they are also right who say that there are other forces hurling towards those foundations; the greatest of these—*Starvation.*

Now it was plain and simple Starvation that rose to rend its starvers when the Catalonian women rose in mobs to cry against the command that was taking away their fathers and sons to their death in Morocco. The Spanish people did not want the Moroccan war; the Government, in the interest of a number of capitalists, did; but like all governments and all capitalists, it wanted workingmen to do the dying. And they did not want to die, and leave their wives and children to die too. So they rebelled. At first it was the conscious, orderly protest of organized workingmen. But Starvation no more respects the commands of workingmen's unions, than the commands of governments, and other orderly bodies. It has nothing to lose: and it gets away, in its fury, from all management; and it riots.

Where Churches and Monasteries are offensively rich and at ease in the face of Hunger, Hunger takes its revenge. It has long fangs, it rends, and tears, and tramples—the innocent with the guilty—always. It is very horrible! But remember—remember how much more horrible is the long, slow systematic crushing, wasting, drying of men upon their bones, which year after year, century after century, has begotten the Monster, Hunger. Remember the 50,000 innocent children annually slaughtered, the blinded and the crippled children, maimed and forsaken by social power; and behind the smoke and flame of the burning convents of July 1909, see the staring of those sightless eyes.

Ferrer instigate that mad frenzy! Oh, no; it was a mightier than Ferrer!

"Our Lady of Pain"—Our Lady of Hunger—Our Lady with uncut nails and wolf-like teeth—Our Lady who bears the Man-flesh in her body that cannons are to tear—Our Lady the Workingwoman of Spain, ahungered. She incarnated the Red Terror.

And the enemies of Ferrer in 1906, as in 1909, knew that such things would come; and they bided their time.

It is one of those pathetic things which destiny deals, that it was only for love's sake—and most for the love of a little child—who died moreover—that the uprising found Ferrer in Spain at all. He had been in England, investigating schools and methods there from April until the middle of June. Word came that his sister-in-law and his niece were ill, so the 19th of June found him at the little girl's bedside. He intended soon after to go to Paris, but delayed to make some inquiries for a friend concerning the proceedings of the Electrical Society of Barcelona. So the storm caught him as it caught thousands of others.

He went about the business of his publishing house as usual, making the observations of an interested spectator of events. To his friend Naquet he sent a postal card on the 26th of July, in which he spoke of the heroism of the women, the lack of coordination in the people's movements, and the total absence of leaders, as a curious phenomenon. Hearing soon after that he was to be arrested, he secluded himself for five weeks. The "White Terror" was in full sway; 3,000 men, women, and children had been arrested, incarcerated, inhumanly treated. Then the Chief Prosecutor issued the statement that Ferrer was "the director of the revolutionary movement."

Too indignant to listen to the appeals of his friends, he started to Barcelona to give himself up and demand trial. He was arrested on the way.

And they court-martialed him.

The proceedings were utterly infamous. No chance to confront witnesses against him; no opportunity to bring witnesses; not even the books accused of sedition allowed to offer their mute testimony in their own defense; no opportunity given to his defender to prepare; letters sent from England and France to prove what had been the doomed man's purposes and occupations during his stay there, "lost in transit"; the old articles of twenty-four years before, made to appear as if recent utterances; forgeries imposed and with all this, nothing but hearsay evidence even from his accusers; and yet—he was sentenced to death.

Sentenced to death and shot.

And all Modern Schools closed, and his property sequestrated.

And the Virgin of Toledo may wear her gorgeous robes in peace, since the shadow of the darkness has stolen back over the circle of light he lit.

Only—somewhere, somewhere, down in the obscurity—hovers the menacing figure of her rival, "Our Lady of Pain." She is still now—but she is not dead. And if all things be taken from her, and the light not allowed to come to her, nor to her children—then—someday—she will set her own lights in the darkness.

Ferrer—Ferrer is with the immortals. His work is spreading over the world; it will yet return, and rid Spain of its tyrants.

Tributes from Prominent Figures[54]

Ernst Haeckel

I send you an expression of my warmest sympathy with your plan to commemorate the first anniversary of the martyrdom of Francisco Ferrer by a great public meeting on October 13.

I admire in the great Spanish martyr not only an excellent Freethinker and founder of the Modern Schools, but also one of those heroes of humanity who devote their whole lives and forces to the free development and progress of the human race.

My late illustrious friend, Professor Ernst Abbe, of Jena, the celebrated founder of the Carl Zeiss Institute at Jena, who was also a talented physicist, monistic philosopher and social reformer, had quite the same ideas and aims as our much lamented Francisco Ferrer.

I hope that the commemoration of these venerable benefactors of true humanity and liberators from superstition and clerical tyranny will be of great advantage for the propagation of true natural religion.

Jena, Germany, July 1910

Maxim Gorky

When the dark power of fanaticism kills before our eyes a man for the reason that he honestly and humanely labored for the good of humanity, we are all equally guilty in that murder.

Is not the work of Ferrer familiar and is it not dear to us all, the work which aims to increase the number of honest and reasoning men in this world?

Should we not be close to one another, and give support in the moments of dejection and weariness, help in the work, and protect one another in danger? We live solitary lives, divided not by space, but by the absence of an idea that would unite us into a strong army of honest men.

We are too individualistic; we esteem one another too little; we often criticize the work of friends, and so our enemies murder us one by one.

When one of us is killed we complain and we weep. It is endless.

We would have done better if we had defended the *living*, if we had kept up with his activities from day today, had guessed in advance the danger that could threaten him, and had surrounded him with the close embrace of friendship and esteem.

Capri, Italy, August 1910

Havelock Ellis

I never met Ferrer or came in contact with his work, and can, therefore, say little about him, but I am glad to be allowed to associate myself with the Ferrer commemoration.

We are told by distinguished Spaniards whose opinion is entitled to respect that Ferrer was by no means a man of great intellectual distinction. It is possible that they are right and that we are scarcely entitled to class him among those supreme teachers with whom he is sometimes grouped.

But the evidence of those who knew him best seems to show conclusively that he was not only a man of great character, but that he possessed a clear vision of the special needs of his country at the present time. He realized, I take it, that what Spain requires at present is not a violent political revolution, but a sound educational system on non-clerical lines, with, it seems, a stress on the moral side of education.

Against immense difficulties, Ferrer devoted himself with persistency and success to the establishment of such a system of education. His death was due to his devotion to this cause.

I think, therefore, that, whatever Ferrer's limitations may have been, he deserves to rank not only among the Spanish heroes who have always known how to die, but also among those great men who by their inspiring example have deserved well of humanity and all over the world. He is rightly revered as a martyr.

Carbis Bay, Cornwall, England, August 1910

Edward Carpenter

It is high time indeed that the mass populations of modern lands should be able to look around, take intelligent reckoning of their position, and set about the management of their own affairs—instead of being kept under, in a state of chronic fear and ignorance, by the threats of armed Property and the incantations of Religion.

This liberation is already rapidly taking place in America, but in the old countries of Europe it goes slowly. In Spain it has gone *very* slowly hitherto, but in the future it will more rapidly; and the death of Ferrer will become the signal of a new era to that country and to the world.

Sheffield, England, August 1910

Jack London

Had the noble Ferrer been killed in any other century than this, he would have been one of the host of martyrs. But to be killed as he was killed, by a modern state, at the end of the first decade of the twentieth century, is to make his martyrdom not only an anachronism, but a startlingly conspicuous historical event.

It were as if New England had, in the twentieth century, resumed her ancient practice of burning witches.

This killing of Ferrer is inconceivable and monstrous. And yet it happened. And we stand aghast and cannot quite believe. We know it did happen, and yet it is too impossible to believe.

Glen Ellen, California, September 1910

Upton Sinclair

Capitalism is a hideous thing in all its aspects, and hateful in all the methods by which it seeks to perpetuate itself, but it becomes especially hateful when it employs superstition and bigotry in its aid and seeks to turn the religious instincts of the ignorant people into engines of cruelty and oppression. It is doing that today in Russia and in Spain, and it is well

Drawing of Ferrer. UCSD, Box 17, Folder 5.

that we who live in America should bear in mind that if it does not do so in our country, it is simply because it does not dare to. We have here many millions of ignorant and helpless foreigners who have been its victims abroad. They bring their priests and their ideals with them, and if we preserve the institutions of freedom in America it will only be because we make it our business to free these people from the shackles of superstition and guard against the slightest attempt at the introduction of repression. Such attempts are being made today in every part of our country, and this, it seems to me, is the lesson which we have to learn from the martyrdom of Ferrer. The Roman Catholic Church is here, and here, as everywhere in the world, it is the enemy of civilization.

Arden, Delaware, September 1910

Albert Camus[55]

Francisco Ferrer thought that no one is deliberately wicked and that all of the evil that exists in the world comes from ignorance. That is why the ignorant murdered him and criminal ignorance still continues today through new and tireless inquisitions. Before them, however, victims such as Ferrer will live forever.

The Need of Translating Ideals into Life by Alexander Berkman[56]

One year has passed since the death of Francisco Ferrer. His martyrdom has called for an almost universal indignation against the cabal of priest and ruler that doomed a noble man to death. The thinking, progressive elements throughout the world have voiced their protest in no ambiguous manner. Everywhere sympathy has been manifested for Ferrer, the modern victim of the Spanish Inquisition, and deep appreciation expressed for his work and aims. In short, the death of Ferrer has succeeded—as probably no other martyrdom of recent history—in rousing the social conscience of man. It has clarified the eternally unchanging attitude of the Church as the enemy of progress; it has convincingly exposed the State as the crafty foe of popular advancement; it has, finally, roused deep interest in the destiny of the child and the necessity of rational education.

It would indeed be a pity if the intellectual and emotional energies thus wakened should exhaust themselves in mere indignation and unprofitable speculation concerning the unimportant details of Ferrer's personality and life. Protest meetings and anniversary commemorations are quite necessary and useful, in proper time and place. They have already accomplished, so far as the world at large is concerned, a great educational work. By means of these the social consciousness has been led to realize the enormity of the crime committed by the Church and State of Spain. But "the world at large" is not easily moved to action; it requires many terrible martyrdoms to disturb its equilibrium of dullness; and even when disturbed, it tends quickly to resume its wonted immobility. It is the thinking, radical elements which are, literally, the movers of the world, the intellectual and emotional disturbers of its stupid equanimity. They must never be suffered to become dormant, for they, too, are in danger of growing absorbed in mere adulation of the martyr and rhetorical admiration of his great work. As Ferrer himself has wisely cautioned us: "Idols are created when men are praised, which is very bad for the future of the human race. The time devoted to the dead would be better employed in improving the condition of the living, most of whom stand in great need of this."

These words of Francisco Ferrer should be italicized in our minds. The radicals, especially—of whatever creed—have much to atone for in this respect. We have given too much time to the dead, and not enough to living. We have idealized our martyrs to the extent of neglecting the practical needs of the cause they died for. We have idealized our ideals to the exclusion of their application in actual life. The cause of it was an immature appreciation of our ideals. They were too sacred for everyday use. The result is evident, and rather discouraging. After a quarter of a century—and more—of radical propaganda, we can point to no very particular achievement. *Some* progress, no doubt, has been made; but by no means commensurate with the really tremendous efforts exerted. This comparative failure, in its turn, produces a further disillusioning effect: old-time radicals drop from the ranks, disheartened; the most active workers become indifferent, discouraged with lack of results.

It is this the history of every world-revolutionizing idea of our times. But especially is it true of the Anarchist movement. Necessarily so, since by its very nature it is not a movement that can conquer immediate, tangible results, such as a political movement, for instance, can accomplish. It may be said that the difference between even the most advanced political movement, such as Socialism, and Anarchism is this: the one seeks the transformation of political and economic conditions, while the goal of the other includes a complete transvaluation of individual and social conceptions. Such a gigantic task is necessarily of slow progress; nor can its advancement be counted by noses or ballots. It is the failure to realize fully the enormity of the task that is partly responsible for the pessimism that so often overtakes the active spirits of the movement. To that is added the lack of clarity regarding the manner of social accoutrements.

The Old is to give birth to the New. How do such things happen?—as little Wendla asks her mother in Wedekind's *Frühlings Erwachen*. We have outgrown the stork of Social Revolution that will deliver us the newborn child of readymade equality, fraternity, and liberty. We now conceive of the coming social life as a condition rather than a system. A condition of mind, primarily; one based on solidarity of interests arising from social understanding and enlightened self-interest. A system can be organized, made. A condition must be developed. This development is determined by existing environment and the intellectual tendencies of the times. The causation of both is no doubt mutual and interdependent, but the factor of individual and propagandistic effort is not to be underestimated.

The social life of man is a centre, as it were; whence radiate numerous intellectual tendencies, crossing and zigzagging, receding and approaching each other in interminable succession. The points of convergence create new centres, exerting varying influences upon the larger centre, the general life of humanity. The new intellectual and ethical atmospheres are established, the degree of their influence depending, primarily, on the active enthusiasm of the adherents; ultimately, on the kinship between the new ideal and the requirements of human nature. Striking this true chord, the new ideal will affect ever more intellectual centres which gradually begin interpreting themselves into life and transvaluing the values of the great general centre, the social life of man.

Anarchism is such an intellectual and ethical atmosphere. With sure hand it has touched the heart of humanity, influencing the world's foremost minds in literature, art, and philosophy. It has resurrected the individual from the ruins of the social debacle. In the forefront of human events, its progress is necessarily painfully slow: the leaden weight of ages of ignorance and superstition hangs heavily at his heels. But its slow progress should by no means prove discouraging. On the contrary: it evidences the necessity of greater effort, of solidifying existing libertarian centres, and of ceaseless activity to create new ones.

The immaturity of the past has blinded our vision to the true requirements of the situation. Anarchism was regarded, even by his adherents, as an ideal for the future. Its practical application to current life was entirely ignored. The propaganda was circumscribed by the hope of ushering in the

Social Revolution. *Preparation* for the new social life was not considered necessary. The gradual development and growth of the coming day did not enter into revolutionary concepts. The dawn had been overlooked. A fatal error, for there is no day without dawn.

The martyrdom of Francisco Ferrer will not have been in vain if, through it, the Anarchists—as well as other radical elements—will realize that, in social as well as in individual life, conception precedes birth. The social conception which we need, and must have, is the creation of libertarian centres which shall radiate the atmosphere of the dawn into the life of humanity.

Many such centres are possible. But the most important of all is the young life, the growing generation. After all, it is they upon whom will devolve the task of carrying the work forward. Just in the proportion that the young generation grows more enlightened and libertarian, will we approach a freer society. Yet in this regard we have been, and still are, unpardonably negligent; we Anarchists, socialists, and other radicals. Protesting against the superstition breeding educational system, we nevertheless continue to subject our children to its baneful influence. We condemn the madness of war, yet we permit our offspring to be inculcated with the poison of patriotism. Ourselves more or less emancipated from false bourgeois standards, we still suffer our children to be corrupted by the hypocrisy of the established. Every such parent directly aids in the perpetuation of dominant ignorance and slavery. Can we indeed expect a generation reared in the atmosphere of the suppressive, authoritarian educational regime, to form the cornerstone of a free, self-reliant humanity? Such parents are criminally guilty toward themselves and their children: they rear the ghost that will divide their house against itself, and strengthen the bulwarks of darkness.

No intelligent radical can fail to realize the need of the rational education of the young. The rearing of the child must become a process of liberation by methods which shall not impose readymade ideas, but which should aid the child's natural self-unfoldment. The purpose of such an education is not to force the child's adaptation to accepted concepts, but to give free play to his originality, initiative, and individuality. Only by freeing education from compulsion and restraint can we create the environment for the manifestation of the spontaneous interest and inner incentives on the part of the child. Only thus can we supply rational conditions favorable to the development of the child's natural tendencies and his latent emotional mental faculties. Such methods of education, essentially aiding the child's imitative quality and hunger for knowledge, will develop a generation of healthy intellectual independence. It will produce men and women capable, in the words of Francisco Ferrer, "of evolving without stopping, of destroying and renewing their environment without cessation; of renewing themselves also; always ready to accept what is best, happy in the triumph of new ideas, aspiring to live multiple lives in one life."

Upon such men and women rests the hope of human progress. To them belongs the future. And it is, to a very considerable extent, in our own power to pave the way. The death of Francisco Ferrer were in vain, our indignation, sympathy, and admiration worthless, unless we translate the ideals of the martyred educator into practice and life, and thus advance the human struggle for enlightenment in liberty.

A beginning has already been made. Several schools, along Ferrer lines, are being conducted in New York and Brooklyn; Philadelphia and Chicago are also about to open classes. At present the efforts are limited, for lack of aid and teachers, to Sunday schools. But they are the nucleus of grand, far-reaching potentiality. The radical elements of America, and chiefly the Francisco Ferrer Association, could rear no worthier nor more lasting monument to the memory of the martyred educator, Francisco Ferrer, than by a generous response to this appeal for the establishment of the first Francisco Ferrer Day School in America.

Poems for Ferrer

To Francisco Ferrer[57]

J. William Lloyd

O Hero of the Unbound Brain!
    From thy great heart the bullets tore,
From thy great agony of pain,
    There comes to us, forevermore,

The sign of courage, faithfulness
    In face of death to human need;
And tho these hounds thy flesh possess
    Thy soul goes sowing Freedom's seed

Woodcut image of Ferrer. *Solidaridad: Órgano de la Federación Obrera Regional Uruguaya*, Oct-Nov, 1957. UCSD, Box 17, Folder 5.

Eternally. They murdered thee,
    But on the black cloud of their shame,
Where all mankind for aye must see,
    In blood and fire they wrote thy name.

Ferrer[58]

Herman Scheffauer

Who armed the hands of the butchers? what powers
    crouched in the crypts of night?
What fools, fat-blown with their hate like toads, plotted
    to throw in eclipse this light?
Not enough the curse and blight they brought on the
    house of Spain with pyre and bar—
Their mildewed hands as of old must stretch from
    ancient darkness to quench a star!

Yet blindly they wrought in their rage, nor learned the
    lesson of newborn centuries,
Nor saw, ere they trod on the torch of truth, what hands
    shook dust from their dynasties,
What ghostly chisels gnawed deep upon the mouldered
    mortar that bound the vault,
Nor their cold lips knew that the taste of blood like that
    of tears is accurst with salt.

Wherefore from their baleful tomes they dragged the
    words of an iron doom in vain,
While the blood-splashed Torquemada again sprang
    howling out of the ribs of Spain,
And lies like serpents crept from their throats to weave
    a halter for men to wear,
Yea, charnels stank 'mid manacle-clank as they fusilladed
    a greybeard there!

But the musket-roar and the smoke o'er Earth grew
    straightway a bolted thundercloud,

And the dumb lips of the slain reopen, and his hand
    moves blazing beyond his shroud,
While she that slew him—the crumbling realm—hath
    felt new life in her ashen womb—
E'en she is freed by this blood!—for blood, like a fire
    may shine—like a flower, bloom.

In the Evil Castle
(For the Life of Francisco Ferrer)
Pietro Gori, October 10, 1909[59]

Prison, court, and slaughterhouse,
Montjuich, lair of ambushes and conflict,
overlooking the city, like a vulture,
ready to strike in the darkness of night. . .

The innocent sleep: but threatening
priests awarded with a perverse
plot, in the name of the Bourbons of Spain,
the secular swindle of justice.

Once again intensifies the black
ferment of hate against human
reason . . . it is the tragedy of thought
afflicted by the inquisition.

The insane game that steals lives, of the
new truths that didn't hear the sound:
Like they kill in Jerez and like in Cuba and
still—"Germinal! . . ."—shouts Angiolillo.[60]

—"Catholic king, already over your reign,
(Carlos V is stone dead) the sun sets;
and you cannot kill the truth with the
popular masses, nor confront the future

with the chains of a vile past.
From the ashes of the bonfires the immortal

idea shone, more than the scepter and the steel
of the skeletons of the Escorial.

It was the blood tax, that brought
Barcelona to refuse more meat for the
War ... today they die over there, and in those
trenches Iberian lead bloodies the earth. . .

Be careful, oh king, for the executioner is the
saddest instigator, and the martyr is the
strongest. . . . He who was vanquished on the cross was not Christ
and he who dies for the idea defeats death.

The Death of Ferrer
Ricardo Gómez
(*El Libertario*, November 7, 1909)

Your death was beautiful for the artists,
it was frightening and tragic for the slaves,
it was just vengeance for your executioners,
your death ... it was a path for your brothers.
The mouths of your enemies laughed,
the eyes of millions of pariahs sobbed,
but the spirits of your compañeros
watched your rough torment with serenity.
Why cry about the effects of struggles
that keep men in high spirits?
Yes, romantic tears are for the poets!
Yes, impotent tears are for slaves!
That is why we, strong and serene,
not wanting to be poets, or slaves,
calmly watch your tragic fate
with dry eyes ... with a bitter gaze.

Notes
1   Daniel Laqua, "Freethinkers, Anarchists and Francisco Ferrer: The Making of a Transnational Solidarity Campaign," *European Review of History / Revue euro-péenne d'histoire* 21, no. 4 (2014): 471.

2   *L'Humanité*, September 4–5, 1909.

3   Dreyfus was also part of the Ferrer statue committee. APP Ba 1075; *L'Humanité*, October 9, 1909; Peter Tiidu Park, "The European Reaction to the Execution of Francisco Ferrer" (PhD diss., University of Virginia, 1970), 224–26; *Le Journal*, September 10, 1909; *L'Humanité*, September 10 and 12, 1909; *Le Libertaire*, September 12, 1909; AN, F7 13066; Vincent Robert and Eduard J. Verger, "'La protesta universal' contra la ejecución de Ferrer: las manifestaciones de octubre de 1909," *Historia Social* 14 (Autumn 1992): 61–82.

4   Pedro Voltes Bou, *La semana trágica* (Madrid: Espasa Calpe, 1995), 199–206.

5   *L'Humanité*, October 14, 1909; *L'Intransigeant*, October 14, 1909; *Le Temps*, October 15, 1909; AN F7 13066.

6   Park, "The European Reaction," 266–69; Juan Avilés, *Francisco Ferrer y Guardia: pedagogo, anarquista y mártir* (Madrid: Marcial Pons, 2006), 253; Sol Ferrer, *La vie et l'oeuvre de Francisco Ferrer: un martyr au XXe siècle* (Paris: Librairie Fischbacher, 1962), 175–84; Madeleine Rebérioux, "Manifester pour Ferrer Paris Octobre 1909," in Francine Best et al., *L'affaire Ferrer* (Castres, France: Centre national et Musée Jean Jaurès, 1991), 79–100.

7   Park, "The European Reaction," 351–411; Avilés, *Francisco Ferrer y Guardia*, 254–55; AHN, Asuntos Exteriores, Sección Histórica, 2751; Ferrer, *La vie et l'oeuvre de Francisco Ferrer*, 190–92; Laqua, "Freethinkers, Anarchists and Francisco Ferrer," 477; Fernando García Sanz, *Historia de las relaciones entre España e Italia: imágenes, comercio y política exterior (1890–1914)* (Madrid: Consejo Superior de Investigaciones Científicas, 1994), 328–77.

8   Park, "The European Reaction," 312–29.

9   Park, "The European Reaction," 570–82; Ferrer, *La vie et l'oeuvre*, 185–99.

10   Avilés, *Francisco Ferrer y Guardia*, 256–58; Park, "The European Reaction," 414–592; Ferrer, *La vie et l'oeuvre*, 192–99; Pietro Di Paola, *The Knights Errant of Anarchy: London and the Italian Anarchist Diaspora (1880–1917)* (Liverpool: Liverpool University Press, 2013), 114–15; Ilham Khuri-Makdisi, *The Eastern Mediterranean and the Making of Global Radicalism, 1860–1914* (Berkeley: University of California Press, 2010), 60–62.

11   AHN, Asuntos Exteriores, Sección Histórica, 2752; Pere Solà i Gussinyer, "Los grupos del magisterio racionalista en Argentina y Uruguay hacia 1910 y sus actitudes ante la enseñanza laica oficial," *Historia de la Educación* 1 (1982): 236–37; Avilés, *Francisco Ferrer y Guardia*, 258; Park, "The European Reaction," 591; Ferrer, *La vie et l'oeuvre*, 199–202; *San Francisco Call*, October 25, 1909; Amparo Sanchez Cobos, *Sembrando ideales: anarquistas españoles en Cuba, 1902–1925* (Sevilla: Consejo Superior de Investigaciones Científicas, 2008), 234–35; Frank Fernández, *Cuban Anarchism: The History of a Movement*, trans. Charles Bufe (Tucson: See Sharp Press, 2001), 47; Leoncio Lasso de la Vega, *El asesinato de Ferrer: la protesta del Uruguay* (Montevideo, 1909) [IISG]; Maria del Mar Araus Segura, "La escuela moderna en Iberoamérica: repercussion de la muerte de Francisco Ferrer Guardia," *Boletín americanista* 52 (2002): 13–22.

12   Laqua, "Freethinkers, Anarchists and Francisco Ferrer," 471.

13   Gabriel Maura y Gamazo and Melchor Fernández Almagro, *Por qué cayó Alfonso XIII? Evolución y disolución de los partidos históricos durante su reinado* (Madrid: Ediciones Ambos Mundos, S. L., 1948), 154–56.

14   Eduardo González Calleja, *La razón de la fuerza: orden público, subversión y violencia política en la España de la Restauración (1875–1917)* (Madrid: Consejo Superior de Investigaciones Científicas, 1998), 438; *El proceso Ferrer en el Congreso: recopilación de los discursos pronunciados por various diputados durante el debate* (Barcelona: Imprenta Lauria, 1911).

15   UCSD, Box 2, Folder 13.

16   *L'Anarchie*, October 27, 1910; APP, Ba 1075.

17   In Paris someone covered several street signs such as "rue de l'Eglise" and "rue des Moines" with paper that read "rue Ferrer." APP, Ba 1075; Park, "The European Reaction to the Execution of Francisco Ferrer," 314–591; Ferrer, *La vie et l'oeuvre*, 187–92; Jean-François Aguinaga, "Ferrer i Guàrdia: llocs de memòria a Bèlgica," *Espai de Llibertat: revista d'esquerres per a la formació, la reflexió i l'agitació política* 54 (2009): 13–16; Segura, "La escuela moderna en Iberoamérica," 14.

18   UCSD, Box 17, Folder 7.

19   Ferran Aisa, *La cultura anarquista a Catalunya* (Barcelona: Edicions de 1984, 2006), 319–20.

20   Laqua, "Freethinkers, Anarchists and Francisco Ferrer," 476.

21   Kirwin R. Shaffer, "Freedom Teaching: Anarchism and Education in Early Republican Cuba, 1898–1925," *The Americas* 60, no. 2 (October 2003): 151–83; Kirwin R. Shaffer, *Anarchism and Countercultural Politics in Early Twentieth-Century Cuba* (Gainesville: University Press of Florida, 2005), 173–94; Sánchez Cobos, *Sembrando ideales*, 228–42.

22   John M. Hart, "The Urban Working Class and the Mexican Revolution: The Case of the Casa del Obrero Mundial," *The Hispanic American Historical Review* 58, no. 1 (February 1978): 1–20; John M. Hart, *Anarchism and The Mexican Working Class, 1860–1931* (Austin: University of Texas Press, 1978), 112–19, 156; Claudio Lomnitz, *The Return of Comrade Ricardo Flores Magón* (Brooklyn: Zone Books, 2014), 437; Lucien van der Walt and Steven J. Hirsch, "Rethinking Anarchism and Syndicalism: The Colonial and Postcolonial Experience, 1870–1940," in *Anarchism and Syndicalism in the Colonial and Postcolonial World, 1870–1940: The Praxis of National Liberation, Internationalism, and Social Revolution*, ed. Steven Hirsch and Lucien van der Walt (Leiden, NL: Brill, 2010), xlii; Práxedis G. Guerrero, "Impulsemos la enseñanza racionalista," in *El anarquismo en America Latina*, ed. Carlos M. Rama and Angel J. Cappelletti, (Caracas: Biblioteca Ayacucho, 1990), 422–23; Kevan Antonio Aguilar, "Peripheries of Power, Centers of Resistance: Anarchist Movements in Tampico and the Huasteca Region, 1910–1945" (MA thesis, University of California, San Diego, 2014), 39, 83–84; Segura, "La escuela moderna en Iberoamérica," 15–16.

23   Juan Suriano, *Anarquistas: cultura y política libertaria en Buenos Aires, 1890–1910* (Buenos Aires: Manatial, 2001), 217–49; Pamela De Seta, Flavia Fanello, and Ignacio Kuppe, "Las escuelas anarquistas en Argentina a principios del siglo XX," presentation, XXVIII Congreso ALAS, "Fronteras Abiertas de América Latina,"

UFPE, Recife, Brasil, September 6–10, 2011; Segura, "La escuela moderna en Iberoamérica," 12–14.

24 Leonora Reyes-Jedlicki, "The Crisis of the Estado docente and the Critical Education Movement: The Escuelas Obreras Federales Racionalistas in Chile (1921–1926)," *Journal of Latin American Studies* 39, no. 4 (2007): 827–55; Jorge Rojas Flores, *Moral y prácticas cívicas en los niños chilenos, 1880–1950* (Santiago: Ariadna Ediciones, 2004), 244–62; Iván Núñez, *Educación popular y movimiento obrero: un estudio histórico* (Santiago: Academia de Humanismo Cristiano, 1982), 17–18.

25 Aracely Mehl Gonçalves, "Francisco Ferrer y Guardia: educação e a imprensa anarco-sindicalista—'A PLEBE'" (PhD diss., Universidade Estadual De Ponta Grossa-UEPG, 2007), 88–100; Francisco Furtado Gomes Riet Vargas, "Anarquismo e Educação em Rio Grande (1918–1927): educação de, para e pelos Trabalhadores" (PhD diss., Universidade Federal de Pelotas, 2011), 88–89; Olga Regina Fregoni, "Educação e resistência anarquista em São Paulo: a sobrevivência das prácticas da educação na Academia de Comércio Saldanha Marinho (1920–1945)" (PhD diss., Pontíficia Universidade Católica de São Paulo, 2007), 47–79; Adelino Tavares de Pinho, *Pela educação e Pelo trabalho e outros escritos* (São Paulo: Biblioteca Terra Livre, 2012); Segura, "La escuela moderna en Iberoamérica," 14.

26 Segura, "La escuela moderna en Iberoamérica," 14.

27 Geoffrey C. Fidler, "The Escuela Moderna Movement of Francisco Ferrer: 'Por la Verdad y la Justicia,'" *History of Education Quarterly* 25, no. 1–2 (Spring–Summer, 1985): 117–23; Di Paola, *The Knights Errant of Anarchy*, 35.

28 Paul Avrich, *Anarchist Voices: An Oral History of Anarchism in America* (Oakland: AK Press, 2005), 191–95; Paul Avrich, *The Modern School Movement: Anarchism and Education in the United States* (Princeton: Princeton University Press, 1980); Fidler, "The Escuela Moderna Movement of Francisco Ferrer," 119; Victor Sacharoff et al., *Recollections from the Modern School Ferrer Colony*, ed. Jon Thoreau Scott (Altamont, NY: Friends of the Modern School, 2007); Joseph Jacob Cohen and Alexis C. Ferm, *The Modern School of Stelton: A Sketch* (Stelton, NJ: Modern School Association of North America, 1925); Jeffrey Babcock Perry, *Hubert Harrison: The Voice of Harlem Radicalism, 1883–1918* (New York: Columbia University Press, 2009), 234–38; Kenyon Zimmer, *Immigrants against the State: Yiddish and Italian Anarchism in America* (Urbana: University of Illinois Press, 2015), 56–65; Anatole Dolgoff, *Left of the Left: My Memories of Sam Dolgoff* (Oakland: AK Press, 2016), 116–124, 151; Tom Goyens, *Beer and Revolution: The German Anarchist Movement in New York City, 1880–1914* (Urbana: University of Illinois Press, 2007), 203–4.

29 Fidler, "The Escuela Moderna Movement of Francisco Ferrer," 118–26; Jean Wintsch, *L'école Ferrer: un essai d'institution ouvrière: notice.* (Geneva: Impr. des Unions ouvrières, 1919); IISG, Jean Wintsch Papers; IISG, Max Nettlau Papers, 3358.

30 Initial information of the Dutch Ferrer schools provided by Dennis Bos. J. Snijders, *Doel en streven der ontspanningsscholen: Ten voordeele der ontspanningsschool "Oosterpark en Omstreken"* (Amsterdam: Snijders, 1907); Richard van der Woude,

"Op, mannen, broeders! saam vereenigd! Op, burgers! Sluit u bij ons aan! Het proletariërslied in Nederland, 1872–1914" (BA thesis, Universiteit Utrecht, 2011); Ferdinand Domela Nieuwenhuis, *De kommune van Parijs* (Amsterdam: Uitg. der Ontspanningsschool Haarlemmerpoort en Omstreken—Kinder-bibliotheek no. 3); *Liederen ten dienste [der] Ontspanningsschool te Emmer-Compascuum* (Z.pl. en j.) [IISG].

31 Avrich, *The Modern School Movement*, 33; Fidler, "The Escuela Moderna Movement of Francisco Ferrer," 121; Laqua, "Freethinkers, Anarchists and Francisco Ferrer," 478; IISG, Max Nettlau Papers, 3179; Mar Araus Segura, "La escuela moderna en Iberoamérica, 7.

32 William Archer, *The Life, Trial and Death of Francisco Ferrer* (New York: Moffat, Yard and Co., 1911), 60–61.

33 Richard Purkiss, *Democracy, Trade Unions and Political Violence in Spain: The Valencian Anarchist Movement, 1918–1936* (Brighton: Sussex Academic Press, 2011), 15; Luis M. Lázaro Lorente, *La Escuela Moderna de Valencia* (Valencia: Generalitat Valenciana, 1989); Luis M. Lázaro Lorente, *Las Escuelas Racionalistas en el País Valenciano (1906–1931)* (Valencia: NAU llibres, 1992), 79; Josep González Agàpito, Salomó Marquès, Alejandro Mayordomo, and Bernat Sureda, *Tradició i renovació pedagògica, 1898–1939: història de l'educació: Catalunya, Illes Balears, País Valencià* (Barcelona: Publicacions de l'Abadia de Montserrat, 2002), 62; Miguel Íñiguez, *Enciclopedia histórica del anarquismo español* (Vitoria: Asociación Isaac Puente, 2008), 1694.

34 Avrich, *The Modern School Movement*, 80.

35 Margaret Sanger, *Margaret Sanger: An Autobiography* (New York: W.W. Norton, 1938), 122–63.

36 Alejandro Tiana Ferrer, *Educación libertaria y revolución social (España, 1936–1939)* (Madrid: UNED, 1987), 108, 142.

37 Xavier Cuadrat, *Socialismo y anarquismo en cataluña (1899–1911): los origenes de la C.N.T.* (Madrid: Ediciones de la Revista de Trabajo, 1976), 191–92.

38 Scholars debate just how Ferrerian the CENU really was. Aisa argues it was heavily Ferrerian, while Solà i Gussinyer says it was not. Aisa, *La cultura anarquista*, 201; Pere Solà i Gussinyer, *Educació i moviment llibertari a Catalunya (1901–1939)* (Barcelona: Edicions 62, 1980), 162; Pere Solà, "Prólogo a la edición de 2009 de *La Escuela Moderna*," in Francisco Ferrer Guardia, *La Escuela Moderna: póstuma explicación y alcance de la enseñanza racionalista* (Barcelona: Fábula Tusquets Editores, 2009), 33–34; Íñiguez, *Enciclopedia histórica del anarquismo español*, 1392–93.

39 Solà, "Prólogo," in Ferrer Guardia, *La Escuela Moderna*, 42.

40 Íñiguez, *Enciclopedia histórica del anarquismo español*, 1222.

41 Solà, "Prólogo," in Ferrer Guardia, *La Escuela Moderna*, 41–42.

42 Solà i Gussinyer, *Educació i moviment llibertari a Catalunya*, 148–55; Íñiguez, *Enciclopedia histórica del anarquismo español*, 1705.

43 Excerpt from: Rudolf Rocker, *En la borrasca: años de destierro*, trans. Diego A. de Santillán (Buenos Aires: Editorial Tupac, 1949), 274–76.

44 In 1910, Rocker published a Yiddish-language book on Ferrer and education. Rudolf Rocker, *Fransisko Ferrer un di freie ertzihung fun der jugend* (London: Arbeiter Freind, 1910).

45 Fernando Tarrida del Mármol (1861–1915) was an engineer, professor at the University of Barcelona, and a leading intellectual of late nineteenth-century Spanish anarchism most well-known for coining the phrase "anarchism without adjectives." After his imprisonment during the repression of *el proceso de Montjuich*, Tarrida fled to England, after a stay in France, and published *Les inquisiteurs d'Espagne, Montjuich, Cuba, Philippines* which put him at the forefront of the international campaign against the repression of the Spanish government. "Fernando Tarrida del Mármol," in Íñiguez, *Enciclopedia histórica del anarquismo español*, 1676.

46 Rocker also ended up speaking on behalf of Ferrer at protest meetings in Paris, where he happened to be when Ferrer was executed. His participation in these protests got him deported. Rocker, *En la borrasca*, 266–68.

47 Tcherkesov (also known as Varlaam Cherkesov) was a former Georgian aristocrat turned anarchist-communist who cofounded *Le Révolté* with Kropotkin and Reclus in 1879. George Woodcock, *Anarchism: A History of Libertarian Ideas and Movements* (New York: Meridian, 1962), 202.

48 Alexander ("Sanya") Schapiro was a Jewish anarchist born in Rostov-on-Don, Russia, in 1882. After moving to London, Schapiro was active in the London Anarchist Federation with Kropotkin, Tcherkesov, and Rocker and was named secretary of the International Anarchist Bureau created by the 1907 Amsterdam Congress. Years later he became editor of *Golos Truda* in Russia but emigrated with Emma Goldman and Alexander Berkman after growing disillusioned with the Soviet state. He was a member of the first secretariat of the IWA. Paul Avrich, *Russian Anarchists* (New York: WW Norton & Co., 1980), 138, 232–33, 240; Paul Avrich and Karen Avrich, *Sasha and Emma: The Anarchist Odyssey of Alexander Berkman and Emma Goldman* (Cambridge: The Belknap Press of Harvard University Press, 2012), 314; José Luis Gutiérrez Molina, introduction to Pedro Vallina, *Fermín Salvochea: crónica de un revolucionario* (Sevilla: Editorial Renacimiento, 2012), 69.

49 Emidio Recchioni was an Italian anarchist who may have been involved in plots to assassinate the Italian prime minister before getting locked up in an island prison with Luigi Galleani. Subsequently, he fled to London in 1899, where he opened the delicatessen King Bomba, which became a meeting place for London anarchists and a source of revenue to finance several of Malatesta's newspapers and two attempts on the life of Mussolini years later. He contributed avidly to the anarchist press under the penname "Nemo." Recchioni's son was *Freedom* editor Vernon Richards. Carl Levy, foreword to *Life and Ideas: The Anarchist Writings of Errico Malatesta*, ed. Vernon Richards (Oakland: PM Press, 2015), x.

50 From *Francisco Ferrer: His Life, Work and Martyrdom* (New York: Francisco Ferrer Association, 1910), 6–10.

51 In her autobiography, Margaret Sanger, who visited Ferrer's comrade Lorenzo Portet, describes the constant and completely overt police surveillance that he dealt with. Sanger, *Margaret Sanger*, 153–60.

52 From *Ferrer: His Life, Work and Martyrdom*, 70–72.

53 Voltairine de Cleyre, *Selected Works of Voltairine de Cleyre*, ed. Alexander Berkman (New York: Mother Earth Publishing Association, 1914), 297–320.

54 From *Ferrer: His Life, Work, and Martyrdom*, 75–78.

55 Ferrer, *La vie et l'oeuvre*, 6.

56 Alexander Berkman, "The Need of Translating Ideals into Life," *Mother Earth* (November 1910).

57 From *Ferrer: His Life, Work, and Martyrdom*, 44.

58 From *Ferrer: His Life, Work, and Martyrdom*, 4.

59 Gori also penned another poem "Dopo il delitto a Pace Ferrer" two days after the execution. "La creació," *Espai de llibertat: revista d'esquerres per a la formació, la reflexió i l'agitació política* 54 (2009): 46–47.

60 Angiolillo was an Italian anarchist who assassinated Spanish prime minister Cánovas del Castillo in 1897 to avenge his repression of Spanish anarchists and Cuban revolutionaries. His last word before his execution was "Germinal," a reference to Émile Zola's *Germinal*, which became very popular among anarchists and socialists who often named groups and newspapers after the book. Germinal was the seventh month in the French revolutionary calendar. It occurred during the spring and so took on the connotation of rebirth.

XI

Afterword: Learning from Ferrer

Robert H. Haworth

Throughout this volume there has been an emphasis on building an important historical context to Ferrer's work. Moreover, we also saw a need to acknowledge and expose readers to the way his work has influenced educational spaces and anarchist thinkers in different parts of the world. Within my own field of educational research, I found it interesting that when I first began to look into anarchism and education that not only was the topic (including Ferrer's work) relegated to more obscure conversations, but it often wasn't taken seriously, even within radical circles. I believe part of the problem stems from the absence of educational voices that move the conversation beyond the liberal reformist ideas surrounding public education, as well as some of the current conservative trends and tendencies within our field. In many cases, it feels as though when discussing educational practices outside of tax-based compulsory education or the confines of the liberal state, these ideas end up at the bottom of the conversation or, as some would argue, are outright dismissed as naive and utopian thinking. This is partly why Ferrer's work has fallen out of step with mainstream educational research.

Even within anarchist literature, there is an occasional nod and short reference or brief overview of Ferrer's work, but it is definitely not part of the discussion of different anarchist struggles and ideas about teaching and learning. When Ferrer's name arises in activist's conversations, you might hear someone say, "Wasn't that the guy who was executed in Spain?" Of course, when I bring up his name in class, students usually shake their heads, shrug their shoulders, and ask, "Who's that?" This is not surprising. Nonetheless, I do believe Ferrer's ideas are useful, particularly in helping

students think historically about educational practices that have challenged public / statist institutions. After students have read some excerpts
of Ferrer, they may actually agree with many of his proposals; however,
in many cases, they don't see his educational ideas as viable alternatives
within the larger contemporary society. Students usually maintain that
the dominant social, political, economic, and cultural institutions are too
powerful or ingrained to contest or do away with. Teacher and student
autonomy and a curriculum that challenges authority and existing structures are foreign to many students, particularly those who have only
experienced standardized testing, scripted curricula, and the deskilling of
teachers. In short, current educational experiences stand on a very narrow
ideological base. Consequently, this leaves students with little or no hope
in imagining different educational experiences outside of these confines.
So, why do I continue to bring up Ferrer in classes knowing that students
will ultimately resist thinking about education beyond their own experiences, specifically thinking about ideas that challenge their assumptions
about the purpose of education? Although not directly by name, Ferrer's
educational ideas still exist. Our conversations continue to evolve. Almost
one hundred years after his execution, we can still learn a great deal from
Ferrer's work—specifically through conversations and debates surrounding teaching and learning and, more importantly, by the way his ideas
resonate with contemporary movements to create new educational spaces.

It seems evident that twentieth-century anarchists, as well as other
progressive sympathizers, helped (explicitly and implicitly) to romanticize
Ferrer. Whatever flaws Ferrer may have had, his educational thinking has
had an impact on at least some educators and activists around the world.
His belief in more autonomy for students and teachers, his critiques of
the role of the Church in promoting dogmatic thinking in schools, and
his understanding of how the governing classes needed a particular type
of education to meet their own needs still resonate strongly. He understood that the ruling class needed education to reproduce specific types
of workers and a broader social order, highlighting that "the rulers have
sought to give more and more complete organization to the school, not
because they look to education to regenerate society, but because they
need more competent workers to sustain industrial enterprises and enrich
their cities."[1] He, to the contrary, believed that schools and education in
general could be transformed to support the complete emancipation of
the individual.[2]

Ferrer saw a shift in society, with the ruling class realizing that if workers became more educated, they would be more equipped to contest their conditions; therefore, they had to institute a particular type of education—one that would ensure that workers would uphold their own exploitation. This seems hauntingly relevant today. Public schools are inundated with corporate controlled curricula and state and federal standardized testing, and teachers and students have little or no autonomy. In fact, public schools, particularly in urban areas across the United States, are being dismantled, shut down, and replaced with market-driven charter schools and private universities where the purpose of education to have the individual gain a position within the global capitalist order.

The means and ends of public education should not be surprising. In the mid-1970s, Samuel Bowles and Herbert Gintis wrote a book entitled *Schooling in Capitalist America*, where they discussed what they termed the "correspondence theory." Their argument was that public schools ran parallel with the development of capitalism. Hence, there was a correspondence between the needs of capitalism and how schools functioned in society. Ferrer and anarchist supporters in the U.S. saw these parallels almost seventy years earlier. For example, rebel poet and anarchist Voltairine de Cleyre criticized one of the newer players in educational reform in the early twentieth century, calling him the "statesman." De Cleyre explained that the "[statesman] is not actually interested in the actual work of schools, in the children as persons, but in the producing of a certain type of character to serve subsequent ends."[3] Contemporarily, I believe there is a new statesman (i.e., hedge fund managers, corporate CEOs) who not only want schools to produce particular citizenry and workers but want to also make a profit from public taxpayers. As public schools are being shut down in many urban areas, for-profit charters have become the new philanthropic Gucci handbag of the wealthy—where schools are being run and managed by corporate entities. Do I agree that we need to continue to fight for those public spaces? Yes, but at the same time anarchists and other radicals are continuing to rethink such educational spaces, so that we are not just fixated on liberal reforms or, as folk singer Utah Phillips cautioned, we are not just "rearranging the deckchairs on the Titanic."[4] Moreover, it is vital that we continue to reflect critically on the educational experiments of the past in order to create counternarratives and experiences that are connected to new emerging forms of educational resistance. Of course, Ferrer's work should be a part of that conversation, but there need to be more reflective criticisms of Ferrer's educational ideas and practices in order to help us reimagine current and future educational practices.

Theory and Practice

The connections, or rather *disconnections*, between theory and practice have been an ongoing source of conversation within educational research. Although Ferrer's belief in creating emancipated individuals was a strong challenge to the ruling class, he did have some confusing and sometimes contradictory intersections of theory and practice. In other words, there were tensions between his educational ideas and how they played out in the school. Most of these issues stemmed from advocating for a positivist, rational, and scientific approach to education, while trying to instill a moral message within the curriculum that contested capitalism and promoted cooperation and solidarity. It seems that many radical and progressive educators at that time were struggling to have a factual and science-based approach to teaching and learning, while, at the same time, wanting to instill particular beliefs and ideas about how the world operates and, ultimately, how they could transform it. However, as Judith Suissa points out, "It would be wrong to assume that Ferrer naively believed that he could provide an education, which, as opposed to that of the Church and state, was politically neutral."[5] More importantly, through some of the new translations introduced in this volume, one can see that there were emerging discussions and debates between radical educators on how we should teach children. For example, in the article entitled, "The Problem of Teaching," Mella argues:

> The school that we want, without denomination, is that which best arouses in children the desire to learn for themselves, to form their own ideas. Wherever that takes them, that's where we will be with our modest support.
>
> All the rest, to a greater or lesser extent, is to go back over the same worn-out roads, to voluntarily confine yourself to a single path, to change from one set of crutches to another, but not to get rid of them.
>
> And what's important is precisely to get rid of them for once.[6]

Mella's arguments were not just specific to Spain and parts of Europe but were also replicated in the United States. Emma Goldman also took issue with imposing specific ideologies in schools as well as in the home. Even within radical families she saw imposing specific ways of knowing on children as detrimental to creating free individuals. She states:

> These are by no means exaggerations: they are sad facts that I have met with in my experience with radical parents. What are the results of such methods of biasing the mind? The following is the consequence, and not very infrequent, either. The child, being fed on one-sided, set and fixed ideas, soon grows weary of rehashing the beliefs of its parents, and it sets out in quest of new sensations, no matter how inferior and shallow the new experience may be, the human mind cannot endure sameness and monotony.[7]

Fifty years later, Brazilian educator Paulo Freire discussed similar issues with what he termed the "banking" style of education.[8] This was, and I would add still is, the dominant form of educational practice, with students seen as "empty vessels" when they come to the classroom. Students are then inundated with factual materials, and when asked, they recite those facts back to the teacher. Freire later discusses the importance of a more critical and reflective dialogical process that would not only "respect the autonomy of the student" but would enable the teacher and student to develop a more mutual and horizontal relationship, rather than an authoritarian and vertical one.[9]

In more contemporary discussions on anarchism and education, it seems that pedagogy is a recurring issue. One of the more interesting questions that arises is: How might we create a non-hierarchical, anti-authoritative, mutual, and voluntary way of teaching and learning? Needless to say, there is not a deterministic answer to this question. Rather, it highlights the need for educational experiences that are situational to particular locales. This can be evidenced historically, for example, in the ways that the Modern Schools in Spain differed from the Modern Schools in the United States.[10] Of course, there were many philosophical similarities within the Modern Schools, but the curriculum and interpretations of educational theories and practices differed.

Naturally, different outcomes and interpretations are due to more than particular locales. Learning is a situated process and the human element changes rational scientific thinking. Neil deGrasse Tyson stated, "In science, when human behavior enters the equation, things go nonlinear. That's why Physics is easy and Sociology is hard."[11] It is interesting to introduce Tyson's thoughts, because his words ring true, particularly in how we see educational experiences unfold. Although Ferrer believed in constructing a rational educational process for developing young minds, the subjectivities of the human experience changed how his ideas were implemented and acted out in different locales.

Spontaneity

Throughout Ferrer's work we read that we must encourage spontaneity within our teaching and learning processes. This has fascinated me and affected my thinking regarding educational experiences and philosophical beliefs, particularly how we construct knowledge outside of public and statist institutions. Ferrer argues, "I would rather have the free spontaneity of a child who knows nothing than the verbal knowledge and intellectual deformation of one that has experienced the existing system of education."[12] Questions then emerge in defining spontaneity and how it ultimately connects (if at all) with experiences in rational education. Emma Goldman, who was also a supporter of Ferrer, discussed spontaneity in her article entitled "The Child and Its Enemies," where she criticizes the traditional education system stating, "the systems of education are being arranged into files, classified and numbered. They lack the strong fertile seed which, falling on rich soil, enables them to grow to great heights, they are worn and incapable of awakening spontaneity of character."[13] Although Goldman's piece is more of a criticism of traditional educational practices and the system as a whole, she does offer some insight into how spontaneity might be incorporated into the home and other educational spaces. In an article discussing the Modern School in Stelton, she highlights that it is important that "education is the process of drawing out, not of driving in; it aims at the possibility that the child should be left free to develop spontaneously, directing his own efforts and choosing the branches of knowledge he desires to study."[14]

For Ferrer, the idea of spontaneity still seems to conflict with a rational and scientific approach to education. For example, at the end of his section on the "Reform of the School," Ferrer states, "A scheme of rational education is already possible, and in such schools as we advocate the children may develop freely according to their aspirations."[15] However, is it possible to build a relationship between a rational education and spontaneity? From some of the critiques of Ferrer and the larger literature on rational and positivist methodologies in education, the answer seems to be no.

From a rational educational viewpoint, teaching and learning is based on factual and scientific knowledge. However, if the student is encouraged be autonomous and engage in educational experiences that are spontaneous, there are inevitable tensions within a positivist educational environment. Encouraging a rational and positivist framework for teaching students disconnects the individual from constructing the meaning of information. Even progressive educator and philosopher John Dewey noted, "Learning in the proper sense, is not learning things, but the meaning of things."[16] Rather than basing the learning process within the student's lived experience, the rational and positivist educator leaves little to no room to move beyond just the facts, where the teacher is the expert and the students are passive learners.[17] Judith Suissa describes the methodological tension within the Modern School at Stelton, asserting, "It is a serious failing of the work of anarchist educators that they made little systemic attempt to provide a theoretical account of the relationship between child-centered pedagogical practice and their own anarchist goals and values."[18]

I agree with Suissa's argument that anarchists need to further engage with some of the theoretical tensions within educational experiences. Thus, a deeper understanding of the social and psychological needs of the student and transparency about the purpose of education must be reconciled within anarchist spaces. Moreover, if the purpose of education is to develop anarchist values of anti-capitalism, mutual aid, and solidarity, then it seems that a stronger and more coherent theoretical foundation needs to be further articulated. That is to say, a foundation that might begin with the student, but which enables the teacher to create more participatory learning spaces to help students name the world they live in, as opposed to having someone name it for them. Without doing so, anarchist educational practices, even on paper, seem to have some theoretical hiccups.

Desire

When I ask some of my undergraduate students to reflect upon their ideal or most romanticized vision of what their classroom or school might look like, I usually get responses that are somewhat progressive (with vague ideas of student-centered approaches) but always within the confines of traditional educational practices (standardized assessments, teacher accountability, etc.). Part of why they attach themselves to these types of educational practices is that, in many cases, students view their ideal classroom or school through the narrow lens of how they were educated.

Let's face it, if they have been able to get into a state-run college, they probably have been successful within that educational system, so why change it? Although there is a desire to move away from standardized testing and curriculum because it is "boring," students still remain focused on an education as a means to gain access to the marketplace and jobs. Again, part of these desires is created through the students' experiences. Although they understand that they were "successful" within these educational practices, they don't see how these experiences don't always support or pertain to all students or equate to success. Many of their responses to this contradiction are that as new teachers, they believe they can help students who are unsuccessful within these processes through what many term as "best practices." Unfortunately, this still leads them to believe in and desire an educational system that functions to uphold a set of values and relationships. According to D.W. Smith, desires are "constructed, assembled, and arranged in such a manner that your desire is positively invested in the system that allows you to have this particular interest."[19]

Not only our desire but our imagination becomes narrowed within the confines of the state and capitalist structures. More recently, David Graeber argued that our institutions have waged war on the imagination, constructing our imaginations in ways that meet the interests of a particular system.[20] This can be illustrated by the trend for universities to deemphasize or even do away with the humanities. Philosophy, history, the study of literature, and other subject areas do not meet the system's needs unless you are writing a *New York Times* bestseller or your intellectual work has some monetary value within the market place. Your imagination is then limited to and attached to specific means and ends. Although many supporters of the free market view this as the way to give rise to the "best products," your imagination is still confined within what Max Haiven describes as the vernacular of the market.[21] Take, for example, how for-profit universities create seductive commercials where individuals are shown that that they are able to be creative, imaginative, and innovative in their particular fields, and after graduation (along with accruing an enormous amount of debt) they would ultimately become competitive in the global economy.

Ferrer's work challenges traditional ways of educating students across gender and class lines. For this and other reasons, his practices were considered dangerous to the Church and the ruling class. His belief in removing dogmatic thinking from the curriculum and the classroom contested the foundations of Church doctrine—where ideas and world-views are concrete and not to be questioned. His work also challenged the governing class belief that schools needed to reproduce values of hard work and obedience to the capitalist system. Even the progressive educational philosophies of Dewey and Montessori at this time reproduced a particular type of social order. Anarchists argued against these educational practices and believed that they only prepared students for the world that already exists not a world that might become.

However theoretically flawed Ferrer's work may be within the contemporary landscape of educational research, we can see his sense of desire and urgency to create an educational process that moves beyond the social, political, economic, and cultural constraints of the ruling class. His works stands as an illustration of transformative possibilities. It is through this initial process of desiring something other than dominant educational practices that we can begin to articulate and act out new ways of teaching and learning. Through Ferrer's writings and the subsequent creation of the Modern School, contemporary students, activists, and other community members are allowed a glimpse into how we might think about education differently.

Concluding Thoughts

I tend to look at anarchism and educational practices as experiments in what is possible. For anything new to transpire, we must first have a desire to generate teaching and learning spaces that challenge the dominant paradigms of neoliberal capitalism, patriarchy, racism, sexism, and fascism. This means that we need to take a hard look at the historical experiments in creating and operating anarchist educational spaces, as well as partaking in deeper investigations into the theoretical underpinnings of how those educational experiences emerge over time and in different locations.

Ferrer did not develop the Escuela Moderna in isolation. Rather, it intersected educational ideas and spaces in Europe, the U.S., and other parts of the world. What we can gain from Ferrer's work, particularly in anarchist and radical educational spaces, is not just a criticism of traditional educational practices but ways in which we might begin to have conversations that give way to creating experiments in new and dynamic educational possibilities.

Yes, working to create these educational spaces seems daunting and one feels terribly fatalistic in a climate where students are chanting "build the wall" in high school hallways across United States and the slogans of fascist groups are resonating with youth across Europe. However, just as Ferrer's work, and that of others during his time, seems minute compared to how education was operating on a larger scale, it should still be considered an important point of resistance. We need more experiments in radical educational practices that resist the dying functions of the liberal state.

The conversation about educational practices, especially in radical spaces, has taken on a more interdisciplinary approach. Broader literature on the types of environments and relationships and on how knowledge is produced is emerging. Geographers, sociologists, philosophers, historians, and, of course, educators are seeing their work as much more interconnected, as opposed to fragmented or separated.[22] This interdisciplinary approach enables anarchists to develop a much broader theoretical landscape for their situated educational practices, particularly within the different spaces and places they inhabit.

Pedagogy continues to be one of the major issues that many anarchists grapple with. While we should have what Freire describes as a "respect for the autonomy of the student," at the same time, we cannot, as Suissa argues, disconnect ourselves from the society we would like to create.[23] This doesn't mean that we have to draft concrete blueprints of how to educate our students, but it does mean we need to be aware of, as well as transparent in, how we engage in these educational processes. Ferrer, and others whose voices are included in this volume, have given us some important things to think about regarding education. They should be considered points of departure for beginning to unpack the difficulties in not only creating different teaching and learning processes and relationships, but in how those educational experiences can work toward building more dynamic and sustainable communities. This will be difficult as we move into a considerably dangerous time and as we contest and offer alternatives to market fundamentalism, religious fundamentalism, and the failures of the liberal state. These educational projects should be ongoing and not deterministic. Thus, we must continuously view our work as unfinished.

Notes

1   See p. 81 in chapter 9 of *The Modern School*.
2   Ibid.

3   Voltairine de Cleyre, "Modern Educational Reform," in *Exquisite Rebel: Essays of Voltairine de Cleyre—Anarchist, Feminist, Genius*, ed. Sharon Presley and Crispin Sartwell (New York: State University of New York Press, 2005), 251–65.

4   Utah Phillips and Ani DiFranco, "Candidacy," *The Past Didn't Go Anywhere*, Righteous Babe, 1996.

5   Judith Suissa, *Anarchism and Education: A Philosophical Perspective* (New York: Routledge, 2006), 81.

6   See p. 203 in "The Problem of Teaching."

7   Emma Goldman, "The Child and Its Enemies," *Mother Earth* 1, no. 2 (April 1906).

8   Paulo Freire, *Pedagogy of the Oppressed* (New York: Continuum, 2007).

9   Paulo Freire, *Pedagogy of Freedom: Ethics, Democracy and Civic Courage* (New York: Rowan & Littlefield, 2000), 59.

10 Suissa, *Anarchism and Education*, 77–88.

11 Neil deGrasse Tyson, Twitter correspondence, February 6, 2016.

12 See p. 86 in chapter 9 of *The Modern School*.

13 Goldman, "The Child and Its Enemies."

14 Emma Goldman, "The Social Importance of the Modern School," 1912, accessed June 29, 2018, http://dwardmac.pitzer.edu/anarchist_archives/goldman/socimportms.html.

15 See p. 87 in chapter 9 of *The Modern School*.

16 John Dewey, *How We Think* (Lexington: D.C. Heath & Co., 1910).

17 Patricia Hinchey, *Finding Freedom in the Classroom: A Practical Introduction to Critical Theory* (New York: Peter Lang, 2010).

18 Suissa, *Anarchism and Education*, 85.

19 D.W. Smith, "Deleuze and the Question of Desire: Toward an Immanent Theory of Ethics," *Parrhesia: A Journal of Critical Philosophy* 74 (2007).

20 David Graeber, *Revolutions in Reverse: Essays on Politics, Violence, Art, and Imagination* (London: Minor Compositions, 2011).

21 Max Haiven, *Crises of Imagination, Crisis of Power: Capitalism, Creativity and the Commons* (London: Zed Books, 2014), 242.

22 Robert Haworth and John Elmore, ed., *Out of the Ruins: The Emergence of Radical Informal Learning Spaces* (Oakland: PM Press, 2017).

23 Judith Suissa, "'The Space Now Possible': Anarchist Education as Utopian Hope," in *Anarchism and Utopianism*, ed. Laurence Davis and Ruth Kinna (Manchester: Manchester University Press, 2009), 248.

Bibliography

Newspapers
L'Anarchie (Paris)
Boletín de la Escuela Moderna (Barcelona)
Diario de Barcelona (Barcelona)
El Diluvio (Barcelona)
España Nueva (Madrid)
La Guerre sociale (Paris)
La Huelga general (Barcelona)
L'Humanité (Paris)
L'Intransigeant (Paris)
Le Journal (Paris)
Le Libertaire (Paris)
Mother Earth (New York)
Natura (Barcelona)
Nuevo Mundo (Madrid)
El País (Madrid)
Pro Ferrer (Barcelona)
Le Temps (Paris)
Les Temps nouveaux (Paris)
¡Tierra! (Havana)
San Francisco Call (San Francisco)

Archives
Archives de la préfecture de Police (APP)
Archives nationales (AN)
Ateneu Enciclopèdic Popular (AEP)
Fundació Ferrer i Guardia (FFG)
Internationaal Instituut voor Sociale Geschiedenis (IISG)
New York Public Library (NYPL)
Real Academia de Historia (RAH)

University of California, San Diego Special Collections, Francisco Ferrer Collection MS 248 (UCSD)

Primary Sources

Berkman, Alexander. "The Need of Translating Ideals into Life." *Mother Earth* (November 1910).

Bloch, Albert, and Georges M. Paraf-Javal. *La substancia universal.* Translated by Anselmo Lorenzo. Barcelona: Escuela Moderna, 1904.

Bonnard, Leopoldina. *Nociones de idioma francés.* Barcelona: Escuela Moderna, 1903.

Causa contra Francisco Ferrer Guardia: instruida y fallada por la Jurisdicción de Guerra en Barcelona, año 1909. Madrid: Sucesores de J. A. García, 1911.

Cohen, Joseph Jacob, and Alexis C. Ferm. *The Modern School of Stelton: A Sketch.* Stelton, NJ: Modern School Association of North America, 1925.

Comité de défense des victimes de la répression espagnole. *Un martyr des prêtres: Francisco Ferrer, 10 janvier 1859–13 octobre 1909: sa vie, son oeuvre.* Paris: Schleicher frères, 1909.

de Cleyre, Voltairine. *Exquisite Rebel: The Essays of Voltairine de Cleyre—Anarchist, Feminist, Genius.* Edited by Sharon Presley and Crispin Sartwell. Albany: State University of New York Press, 2005.

———. *Selected Works of Voltairine de Cleyre.* Edited by Alexander Berkman. New York: Mother Earth Publishing Association, 1914.

Dewey, John. *How We Think.* Lexington: D.C. Heath & Co., 1910.

Dolgoff, Anatole. *Left of the Left: My Memories of Sam Dolgoff.* Oakland: AK Press, 2016.

Estévanez, Nicolás. *Resumen de la historia de España.* Barcelona: Escuela Moderna, 1904.

Ferrer, F. *L'Espagnol pratique: enseigné par la méthode Ferrer.* Paris: Garnier Hermanos, 1895.

Ferrer, Sol. *Le véritable Francisco Ferrer: d'après des documents inédits.* Paris: L'Écran du monde, 1948.

———. *La vie et l'oeuvre de Francisco Ferrer: un martyr au XXe siècle.* Paris: Librairie Fischbacher, 1962.

Ferrer Guardia, Francisco. *La Escuela Moderna: póstuma explicación y alcance de la enseñanza racionalista.* Barcelona: Fábula Tusquets Editores, 2009.

Francisco Ferrer: His Life, Work and Martyrdom. New York: Francisco Ferrer Association, 1910.

Grave, Jean. *Las aventuras de Nono.* Barcelona: Escuela Moderna, 1907.

Hamon, Augustin. *Le socialisme et le congrès de Londres: étude historique.* Paris: P.V. Stock, 1897.

Jacquinet, Clemencia. *La sociología en la escuela.* Barcelona: José Miguel Junqueras, 1904.

James, C.L. *Anarchism and Malthus.* New York: Mother Earth, 1910.

Leroy, Constant. *Los secretos del anarquismo.* México, DF: Librería Renacimiento, 1913.

Lerroux, Alejandro. *Mis Memorias.* Madrid: Afrodisio Aguado, 1963.

Malato, Charles. *L'assassinat de Ferrer: eclaircissements.* Geneva: Édition du Réveil, 1911.

————. *León Martín, ó, La miseria: sus causas, sus remedios*. Barcelona: Escuela Moderna, 1905.

Malvert. *El origen del cristianismo*. Barcelona: Escuela Moderna, 1903.

Patriotismo y colonización: con un prefacio de E. Reclus. Barcelona: Escuela Moderna, 1904.

Proceedings of the M.W. Grand Lodge of Free and Accepted Masons of the District of Columbia from November 4, A.L. 5845 to January 21, A. L. 5847. Washington: T. Barnard Printer, 1847.

El proceso Ferrer en el Congreso: recopilación de los discursos pronunciados por varios diputados durante el debate. Barcelona: Imprenta Lauria, 1911.

Regicidio furstrado, 31 Mayo 1906: causa contra Mateo Morral, Francisco Ferrer, José Nakens, Pedro Mayoral, Aquilino Martínez, Isidro Ibarra, Bernardo Mata y Concepción Pérez Cuesta, Vol. 1. Madrid: Sucesores de J.A. García, 1911.

Rocker, Rudolf. *En la borrasca: años de destierro*. Translated by Diego A. de Santillán. Buenos Aires: Editorial Tupac, 1949.

————. *Fransisko Ferrer un di freie ertzihung fun der jugend*. London: Arbeiter Freind, 1910.

Sacharoff, Victor et al., *Recollections from the Modern School Ferrer Colony*. Edited by Jon Thoreau Scott. Altamont, NY: Friends of the Modern School, 2007.

Salillas, Rafael. "La celda de Ferrer." *Revista penitenciaria*, Año IV, Tomo IV, Entrega 1a. Madrid: Eduardo Arias, 1907, 321–47.

Sanger, Margaret. *Margaret Sanger: An Autobiography*. New York: W.W. Norton, 1938.

Snijders, J. *Doel en streven der ontspanningsscholen: Ten voordeele der ontspanningsschool "Oosterpark en Omstreken."* Amsterdam: Snijders, 1907.

Wintsch, Jean. *L'école Ferrer: un essai d'institution ouvrière: Notice*. Geneva: Impr. des Unions ouvrières, 1919.

Books and Articles

Abad de Santillan, Diego. Foreword in *La Huelga general: periódico libertario*. Vaduz-Georgetown: Cabildo, 1975.

Aguilar, Kevan Antonio. "Peripheries of Power, Centers of Resistance: Anarchist Movements in Tampico and the Huasteca Region, 1910–1945." MA thesis, University of California, San Diego, 2014.

Aguinaga, Jean-François. "Ferrer i Guàrdia: llocs de memòria a Bèlgica." *Espai de Llibertat: revista d'esquerres per a la formació, la reflexió i l'agitació política* 54 (2009).

Aisa, Ferran. *La cultura anarquista a Catalunya*. Barcelona: Edicions de 1984, 2006.

Álvarez Junco, José. *El emperador del paralelo: Lerroux y la demogogia populista*. Madrid: Alianza, 1990.

Anderson, Benedict. *Under Three Flags: Anarchism and the Anti-Colonial Imagination*. New York: Verso, 2005.

Anderson, Peter. *The Francoist Military Trials: Terror and Complicity, 1939–1945*. New York: Routledge, 2010.

Araus Segura, Maria del Mar. "La escuela moderna en Iberoamérica: repercussion de la muerte de Francisco Ferrer Guardia." *Boletín americanista* 52 (2002): 7–22.

Archer, William. *The Life, Trial and Death of Francisco Ferrer.* New York: Moffat, Yard and Co., 1911.

Áviles, Juan. *Francisco Ferrer y Guerdia: pedagogo, anarquista y mártir.* Madrid: Marcial Pons, Ediciones de Historia, S. A., 2006.

Avrich, Paul. *Anarchist Voices: An Oral History of Anarchism in America.* Oakland: AK Press, 2005.

———. *The Modern School Movement: Anarchism and Education in the United States.* Princeton: Princeton University Press, 1980.

———. *Russian Anarchists.* New York: W.W. Norton & Co., 1980.

Avrich, Paul, and Karen Avrich. *Sasha and Emma: The Anarchist Odyssey of Alexander Berkman and Emma Goldman.* Cambridge: The Belknap Press of Harvard University Press, 2012.

Balfour, Sebastian. "Riot, Regeneration and Reaction: Spain in the Aftermath of the 1898 Disaster." *The Historical Journal* 38, no. 2 (1995): 405–23.

Bantman, Constance. *The French Anarchists in London, 1880–1914: Exile and Transnationalism in the First Globalisation.* Liverpool: Liverpool University Press, 2013.

Bergasa, Francisco. *¿Quién mató a Ferrer i Guardia?* Madrid: Santillana Ediciones Generales, S.L., 2009.

Best, Francine et al., *L'affaire Ferrer.* Castres: Centre national et Musée Jean Jaurès, 1991.

Bowles, Samuel, and Herbert Gintis. *Schooling in Capitalist America: Educational Reform and the Contradictions of Economic Life.* New York: Basic Books, 1976.

Boyd, Carolyn P. "The Anarchists and Education in Spain, 1868–1909." *The Journal of Modern History* 48 (December 1976): 125–70.

Canals, Salvador. *Los sucesos de España en 1909.* Vol. 2. Madrid: Imprenta Alemana, 1911.

Carr, Raymond. *Spain, 1808–1975.* Oxford: Clarendon Press, 2003.

Casanovas, Joan. *Bread, or Bullets! Urban Labor and Spanish Colonialism in Cuba, 1850–1898.* Pittsburgh: University of Pittsburgh, 1998.

Cuadrat, Xavier. *Socialismo y anarquismo en cataluña (1899–1911): los origenes de la C.N.T.* Madrid: Ediciones de la Revista de Trabajo, 1976.

Dalmau, Antoni. *El Procés de Montjuïc: Barcelona al final del segle XIX.* Barcelona: Editorial Base, 2010.

———. *Set dies de fúria: Barcelona i la setmana tràgica (juliol de 1909).* Barcelona: Columna Edicions, 2009.

Davis, Laurence, and Ruth Kinna, ed. *Anarchism and Utopianism.* Manchester: Manchester University Press, 2009.

de Angulo, Jaime. *The "Trial" of Ferrer: A Clerical Judicial Murder.* New York: New York Labor News Company, 1911.

de Cambra Bassols, Jordi. *Anarquismo y positivismo: el caso Ferrer.* Madrid: Centro de Investigaciones Sociologicas, 1981.

De Seta, Pamela, Flavia Fanello, and Ignacio Kuppe. "Las escuelas anarquistas en Argentina a principios del siglo XX." Presentation, XXVIII Congreso ALAS, "Fronteras Abiertas de América Latina," UFPE, Recife, Brasil, September 6–10, 2011.

de Vroede, Maurice. "Francisco Ferrer et la Ligue Internationale pour l'Éducation Rationnelle de l'Enfance." *Paedagogica Historica* 19 (1979): 278–95.

Delgado, Buenaventura. *La Escuela Moderna de Ferrer i Guardia.* Barcelona: Ediciones CEAC, 1979.

Di Paola, Pietro. *The Knights Errant of Anarchy: London and the Italian Anarchist Diaspora (1880–1917).* Liverpool: Liverpool University Press, 2013.

Elwitt, Sanford. "Education and the Social Questions: The Universités Populaires in Late Nineteenth Century France." *History of Education Quarterly* 22, no. 1 (Spring, 1982): 55–72.

Esdaile, Charles J. *Spain in the Liberal Age: From Constitution to Civil War, 1808–1939.* Oxford: Blackwell Publishers, 2000.

Esenwein, George Richard. *Anarchist Ideology and the Working-Class Movement in Spain, 1868–1898.* Berkeley: University of California Press, 1989.

Fernández, Frank. *Cuban Anarchism: The History of a Movement.* Translated by Charles Bufe. Tucson: See Sharp Press, 2001.

Fidler, Geoffrey C. "The Escuela Moderna Movement of Francisco Ferrer: 'Por la Verdad y la Justicia.'" *History of Education Quarterly* 25, no. 1–2 (Spring–Summer 1985): 103–32.

Fregoni, Olga Regina. "Educação e resistência anarquista em São Paulo: a sobrevivência das prácticas da educação na Academia de Comércio Saldanha Marinho (1920–1945)." PhD diss., Pontíficia Universidade Católica de São Paulo, 2007.

Freire, Paulo. *Pedagogy of Freedom: Ethics, Democracy and Civic Courage.* New York: Rowan & Littlefield, 2000.

———. *Pedagogy of the Oppressed.* New York: Continuum, 2007.

Furtado Gomes Riet Vargas, Francisco. "Anarquismo e educação em Rio Grande (1918–1927): educação de, para e pelos trabalhadores." PhD diss., Universidade Federal de Pelotas, 2011.

García Sanz, Fernando. *Historia de las relaciones entre España e Italia: imágenes, comercio y política exterior (1890–1914).* Madrid: Consejo Superior de Investigaciones Científicas, 1994.

Girón Sierra, Álvaro. *En la mesa con Darwin: evolución y revolución en el movimiento libertario en España (1869–1914).* Madrid: Consejo Superior de Investigaciones Científicas, 2005.

Goldman, Emma. "The Social Importance of the Modern School 1912." Accessed June 29, 2018. http://dwardmac.pitzer.edu/anarchist_archives/goldman/socimportms.html.

Goldstein, Robert Justin. *Political Censorship of the Arts and the Press in Nineteenth-Century Europe.* New York: Palgrave Macmillan, 1989.

González Agàpito, Josep, Salomó Marquès, Alejandro Mayordomo, and Bernat Sureda. *Tradició i renovació pedagògica, 1898–1939: història de l'educació: Catalunya, Illes Balears, País Valencià.* Barcelona: Publicacions de l'Abadia de Montserrat, 2002.

González Calleja, Eduardo. *La razón de la fuerza: orden público, subversión y violencia política en la España de la Restauración (1875–1917).* Madrid: Consejo Superior de Investigaciones Científicas, 1998.

Gori, Pietro. "Poemes." *Espai de Llibertat: revista d'esquerres per a la formació, la reflexió i l'agitació política* 54 (2009): 46–47.

Gorman, Anthony. "Anarchists in Education: The Free Popular University in Egypt (1901)." *Middle Eastern Studies* 41, no. 3 (May 2005): 303–20.

Goyens, Tom. *Beer and Revolution: The German Anarchist Movement in New York City, 1880–1914.* Urbana: University of Illinois Press, 2007.

Graeber, David. *Revolutions in Reverse: Essays on Politics, Violence, Art, and Imagination.* London: Minor Compositions, 2011.

Graham, Robert. *We Do Not Fear Anarchy, We Invoke It: The First International and the Origins of the Anarchist Movement.* Oakland: AK Press, 2015.

Griffiths, Richard. *The Use of Abuse: The Polemics of the Dreyfus Affair and its Aftermath.* New York: Berg, 1991.

Guerrero, Práxedis G. "Impulsemos la enseñanza racionalista." In Rama and Cappelletti, *El anarquismo en America Latina.*

Haiven, Max. *Crises of Imagination, Crisis of Power: Capitalism, Creativity and the Commons.* London: Zed Books, 2014.

Harrington, Thomas S. *Public Intellectuals and Nation Building in the Iberian Peninsula: The Alchemy of Identity.* Lewisburg, PA: Bucknell University Press, 2015.

Hart, John M. *Anarchism and The Mexican Working Class, 1860–1931.* Austin: University of Texas Press, 1978.

———. "The Urban Working Class and the Mexican Revolution: The Case of the Casa del Obrero Mundial." *Hispanic American Historical Review* 58, no. 1 (February 1978): 1–20.

Haworth, Robert, and John Elmore. *Out of the Ruins: The Emergence of Radical Informal Learning Spaces.* Oakland: PM Press, 2017.

Henry, André. *Serviteurs d'idéal: histoire de la longue marche, des associations, des cooperatives, des mutuelles et des syndicats.* Paris: Centre federal FEN, 1987.

Herrerín López, Ángel. *Anarquía, dinamita y revolución social: violencia y represión en la España de entre siglos (1868–1909).* Madrid: Catarata, 2011.

Hinchey, Patricia. *Finding Freedom in the Classroom: A Practical Introduction to Critical Theory.* New York: Peter Lang, 2009.

Hirsch, Steven, and Lucien van der Walt, ed. *Anarchism and Syndicalism in the Colonial and Postcolonial World, 1870–1940: The Praxis of National Liberation, Internationalism, and Social Revolution.* Leiden, NL: Brill, 2010.

Hoffman, Robert L. *More Than a Trial: The Struggle Over Captain Dreyfus.* New York: Free Press, 1980.

Íñiguez, Miguel, ed. *Enciclopedia histórica del anarquismo español.* Vitoria: Asociación Isaac Puente, 2008.

Izrine, Jean-Marc. *Les libertaires dans l'affaire Dreyfus.* Paris: Éditions d'Alternative libertaire, 2012.

Kaplan, Temma. *Anarchists of Andalusia 1868–1903.* Princeton: Princeton University Press, 1977.

———. *Red City, Blue Period: Social Movements in Picasso's Barcelona.* Princeton: Princeton University Press, 1992.

Keep, John. "Terror in 1905." In *Reinterpreting Revolutionary Russia: Essays in Honour of James D. White.* Edited by Ian D. Thatcher. New York: Palgrave Macmillan, 2006.

Khuri-Makdisi, Ilham. *The Eastern Mediterranean and the Making of Global Radicalism, 1860–1914.* Berkeley: University of California Press, 2010.

Laqua, Daniel. "Freethinkers, Anarchists and Francisco Ferrer: The Making of a Transnational Solidarity Campaign." *European Review of History / Revue européenne d'histoire* 21, no. 4 (2014): 467–84.

Lasso de la Vega, Leoncio. *El asesinato de Ferrer: la protesta del Uruguay.* Montevideo: 1909.

Lázaro Lorente, Luis M. *La Escuela Moderna de Valencia.* Valencia: Generalitat Valenciana, 1989.

————. *Las Escuelas Racionalistas en el País Valenciano (1906–1931).* Valencia: NAU llibres, 1992.

Levy, Carl. Foreword to Vernon Richards. *Life and Ideas: The Anarchist Writings of Errico Malatesta.*

Lomnitz, Claudio. *The Return of Comrade Ricardo Flores Magón.* Brooklyn: Zone Books, 2014.

Madrid, Francisco. *Solidaridad Obrera y el periodismo de raíz ácrata.* Badalona: Ediciones Solidaridad Obrera, 2007.

Maitron, Jean. *Le mouvement anarchiste en France: Vol. 1—Des origines à 1914.* Paris: Gallimard, 1992.

Martínez de Sas, M. Teresa, ed. *Cartas, comunicaciones y circulares de la Comisión Federal de la Región Española.* Vol. 7. Barcelona: Edicions de la Universitat de Barcelona, 1987.

Martínez Fiol, David. *La setmana tràgica.* Barcelona: Pòrtic, 2009.

Masjuan, Eduard. *Un héroe trágico del anarquismo español: Mateo Morral, 1879–1906.* Barcelona: Icaria editorial, 2009.

Maura y Gamazo, Gabriel, and Melchor Fernández Almagro. *Por qué cayó Alfonso XIII? Evolución y disolución de los partidos históricos durante su reinado.* Madrid: Ediciones Ambos Mundos, S. L., 1948.

Mehl Gonçalves, Aracely. "Francisco Ferrer y Guardia: educação e a imprensa anarco-sindicalista—'A PLEBE.'" PhD diss., Universidade Estadual De Ponta Grossa-UEPG, 2007.

Merriman, John. *The Dynamite Club: How a Bombing in Fin-de-Siècle Paris Ignited the Age of Modern Terror.* Boston: Houghton Mifflin Harcourt, 2009.

Monés, Jordi, Pere Solà, and Luis Miguel Lázaro, ed. *Ferrer Guardia y la pedagogía libertaria: elementos para un debate.* Barcelona: Icaria Editorial, 1977.

Monés i Pujol-Busquets, Jordi. "Ferrer en la tradición del pensamiento educativo libertario." In *Ferrer Guardia y la pedagogía libertaria.*

Nadal Masegosa, Antonio. "Análisis y valoración de la vigencia de los principios pedagógicos de la Escuela Moderna de Francisco Ferrer Guardia en el estado español en el siglo XXI: estudio de casos." PhD diss., Univerdidad de Málaga, 2015.

Nieuwenhuis, Ferdinand Domela. *De Kommune van Parijs.* Amsterdam: Uitg. der Ontspanningsschool Haarlemmerpoort en Omstreken—Kinder-bibliotheek no. 3.

Núñez, Iván. *Educación popular y movimiento obrero: un estudio histórico.* Santiago: Academia de Humanismo Cristiano, 1982.

Park, Tiidu Peter. "The European Reaction to the Execution of Francisco Ferrer." PhD diss., University of Virginia, 1970.

Paz, Abel et al., ed. *La Barcelona rebelde: guía de una ciudad silenciada.* Barcelona: Octaedro, 2008.

Perry, Jeffrey Babcock. *Hubert Harrison: The Voice of Harlem Radicalism, 1883–1918.* New York: Columbia University Press, 2009.

Phillips, Utah, and Ani DiFranco. "Candidacy." *The Past Didn't Go Anywhere.* Righteous Babe, 1996.

Piqueras Arenas, José Antonio. *Cánovas y la derecha española: del magnicidio a los neocon.* Barcelona: Ediciones Península, 2008.

Pradas Baena, María Amalia. *Teresa Claramunt: la "virgen roja" barcelonesa, biografía y escritos.* Barcelona: Virus, 2006.

Purkiss, Richard. *Democracy, Trade Unions and Political Violence in Spain: The Valencian Anarchist Movement, 1918–1936.* Brighton: Sussex Academic Press, 2011.

Rama, Carlos M., and Angel J. Cappelletti, ed. *El anarquismo en America Latina.* Caracas: Biblioteca Ayacucho, 1990.

Reyes Jedlicki, Leonora. "The Crisis of the Estado docente and the Critical Education Movement: The Escuelas Obreras Federales Racionalistas in Chile (1921–1926)." *Journal of Latin American Studies* 39, no. 4 (2007): 827–55.

Richards, Vernon, ed. *Life and Ideas: The Anarchist Writings of Errico Malatesta.* Oakland: PM Press, 2015.

Robert, Vincent, and Eduard J. Verger, "'La protesta universal' contra la ejecución de Ferrer: las manifestaciones de octubre de 1909." *Historia Social* 14 (Autumn 1992): 61–82.

Rojas Flores, Jorge. *Moral y prácticas cívicas en los niños chilenos, 1880–1950.* Santiago: Ariadna Ediciones, 2004.

Romero Maura, Joaquín. *"La rosa de fuego": el obrerismo barcelonés de 1899 a 1909.* Barcelona: Ediciones Grijalbo, 1975.

———. "Terrorism in Barcelona and Its Impact on Spanish Politics 1904–1909." *Past and Present* 41, (December 1968): 130–83.

Ruiz Berrio, Julio. "La rénovation pédagogique en Espagne de la fin du XIXe siècle à 1939." *Histoire de l'éducation* 78 (1998): 133–65.

Samuel, René, and Georges Bonet-Maury. *Les parlementaires français: II, 1900–1914: dictionnaire biographique et bibliographique des sénateurs, députés, ministres.* Paris: Georges Roustan, 1914.

Sanabria, Enrique A. *Republicanism and Anticlerical Nationalism in Spain.* New York: Palgrave Macmillan, 2009.

Sánchez Cobos, Amparo. *Sembrando ideales: anarquistas españoles en Cuba, 1902–1925.* Sevilla: Consejo Superior de Investigaciones Científicas, 2008.

Shaffer, Kirwin R. *Anarchism and Countercultural Politics in Early Twentieth-Century Cuba.* Gainesville: University Press of Florida, 2005.

———. "Freedom Teaching: Anarchism and Education in Early Republican Cuba, 1898–1925." *The Americas* 60, no. 2 (October 2003): 151–83.

Shubert, Adrian. *A Social History of Modern Spain.* London: Routledge, 1990.

Smith, D.W. "Deleuze and the Question of Desire: Toward an Immanent Theory of Ethics." *Parrhesia: A Journal of Critical Philosophy* 2 (2007): 66–78.

Smith, Virginia. *Clean: A History of Personal Hygiene and Purity.* Oxford: Oxford University Press, 2007.

Solà, Pere. "Prólogo a la edición de 2009 de *La Escuela Moderna*." In Ferrer Guardia, *La Escuela Moderna: Póstuma explicación y alcance de la enseñanza racionalista*.

Solà i Gussinyer, Pere. *Educació i moviment llibertari a Catalunya (1901–1939)*. Barcelona: Edicions 62, 1980.

———. "Escuela y educación para una sociedad autogestionada: la aportación de la pedagogía racionalista de F. Ferrer." In *Ferrer Guardia y la pedagogía libertaria*, 90–1.

———. "Los grupos del magisterio racionalista en Argentina y Uruguay hacia 1910 y sus actitudes ante la enseñanza laica official." *Historia de la Educación* 1 (1982): 229–46.

Sonn, Richard D. *Anarchism and Cultural Politics in Fin de Siècle France*. Lincoln: University of Nebraska Press, 1989.

Suissa, Judith. *Anarchism and Education: A Philosophical Perspective*. New York: Routledge, 2006.

———. "'The Space Now Possible': Anarchist Education as Utopian Hope." In Davis and Kinna. *Anarchism and Utopianism*.

Suriano, Juan. *Anarquistas: cultura y política libertaria en Buenos Aires, 1890–1910*. Buenos Aires: Manatial, 2001.

Tavares de Pinho, Adelino. *Pela educação e pelo trabalho e outros escritos*. São Paulo: Biblioteca Terra Livre, 2012.

Thomson, Guy. *The Birth of Modern Politics in Spain: Democracy, Association and Revolution, 1854–75*. New York: Palgrave Macmillan, 2010.

Tiana Ferrer, Alejandro. *Educación libertaria y revolución social (España, 1936–1939)*. Madrid: UNED, 1987.

———. "Movimiento obrero y educación popular en la españa contemporánea." *Historia Social* 27 (1997): 127–44.

Tone, John Lawrence. *War and Genocide in Cuba, 1895–1898*. Chapel Hill: University of North Carolina Press, 2006.

Turin, Yvonne. *La educación y la escuela en España de 1874 a 1902: liberalismo y tradición*. Translated by Josefa Hernández Alfonso. Madrid: Aguilar, 1967.

Ullman, Joan Connelly. *La semana trágica: estudio sobre las causas socioeconómicas del anticlericalismo en España (1898–1912)*. Barcelona: Ediciones Ariel, 1968.

Vallina, Pedro. *Fermín Salvochea: crónica de un revolucionario*. Sevilla: Editorial Renacimiento, 2012.

van der Woude, Richard. "Op, mannen, broeders! saam vereenigd! Op, burgers! Sluit u bij ons aan! Het proletariërslied in Nederland—1872–1914." BA thesis, Universiteit Utrecht, 2011.

Vázquez Romero, José Manuel, ed. *Francisco Giner de los Ríos: actualidad de un pensador krausista*. Madrid: Marcial Pons, 2009.

Velázquez, Pascual, and Antonio Viñao. "Un programa de educación popular: el legado de Ferrer Guardia y la editorial publicaciones de la Escuela Moderna (1901–1936)." *Educació i Història: Revista d'Història de l'Educació* 16 (2010): 79–104.

Vincent, Mary. *Spain, 1833–2002: People and State*. Oxford: Oxford University Press, 2007.

Voltes Bou, Pedro. *La semana trágica*. Madrid: Espasa Calpe, 1995.

Wagnon, Sylvain. *Francisco Ferrer: une éducation libertaire en héritage*. Lyon: Atelier de création libertaire, 2013.

Walker, D.J. *Spanish Women and the Colonial Wars of the 1890s*. Baton Rouge: Louisiana State University Press, 2008.

Wheeler, Robert F. "Teaching Sport as History, History through Sport." *The History Teacher* 11, no. 3 (1978).

Woodcock, George. *Anarchism: A History of Libertarian Ideas and Movements*. New York: Meridian, 1962.

Zimmer, Kenyon. *Immigrants against the State: Yiddish and Italian Anarchism in America*. Urbana: University of Illinois Press, 2015.

Zuckerman, Fredric S. *The Tsarist Secret Police in Russian Society, 1880–1917*. New York: New York University Press, 1996.

About the Authors

Francisco Ferrer Guardia (1859–1909) was a Catalan educator, writer, and organizer who founded The Modern School in Barcelona in 1901. Although innocent of the charges against him, he was executed by the Spanish Monarchy for being the alleged mastermind of the Tragic Week in 1909.

Joseph McCabe (1867–1955) was an English freethinker and rationalist who authored, edited, and translated more than two hundred books on religion, war, government, and many other topics.

Mark Bray is a historian of Modern European History, a political organizer, and the author of *Antifa: The Anti-Fascist Handbook* and *Translating Anarchy: The Anarchism of Occupy Wall Street*. He is currently a lecturer at Dartmouth College.

Robert H. Haworth is an associate professor in the Department of Educational Foundations and Policy Studies at West Chester University. He teaches courses focusing on the social foundations of education, anarchism, and critical pedagogies. He has published and presented internationally on anarchism, youth culture, informal learning spaces, and critical social studies education. Haworth has been the editor of other PM Press books, including *Anarchist Pedagogies: Collective Actions, Theories, and Critical Reflections on Education* and *Out of the Ruins: The Emergence of Radical Informal Learning Spaces*. In the 1990s, he cofounded the worker-owned and operated Regeneration TV, as well as other academic research collectives. He is also a songwriter / vocalist for the political rock band Second Letter.

Index

Page numbers in *italic* refer to illustrations. "Passim" (literally "scattered") indicates intermittent discussion of a topic over a cluster of pages.

ABOUT PM PRESS

PM Press was founded at the end of 2007 by a small collection of folks with decades of publishing, media, and organizing experience. PM Press co-conspirators have published and distributed hundreds of books, pamphlets, CDs, and DVDs. Members of PM have founded enduring book fairs, spearheaded victorious tenant organizing campaigns, and worked closely with bookstores, academic conferences, and even rock bands to deliver political and challenging ideas to all walks of life. We're old enough to know what we're doing and young enough to know what's at stake.

We seek to create radical and stimulating fiction and non-fiction books, pamphlets, T-shirts, visual and audio materials to entertain, educate, and inspire you. We aim to distribute these through every available channel with every available technology—whether that means you are seeing anarchist classics at our bookfair stalls, reading our latest vegan cookbook at the café, downloading geeky fiction e-books, or digging new music and timely videos from our website.

PM Press is always on the lookout for talented and skilled volunteers, artists, activists, and writers to work with. If you have a great idea for a project or can contribute in some way, please get in touch.

PM Press
PO Box 23912
Oakland, CA 94623
www.pmpress.org

PM Press in Europe
europe@pmpress.org
www.pmpress.org.uk

FRIENDS OF PM PRESS

These are indisputably momentous times—the financial system is melting down globally and the Empire is stumbling. Now more than ever there is a vital need for radical ideas.

In the years since its founding—and on a mere shoestring—PM Press has risen to the formidable challenge of publishing and distributing knowledge and entertainment for the struggles ahead. With over 300 releases to date, we have published an impressive and stimulating array of literature, art, music, politics, and culture. Using every available medium, we've succeeded in connecting those hungry for ideas and information to those putting them into practice.

Friends of PM allows you to directly help impact, amplify, and revitalize the discourse and actions of radical writers, filmmakers, and artists. It provides us with a stable foundation from which we can build upon our early successes and provides a much-needed subsidy for the materials that can't necessarily pay their own way. You can help make that happen—and receive every new title automatically delivered to your door once a month—by joining as a Friend of PM Press. And, we'll throw in a free T-shirt when you sign up.

Here are your options:

• **$30 a month** Get all books and pamphlets plus 50% discount on all webstore purchases

• **$40 a month** Get all PM Press releases (including CDs and DVDs) plus 50% discount on all webstore purchases

• **$100 a month** Superstar—Everything plus PM merchandise, free downloads, and 50% discount on all webstore purchases

For those who can't afford $30 or more a month, we have **Sustainer Rates** at $15, $10 and $5. Sustainers get a free PM Press T-shirt and a 50% discount on all purchases from our website.

Your Visa or Mastercard will be billed once a month, until you tell us to stop. Or until our efforts succeed in bringing the revolution around. Or the financial meltdown of Capital makes plastic redundant. Whichever comes first.

Anarchist Pedagogies: Collective Actions, Theories, and Critical Reflections on Education

Edited by Robert H. Haworth
with an afterword by Allan Antliff

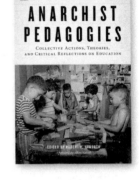

ISBN: 978-1-60486-484-7
$24.95   352 pages

Education is a challenging subject for anarchists.
Many are critical about working within a state-run
education system that is embedded in hierarchical, standardized, and authoritarian
structures. Numerous individuals and collectives envision the creation of
counterpublics or alternative educational sites as possible forms of resistance,
while other anarchists see themselves as "saboteurs" within the public arena—
believing that there is a need to contest dominant forms of power and educational
practices from multiple fronts. Of course, if anarchists agree that there are no
blueprints for education, the question remains, in what dynamic and creative
ways can we construct nonhierarchical, anti-authoritarian, mutual, and voluntary
educational spaces?

Contributors to this edited volume engage readers in important and challenging
issues in the area of anarchism and education. From Francisco Ferrer's modern
schools in Spain and the Work People's College in the United States, to
contemporary actions in developing "free skools" in the U.K. and Canada, to
direct-action education such as learning to work as a "street medic" in the
protests against neoliberalism, the contributors illustrate the importance of
developing complex connections between educational theories and collective
actions. Anarchists, activists, and critical educators should take these educational
experiences seriously as they offer invaluable examples for potential teaching and
learning environments outside of authoritarian and capitalist structures. Major
themes in the volume include: learning from historical anarchist experiments
in education, ways that contemporary anarchists create dynamic and situated
learning spaces, and finally, critically reflecting on theoretical frameworks and
educational practices. Contributors include: David Gabbard, Jeffery Shantz,
Isabelle Fremeaux & John Jordan, Abraham P. DeLeon, Elsa Noterman, Andre
Pusey, Matthew Weinstein, Alex Khasnabish, and many others.

*"Pedagogy is a central concern in anarchist writing and the free skool has played
a central part in movement activism. By bringing together an important group of
writers with specialist knowledge and experience, Robert Haworth's volume makes an
invaluable contribution to the discussion of these topics. His exciting collection provides
a guide to historical experiences and current experiments and also reflects on anarchist
theory, extending our understanding and appreciation of pedagogy in anarchist
practice."*
—Dr. Ruth Kinna, Senior Lecturer in Politics, Loughborough University, author of
Anarchism: A Beginners Guide and coeditor of *Anarchism and Utopianism*

Out of the Ruins: The Emergence of Radical Informal Learning Spaces

Edited by Robert H. Haworth and
John M. Elmore

ISBN: 978-1-62963-239-1
$24.95   288 pages

OUT OF THE RUINS
The Emergence of
Radical Informal Learning Spaces

Edited by Robert H. Haworth & John M. Elmore

Contemporary educational practices and policies
across the world are heeding the calls of Wall Street for
more corporate control, privatization, and standardized accountability. There are
definite shifts and movements towards more capitalist interventions of efficiency
and an adherence to market fundamentalist values within the sphere of public
education. In many cases, educational policies are created to uphold and serve
particular social, political, and economic ends. Schools, in a sense, have been tools
to reproduce hierarchical, authoritarian, and hyper-individualistic models of social
order. From the industrial era to our recent expansion of the knowledge economy,
education has been at the forefront of manufacturing and exploiting particular
populations within our society.

The important news is that emancipatory educational practices are emerging.
Many are emanating outside the constraints of our dominant institutions and
are influenced by more participatory and collective actions. In many cases, these
alternatives have been undervalued or even excluded within the educational
research. From an international perspective, some of these radical informal
learning spaces are seen as a threat by many failed states and corporate entities.

Out of the Ruins sets out to explore and discuss the emergence of alternative
learning spaces that directly challenge the pairing of public education with
particular dominant capitalist and statist structures. The authors construct
philosophical, political, economic and social arguments that focus on radical
informal learning as a way to contest efforts to commodify and privatize our
everyday educational experiences. The major themes include the politics of
learning in our formal settings, constructing new theories on our informal practices,
collective examples of how radical informal learning practices and experiences
operate, and how individuals and collectives struggle to share these narratives
within and outside of institutions.

Contributors include David Gabbard, Rhiannon Firth, Andrew Robinson, Farhang
Rouhani, Petar Jandrić, Ana Kuzmanić, Sarah Amsler, Dana Williams, Andre Pusey,
Jeff Shantz, Sandra Jeppesen, Joanna Adamiak, Erin Dyke, Eli Meyerhoff, David I.
Backer, Matthew Bissen, Jacques Laroche, Aleksandra Perisic, and Jason Wozniak.

Anarchism and Education: A Philosophical Perspective

Judith Suissa

ISBN: 978-1-60486-114-3
$19.95   184 pages

While there have been historical accounts of the anarchist school movement, there has been no systematic work on the philosophical underpinnings of anarchist educational ideas—until now.

Anarchism and Education offers a philosophical account of the neglected tradition of anarchist thought on education. Although few anarchist thinkers wrote systematically on education, this analysis is based largely on a reconstruction of the educational thought of anarchist thinkers gleaned from their various ethical, philosophical, and popular writings. Primarily drawing on the work of the nineteenth-century anarchist theorists such as Bakunin, Kropotkin, and Proudhon, the book also covers twentieth-century anarchist thinkers such as Noam Chomsky, Paul Goodman, Daniel Guérin, and Colin Ward.

This original work will interest philosophers of education and educationalist thinkers as well as those with a general interest in anarchism.

"This is an excellent book that deals with important issues through the lens of anarchist theories and practices of education… The book tackles a number of issues that are relevant to anybody who is trying to come to terms with the philosophy of education."
—*Higher Education Review*

Collectives in the Spanish Revolution

Gaston Leval

With a foreword by Vernon Richards, and an introduction by Pedro García-Guirao

ISBN: 978-1-62963-447-0

$27.95   416 pages

Revolutionary Spain came about with an explosion of social change so advanced and sweeping that it remains widely studied as one of the foremost experiments in worker self-management in history. At the heart of this vast foray into toppling entrenched forms of domination and centralised control was the flourishing of an array of worker-run collectives in industry, agriculture, public services, and beyond.

Collectives in the Spanish Revolution is a unique account of this transformative process—a work combining impeccable research and analysis with lucid reportage. Its author, Gaston Leval, was not only a participant in the Revolution and a dedicated anarcho-syndicalist but an especially knowledgeable eyewitness to the many industrial and agrarian collectives. In documenting the collectives' organisation and how they improved working conditions and increased output, Leval also gave voice to the workers who made them, recording their stories and experiences. At the same time, Leval did not shy away from exploring some of the collectives' failings, often ignored in other accounts of the period, opening space for readers today to critically draw lessons from the Spanish experience with self-managed collectives. The book opens with an insightful examination of pre-revolutionary economic conditions in Spain that gave rise to the worker and peasant initiatives Leval documents and analyses in the bulk of his study. He begins by surveying agrarian collectives in Aragón, Levante, and Castile. Leval then guides the reader through an incredible variety of urban examples of self-organisation, from factories and workshops to medicine, social services, Barcelona's tramway system, and beyond. He concludes with a brief but perceptive consideration of the broader political context in which workers carried out such a far-reaching revolution in social organisation—and a rumination on who and what was responsible for its defeat.

This classic translation of the French original by Vernon Richards is presented in this edition for the first time with an index. A new introduction by Pedro García-Guirao and a preface by Stuart Christie offer a précis of Leval's life and methods, placing his landmark study in the context of more recent writing on the Spanish collectives—eloquently positing that Leval's account of collectivism and his assessments of their achievements and failings still have a great deal to teach us today.

Anarchy and the Sex Question: Essays on Women and Emancipation, 1896–1926

Emma Goldman
Edited by Shawn P. Wilbur

ISBN: 978-1-62963-144-8
$14.95   160 pages

For Emma Goldman, the "High Priestess of Anarchy," anarchism was "a living force in the affairs of our life, constantly creating new conditions," but "the most elemental force in human life" was something still more basic and vital: sex.

"The Sex Question" emerged for Goldman in multiple contexts, and we find her addressing it in writing on subjects as varied as women's suffrage, "free love," birth control, the "New Woman," homosexuality, marriage, love, and literature. It was at once a political question, an economic question, a question of morality, and a question of social relations.

But her analysis of that most elemental force remained fragmentary, scattered across numerous published (and unpublished) works and conditioned by numerous contexts. *Anarchy and the Sex Question* draws together the most important of those scattered sources, uniting both familiar essays and archival material, in an attempt to recreate the great work on sex that Emma Goldman might have given us. In the process, it sheds light on Goldman's place in the history of feminism.

"Emma Goldman left a profound legacy of wisdom, insight, and passionate commitment to life. Shawn Wilbur has carefully selected her best writings on that most profound, pleasurable, and challenging of topics: sex. This collection is a great service to anarchist, feminist, and queer communities around the world."
—Jamie Heckert, coeditor of *Anarchism & Sexuality: Ethics, Relationships and Power*

"Shawn Wilbur has done a great job assembling and introducing Emma Goldman's writings on women, feminism, and sexuality. As he notes, Goldman's essays continue to provoke and inspire. The collection artfully documents the evolution of Goldman's views on freedom, sex, and human liberation."
—Robert Graham, editor of *Anarchism: A Documentary History of Libertarian Ideas*

The Paul Goodman Reader

Edited by Taylor Stoehr

ISBN: 978-1-60486-058-0
$28.95   500 pages

A one-man think-tank for the New Left, Paul Goodman wrote over thirty books, most of them before his decade of fame as a social critic in the Sixties. A Paul Goodman Reader that does him justice must be a compendious volume, with excerpts not only from best-sellers like *Growing Up Absurd*, but also from his landmark books on education, community planning, anarchism, psychotherapy, language theory, and poetics. Samples as well from *The Empire City*, a comic novel reviewers compared to *Don Quixote*, prize-winning short stories, and scores of poems that led America's most respected poetry reviewer, Hayden Carruth, to exclaim, "Not one dull page. It's almost unbelievable."

Goodman called himself as an old-fashioned man of letters, which meant that all these various disciplines and occasions added up to a single abiding concern for the human plight in perilous times, and for human promise and achieved grandeur, love and hope.

"*It was that voice of his that seduced me—that direct, cranky, egotistical, generous American voice… Paul Goodman's voice touched everything he wrote about with intensity, interest, and his own terribly appealing sureness and awkwardness… It was his voice, that is to say, his intelligence and the poetry of his intelligence incarnated, which kept me a loyal and passionate fan.*"
—Susan Sontag, novelist and public intellectual

"*Goodman, like all real novelists, is, at bottom, a moralist. What really interests him are the various ways in which human beings living in a modern metropolis gain, keep or lose their integrity and sense of selfhood.*"
—W. H. Auden, poet

"*Any page by Paul Goodman will give you not only originality and brilliance but wisdom, that is, something to think about. He is our peculiar, urban, twentieth-century Thoreau, the quintessential American mind of our time.*"
— Hayden Carruth, poet and essayist

"*No one writing now in America makes better sense of literary subjects. His ability to combine linguistic criticism, politics, a version of the nature of man, anthropology, the history of philosophy, and autobiographical testament with literary analysis, and to make a closely woven fabric of argument, seems magical.*"
—Robert Meredith, *The Nation*

The CNT in the Spanish Revolution Vols. 1–3

José Peirats
with an introduction by Chris Ealham

Vol. 1 **ISBN: 978-1-60486-207-2**
   $28.00   432 pages

Vol. 2 **ISBN: 978-1-60486-208-9**
   $22.95   312 pages

Vol. 3 **ISBN: 978-1-60486-209-6**
   $22.95   296 pages

The CNT in the Spanish Revolution is the history of one of the most original and audacious, and arguably also the most far-reaching, of all the twentieth-century revolutions. It is the history of the giddy years of political change and hope in 1930s Spain, when the so-called 'Generation of '36', Peirats' own generation, rose up against the oppressive structures of Spanish society. It is also a history of a revolution that failed, crushed in the jaws of its enemies on both the reformist left and the reactionary right. José Peirats' account is effectively the official CNT history of the war, passionate, partisan but, above all, intelligent. Its huge sweeping canvas covers all areas of the anarchist experience—the spontaneous militias, the revolutionary collectives, the moral dilemmas occasioned by the clash of revolutionary ideals and the stark reality of the war effort against Franco and his German Nazi and Italian Fascist allies.

This new edition is carefully indexed in a way that converts the work into a usable tool for historians and makes it much easier for the general reader to dip in with greater purpose and pleasure.

"José Peirats' The CNT in the Spanish Revolution *is a landmark in the historiography of the Spanish Civil War. . . . Originally published in Toulouse in the early 1950s, it was a rarity anxiously searched for by historians and others who gleefully pillaged its wealth of documentation. Even its republication in Paris in 1971 by the exiled Spanish publishing house, Ruedo Ibérico, though welcome, still left the book in the territory of specialists. For that reason alone, the present project to publish the entire work in English is to be applauded."*
—Professor Paul Preston, London School of Economics

Demanding the Impossible:
A History of Anarchism

Peter Marshall

ISBN: 978-1-60486-064-1
$28.95   840 pages

Navigating the broad "river of anarchy," from Taoism
to Situationism, from Ranters to Punk rockers, from
individualists to communists, from anarcho-syndicalists
to anarcha-feminists, *Demanding the Impossible* is an
authoritative and lively study of a widely misunderstood
subject. It explores the key anarchist concepts of society and the state, freedom
and equality, authority and power, and investigates the successes and failure of
the anarchist movements throughout the world. While remaining sympathetic
to anarchism, it presents a balanced and critical account. It covers not only the
classic anarchist thinkers, such as Godwin, Proudhon, Bakunin, Kropotkin, Reclus
and Emma Goldman, but also other libertarian figures, such as Nietzsche, Camus,
Gandhi, Foucault and Chomsky. No other book on anarchism covers so much so
incisively.

In this updated edition, a new epilogue examines the most recent developments,
including "post-anarchism" and "anarcho-primitivism" as well as the anarchist
contribution to the peace, green and Global Justice movements.

Demanding the Impossible is essential reading for anyone wishing to understand
what anarchists stand for and what they have achieved. It will also appeal to those
who want to discover how anarchism offers an inspiring and original body of ideas
and practices which is more relevant than ever in the twenty-first century.

"Demanding the Impossible *is the book I always recommend when asked—as I often
am—for something on the history and ideas of anarchism.*"
—Noam Chomsky

"*Attractively written and fully referenced… bound to be the standard history.*"
—Colin Ward, *Times Educational Supplement*

"*Large, labyrinthine, tentative: for me these are all adjectives of praise when applied to
works of history, and* Demanding the Impossible *meets all of them.*"
—George Woodcock, *Independent*

Archive That, Comrade! Left Legacies and the Counter Culture of Remembrance

Phil Cohen

ISBN: 978-1-62963-506-4
$19.95   160 pages

Archive That, Comrade! explores issues of archival theory and practice that arise for any project aspiring to provide an open-access platform for political dialogue and democratic debate. It is informed by the author's experience of writing a memoir about his involvement in the London underground scene of the 1960s, the London street commune movement, and the occupation of 144 Piccadilly, an event that hit the world's headlines for ten days in July 1969.

After a brief introduction that sets the contemporary scene of 'archive fever,' the book considers what the political legacy of 1960s counter culture reveals about the process of commemoration. The argument then opens out to discuss the notion of historical legacy and its role in the 'dialectic of generations'. How far can the archive serve as a platform for dialogue and debate between different generations of activists in a culture that fetishises the evanescent present, practices a profound amnesia about its past, and forecloses the sociological imagination of an alternative future? The following section looks at the emergence of a complex apparatus of public fame and celebrity around the spectacle of dissidence and considers whether the Left has subverted or merely mirrored the dominant forms of reputation-making and public recognition. Can the Left establish its own autonomous model of commemoration?

The final section takes up the challenge of outlining a model for the democratic archive as a revisionary project, creating a resource for building collective capacity to sustain struggles of long duration. A postscript examines how archival strategies of the alt-right have intervened at this juncture to elaborate a politics of false memory.

"Has the Left got a past? And if so, is that past best forgotten? Who was it who said, 'Let the dead bury their dead'? Phil Cohen's book is a searing meditation on the politics of memory, written by someone for whom 'the '60s' are still alive—and therefore horrible, unfinished, unforgivable, tremendous, undead. His book brings back to life the William Faulkner cliché. The past for Cohen is neither dead nor alive. It's not even past, more's the pity."
—T.J. Clark, author of *The Sight of Death*

Understanding Jim Crow: Using Racist Memorabilia to Teach Tolerance and Promote Social Justice

David Pilgrim with a foreword by
Henry Louis Gates Jr.

ISBN: 978-1-62963-114-1
$19.95   208 pages

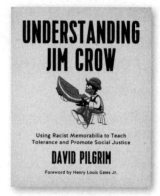

For many people, especially those who came of age after landmark civil rights legislation was passed, it is difficult to understand what it was like to be an African American living under Jim Crow segregation in the United States. Most young Americans have little or no knowledge about restrictive covenants, literacy tests, poll taxes, lynchings, and other oppressive features of the Jim Crow racial hierarchy. Even those who have some familiarity with the period may initially view racist segregation and injustices as mere relics of a distant, shameful past. A a proper understanding of race relations in this country must include a solid knowledge of Jim Crow—how it emerged, what it was like, how it ended, and its impact on the culture.

Understanding Jim Crow introduces readers to the Jim Crow Museum of Racist Memorabilia, a collection of more than ten thousand contemptible collectibles that are used to engage visitors in intense and intelligent discussions about race, race relations, and racism. The items are offensive. They were meant to be offensive. The items in the Jim Crow Museum served to dehumanize blacks and legitimized patterns of prejudice, discrimination, and segregation.

Using racist objects as teaching tools seems counterintuitive—and, quite frankly, needlessly risky. Many Americans are already apprehensive discussing race relations, especially in settings where their ideas are challenged. The museum and this book exist to help overcome our collective trepidation and reluctance to talk about race.

Fully illustrated, and with context provided by the museum's founder and director David Pilgrim, *Understanding Jim Crow* is both a grisly tour through America's past and an auspicious starting point for racial understanding and healing.

"One of the most important contributions to the study of American history that I have ever experienced."
—Henry Louis Gates Jr., director of the W.E.B. Du Bois Institute for African American Research

Girl Gangs, Biker Boys, and Real Cool Cats: Pulp Fiction and Youth Culture, 1950 to 1980

Edited by Iain McIntyre and Andrew Nette with a foreword by Peter Doyle

ISBN: 978-1-62963-438-8
$29.95   336 pages

Girl Gangs, Biker Boys, and Real Cool Cats is the first comprehensive account of how the rise of postwar youth culture was depicted in mass-market pulp fiction. As the young created new styles in music, fashion, and culture, pulp fiction shadowed their every move, hyping and exploiting their behaviour, dress, and language for mass consumption and cheap thrills. From the juvenile delinquent gangs of the early 1950s through the beats and hippies, on to bikers, skinheads, and punks, pulp fiction left no trend untouched. With their lurid covers and wild, action-packed plots, these books reveal as much about society's deepest desires and fears as they do about the subcultures themselves.

Girl Gangs features approximately 400 full-color covers, many of them never reprinted before. With 70 in-depth author interviews, illustrated biographies, and previously unpublished articles from more than 20 popular culture critics and scholars from the US, UK, and Australia, the book goes behind the scenes to look at the authors and publishers, how they worked, where they drew their inspiration and—often overlooked—the actual words they wrote. Books by well-known authors such as Harlan Ellison and Lawrence Block are discussed alongside neglected obscurities and former bestsellers ripe for rediscovery. It is a must read for anyone interested in pulp fiction, lost literary history, retro and subcultural style, and the history of postwar youth culture.

Contributors include Nicolas Tredell, Alwyn W. Turner, Mike Stax, Clinton Walker, Bill Osgerby, David Rife, J.F. Norris, Stewart Home, James Cockington, Joe Blevins, Brian Coffey, James Doig, David James Foster, Matthew Asprey Gear, Molly Grattan, Brian Greene, John Harrison, David Kiersh, Austin Matthews, and Robert Baker.

"Girl Gangs, Biker Boys, and Real Cool Cats *is populated by the bad boys and girls of mid-twentieth-century pulp fiction. Rumblers and rebels, beats and bikers, hepcats and hippies—pretty much everybody your mother used to warn you about. Nette and McIntyre have curated a riotous party that you won't want to leave, even though you might get your wallet stolen or your teeth kicked in at any given moment."*
—Duane Swierczynski, two-time Edgar nominee, author of *Canary* and *Revolver*

Revolutionary Mothering: Love on the Front Lines

Edited by Alexis Pauline Gumbs, China Martens, and Mai'a Williams with a preface by Loretta J. Ross

ISBN: 978-1-62963-110-3
$17.95   272 pages

Inspired by the legacy of radical and queer black feminists of the 1970s and '80s, *Revolutionary Mothering* places marginalized mothers of color at the center of a world of necessary transformation. The challenges we face as movements working for racial, economic, reproductive, gender, and food justice, as well as anti-violence, anti-imperialist, and queer liberation are the same challenges that many mothers face every day. Oppressed mothers create a generous space for life in the face of life-threatening limits, activate a powerful vision of the future while navigating tangible concerns in the present, move beyond individual narratives of choice toward collective solutions, live for more than ourselves, and remain accountable to a future that we cannot always see. *Revolutionary Mothering* is a movement-shifting anthology committed to birthing new worlds, full of faith and hope for what we can raise up together.

Contributors include June Jordan, Malkia A. Cyril, Esteli Juarez, Cynthia Dewi Oka, Fabiola Sandoval, Sumayyah Talibah, Victoria Law, Tara Villalba, Lola Mondragón, Christy NaMee Eriksen, Norma Angelica Marrun, Vivian Chin, Rachel Broadwater, Autumn Brown, Layne Russell, Noemi Martinez, Katie Kaput, alba onofrio, Gabriela Sandoval, Cheryl Boyce Taylor, Ariel Gore, Claire Barrera, Lisa Factora-Borchers, Fabielle Georges, H. Bindy K. Kang, Terri Nilliasca, Irene Lara, Panquetzani, Mamas of Color Rising, tk karakashian tunchez, Arielle Julia Brown, Lindsey Campbell, Micaela Cadena, and Karen Su.

"This collection is a treat for anyone that sees class and that needs to learn more about the experiences of women of color (and who doesn't?!). There is no dogma here, just fresh ideas and women of color taking on capitalism, anti-racist, anti-sexist theory-building that is rooted in the most primal of human connections, the making of two people from the body of one: mothering."
—Barbara Jensen, author of *Reading Classes: On Culture and Classism in America*

"For women of color, mothering—the art of mothering—has been framed by the most virulent systems, historically: enslavement, colonialism, capitalism, imperialism. We have had few opportunities to define mothering not only as an aspect of individual lives and choices, but as the processes of love and as a way of structuring community. *Revolutionary Mothering* arrives as a needed balm."
—Alexis De Veaux, author of *Warrior Poet: A Biography of Audre Lorde*

A Letter to My Children and the Children of the World to Come

Raoul Vaneigem
with an afterword by John Holloway

ISBN: 978-1-62963-512-5
$15.95   128 pages

Readers of Vaneigem's now-classic work *The Revolution of Everyday Life*, which as one of the main contributions of the Situationist International was a herald of the May 1968 uprisings in France, will find much to challenge them in these pages written in the highest idiom of subversive utopianism.

Some thirty-five years after the May "events," this short book poses the question of what kind of world we are going to leave to our children. "How could I address my daughters, my sons, my grandchildren and great-grandchildren," wonders Vaneigem, "without including all the others who, once precipitated into the sordid universe of money and power, are in danger, even tomorrow, of being deprived of the promise of a life that is undeniably offered at birth as a gift with nothing expected in return?"

A Letter to My Children provides a clear-eyed survey of the critical predicament into which the capitalist system has now plunged the world, but at the same time, in true dialectical fashion, and "far from the media whose job it is to ignore them," Vaneigem discerns all the signs of "a new burgeoning of life forces among the younger generations, a new drive to reinstate true human values, to proceed with the clandestine construction of a living society beneath the barbarity of the present and the ruins of the Old World."

"In this fine book, the Situationist author, whose writings fueled the fires of May 1968, sets out to pass down the foundational ideals of his struggle against the seemingly all-powerful fetishism of the commodity and in favor of the force of human desire and the sovereignty of life."
—Jean Birnbaum, *Le Monde*

"A startling and invigorating restatement for the present ghastly era of humanity's choice: socialism or barbarism."
—Dave Barbu, *Le Nouveau Père Duchesne*

Practical Utopia: Strategies for a Desirable Society

Michael Albert with a preface by Noam Chomsky

ISBN: 978-1-62963-381-7
$20.00   288 pages

Michael Albert's latest work, *Practical Utopia* is a succinct and thoughtful discussion of ambitious goals and practical principles for creating a desirable society. It presents concepts and their connections to current society; visions of what can be in a preferred, participatory future; and an examination of the ends and means required for developing a just society. Neither shying away from the complexity of human issues, nor reeking of dogmatism, *Practical Utopia* presupposes only concern for humanity.

Part one offers conceptual tools for understanding society and history, for discerning the nature of the oppressions people suffer and the potentials they harbor. Part two promotes a vision for a better way of organizing economy, polity, kinship, culture, ecology, and international relations. It is not a blueprint, of course, but does address the key institutions needed if people are to be free to determine their own circumstances. Part three investigates the means of seeking change using a variety of tactics and programs.

"*Practical Utopia immediately struck me because it is written by a leftist who is interested in the people winning and defeating oppression. The book is an excellent jumping off point for debates on the framework to look at actually existing capitalism, strategy for change, and what we need to do about moving forward. It speaks to many of the questions faced by grassroots activists who want to get beyond demanding change but who, instead, want to create a dynamic movement that can bring a just world into existence. As someone who comes out of a different part of the Left than does Michael Albert, I was nevertheless excited by the challenges he threw in front of the readers of this book. Many a discussion will be sparked by the arguments of this work.*"
—Bill Fletcher Jr., author of *"They're Bankrupting Us!" And 20 Other Myths about Unions*

"*Albert mulls over the better society that we may create after capitalism, provoking much thought and offering a generous, hopeful vision of the future. Albert's prescriptions for action in the present are modest and wise, his suggestions for building the future are ambitious and humane.*"
—Milan Rai

(H)afrocentric Comics: Volumes 1-4

Juliana "Jewels" Smith, illustrated by
Ronald Nelson, with colors/lettering by
Mike Hampton, and a foreword by Kiese
Laymon

ISBN: 978-1-62963-448-7
$20.00   136 pages

Glyph Award winner Juliana "Jewels" Smith and
illustrator Ronald Nelson have created an unflinching visual and literary tour-de-
force on the most pressing issues of the day— including gentrification, police
violence, and the housing crisis—with humor and biting satire. *(H)afrocentric*
tackles racism, patriarchy, and popular culture head-on. Unapologetic and
unabashed, *(H)afrocentric* introduces us to strong yet vulnerable students of color,
as well as an aesthetic that connects current Black pop culture to an organic
reappropriation of hip hop fashion circa the early 90s.

We start the journey when gentrification strikes the neighborhood surrounding
Ronald Reagan University. Naima Pepper recruits a group of disgruntled
undergrads of color to combat the onslaught by creating and launching the first
and only anti-gentrification social networking site, mydiaspora.com. The motley
crew is poised to fight back against expensive avocado toast, muted Prius cars,
exorbitant rent, and cultural appropriation. Whether Naima and the gang are
transforming social media, leading protests, fighting rent hikes, or working as
"Racial Translators," the students at Ronald Reagan University take movements to
a new level by combining their tech-savvy, Black Millennial sensibilities with their
individual backgrounds, goals, and aspirations.

"Smith's comics ooze with originality."
—AFROPUNK

*"(H)afrocentric is a book that is incredibly contemporary and fits the progressive minds
of today's readers. It tackles issues of intersectionality and gentrification in ways that
are not only informative but also entertaining. It's unlike any comic book I've ever read."*
—Jamie Broadnax, founder and managing editor of Blackgirlnerds.com

*"(H)afrocentric is fully dope, artistic, brilliantly drawn, styled, and wonderfully radical
with an awesomely fiery heroine! Juliana Smith and her team are to be commended
for this desperately needed political and cultural contribution. Get into it and grab your
soapboxes!"*
—Jared A. Ball, author of *I Mix What I Like! A Mixtape Manifesto*

Revolution at Point Zero: Housework, Reproduction, and Feminist Struggle

Silvia Federici

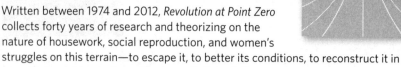

ISBN: 978-1-60486-333-8
$15.95   208 pages

Written between 1974 and 2012, *Revolution at Point Zero* collects forty years of research and theorizing on the nature of housework, social reproduction, and women's struggles on this terrain—to escape it, to better its conditions, to reconstruct it in ways that provide an alternative to capitalist relations.

Indeed, as Federici reveals, behind the capitalist organization of work and the contradictions inherent in "alienated labor" is an explosive ground zero for revolutionary practice upon which are decided the daily realities of our collective reproduction.

Beginning with Federici's organizational work in the Wages for Housework movement, the essays collected here unravel the power and politics of wide but related issues including the international restructuring of reproductive work and its effects on the sexual division of labor, the globalization of care work and sex work, the crisis of elder care, the development of affective labor, and the politics of the commons.

"Finally we have a volume that collects the many essays that over a period of four decades Silvia Federici has written on the question of social reproduction and women's struggles on this terrain. While providing a powerful history of the changes in the organization of reproductive labor, Revolution at Point Zero *documents the development of Federici's thought on some of the most important questions of our time: globalization, gender relations, the construction of new commons."*
—Mariarosa Dalla Costa, coauthor of *The Power of Women and the Subversion of the Community* and *Our Mother Ocean*

"As the academy colonizes and tames women's studies, Silvia Federici speaks the experience of a generation of women for whom politics was raw, passionately lived, often in the shadow of an uncritical Marxism. She spells out the subtle violence of housework and sexual servicing, the futility of equating waged work with emancipation, and the ongoing invisibility of women's reproductive labors. Under neoliberal globalization women's exploitation intensifies—in land enclosures, in forced migration, in the crisis of elder care. With ecofeminist thinkers and activists, Federici argues that protecting the means of subsistence now becomes the key terrain of struggle, and she calls on women North and South to join hands in building new commons."
—Ariel Salleh, author of *Ecofeminism as Politics: Nature, Marx, and the Postmodern*